Women Novelists Before Jane Austen:
The Critics and Their Canons

BRIAN CORMAN

# Women Novelists
# Before Jane Austen:

## The Critics and Their Canons

UNIVERSITY OF TORONTO PRESS
Toronto   Buffalo   London

© University of Toronto Press Incorporated 2008
Toronto   Buffalo   London
www.utppublishing.com
Printed in Canada

ISBN 978-0-8020-9770-5

Printed on acid-free paper

**Library and Archives Canada Cataloguing in Publication**

Corman, Brian, 1945–
Women novelists before Jane Austen: the critics and their canons / Brian
Corman.

Includes bibliographical references and index.
ISBN 978-0-8020-9770-5

1. Women novelists, English – History.   2. English fiction – Women authors
– History and criticism.   3. English fiction – 18th century – History and
criticism.   4. Criticism – Great Britain – History.   5. Women and literature
– Great Britain – History.   I. Title.

PR448.W65C67 2008      823'.5099287      C2007-907472-3

University of Toronto Press acknowledges the financial assistance to its
publishing program of the Canada Council for the Arts and the
Ontario Arts Council.

University of Toronto Press acknowledges the financial support for its
publishing activities of the Government of Canada through the Book
Publishing Industry Development Program (BPIDP).

*For Linda and Sarah*

# Contents

# Acknowledgments

I have had the benefit of considerable advice, help, and support from friends, colleagues, and students in preparing this study. I would like to take this opportunity to record my thanks to: John Baird, Joseph Bartolomeo, Alan Bewell, Thomas Bonnell, Patricia Brückmann, Gillian Fenwick, Jocelyn Harris, Heather Jackson, Elizabeth Kraft, Jill Matus, and Laura Runge; my research assistants: Darryl Domingo, Anne Lyden, Lenore Morra, Margaret Reeves, and Rebecca Tierney-Hynes; the students in my Research Opportunities group: Alexandra Bolintineanu, Sarah Neville, and Katherine Rentschler; my editor and copy-editor at the University of Toronto Press: Jill McConkey and Allyson May. I am also grateful for the generous support of the Department of English and the Faculty of Arts and Sciences at the University of Toronto.

Women Novelists Before Jane Austen:
The Critics and Their Canons

# Introduction

This study evolved from my interest in the historiography of the early English novel. Questions like 'What was the first novel?' or 'Who was the first novelist?' and 'Why did the novel "rise" in the eighteenth century?' have occupied literary historians since they first decided to consider the history of the form. As a habitual reader of early and out-of-date literary histories and someone long fascinated by the ever-changing answers to a limited number of central problems, I originally contemplated a history of histories of the novel. Eventually, I came to focus on a single problem in the literary histories.

The choice of which problem to take on was settled for me some time ago when I read Dale Spender's *Mothers of the Novel* (1986). Spender's book was published as the polemical critical introduction to the Pandora series of reprints of (usually out-of-print) novels by women. As an attempt to introduce forgotten writers and to make a strong case for their inclusion in a revamped canon, it is largely successful. In the process of that recovery, Spender raises a number of important critical and historical issues. Her discussion of Walter Allen's failure to include many women in *The English Novel* (1954) is punctuated by the assertion that 'the exclusion of women from the literary heritage has not been confined to efforts to keep [women] out of print but has extended to keep them out of consideration even when they are in print' (45). This hypothesis is later expanded into the following pronouncement: 'The removal of these women writers from the literary heritage cannot be explained by the subsidiary nature of their concerns, the silly nature of their content, or the sensational nature of their style. And it cannot be explained by comparison with their male colleagues, for the men who wrote in similar vein have been retained within the tradition. The only explanation that suffices to account for women's crime – is their sex' (168).

My own education in the 1960s offers clear and concrete evidence of the exclusion of women writers from accounts of the eighteenth-century novel by mid-twentieth-century critics. A standard critical work in the field I was required to read was called *The Early Masters of English Prose Fiction* (1956). For its author, A.D. McKillop, there were five such masters: Defoe, Richardson, Fielding, Smollett, and Sterne. I also studied Bunyan, Swift, Johnson, Goldsmith, and, the exception to prove the rule, Burney. The other standard critical work at the time, Ian Watt's still-important *The Rise of the Novel* (1957), traced the novel back to Defoe, Richardson, and Fielding, with no mention of a woman of consequence before Burney. On page 298 of his 301-page study, in the context of an argument for seeing Austen 'as the climax of many aspects of the 18th-century novel,' Watt notes that 'the majority of eighteenth-century novels were actually written by women, but this had long remained a purely quantitative assertion of dominance; it was Jane Austen who completed the work that Fanny Burney had begun, and challenged masculine prerogative' in the writing of novels. With hindsight, this is an astonishing assertion. The question it now raises for me is: how was it possible for Watt's claim, unsupported by evidence or serious argument, to be accepted by the scholarly community without debate?[1] Since I do not believe in 'only' explanations for interesting problems in literary history, I found Spender's hypothesis inadequate. It raised far more questions than it answered. Have women always been excluded? Was their erasure from the story of the development of the novel part of 'the systematic devaluation of women writers and their concerns' by nineteenth-century critics intent on removing the mothers of the novel from the places of 'very high repute' (161) many of them had earned? A desire to offer a fuller explanation for what struck me as a far more complex series of problems provided the initial impetus for this book.

My narrative is based on an examination of as many 'historical' accounts of the 'novel,' both terms generously defined, as I could find. In approaching my 'histories,' I was looking for comments about women 'novelists' before Austen; absence of comment was also significant evidence. Which novelists merit attention? Why? Is there a master narrative? Virtually every critic and historian begins with or seeks a canon of writers, and the changing nature of that canon is a central concern of this study. Most critics and historians also bring to their work a set of axiomatic assumptions that determine much of the result.

These assumptions are as contested as the canon; they, too, are central to my study. Much of what follows presents the views of the critics I have selected on the questions central to my enquiry. I do this for the same reason that many of the critics summarize the plots of the works of the early women novelists: they are not likely to be familiar to my readers. (Those who have read widely in the early histories of the novel will be able to skip over the summaries.) Had Spender been familiar with the texts I have chosen to examine, she would not have leaped to the conclusion offered in her own work. Since I do not find Spender's neglect of early criticism and literary history exceptional, I have provided a 'history of histories' of the novel, a reception history of the eighteenth-century novel, and a history of the canon of the novel by way of tracing the critical histories of the women novelists central to my study. I find it impossible to assess a critic's evaluation of women novelists without knowing that critic's evaluation of their male contemporaries and the critical principles and personal biases informing those evaluations; I also find it essential to identify the recurring narratives that structure so much of the historical thinking about the novel. For all the interesting variants, there is a remarkable consistency in most novel criticism through to the middle of the twentieth century, just as there is a remarkable consistency in the core canon of the novel. Changes occur in both the histories and the canons, but they tend to be cautious and slow. The fundamental conservatism informing novel criticism is one of my central themes.

Publishing this study in the early twenty-first century, twenty some years after Spender's and a half-century after Watt set the terms for what became a robust debate about the origin and development of English prose fiction, I am attempting to revisit the critical tradition that led up to *The Rise of the Novel* and the important feminist (and other) responses that continue to follow. It should become clear that my own critical views and practice have been informed by the past two generations of scholarship on the novel, and especially by the many studies that have complicated Watt's tale of the rise of formal realism. Still more relevant are the recent histories of the place of women novelists in the history of the novel and the extensive work of the past several decades to recover early women novelists and assert their claims to canonical status.

Although this past half-century's work on the early novel permeates everything that follows, my study remains an attempt to provide the pre-history of that valuable scholarship, or, as one of the readers of an earlier draft put it, 'a prolegomenon to contemporary feminist studies.' One result is that I make little reference to criticism after Watt, preferring to try to understand the two hundred years of responses to the novel leading up to him in their own terms before imposing my own narrative on the vast body of data I have reviewed. My organization of that data, in other words, imprints my own twenty-first-century perspective. I have not continued my study beyond Watt to include the views of the many scholars who have enriched my understanding of the early novel and its history. To incorporate such a challenging extension would be rewarding, but it would require a second volume to do justice to so rich, complex, and diverse a body of scholarship. In short, that is not the project I have undertaken here. Consequently, this is a book with very few notes: little has been written about early critics and historians of the novel. I began with the temptation to footnote subsequent responses to the questions raised by these early critics and historians, particularly those that are part of current debates and discussions, but soon discovered that my book was in danger of containing more notes than text. As a result, I have resisted the temptation to discuss in notes the rich and varied contributions of critics and historians since Watt, the very writers whose views have helped to form and most closely resemble my own. By way of apology, I have also resisted the opportunity to provide my own critical correctives to early critics and their histories.

Histories of the novel are generally recognized as an invention of the early nineteenth century. But like most new kinds of inquiry, they do not emerge fully formed. Questions about the nature of the novel, its origin, and its greatest practitioners go back to the beginning – whenever that was. By the late eighteenth century there is a considerable body of criticism, much of it historical, about the rise of the novel, enough to call into question Spender's assertion – provoked as it was by Watt's ingenuous announcement that 'the majority of eighteenth century novels were actually written by women' – that 'in the eighteenth century it was not known that women writers did not count. Quite the reverse. Charlotte Lennox, Mary Wollstonecraft, Fanny Burney, Elizabeth Inchbald, Mary Hays, Amelia Opie and Maria Edgeworth were not just "actually" the majority, they were the *esteemed* majority' (139). Spender's list of novelists points to part of the problem in what it includes, and to more of the problem in what it excludes. With the exception of Lennox, these novelists wrote at the very end of the century; none published a novel before 1750. Wollstonecraft was indeed a famous writer during her lifetime, but not a famous novelist. Mary Hays was anything but esteemed in her lifetime. And the most admired woman novelist of the century, Ann Radcliffe, is excluded from this list. The body of Spender's text provides some important qualifications, but the thrust of her polemic remains fundamentally unchallenged. It exemplifies an extreme version of the problems I would have had to confront had I included discussions of critics since Watt, especially feminist critics, and most especially those who offer more sophisticated and more highly nuanced accounts of the early novel than those I survey in this study. I have instead limited myself to attempting to determine which women novelists counted, which were esteemed, when, and why, in the histories and criticism up to 1957. It should soon be clear that, from my perspective, many of the critics I discuss are wanting. I rarely quarrel directly with them, preferring to allow them to point out their own limitations in their own words. My analysis is more concerned with trends and developments over time.

A corollary to this approach is that I do not attempt to define contested terms such as 'novel,' as my study requires that I include the many uses made of such terms by the critics and historians I discuss – uses that are themselves rarely defined with any precision. Though I try throughout where possible to indicate what individual critics and historians mean by 'the novel,' I am better able to identify qualities they value in it; most of the critics I discuss are not overly interested in defining the novel's form or genre. Since what interests me most here is identifying continuities and changes in critical views of the novel and its history, my fluid use of such terms as 'novel' should not cause unnecessary confusion.

This study is arranged chronologically in order to unpack the complex histories of early women novelists and their place in histories and canons of the novel. Chapter 1 examines early British novel criticism – that is, the criticism that predates the first systematic attempts to provide assessments and a history of the form. It covers the early canon-making of the mid- and late eighteenth century and the early historical studies of the late eighteenth century. Chapter 2, covering the opening decades of the nineteenth century, looks at the first self-conscious attempt at establishing a canon of the British novel, the first complete history of the novel in English, and the first biographical studies of British novelists. I argue that Georgian and Romantic tastes informed these efforts and subsequently set the terms for future debates. Chapter 3 examines the impact of Victorian realism on tastes and assessments of the novel; chapter 4 turns to the fin-de-siècle responses to the Victorians. Chapter 5 looks at the criticism and literary history at the time of high Modernism, with its formalist tendencies. Each of these periods has dominant voices, but none is without dissenting views. I have tried to capture a representative selection of these voices in each chapter. Although there are many continuities from period to period, there are also significant incremental changes. My belief is that the only way to understand the shifting fortunes of early women novelists is through a survey of where they are placed by the full range of critics operating in each of my periods. The result is messier than a more Whiggish narrative of neglect that looks for early intimations of more enlightened views to follow. My hope is that it also provides a more accurate view of how it came to be that, by the time of Watt's *The Rise of the Novel*, so many women novelists had been forgotten.

# 1 The Eighteenth Century

John Dunlop claims that his *History of Fiction* is the first 'attempt towards a general History of fiction' (11) in Britain. Given the range and inclusiveness of his work the claim is a just one, but like all histories, his is not without a prehistory. Dunlop acknowledges the work of Percy and Warton on the origins of what he calls 'Romantic' fiction but ignores his three important predecessors, Clara Reeve, John Moore, and Anna Laetitia Barbauld, the three critics with the greatest expertise on the history of the novel – though to be fair to Dunlop, none produced a full 'general' history. One important reason for the limited amount of earlier historical inquiry was the success of the campaign by Richardson and Fielding – a rare example of common goals for these two rivals – to establish their fiction as entirely new, that is, without a history or a past.[1] If the so-called fathers of the novel were notoriously reluctant to acknowledge the contributions of their mothers, or even their sisters, they were scarcely more generous to their fathers or brothers. Richardson, Fielding, and Smollett, to a greater or lesser degree, credit the occasional, carefully selected male predecessor, who is usually foreign. Fielding on Cervantes and Smollett on Lesage offer the most familiar and ungrudging examples. But these examples are understandably few, as they offer evidence against the claims for the mid-century novel as 'a new species of writing,' one without important predecessors. The old species, usually identified as 'romance,' was the evil other against which the new novel was to be compared; among other things, it was invariably presented as a tired, worn-out, feminized other, and one of questionable morality as well. The likes of Cervantes and Lesage were useful to the 'fathers' for diverting attention from a more local tradition. The key to their establishment of the novel and its history as we have come to know it was to obliterate their debts to their British predecessors, the outmoded and disreputable prose fiction. Fielding's acolyte, Francis Coventry, argued that Fielding and Richardson successfully inoculated themselves from the 'disease' carried by their predecessors. As William Warner has shown, Coventry's choice of metaphor reveals as much as it conceals: 'Just as a vaccine can achieve its antidotal function only by introducing a mild form of the disease into the body of the patient, their novels incorporated many elements of the dangerous old novels of Behn, Manley, and Haywood into this "new species" of fiction' ('Licensing Pleasure,' 6). Nowhere is this more true than in the case of Coventry himself (xviii).[2]

For my purposes, Richardson and Fielding's demonization of pre-1740 prose fiction had two important effects. First is the ahistorical nature of most mid-century novel criticism. Gifted writers of the previous several generations might as well not have written. The four most obvious examples, Behn, Defoe, Manley, and Haywood, were the highest-profile victims. Second, as the gender balance of Behn, Defoe, Manley, and Haywood suggests, a large number, if not the majority, of the neglected novelists were women. Richardson and Fielding were right to recognize that the novel was a disreputable form in 1740, and they were successful in curing its illness by isolating and quarantining the infected to disguise their own symptoms of infection. Their propaganda was so successful that by the time historical questions were asked, their critics were not inclined to look back for a continuous tradition of English fiction. Instead, they were diverted by the early forms of the dialectic that continues to dominate criticism of the eighteenth-century novel, Richardson versus Fielding.[3] Since one of the few things these two novelists had in common was their rejection of the kind of prose fiction produced by their predecessors, the dialectic was formed in terms that left Behn, Manley, and (the pre-Richardson) Haywood out of the equation entirely. Choose which side you would, it made no difference to the stature or reputation of earlier English male novelists; any praise was directed at Continental male writers. Women novelists were nowhere to be found.

### Sarah Fielding (1710–1768)

The success of the combined onslaught of the rival camps of Richardson and Fielding was both immediate and lasting. Consider, for example, the following passage:

From the same Taste of being acquainted with the various and surprising Incidents of Mankind, arises our insatiable Curiosity for Novels or Romances: Infatuated with a Sort of Knight errantry, we draw these fictitious Characters into a real Existence; and thus, pleasingly deluded, we find ourselves as warmly interested, and deeply affected by the imaginary scenes of *Arcadia*, the wonderful Atchievements of Don *Quixote*, the merry Conceits of *Sancho*, rural Innocence of a *Joseph Andrews*, or the inimitable virtues of Sir *Charles Grandison*, as if they were real, and those romantic Heroes had experienced the capricious Fortunes attributed to them by the fertile Invention of the Writers. (54)

The passage is from Sarah Fielding's 1757 introduction to *The Lives of Cleopatra and Octavia*, an introduction that concludes with her defence of her use of the 'Interview' – a defence from authority, the authority established by Homer, Virgil, Aristophanes, and Lucan. Sarah Fielding's prefaces and introductions display broad learning and reading. They abound in allusions, quotations, and other literary references, but those references seem always to be from male writers. She prefers to quote from poets: novelists were not really respectable. But when she does look to the novel, it is to the canon of her brother and of her friend Richardson. In forming a single canon from the great rivals she shows just how effective was their campaign to erase their predecessors.[4] She also anticipates the claims that will later legitimize both Burney and Austen, that in them the only two great traditions of the English novel are united.

### Frances Burney (1752–1840)

Burney herself makes a similar point in her well-known Preface to *Evelina* (1778), where in the voice of an anonymous, implicitly male, 'humble Novelist,' she expresses 'his' lament that 'among the whole class of writers, perhaps not one [novelist] can be named, of whom the votaries are more numerous but less respectable.' Soon after, however, she is able to argue that there has been a change: while 'in the annals of these few of our predecessors, to whom this species of writing is indebted for being saved from contempt, and rescued from depravity, we can trace such names as Rousseau, Johnson, Marivaux, Fielding, Richardson, and Smollett, no man need blush at starting from the same post, though many, nay, most men, may sigh at finding themselves distanced' (7). Although never an enthusiastic defender of the genre, Burney was a keen reader of novels. Generations of critics have seen the influence of her popular, female predecessors, particularly that of Eliza Haywood's *History of Miss Betsy Thoughtless* (1751), on *Evelina*, but it was an influence that Burney was not eager to acknowledge. Instead, she adopts a very small, all-male canon, none of the members of which is still writing novels in the late 1770s.

In finding no contemporary to rival the achievement of the past masters of the novel, Burney is among the earliest to record a late-century commonplace about the novel: by the 1770s it was already in a state of decline. Just two years later, Thomas Holcroft (1745–1809) declares that 'novels have fallen into disrepute,' because novelists cannot live up to the standards of their mid-century predecessors. 'Novels shall continue to want admirers: but Tom Jones shall never want admirers' (quoted in Bartolomeo, *New Species of Criticism*, 93–4). Holcroft's view is echoed by the reviewers for the rest of the century. As J.M.S. Tompkins comments, there was 'a real conviction that the novel was played out.' She cites these lines from the *Monthly Review* of August 1790 as a late representative example: 'The manufacture of novels has been so long established, that in general they have arrived as mediocrity … We are indeed so sickened with this worn-out species of composition, that we have lost all relish for it' (*The Popular Novel*, 5). This reading of the history of the novel did not survive the new century, but it has remained the dominant reading of the late-eighteenth-century novel for two hundred years, a fact of central importance to my study. The gradual, steady increase of respectability for the novel in the view of critics and historians did little for the status of the generation or two of novelists immediately following that of Richardson and Fielding. Again, the majority of these novelists are probably women.

## Hugh Blair (1718–1800)

Though Burney shared with professional reviewers the conviction that the novel was in a state of decline, the reviewers continued to take the genre more seriously. Most new novels were reviewed, and, as recent studies have shown, the better reviewers were, for the most part, generous and receptive if patronizing.[5] The academic critics were more severe, tending to share Burney's sense of a very small canon of novelists worthy of their attention. For them, the novel remains what it had always been for serious-minded moralists and pedagogues, a form not to be trusted, a form best ignored. By the time Hugh Blair published his *Lectures on Rhetoric and Belles Lettres* (1783) – a survey course for nearly a quarter of a century at the University of Edinburgh – he found it necessary to recognize 'a very insignificant class of Writings, known by the name of Romance and Novels.' Though 'these may, at first view, seem too insignificant, to deserve that any particular notice should be taken of them,' Blair must allow that 'any kind of Writing, however trifling soever in appearance, that obtains a general currency, and especially that early pre-occupies the imagination or the youth of both sexes, must demand particular attention. Its influence is likely to be considerable, both on the moral and taste of a nation' (3: 74–5).

Blair devotes a mere nine pages to 'fictitious histories' (3: 75), emphasizing their potential to outdo real, lived history in presenting 'heroic and illustrious deeds' and distributing 'rewards and punishments' more in line with things as they should be. The movement of the novel is from the noble and moral tales of the ancients (the first stage) to the more refined and realistic but diminished romances of seventeenth-century France, including those of 'Mad. Scuderi' (the second stage), to the 'dwindled,' amoral 'familiar novel that came into fashion during the reigns of Louis XIV and Charles II' (3: 80). To Blair's great relief, this long decline was finally broken by the appearance of a new, realistic novel, complete with the restoration of a much-needed component of instruction. It is a tradition to date better established in France, and one that has yet to succeed in discouraging the large number of unnamed 'trivial performances' that 'oftener tend to dissipation and idleness, than to any good purpose' (3: 83). Blair's canon of new novels is very small: Lesage, Marivaux, and Rousseau, and among the English, the unnamed author of *Robinson Crusoe* (1719), Fielding, and Richardson. It takes little effort to infer where women novelists fit in his history.

### James Beattie (1735–1803)

James Beattie's 'On Fable and Romance' (also 1783) is far more systematic in surveying the history of prose fiction and far more generous in evaluating it. It is the first extensive treatment of the novel in English (seventy-one pages to Blair's nine). Beattie traces the novel back to the ancients, through the medieval and French romances to the various forms of what he calls the 'new romance,' serious and comic tales that differ from their predecessors because of the attention now given to common life and to 'probability.' For Beattie, Cervantes 'occasioned the death of the Old Romance and gave birth to New' (564). The French romances lie between the two. The canon runs from Petrarch, Vidal, Dante, Boccaccio, and Chaucer to Cervantes, Lesage, Marivaux, Richardson, Fielding, and Smollett. Both serious and comic novels are divided into those arranged as historical narratives and those arranged like the epic; each canonical work is evaluated in some detail. Beattie also notes a number of English writers of more old-fashioned romances: John Barclay, Bunyan, John Arbuthnot, Swift, Addison, Hawkesworth, and Johnson. His more thorough survey does not, however, find room for a single woman novelist, 'no doubt' since 'romances are a dangerous recreation'; only 'the best may be friendly to good taste and good morals' (573).

### Vicesimus Knox (1752–1821)

Moving from these university critics to Vicesimus Knox, the influential master of Tonbridge School, reveals a still more limiting view of the novel. Knox holds a common, late-century view that the new, realistic novels have contributed significantly to the 'corrupt' state of the 'present age.' Unlike the old romances, which 'filled the heart with pure, manly, bold, and liberal sentiments' (*Essays Moral and Literary*, 131), the more recent forms of fiction, from the licentious and coarse tales of the reign of Charles II to the sentimental novel, which gives 'an amiable name to ·vice,' excusing 'extravagance of the passions … as the effect of lovely sensibility' (134), are too dangerous for most of their vulnerable readership of women and children. Knox prefers to recommend a diet of more wholesome fare: *Robinson Crusoe*, *The Pilgrim's Progress* (1678–84), *Don Quixote*, various Oriental and Eastern tales, the *Tales of the Genii*, the *Death of Abel*, and, above all, the Bible. Only four recent novelists are mentioned by name: Richardson and Fielding are the best of the lot and, if necessary, are to be tolerated. Smollett and Sterne are named, too, but only to sound strong warnings against them. It is hardly surprising, then, to find Knox joining Blair and Beattie in ignoring the women novelists entirely.

### Clara Reeve (1729–1807)

By far the richest and most inclusive historical treatment of the novel in the eighteenth century is Clara Reeve's *The Progress of Romance* (1785), which chronicles dozens of writers and novels and offers brief but important judgments of most of them. Reeve makes it clear that she knows most of the earlier novel criticism well; the text of *The Progress of Romance* is filled with quotations and citations from virtually every authority. Though she notes in her preface that she did not see Beattie's 1783 *Dissertation* before completing her own study, she acknowledges that he, too, has 'walked over the ground, and marked its boundaries.' But she quickly and rightly adds that 'he has paid little attention to its various produce, whether of flowers, herbs, or weeds; except a very few works of capital merit (some of which he confessed he had not read through), he consigns all the rest to oblivion' (viii). Beattie's value, in other words, lies not in his criticism of eighteenth-century novels but rather in his honouring of earlier romances. Reeve finds no shortage of French and Italian critics who consider romances 'worthy their own attention'; but 'the learned men of [her] own country, have in general affected a contempt for this kind of writing, and looked upon Romances, as proper furniture only for a lady's Library' (xi). Along with Beattie, the short list of exceptions includes only Hurd, Warton, Percy, Mallet, and Susannah Dobson.

In the process of surveying the literature in the field in her preface, Reeve also notes the general neglect of pre-sixteenth-century prose romances compared to the attention given to romances in verse, the inattention to distinguishing properly between the romance and the novel, and the lack of a thorough, evaluative survey of the works of the many writers of prose fiction. In other words, by the end of the preface Reeve has made clear her agenda for *The Progress of Romance*. The body of the text delivers all she promises, and more.

*The Progress of Romance* consists of a series of twelve dialogues between two women, the learned, novel-friendly Euphrasia and her less learned but equally novel-friendly friend Sophronia, and one man, the more novel-resistant Hortensius. These three voices allow Reeve to present a full range of opinions in the same way that Dryden did in 'An Essay of Dramatic Poesie' (1668). Euphrasia's views, like Neander's in Dryden's text, dominate, but the other characters offer widely held alternative positions and even score occasional points. Euphrasia, however, even more than Neander, follows the Platonic model of the single, dominant voice of reason. What emerges is a unique resource for students of late-eighteenth-century criticism of the novel.

Reeve traces the novel back to the ancient war songs and historical narratives that predate the epic, 'the parent of Romance' (1: 25). She (I take Euphrasia's predominant narrative to express Reeve's own views) then surveys the ancient and medieval romances and the modern romances of the sixteenth and seventeenth centuries, including those by Lyly, Boyle, Sidney, and Barclay. Crucial to her defence of the romance and the novel is Euphrasia's argument that the romance must be understood as a prose development of the epic. Respectable

parentage, especially male parentage, helps subvert the instinct, represented by Hortensius, to downgrade prose fiction through feminization.
So important is it to Reeve that roughly half of *The Progress of Romance* is
dedicated to making the point that the difference between epic and
romance is as much one of degree as of kind. Once that point has been
made, she can then make a similar point about the difference between
romance and the novel. Her well-known distinction between 'an heroic
fable which treats of fabulous persons and things' and 'a picture of real
life and manners, and of the times in which it is written' again insists
upon both similarities and differences. She refuses, unlike some critics,
to collapse the generic differences into a single form of prose fiction; the
novel is, as its name suggests, something new and different. But she
won't side with Richardson and Fielding and remove the novel from the
broader history of prose fiction. Reeve's understanding of novel and
romance, in other words, is deep, nuanced, and historically informed.

After she has discussed the nature of romance Reeve turns to the
novel, distinguishing it from romance in typical eighteenth-century
fashion as 'familiar,' 'probable,' and 'real' (1: 111). Cinthio and Boccaccio
are its early masters, followed by Cervantes, Scarron, and Segrais (she
thought that he had written Lafayette's *Zaïde*). When she turns to the
novel in English, the first author she 'must reckon' is Aphra Behn:
'There are strong marks of Genius in all the lady's works, but unhap-
pily, there are some parts of them, very improper to be read by, or recommended to virtuous minds, and especially to youth' (1: 117). Since
Behn wrote in a licentious age, her faults are treated with a 'veil of
compassion' and a plea to do 'justice to her merits' (1: 118). Euphrasia
rejects Hortensius's accusation that she tolerates in a woman what she
would condemn in a man, but, in the end, agrees that Behn's works
cannot be recommended.

The other 'female wits' follow, and do less well. Delarivier Manley is
'still more exceptionable' than Behn; her early reputation was based on
scandal, and Reeve is sorry that her works 'were once in fashion,' the only
reason she feels compelled to mention them at all (thus requiring her to
condemn a woman writer). The good news is that it will not be necessary
to mention Manley much longer as her works 'are sinking gradually into
oblivion' (1: 119). When Hortensius then tries to tar Eliza Haywood with
the same brush, Euphrasia offers what would fast become the standard
reading of Haywood: though she is guilty of 'some amorous novels in
her youth, and also two books of the same kind as Mrs. *Manley*'s capital
work ... she repented her faults, and employed the latter part of her life in

expiating the offences of the former' (1: 120–1). Haywood's career is thus presented in two discrete halves; the early works are best 'forgotten,' but 'none of her latter works are destitute of merit.' She may not share Behn's genius (her works 'do not rise to the highest pitch of excellence') but her best novel, *Betsy Thoughtless*, is worth recommending, along with *The Female Spectator* (1744–6) and *The Invisible Spy* (1755). Reeve condemns Pope's influential assessment of the three female wits in *The Dunciad* (1728–43) as too severe, especially in its attack on Haywood (1: 121). But what remains is an account of the novel that is uneasy with the three most important women novelists before 1740: Behn and Manley are best left unread, and Haywood's late works are the only ones worth salvaging. All that remains is to credit what is good in Haywood to the influence of Richardson and the place of the triumvirate in the standard histories to follow will be complete.

Reeve concludes her survey of early English fiction with a brief reference to *Cleveland* (Prévost's authorship was unknown to her), and more extensive attention to *Robinson Crusoe* and Simon Berington's *Gaudentio di Lucca* (1737), both 'strongly recommended' to 'warm the heart with the love of virtue, and ... excite the reader to the practice of it' (1: 126). She then moves on to the recent French fiction, discussing the merits of Marivaux and, especially, Riccoboni, and the shortcomings of Mouhy, Crébillon, St Aubin, and Prévost. She is now ready to talk about Richardson and Fielding. For Reeve, Richardson is clearly the greatest novelist ever, and *Pamela* is his greatest novel (a judgment that Anna Seward considered an attempt to harm Richardson's reputation).[6] Hortensius counters that '*Richardson* is a writer all your own; your sex are more obliged to him and *Addison*, than to all other men-authors' (1: 135), a charge Euphrasia denies but does not address. Instead, she catalogues Richardson's virtues and concludes that he offers young women a far better model than Behn, Manley, and Haywood did to the previous generation.

Fielding is credited with superiority to Richardson in wit and learning, but not in the more important areas of morality and exemplary characters. Hortensius makes the case for his virtues and Euphrasia is willing to grant them, but she ends by asserting that Fielding 'certainly painted human nature as it is, rather than as *it ought to be*' (1: 141); the reader is left to draw the appropriate conclusion. Richardson and Fielding emerge as England's greatest novelists, as Reeve rejects the commonly held extremes that encourage critics to make a choice between them. She prefers Richardson, but sees no reason to denigrate

Fielding because of it. Reeve remains a non-confrontational critic throughout *The Progress of Romance*, refusing to allow the views of her characters ever to exceed the most polite difference of opinion.

Volume 1 ends with high praise for that 'truly estimable' (1: 143) writer Sarah Fielding. Euphrasia begins the second volume with an expression of apprehension over moving into the realm of living authors. Reeve's inclination to focus on the positive is only strengthened by the difficulty of evaluating the large number of still active writers. The company agrees to consult the critics and reviewers to help them through their difficult task. What follows is the most inclusive contemporary discussion of late-eighteenth-century fiction I have seen. Reeve surveys a remarkable number of works of prose fiction and gently assesses their relative importance. Her judgments are always predicated first and foremost on moral soundness, but in order to be ranked in 'the first class of excellence,' more is required. She cannot, for example, give her highest approval to the novels of Elizabeth Griffith. She values sensibility and pathos only so long as they are not at odds with morality, and has severe reservations about Rousseau and Sterne (despite Hortensius's defence of each). She expresses concern about the excessive gloom in otherwise admirable works such as *Sidney Bidulph* (1761) and *Rasselas* (1759); similar concern is occasioned by the 'shocking representations of human nature' (2: 46) in *The Man of Feeling* (1771). She also objects to departures from mainline Christianity, from the atheism of Voltaire to the 'enthusiasm' tending to 'fanaticism' of Henry Brooke and Elizabeth Rowe. Finally, some novels, Margaret Minifie's for example, though 'innocent and moral' are too mediocre to merit serious attention (2: 46).

Reeve rarely, in fact, attends to novels she considers unworthy. Rather, she limits herself to the best, generously defined, though her praise is often qualified by her principles. Her taste is unusually catholic; she is receptive to all forms of fiction. She covers roughly a hundred modern novelists, including roughly thirty-five living novelists, in completing an unusually early exercise in canon making. No distinctions are drawn between translations (usually from the French) and native English texts. Fewer of the women she recognizes require qualifications on moral or religious grounds. The women she rates most highly include Charlotte Lennox, Frances Sheridan (*Nourjahad*), Frances Brooke, Sarah Scott, Anne Louise Elie de Beaumont, Madam le Prince de Beaumont, Marie-Jeanne Riccoboni, and Helen-Maria Williams (if *Anecdotes of a Convent* and/or *Letters Between an English Lady and her Friend at Paris* are hers).

Others receive a more qualified recognition: Elizabeth Rowe, Frances Sheridan (*Sidney Bidulph*), Elizabeth Griffith, Maria Susanna Cooper, and Sophie Briscoe. (Euphrasia says she has stopped at 1770, but she discusses several works published in the 1770s.)

Reeve concludes *The Progress of Romance* with (among other things) a series of lists: of 'Novels and Stories Original and Uncommon,' of 'Tales and Fables ancient and modern,' of 'Eastern Tales,' of modern imitations of Eastern tales, of 'German books,' of 'Books for Children,' and of 'Books for Young Ladies.' She has little good to say about either the Eastern or German tales. Among the original and uncommon novels, tales and fables, and imitations of Eastern tales, all of which she admires, Frances Sheridan's *Nourjahad* (1767) and three translations from Marianne Agnès Pillement, dame de Fauques, are the only ones by women. And Richardson is the only novelist suitable for young women (no novels are recommended for children).

*The Progress of Romance* provides the most extensive and thoughtful canon of novels in the eighteenth century. It appeared at a time when critics were taking the novel increasingly seriously, largely because of its ever-growing popularity. Reeve's is the list of novels that attracted the attention of the best, and probably best-read, novel critic of her time. Hers is a canon of the novel for 1785, a late-century canon produced, albeit by a pioneer of the British Gothic, prior to the Gothic rage of the end of the century and prior to the French Revolution and the changing tastes in fiction it spawned. Anne Mellor may wish to claim Reeve as a 'feminine Romantic' ('A Criticism of Their Own,' 30) critic, but her novel criticism will not sustain that claim. Reeve retains a fondness for seventeenth-century romances, and she has clearly read a large number of them. She is predisposed in favour of imaginary voyages and of Western reworkings of the Oriental tale. She insists on a strong didactic commitment from her novelists. She has read and enjoyed a very long list of novels by her contemporaries, most of which will be forgotten by the time Barbauld prepares her 1810 anthology of the best novels. She does welcome the early signs of revival of romance, but not at the expense of other forms of prose fiction. Her approach to prose fiction seeks to obliterate all hierarchical distinctions among fictive forms.

Gary Kelly considers Reeve an upper-middle-class Republican whose criticism breaks down traditional hierarchies, especially gender-based hierarchies. The first part of his equation is problematic; it is difficult to square the social and religious conservative so well captured by Miriam Lerenbaum, Laura Runge, and Homer Obed Brown with the proto-Jacobin Kelly would like to find in Reeve. It is difficult to find a single novelistic mode being given a strong indication of preference in *The Progress of Romance*, and more difficult still to detect signs of endorsement of any form of radical ideology. Reeve is far too concerned with the ill effects of circulating libraries to have much time for fiction promoting Republican politics. Runge and others are right to point to the fundamental commitment to a defence of the novel as a form that serves the needs of women readers as well as one that has profited from the many contributions of women writers. They are right, too, to observe that in support of her version of a feminist criticism Reeve appropriates a number of traditional masculine literary values, most notably a high regard for the epic and things heroic, while making her case in the most humble of feminine voices, frequently citing the authority of male writers and critics. There can be little doubt that hers is the first important feminist voice to present an account of the novel in English. Finally, Reeve's is the voice of a practising novelist concerned to see an end of talk about the decline of the novel, the prototype of the Regency voices who were to declare an end to the decline and to maintain a progressive rhetoric in their historical accounts of the novel – a rhetoric that prevailed for at least the following hundred years.

What has often been overlooked in *The Progress of Romance* is the overwhelming volume of fiction it covers from the 1760s and 1770s, including translations of many of the French works she cites. Reeve pretends to a great reticence about discussing relatively contemporary works of fiction; in fact, for all the delicacy of the discussion, she pays a great deal of attention to her contemporaries. I would argue that the promotion of recent fiction provides one of the strongest agendas behind *The Progress of Romance*, and one of the most successful. I would also argue that Reeve's proactive agenda contributes significantly to making *The Progress of Romance* a unique indicator of late-century taste, of the novel canon, generously defined, for 1785. Not for another twenty-five years would there be as thorough a survey of the English novel. But before moving to the work of the formative Regency histories of the novel, it is worth noting the work of other, more limited canon-makers among Reeve's contemporaries. I divide this work into three groups: collections, reviews, and the rest, this last group consisting largely of miscellaneous essays by novelists and critics, including prefaces to novels.

## Collections, Reviews, and Other Contributors
## to the Eighteenth-Century Canon

The introduction of commercially viable, large, multi-volume collections of literature was an eighteenth-century phenomenon, but its impact was first and most strongly felt in other areas of the literary marketplace, particularly poetry and drama. Enterprising publishers put together collections of novels, and their contents reveal something about the late-century canon. Elizabeth Griffith (1727–93) selected the texts for a three-volume set, *A Collection of Novels*, published by G. Kearsly in 1777. It consists of seven titles, six by women: Lafayette's *Zaïde* (translated by Griffith as *Zayde* and attributed to Segrais), *Oroonoko*, *The Princess of Clèves*, *The Fruitless Enquiry* (abridged and expurgated by Griffith), *Agnes de Castro*, Aubin's *The Noble Slaves* (a self-conscious attempt to recover a deserving but little-known text), and *The History of the Count de Belflor and Leonora de Cespedes* (translated from the French by Griffith from what she identifies as the anonymous source text both for Beaumarchais's *Eugénie* and her own *The School for Rakes*). The *Novelist's Magazine*, published in the 1780s by Harrison in twenty-three volumes, includes sixty titles, many of them translations. Ten are by women: Fielding's *David Simple* and *Ophelia*; Grafigny's *Peruvian Princess*; Lennox's *Female Quixote* and *Henrietta*; Haywood's *Betsy Thoughtless*, *Jemmy and Jenny Jessamy*, and *Invisible Spy*; and Sheridan's *Sidney Bidulph* and *Nourjahad*. Between Harrison and Barbauld, the London publisher C. Cooke published at least forty-two novels in uniform format under the advertised title of 'Select Novels.' Only four are by women: *Nourjahad*, *The Peruvian Princess*, *The Female Quixote*, and *Henrietta*.[7]

After fifty years of rehabilitation, eighteenth-century reviewers no longer have the bad name they once had. The *Monthly Review* (1749–1845) and the *Critical Review* (1756–90) instituted a tradition of paying attention to and offering serious criticism of new fiction. Reviewers were receptive to good novels, regardless of author and genre; they took their responsibilities seriously and dispensed their judgments fairly and professionally.[8] Their standards changed with the times – they tended to favour realism in the 1740s and 1750s, sensibility in the 1760s and 1770s, the Gothic in the 1790s, and so forth – but regardless of the trends of the moment, any novel that appealed to a reviewer was treated favourably. The magazine reviewers considered Richardson, Fielding and, to a somewhat lesser extent, Smollett, the old masters of the English novel, but they respected and attended to the work of many others, including a core of women: Fielding, Lennox, Brooke, Sheridan, and Griffith from the group of recent novelists covered by Reeve, and, from the next generation, Reeve herself, More, Burney, Smith, Radcliffe, Sophia Lee, Inchbald, and Edgeworth.

## John Moore (1729–1802)

The only other substantial historical study of the novel published between Reeve's and the end of the century is Dr John Moore's 'A View of the Commencement and Progress of Romance' (1797; though possibly written many years earlier), published as the preface to his edition of Smollett's *Works*. Most of its ninety-five pages focus on the 'commencement,' Moore finding the origin of romance in medieval history, especially in Arabian, Celtic, and Gothic social history. Boccaccio and Chaucer first appear on page 75, quickly followed by Rabelais, Sidney, Orrery, the French romance writers, and, at last, on page 80, 'the immortal Cervantes,' the hero of Moore's narrative because he exploded the old romance conventions and initiated the novel that will lead to Smollett – and providing a context for Smollett's works is the purpose of Moore's study. Though he acknowledges 'so many others' (lxxxii), the line of novelists who count for Moore is very limited: he names only Lesage, Marivaux, Rousseau, Richardson, Fielding, and Smollett. Moore comments that it seems 'strange that no Spanish writer appears in this list' after Cervantes (lxxxi). He mentions Madeleine de Scudéry (along with La Calprenède) among the French writers of romance, commenting that her works were considered 'entertaining' during the reign of Louis XIV; he also notes that she 'was remarkably ugly,' perhaps his explanation for her success as a writer. He does not seem to find it strange that there are no women among the novelists he values; he sees no need to comment on their absence. Moore's history of the novel, especially the eighteenth-century novel, is unusually limited: most serious critics of the novel are much more open. But his narrowness did not prevent his essay from being reprinted with Smollett's works for the following century.

## Germaine de Staël (1766–1817)

An influential Continental view of the novel, its history, and its canon is offered by Germaine de Staël's 'Essai sur les fictions' (1795; translated as 'An Essay on Fictions,' 1813). Staël's work is fundamentally a defence of the novel as, at its best, moral and uniquely able to improve its readers: 'If fictions please nothing but the eye, they do nothing but amuse; but if they touch our hearts, they can have a great influence on all our moral ideas. This talent may be the most powerful way there is of controlling behavior and enlightening the mind' (60–1), a sentiment worthy of the Evangelical reformers in principle, but quite at odds with their position in practice.

Staël divides novels into three types: '(1) marvelous and allegorical fictions, (2) historical fictions, (3) fictions in which everything is both invented and imitated, where nothing is true and everything is likely' (61). The marvellous, including the Gothic, 'casts a pall on every feeling associated with it' (62) because it is so unreal and improbable; allegories are even worse, so abstracted are they from reality. Historical fiction must sacrifice the morality of invention to an already determined story, always the worse for fictional accretions. It is, of course, only the third category, 'natural fictions' (70), that can realize the potential of the novel by allowing a reader to believe that 'he is being spoken to directly, with no artifice but the tactfulness of changing the names.' Few authors have the genius to achieve this greatness, and only they can save the novel from the 'throng of bad writers overwhelming us with their colorless productions,' the 'mediocrity' that has been so easy for the majority of novel writers to produce (71).

Because so few novelists have the 'talent to teach us,' the key to making 'almost all moral truths … tangible,' and thus enabling the noble end of fiction, promoting virtue through moving and controlling the passions and feelings (74), the canon Staël offers is very select, dominated by novelists of sensibility, and far more cosmopolitan than most offered by her British contemporaries. She cites Lafayette, Tencin, St Pierre, Richardson, Fielding, Riccoboni, Marmontel, Sterne, Burney, Montolieu, Charrière, Godwin, and, though not the authors of what she can call proper novels, Pope (for 'Eloisa to Abelard'), Rousseau, Goethe, and the author of *The Portuguese Letters*. For Staël, realism is clearly not what it was to become for succeeding generations of critics, who would dismiss most of her favourites for not being realistic. In this sense, she helps to document an important transition. It is also significant that, although her canon is equally divided between men and women, Burney is the only English woman novelist Staël recognizes.

## Hannah More (1745–1833)

Staël's emphasis on the primacy of moral improvement is about all she shares with the more conservative critics of the novel, from those who would have been happy to ban all publication to those, like Hannah More, who realized that it is far more effective to write novels than to fight them. It is worth noting that More's only novel, *Cœlebs in Search of a Wife* (1808), was one of the most popular novels of the early nineteenth century, with twelve editions in its first year alone (Jones, *Ideas and Innovations*, 10). But More approached the novel only with the greatest caution. In 1799 she had declared that 'Novels, which used to be dangerous in one respect, are now become mischievous in a thousand. They are continually shifting their ground and enlarging their sphere, and are daily becoming vehicles of wide mischief.' Her *Hints towards Forming the Character of a Young Princess* (1805) contains three chapters on what young women should read: 'Books' (extracts from classic male writers such as Fénelon and Xenophon), 'Periodicals' (Addison and Steele and Johnson), and 'Books for Amusement.' In this last group she argues for romances over novels, developing the argument of Johnson's *Rambler* #4 (31 March 1750) far more fully. Her fear of realism is acknowledged as the basis for her preference for Oriental tales: *Zobeide* (1762) or *Almoran and Hamet* (1761) rather than *Tom Jones* (1749) or *The Princess of Clèves* (trans. 1679) (4: 283).

It must have been something of a surprise for her admirers to discover that More had turned novelist, and not all of them approved. But, as Ann H. Jones has pointed out, most of the various Evangelicals and many other readers, too, found that a novel like *Cœlebs* met their requirements for 'amusement' because it was sufficiently attentive to their moral and religious principles. Jones concluded that even when the public grew to demand less 'obtrusive' morality in their fiction, the Evangelicals continued to have a residual and 'beneficial' effect by giving 'the novel a respectability which encouraged better writers to adopt the form, and critics, therefore, to give it more attention' (*Ideas and Innovations*, 14). That view, one which clearly continues to be held, goes a long way towards explaining the critical fate of most early women novelists. When critics increasingly began to demand high moral seriousness in addition to high moral standards, they had less patience than ever for early women novelists. The shift from a criticism that valued the morality of More's *Cœlebs* to one that valued the artistry of George Eliot, in other words, had little impact on the status of eighteenth-century women novelists, as I argue in greater detail below.

## Robert Alves (1745–1794)

Robert Alves's *Sketches of a History of Literature* (1794) is typical of the odd, miscellaneous essays that evaluate the English novel. 'Sketch' is a good description of his four-page 'Parallel between History and Novel Writing,' where he defines the novel as history 'in a private capacity' (232). Alves sees the novel as a recently developed kind of writing, perfected by 'Fielding, Richardson, Brook, Smollet, and others.' When he looks to expand the core canon, he declares that 'Mrs. Griffith's Novels; the Tale of Other Times [possibly Anna Maria Porter's 'A Tale of Other Times' from *Artless Tales*, 1793–5], and Cecilia, by Miss Burney, are among the best I know' (233–4). This is not surprising to Alves. He considers the novel a genre especially appropriate for women writers, so much so that 'were women of genius and virtue always to attempt this kind of writing, it is to be presumed, from their greater sensibility and sense of character, that they would not only succeed better than the men in their descriptions, but conduct them with more delicacy' (234).

Alves's view of the novel as a feminized genre is, of course, not uncommon. It is a view that worked against the status of the novel as a literary form. But it also helped to establish women writers among novelists, in many cases giving them an advantage with the critics. At the end of the eighteenth century it is unusual to find a discussion of the novel that excludes women writers in the way that Fielding and Richardson or Beattie and Blair did just a generation or two earlier. The novels chosen for discussion, like Alves's, are often quite contemporary; there are few attempts at what later critics would consider genuine histories or canons. Few lists exclude women.

## William Beckford (1760–1844)

Novelists themselves are among the most frequent contributors of criticism of prose fiction, and while their criticism is usually self-promotional their commitment to the novel is rarely in doubt. They look to the history of the novel to create their own genesis, a process in no way disinterested, but guaranteed to take canon-making very seriously indeed – even when it assumes the form of parody, as in William Beckford's *Modern Novel Writing* (1796) and *Azemia* (1797). Beckford sends up the conventions of

sentimental and Gothic novels, takes passing swipes at most other novelistic genres, and concludes with parodies of the reviewing styles of the
most important magazines. Like most good parodists, he reveals so thorough a familiarity with his victims that his motives cannot be written off
as mere hostility. His parodies are the products of a keen reader of novels.

The parody of the reviews takes the form of an open letter to the
reviewers appended to *Azemia* by its putative author, Jacquetta Agneta
Mariana Jenks. Miss Jenks assures the reviewers that she has 'studied with
unwearied attention *all* the most approved novels of this present as well as
the past day' (235). The catalogue that follows can be taken as another
example of early canon formation: Fielding, Cervantes, Richardson,
Cumberland, Burney, Radcliffe, Mary Robinson, Mrs and Miss Gunning
(Susannah Minifie Gunning, Elizabeth Gunning Plunkett), Piozzi, Samuel Jackson Pratt (Courtney Melmoth), Sophia Lee, Inchbald, and Smith
are among those clearly acknowledged. There are no doubt more subtle,
passing references to others in this appendix; others are certainly sent up
in the main texts of *Azemia* and *Modern Novel Writing*. But like Alves, and
like the reviewers, Beckford has a clear sense of a developing canon of
novelists, and his, too, includes a large proportion of women novelists.

## Conclusion

To return, then, to Spender's three central claims about the status and
recognition of women novelists in the eighteenth century. (1) 'It was then
widely appreciated that women wrote novels, and wrote them well'
(*Mothers of the Novel*, 118). There can be little doubt about this assertion. It
is very rare to find a discussion of the novel that does not include women
novelists; the reviewers took them seriously and recognized their talents.
Those most likely to ignore them did so in the context of a fundamental
dislike or distrust of all novels. (2) 'In the beginning, and for quite a long
time thereafter, the novel was seen as the female forte' (118). This is a
more problematic claim. Whether Watt was right about the majority of
eighteenth-century novels being written by women is still under discussion and difficult to resolve, in part because the gender of the writers of
many anonymously published novels is unlikely ever to be known. The
novel was recognized as a form especially welcoming to women writers,
and many critics thought that women had special gifts or instincts for the
novel. But Richardson and Fielding were so successful in establishing
their founders' claims and rights that they continued to be seen as the
greatest novelists throughout the eighteenth century, and, after the death

of Smollett, many critics thought that the novel had entered a period of decline. There were, too, always critics unable to respond to women's writing without patronizing condescension or contempt. (3) Women writers 'were not just "actually" the majority, they were the *esteemed* majority' (137). Again, this is an assertion requiring qualification. Most novelists, including most women novelists, were not respected at all, let alone esteemed. They produced a popular form of literature that itself was widely held in low regard. Even when it enjoyed the respect of the more prestigious genres, the novel was produced by a great many writers of whom only a few could be considered the best. The most esteemed novelists were its fathers. The mothers – Behn, Manley, and Haywood – had been virtually written out of the history of the novel before there was one, that is, well before the end of the century. There is no question, however, that the various canons that were proposed include significant numbers of novels by women, and that women novelists were among those most highly respected by the critics.

Spender's assertions leave her with a number of interesting, unanswered questions. For me, the most important is: 'Now when we are presented with an exclusively male literary tradition – and this is how the early novel is presented – we must bear in mind that this is not because women did not write, could not get published, or went unacclaimed … How do we explain this transition from prominence to negation?' (138). Her answer takes the form of some brief speculations; most of her study is devoted to detailed discussion of the work of the women novelists of the eighteenth century she considers most worth recovering. So successful has the recovery been that the early novel is no longer presented as an exclusively male literary tradition.

The transition from recognition and appreciation to omission and denial – and back – is the subject of the following chapters. The new century was soon to bring more thorough and systematic studies of the novel, but not before these early critics had set the terms for much of the debate. These eighteenth-century critics did not attempt to write histories as they would soon be understood, but late-century critics like Reeve and Moore were the first to historicize the novel in English. Few saw canon-making as their goal, but insofar as they were evaluative critics, a canon of prose fiction can often be inferred from their work, especially from those with pedagogical impulses. But even Reeve, the best of the eighteenth-century critics, had little influence on criticism to follow.

The critics of the next generation cite very few of their predecessors, even when they return to the concerns that dominated the earlier criticism: the newness of the novel of the 1740s; the relationship and relative merit of the novel and romance; the relationship and relative merit of Richardson and Fielding; the degree to which the novel was a feminized form and the place of Richardson in that feminization; the decline of the novel after the death of Smollett; the problematic place of the 'female wits' in the development of the novel; and the moral value and potential of the novel as a popular form with an audience that included the uneducated, women, and children.

It is also the case that a number of ongoing obstacles to understanding the debates about these questions have already surfaced. Foremost is the absence of consistent definitions of terms such as 'novel,' 'romance,' and 'realism' (and its many synonyms). Other substantive problems include changing moral and cultural values; the different agendas of academic and more general critics; and the different agendas of reviewers and more historically driven critics. These problems all multiply with increasing attention to the novel in the nineteenth century, beginning with the unprecedentedly influential contributions of the Regency critics.

# 2 1800–1840

The history of the English novel is a Regency invention; the tastes and values of the Regency historians set the tone for all subsequent study. This was the time of the first serious attempts at canon making, and the canon established by the critics of the Romantic period became the canon to be modified thereafter. It is a period of ever-increasing reviews of novels, anthologies and collections of novels, and general novel criticism and theory. The three most important Regency novel critics, Anna Laetitia Barbauld, John Colin Dunlop, and Sir Walter Scott, merit special and fuller attention. A number of others, some more famous and important in other contexts, also deserve serious, if less full, discussion.

## Anna Laetitia Barbauld (1743–1825)

In 1931 Byron Hall Gibson praised Barbauld for producing 'the most complete and the most accurate history of prose fiction to appear during the years intervening between the publication of John Moore's "A View of the Commencement and Progress of Romance" (1797) and John Colin Dunlop's *History of Fiction* (1814)' (C. Moore, 'Ladies ... Taking the Pen in Hand, 384). This was no doubt intended as high praise, and not merely because of the lack of competition from other novel critics between Moore and Dunlop. But it does not begin to do justice to Barbauld as critic-historian of the novel. 'On the Origin and Progress of Novel-Writing,' the essay prefixed to her fifty-volume collection, *The British Novelists* (1810), is a quantum leap beyond the limited and narrow historical criticism offered by Moore. Barbauld is less well-informed about the novel before Cervantes, but as soon as she reaches post-medieval prose fiction her greater gifts as a novel critic become evident.

Barbauld had rehearsed the early history of the novel in her 'Life of Richardson,' the introduction to her edition of Richardson's *Correspondence* (1804).[1] In 'On the Origin' she fleshes out the earlier version (without altering her earlier judgments) while bringing the narrative up to date. She here introduces a collection of twenty-eight novels by twenty-one writers rather than the letters of 'the father of the novel of the serious or pathetic kind' ('Life,' xi). The Richardson edition had already shown that, although Barbauld herself was not a novelist, she had given much productive thought to the genre's formal qualities. In the 'Life of Richardson,' she begins by making a case for grouping epic, dramatic, didactic, and satiric with romantic narratives under the general class of *'fictitious adventures'* (vii). She then asks why it is that writers of romance alone among adventure writers have such a low reputation. This is followed by a division of novels into three kinds based on mode of narration: the 'narrative or epic,' the 'most common way,' and also Barbauld's favourite because of the flexibility it enables (xxiii–xxiv); the mode of 'memoirs,' that is, the first-person narrative, Barbauld's least favourite because of the limitations imposed by the single voice and perspective; and the mode of Richardson, the *'epistolary correspondence,'* able to capture the moment dramatically with the variety allowed by as many voices as the author chooses, but nonetheless 'the least probable way of telling a story' (xxvi–xxviii). A critic who had already written so attentively and thoughtfully about the art of the novel was well-prepared to provide a more sophisticated history than either Reeve's or Moore's.

'On the Origin and Progress of Novel-Writing' focuses on different critical issues, a shift made evident by its opening sentence: 'A Collection of Novels has a better chance of giving pleasure than of commanding respect' (1: i). The expected defence of the novel with a full literary pedigree does follow, but it is accompanied by a repeated insistence on the value of pleasure – though, of course, pleasure that is not at odds with morality – in a work of literature: 'To measure the dignity of a writer by the pleasure he affords his readers is not perhaps using an accurate criterion; but the invention of a story, the choice of proper incidents, the ordonnance of the plan, occasional beauties of description, and above all, the power exercised over the reader's heart by filling it with the successive emotions of love, pity, joy, anguish, transport, or indignation, together with the grave impressive moral resulting from the whole, imply talents of the highest order, and ought to be appretiated accordingly' (1: 2–3). The following sentence introduces the other central concept to be developed throughout the essay, that realism is the defining characteristic of the modern novel: 'A good novel is an epic in prose, with more of character and less (indeed in modern novels nothing) of the supernatural machinery' (1: 3). Although the emphases on pleasure and realism are already present, at least implicitly, in Barbauld's earlier novel criticism, they now loom large in determining which novels are most worthy of inclusion in an English canon.

Well into her essay Barbauld declares, in language anticipating critics like E.M. Forster, that 'It is sufficient therefore as an end, that these writings add to the innocent pleasures of life; and if they do no harm, the entertainment they give is sufficient good ... The unpardonable sin in a novel is dullness: however grave or wise it may be, if its author possesses no powers of amusing, he has no business to write novels' (1: 48). Barbauld's discussions of novels always take into account their power to give pleasure.

For Barbauld, the rise of the novel is tied closely to the development of realism. 'If the stage is a mirror of life, so is the novel, and perhaps a more accurate one, as less is sacrificed to effect and representation' (1: 51). Novels are thus in the best position to present the world as it is in order to prepare young readers for what they will find when they enter it. That preparation also requires, however, some protection from the most vicious realities, and considerable discretion in presenting vice triumphant: in 'good novels,' vice always leads to 'infamy and ruin' (1: 51). Barbauld calls attention to the varieties of prose fiction that make up the history of the novel, but she gives special attention to those like Cervantes, who attacked the old romances, and Lafayette, whose works 'are esteemed to be the first which approach the modern novel of the serious kind' (1: 18). She runs through English fiction from Chaucer to Behn in a couple of pages before reaching 'the first author amongst us who distinguished himself by natural painting ... that truly original genius De Foe' (1: 37). The next generation brings Richardson, 'the first author who has given celebrity to the modern novel' (1: i).

Women play a prominent role in Barbauld's history. She holds the French novel in very high esteem, and of the twenty-five French novelists she names, nine are women. Of the twenty-seven English novels in her history, six are by women. And, of greater importance, of the twenty-one novelists whose works are reprinted in the subsequent volumes, eight are women, accounting for twelve of the twenty-eight titles.[2] It is, of course, true that Barbauld was not entirely free to choose which novels to anthologize. They are, however, some of 'the most approved novels,' though of 'very different degrees of merit,' chosen in part to ensure variety, in part in response to 'the taste and preference of the public,' and in part by the constraints of copyright (1: 61). Barbauld acknowledges the place and the importance of personal taste in the selection process. She thus ends 'On the Origin' with a claim that might very well have seemed extravagant at the time: 'It was said by Fletcher of Saltoun, "Let me make the ballads of a nation, and I care not who makes the laws." Might it not be said with as much propriety, Let me make the novels of a country, and let who will make the systems?' (1: 62).

As Elizabeth Kraft has pointed out, the list of titles and authors covered in 'On the Origin' far exceeds the number in the collection and 'is notable for the few titles it shares' in common ('Anna Barbauld's Edition of the British Novelists,' 5). Barbauld's history is far more inclusive, covering novels from other countries and earlier periods. The anthology, on the other hand, accurately named *The British Novelists*, begins with Richardson. The area that interests her least is the British novel before 1740. Aside from two sentences of high praise for Defoe Barbauld has little good to say about the early British novelists: her discussion totals under two pages, and nearly half of it is devoted to a relatively extensive treatment of *Gaudentio di Lucca*. The only women Barbauld mentions before 1740 are Margaret Cavendish, Duchess of Newcastle, and the long-notorious 'Female Wits,' Behn, Manley, and Haywood. Newcastle is dismissed as an 'indefatigable writer' of 'ponderous performances.' Because 'Behn's novels were licentious,' they have 'fallen.' Manley provided her readers with nothing more than 'fashionable scandal'; she is remembered only because of her place in *The Dunciad*. Haywood was able to profit from Pope's just chastisement; 'her later works are by no means void of merit' (1: 35–7). In short, Barbauld has even less desire than Reeve to revive interest in the earliest women novelists.

Barbauld is scarcely more impressed by the first generation of women novelists to appear after the publication of *Pamela* (1740). She mentions only two in 'On the Origin,' Sarah Fielding and Frances Sheridan, in the context of a discussion of novels 'which are, or have been popular, though not of high celebrity.' Fielding was 'a woman of good sense and cultivation; and if she did not equal her brother in talent, she did not, like him, lay herself open to moral censure' (1: 43). Sheridan, 'an ingenious and amiable woman,' nonetheless produced in *Sidney Bidulph* a work that heaps 'distress upon virtue and innocence, merely to prove, what no one will deny, that the best dispositions are not always sufficient to ward off the evils of life' (1: 44). She shares Reeve's concern about excessive melancholy in the novel and suggests that, for reasons she does not understand, women novelists are especially vulnerable to what she considers sentimental weaknesses.[3] Three other women of the earlier generation are discussed in the introductions Barbauld provides within the collection proper. Clara Reeve has 'but a moderate degree of merit,' though she has always been 'a great favourite.' 'Subsequent publications of more elegance and invention' have caused *The Old English Baron* (1778) 'to slide from the place it once held' (22: i). Its plot is too easy to predict, though it remains a good, moral tale for young readers. Charlotte Lennox was 'a diligent and successful author,' and *The Female Quixote* (1752) 'an agreeable and ingenious satire' (24: i) (Romantic critics' adjectives of praise are as telling as ours), but Lennox did not know how to end her novel: 'the grave moralizing of a clergyman is not the means by which the heroine should have been cured of her reveries' (24: iii). Though 'the style of Mrs. Lennox is easy,' it 'does not rise to the elegance attained by many more modern female writers' (24: iv). Finally, Frances Brooke, an 'elegant and accomplished woman,' was 'perhaps the first novel-writer who attained a perfect purity and polish of style' (27: i). Her greatest strength is as a descriptive writer, especially of the climate, landscape, and people of Canada.

This is not to suggest that Barbauld held earlier women novelists in contempt. On the contrary, she takes those she mentions quite seriously, seriously enough to engage in thoughtful criticism of their work. She does not choose to recover or include women writers neglected by Reeve, and she excludes from her history a number of women mentioned by Reeve: Elizabeth Rowe, Sarah Scott, Maria Susanna Cooper, Elizabeth Griffith, Helen Maria Williams, Susannah Minifie [Gunning], the dame de Fauques; she also excludes Frances Sheridan's *Nourjahad*. (She, of course, excludes a number of male novelists Reeve mentioned too.) There are a number of likely reasons for these changes. Barbauld (and, I expect, her publishers) did not share Reeve's enthusiasm for the Eastern tale, a form that had fallen out of fashion. Rowe is too didactic for her taste, and the others are probably rejected as second- or third-rate writers, judgments few would quarrel with today.

But the main reason for Barbauld's relative lack of interest in the earlier generation is her far greater enthusiasm for more recent fiction, especially fiction by women. She accepts a number of the earlier historical commonplaces, especially those that see a decline in the novel after Richardson and Fielding, aided and abetted by the circulating libraries, which encourage 'a great deal of trash' to be published year after year (1: 58). Yet despite the 'many paltry books' that continue to appear, 'it may safely be affirmed that we have more good writers in this walk living at the present time, than at any period since the days of Richardson and Fielding' (1: 58–9). She argues that the decline is over, that progress has been restored, largely thanks to the efforts of the current generation of women: 'A very great proportion of these [good writers] are ladies: and surely it will not be said that either taste or morals have been losers by their taking the pen in hand. The names of D'Arblay, Edgeworth, Inchbald, Radcliffe, and a number more, will vindicate this assertion' (1: 59).

Additional vindication comes in the introductions to the novels of Inchbald, Burney, Radcliffe, and Edgeworth in the collection proper. A sample of Barbauld's superlatives should be sufficient: 'To readers of taste it would be superfluous to point out the beauties of Mrs. Inchbald's novels' (28: i); 'Scarcely any name, if any, stands higher in the history of novel-writers than that of Miss Burney, now Mrs. D'Arblay' (38: i); 'A greater distinction is due to those who stand at the head of a class; and such are undoubtedly the novels of Mrs. Radcliffe, – which exhibit a genius of no common stamp' (43: i); 'The editor feels it would be superfluous to indulge her feelings in dwelling on the excellencies of an author [Edgeworth] so fully in possession of the esteem and admiration of the public' (49: i). Even after discounting the tact required in treating authors still living (and personal friends at that), there can be little doubt about Barbauld's critical agenda. *The British Novelists* offers a forum for furthering the reputations of contemporary novelists, the best of whom are women. In reflecting and voicing the taste of her time as well as her personal taste, Barbauld is simply doing what most critics have always done. What makes her effort unusually significant is that it is one of the formative attempts at canon making for the British novel. Once there is a canon in place, subsequent critics must address it as their starting point. That the first canons of the British novel are the products of early nineteenth-century critics is of enormous importance to the critical histories of eighteenth-century women novelists.

## John Colin Dunlop (1785–1842)

With the appearance of *The British Novelists*, it becomes possible to talk about a fully realized canon of the novel. A fully realized history of the novel in English, John Colin Dunlop's *The History of Fiction* (1814), was published a mere four years later, perhaps just a coincidence, but one which helped cement the nineteenth-century base upon which subsequent structures had to be built. Dunlop's plan is encyclopedic, a historical account of all prose fiction from earliest times (though very little non-European fiction is, in fact, included). Acknowledging the contributions of few of his predecessors – Percy and Warton, but not Reeve, Moore, or Barbauld – Dunlop considers his work the first 'attempt towards a general History of Fiction' (11). In terms of comprehensive coverage, his claim is warranted. Of his fourteen chapters, only the final two cover 'the novel.' The first two discuss ancient prose fiction; the remaining ten discuss medieval and Renaissance 'romance.' All these works share a number of things in common: 'fictitious narratives' (7) are as ubiquitous as Barbauld's 'fictitious adventures.'

Dunlop's theory of fiction, a phrase he would disdain since he considers 'the establishment of a theory' in conflict with 'the investigation of truth' (11), is traditional and inclusive. He follows Bacon's lead in preferring fiction to history because fiction 'presents us with the fates and fortunes of persons rewarded or punished according to merit. And as real history disgusts us with a familiar and constant similitude of things, *Fiction* relieves us by unexpected turns and changes, and thus not only delights, but inculcates morality and nobleness of soul. It raises the mind by accommodating the images of things to our desires, and not, like history and reason, subjecting the mind to things' (8).

Dunlop continues in this vein, arguing that prose fiction is superior to poetry, since it 'can discriminate without impropriety, and enter into detail without meanness.' Even if the 'utility' of 'Fiction were less than it is, how much are we indebted to it for pleasure and enjoyment!' (8). Fiction is thus unique among human products as a 'powerful instrument of virtue and happiness.' Like Barbauld, he thinks it has been too long 'despised.' His own project is part of a wider and timely effort to see fiction 'more justly appreciated' (9). A history of fiction is another important sign that the novel has come of age.

Dunlop's discussion of the Greek romances provides an interesting introduction of some of the characteristics he values most in the novel. He criticizes all early fiction for consisting largely of 'a succession of strange, and often improbable adventures.' What distinguishes the Greek from the other early romances, and as a result makes them 'extremely pleasing,' is that they are 'almost the first productions in which woman is in any degree represented as assuming her proper station of the friend and companion of man.' Dunlop is unequivocal in his privileging of 'manners and character' over 'adventure' as the most important and valuable constituents of the best novels (46).

Dunlop recognizes that literary forms develop and change over time, 'that one species of fable has scarcely disappeared, when it has been succeeded by another,' a consequence of the constant need of fiction to satisfy the requirements of 'the human mind' for 'amusement and relaxation' (360). He credits the French with the most important recent changes in the kinds of fictions that now attempt to satisfy these basic human desires. Recent French fiction is divided into four 'classes': fictionalized history, romances describing European manners through foreign eyes, fairy tales (including Oriental tales and *les voyages imaginaires*), and 'novels ... of which the incidents, whether serious or comical, are altogether imaginary' (361).

The last class, which is the most important in the history of fiction, is given the most thorough treatment. Dunlop adopts Johnsonian language in considering *La Princesse de Clèves* 'the earliest of those agreeable and purely fictitious productions, whose province it is to bring about natural events by natural means, and which preserve curiosity alive without the help of wonder – in which human life is exhibited in its true state, diversified only by accidents that daily happen in the world, and influenced only by passions which are actually to be found in our intercourse with mankind' (362). *La princesse de Clèves* and Lafayette's other novel, *Zaïde* (trans. 1678), 'may justly be regarded as forming a new æra in fiction, and as effecting the most fortunate revolution we have witnessed in the course of our survey.' Since that time, novels 'no longer attempted to please by unnatural or exaggerated representations, but emulated each other in the genuine exhibition of human character, and the manners of real life' (366). Dunlop welcomes the new demands for realism, though his judgments of specific works point to a very different standard of realism from those made familiar by Victorian and twentieth-century critics. The other French novelists Dunlop treats extensively are Marivaux, Prévost, Riccoboni, Rousseau, Crébillon, and Voltaire. Three of the seven writers of historical romance mentioned by Dunlop are women, and Grafigny is one of the five writers of fictions examining manners from the perspective of a foreigner.

Dunlop shares Barbauld's preference of French to British fiction, though his canon is far more selective than hers. His discussion of French fiction is twice the length of his discussion of British fiction, the final chapter of his *History*. He apologizes for the 'compression' of his discussion of 'modern French tales and novels' (400); his rationale is that these works are more familiar to his readers than the earlier romances. That is still more the case for modern British novels, so he limits himself to 'a very short and general survey' (401), though not without acknowledging that a proper analysis of British novels 'would require some volumes' (413). One of the more interesting reasons Dunlop offers for the difficulty in covering modern novels is that the recent explosion in number has also multiplied the kinds of fiction being written: 'In former periods, when readers were few, and when only one species of fiction was written at a time, it was easy to judge what were the circumstances which gave birth to it, and to which it gave birth in turn.' It is no longer the case that novels are clearly 'expressive of the taste and feelings of the period of their composition' (400–1), a view at odds with most of his predecessors, and one that Dunlop's many readers would increasingly reject.

English prose fiction of the Middle Ages and romances of the Renaissance are covered in earlier chapters. Dunlop begins his final chapter with the other kinds of Renaissance fictions, especially those of Lyly, Lodge, and Greene. There is little of importance between them and the Restoration, when the demand for prose fiction was restored with the monarchy. He mentions Newcastle and Orrery as worthy of notice, though without influence. They are followed by the 'Female Wits,' and here Dunlop repeats the familiar tale. Manley was popular because she provided her readers with the 'fashionable scandal' they craved; her popularity could not last. Behn is clearly a far greater writer, but 'her writings have not escaped the moral contagion which infected the literature of that age.' *Oroonoko* is the least indecent of her novels, the only one still worthy of mention. Haywood's early novels are too corrupt for a more refined age, but *Betsy Thoughtless*, 'though not free in every passage from the objections that may be charged against her former compositions, is deserving of notice, both on account of its merit, and of having apparently suggested the plan of Miss Burney's Evelina' (409).

There are so many novels by mid-century that it is useful to subdivide them, and Dunlop chooses to consider them in three groups, 'the *serious*, the *comic*, and the *romantic*.' 'At the head of the first class' (410) is Richardson, who is joined by Sheridan and Godwin. The only comic novelists noticed are Fielding and Smollett; the British comic novelists are no more successful than the French in commanding Dunlop's respect. It is the romantic novel, 'which seems in a great measure peculiar to the English' (413), that excites his greatest interest and enthusiasm. Here again the examples are limited: to the pioneers, Walpole and Reeve, and to the master, Radcliffe, 'this justly celebrated woman' (415), who is treated at greater length than any other British novelist, with more than double the space given to Richardson, her nearest rival. Dunlop concludes his account of the British novel with brief discussions of the important fiction from the other three categories he established in his discussion of French fiction. Fictionalized history has produced nothing worth noting in English – this in 1814. The Citizen of the World (1762) is the only romance of manners through foreign eyes of genuine merit. Fairy tales and Oriental tales have produced nothing of value. But le voyage imaginaire is a form in which British writers are unsurpassed; Robinson Crusoe, Gulliver's Travels (1726), and Gaudentio di Lucca provide conclusive evidence, while Peter Wilkins (1751), William Bingfield (1753), and John Daniel (1751) show that the tradition established by Defoe continued to thrive for at least another generation.

Dunlop's History is important as the first comprehensive history of the novel in English. It was frequently reprinted throughout the nineteenth century and remained the standard work in the field until Ernest Baker's eleven-volume History of the English Novel was published over a hundred years later. As a standard reference work, even its brief discussion of the British novel had considerable influence. Dunlop was clearly an elitist in his tastes, with a strong preference for serious fiction; he had little patience for humour or immorality, though he took great pleasure in the Gothic. While small and exclusive, his canon is also gender neutral. It includes only eight of the twenty-one authors in Barbauld's collection; even in 1814, there is no single canon. Especially significant for this study is Dunlop's reinforcement of Barbauld's treatment of the women novelists before the generation of Burney: only Frances Sheridan survives.

### Sir Walter Scott (1771–1832)

Barbauld edited an important collection of novels; Dunlop provided a history. A third monument to the growing status of the novel is the writing of a series of 'Biographical and Critical Sketches,' on the model of Johnson's Lives of the Poets (1779–81) by Sir Walter Scott. Scott's essays were originally written as prefaces to Ballantyne's Novelists

*Library* (1821–4), a project that was neither successful nor completed. Like Johnson's, however, they were later collected, first in a pirated edition by the French publisher, Galignani, and subsequently as part of Scott's collected *Miscellaneous Prose Works* (1827), and later still in a single volume as *Lives of the Novelists*, the title they are best known by today. When taken together with Scott's occasional essays and reviews, they form one of the most important bodies of novel criticism in English. It is surprising that such a statement is necessary, but Scott is remarkably underrated as a critic. Wellek devotes a mere two paragraphs to him in *A History of Modern Criticism* (1955–92), asserting that he is not 'an important critic.' The highest praise he offers is to note that 'there is some rudimentary criticism in the *Lives of the Novelists* (1821 [*sic*]).' He also observes that 'Scott preferred Smollett to Fielding and praised Jane Austen, as he should. But he praised almost everyone of whom he wrote' and 'lacked discernment, and even critical pretensions and principles' (2: 122).

Scott's extended comparison of Fielding and Smollett in the 'Memoir of Tobias Smollett,' modelled on Johnson's comparison of Dryden and Pope in 'The Life of Pope,' argues for granting Smollett 'an equal rank with his great rival Fielding,' as the conclusion to an essay that places both novelists 'far above any of their successors in the same line of fictitious composition' (3: 181).[4] Scott indeed praised Austen long before most others, and his approach to criticism is one that looks for the best. Like Johnson, though, Scott always offers a balanced view of the strengths and weaknesses of his subjects, however much his presentation accentuates the positive. Perhaps most unforgivable for Wellek is Scott's indifference to principles and his complete lack of pretension. Peter Morgan accurately captures Scott's values as a critic with the following adjectives: 'untheoretic, sincere, careless, modest, generous, good-tempered, judicious, gentlemanly' ('Scott as Critic,' 91). These were not qualities highly prized in critics at the end of the twentieth century, but their presence should not hide the fact that in quantity, quality, range, and insight, Scott's criticism earns him a high place in any study of the criticism of the novel.[5]

*Ballantyne's Novelists Library* consists of novels by fourteen writers, of whom only two are women, Clara Reeve and Ann Radcliffe. With the exception of Lesage, all are British. None were still active in 1821; most were dead. Scott's choices of recent novelists, if they were his, were limited by copyright; his choice of earlier writers was more clearly an expression of his taste. When Galignani issued his piracy and the *Lives* came to the attention of Scott's friend Lady Louisa Stuart, she wrote him to urge him to publish a British edition and to inquire about omissions from his canon: 'Either Galignani has not printed all, or many are wanting whom you certainly do not mean to pass by: Moore's "Zeluco," Godwin's "Caleb Williams" and "St. Leon," Charlotte Smith, Miss Burney, Miss Hamilton, Miss Edgeworth, Miss Austen, and may I petition a word in favour of Charlotte Lennox, Dr, Johnson's favourite, whose female Quixote delighted my childhood so much that I cannot tell whether the liking I still have for it is from taste or memory' (234). Lady Louisa's list of recent novels seems to her beyond dispute, but her case for Lennox is far less assured. She recognizes that tastes change, and that books that once pleased do not necessarily continue to do so. She includes the following anecdote with reflections in her letter:

> I am lately returned from a friend's house where these prefaces have been *devoured* by man, woman, and child. One evening after they were finished, a book was wanting to be read aloud, and what you said of Mackenzie made the company choose the 'Man of Feeling,' though some apprehended it would prove too affecting. However, we began. I, who was the reader, had not seen it for several years, the rest did not know it at all. I am afraid I perceived a sad change in it, or myself, which was worse, and the effect altogether failed. Nobody cried, and at some of the passages, the touches that I used to think so exquisite – oh dear! they laughed. (234–5)

It is an anecdote worthy of attention for its own sake, revealing as it does the always unstable nature of any literary canon, and it is additionally important for the reply it provoked from Scott, a reply that only indirectly deals with Lady Louisa's excluded favourites, but one which reveals Scott's complete agreement with her about the effect of changing tastes on the canon:

> It is very difficult to resolve your Ladyships curious question concerning change of taste but whether in young or old it takes place insensibly without the parties being aware of it. A grand aunt of mine old Mrs. Keith of Ravelstone ... lived with unabated vigour of intellect to a very advanced age. She was very fond of reading and enjoyd it to the last of a long life. One day she asked me when we happened to be alone together whether I had ever seen Mrs Behns novels – I confessd the charge. – Whether I could get her a sight of them – I said with some hesitation I believed I could but that I did not think she would like either the manners or the language which

approached too near that of Charle[s] IIds time to be quite proper reading. Nevertheless said the good old Lady I remember them so much admired & recollect being so much interested in them myself that I wish to look at them again. To hear was to obey. So I sent Mrs. Afra Behn curiously seald up with 'private & confidential' on the pacquet to my gay old grand aunt. The next time I saw her afterwards she gave me back Afra wrapd up with nearly these [words] 'Take back your bonny Mrs Behn and if you will take my advice you will put her in the fire for I found it impossible to get through the very first of the novels – But is it not she said a very odd thing that I an old woman of eighty and upwards sitting alone feel myself ashamd to read a book which sixty years ago I have heard read aloud for the amusement of large circles of the first and most creditable society. [10: 96]

The optimistic Scott's nod to progress aside, these passages document the changing responses to the first several generations of women novelists by two generous and unusually well-informed readers, themselves of different generations, in the 1820s.

Scott's choice of recent writers, he explains, has been limited by factors other than taste: 'I thought of Charlotte Smith whom I admire very much. Miss Edgeworths novels & Miss Austens are inimitable but being both copy-rights could not come within my plan' (10: 95–6). Smith had been included in the original plan, but the series failed before it reached her; his 'Memoir' of her is included in the *Miscellaneous Prose Works*. The only other 'Memoir' not part of the original collection is of Defoe; any other additional authors part of Scott's original plan remain unrecorded. But he does record a number of other recent women novelists he considers important in the 'Memoir' of Smith:

We cannot but remark the number of highly-talented women, who have, within our time of novel-reading, distinguished themselves advantageously in this department of literature. Besides the living excellence of Mrs D'Arblay, and of Maria Edgeworth, of the Authoress of *Marriage* and the *Inheritance*, and of Mrs Opie, the names arise on us of Miss Austen, the faithful chronicler of English manners, and English society of the middling, or what is called the genteel class; besides also Mrs Radcliffe, Miss Reeves, and others, to whom we have endeavoured to do some justice in these sheets. We have to thank Mrs Inchbald, the authoress of *Frankenstein*, Mrs Bennett, too, and many other women of talents, for the amusement which their works have afforded; and we must add, that we think it would be impossible to match against these names the same number of masculine competitors, arising within the same space of time. (4: 69)

Scott's list is remarkably inclusive, ranging from popular favourites like Burney and Edgeworth to writers without strong critical reputations like Austen and Shelley. Like Barbauld and Dunlop, he recognized the novel as an international form with a long tradition and a wide range of species within the umbrella of prose fiction. The above passage testifies to the inclusiveness of his taste: unlike most of his predecessors and still more of the critics of the next generations, he was receptive to good writing regardless of form. He recognized faults within individual writers as well as the inevitable shortcomings of the various novelistic genres, but no writer is dismissed for choice of form and no form dismissed because of weak practitioners.

Scott accepts the basic distinction between 'novel' and 'romance,' but happily embraces both. He condemns coarseness, crudeness, and indecency, but forgives Defoe, Smollett, and Sterne when they are guilty. He thinks it misguided to provide rational explanations for the supernatural, but finds Radcliffe's fertile imagination and poetic gifts, particularly of natural description, more than sufficient compensation. He claims that Mackenzie's originality in portraying human feeling excuses his neglect of plot and character.

In two important areas, Scott anticipates critical trends that will later be developed by far less tolerant writers. Though Scott recognized that the novel was an international form he had a much stronger predilection for the British novel than most of his predecessors. He credits Fielding with retrieving the novel from 'the disgrace in which he found it,' and rendering it 'a classical department of British literature' (3: 93). He even wonders whether Fielding's novels, quintessentially English as they are, 'can be fully understood, or relished to the highest extent, by such natives of Scotland and Ireland, as are not habitually and intimately acquainted with the characters of Old England' (3: 77). For Scott, Fielding's Englishness is an essential quality of his writing, but not an honorific. Later critics would build upon such observations as part of a nationalistic agenda for the novel.

Nor does Scott use his admiration for Fielding to denigrate Richardson, whom he recognizes as a great innovator, and as the author of the 'most affecting and sublime' *Clarissa* (1747–8), the writer of a 'classic' whose 'fame' is guaranteed 'for ever' (3: 41, 38). The 'gentleness of [Richardson's] mind was almost feminine' (3: 13); yet 'his manly and virtuous application of his talents [has] been of service to morality, and to human nature in general' (3: 76). It is interesting that one of the qualities that impressed Richard Whately in his review of *Northanger Abbey* (1818) and *Persuasion* (1818) in the *Quarterly Review,* attributed to Scott and collected in the *Miscellaneous Prose Works,* about Austen's 'new style of novel' (18: 210), was 'the insight she gives us into the peculiarities of female character' (18: 235). At last a woman novelist supplanted the 'interloping male' (18: 236), Richardson, at the representation of women in fiction, an anticipation of a much later development in novel criticism. Richardson remains for Scott what he was for Johnson, a great novelist through mastery of the affective and instructive powers of fiction, powers undiminished by Scott's recognition of Fielding's different but equivalent excellence. Scott will not condemn Richardson any more than Radcliffe for not possessing 'the excellence proper to a style of composition totally different from that which she has attempted' (3: 363). Yet Scott is writing at a time when the Fielding versus Richardson dialectic had long been established, and the balance had clearly shifted in favour of Fielding.[6] The increasingly feminized Richardson continued to be out of favour with most critics for well over a century. It is no coincidence that most eighteenth-century women novelists shared his fate. Responses to Richardson remain an important bellwether for responses to eighteenth-century women novelists and provide a recurring theme in this study.

Scott is never unaware of gender issues in his criticism, but his evaluations are notable for their gender neutrality. Susan Buchan is right to argue that 'Walter Scott had no vanity of sex, and he never condescended' (*Lady Louisa Stuart,* 208). Others responded quite differently to a literary form with an enormous readership and increasing respectability (as evidenced by the critical work of Barbauld, Dunlop, Scott) dominated, almost controlled, by women writers. This is not the place to repeat Scott's critical history, but that history has consequences for the women novelists who preceded him. It is ironic that Scott the novelist was welcomed by so many of his contemporaries and for some time thereafter as 'a robust and manly writer,' a novelist free of the influence of women writers, 'a novelist without origins except in the legends and traditions of oral culture' (Robertson, *Legitimate Histories,* 21, 14), and one who finally 'validates novel reading as a male practice' (Ferris, *The Achievement of Literary Authority,* 10). Scott's own criticism, as well as his novels, continued to provide a powerful influence on his successors; no critic of the novel is cited more frequently in the nineteenth century.

## William Hazlitt (1778–1830)

A useful contrast to Scott as critic of the novel is offered by one of the keener admirers of 'the author of Waverley,' William Hazlitt. Hazlitt is much more systematic in his thinking about the novel, and far more limited in his taste. A committed defender of the novel, he argued for its importance as a form that can 'profit' and 'delight' through 'a close imitation of men and manners ... the very web and texture of society as it really exists, and as we meet with it when it comes into the world,' and as an invaluable 'record of past manners and opinions' (*Complete Works of William Hazlitt*, 6: 134). The novel, for Hazlitt, is the realist novel; and while he values within his model of the realist novel 'sentiment,' 'imagination,' 'wit,' and 'humour,' he places the highest value on the 'profound knowledge of human nature' as evidenced by 'masterly pictures of the characters of men,' the qualities that make Fielding the pre-eminent British novelist, 'equal to Hogarth' and 'little inferior to Shakespeare, though without any of the genius and poetical qualities of his mind' (6: 113). Smollett may be his superior in humour, Sterne and Richardson in pathos, but it is Fielding who best realizes the qualities Hazlitt respects in the novel.

Where Scott is generous and inclusive in his novel-reading tastes, Hazlitt is far more exclusive: 'the first-rate writers' of novels 'are few.' 'The principal of these are Cervantes and Le Sage, who may be considered as having been naturalised among ourselves; and, of native English growth, Fielding, Smollett, Richardson, and Sterne' (6: 107). A footnote acknowledges Defoe, another *The Fool of Quality* (1765–70), *David Simple* (1744), *Sidney Bidulph*, and *The Vicar of Wakefield* (1766). That the 'four best novelwriters' are roughly contemporary is important to Hazlitt. He echoes the late-eighteenth-century view of a golden age of novel writing, adding a historical explanation. He credits the age of George II with allowing 'a security of person and property, and a freedom of opinion' that allowed manners to become 'more domesticated'; there was also 'a general spirit of sturdiness and independence, which made the English character more truly English than perhaps at any other period – that is more tenacious of its own opinions and purposes ... The reign of George II. was, in a word, the age of *hobby-horses*' (6: 122).

The age of George III brought unfortunate changes to English society and, necessarily, to the novel. Revolution and war are just two highprofile examples of the concerns of a society no longer tolerant of the independence that fuelled the great British novel. 'It is not to be wondered at,' Hazlitt observes, 'if amidst the tumult of events crowded into this period, our literature has partaken of the disorder of the time'

(6: 123). He mentions very few recent novels and is positive about fewer still. He admires Radcliffe's ability to harrow 'up the soul with imaginary horrors; she has all the poetry of romance, all that is obscure, visionary, and objectless, in the imagination.' But unlike Barbauld, Dunlop, and Scott, he is unimpressed by her descriptive powers ('vague and wordy to the last degree') or her characters ('insipid,' and always the same) or her stories, which always come to 'nothing' (6: 125–6). She is, however, much to be preferred to most Gothic writers (Walpole, Sophia Lee, and Reeve are offered as representative examples). The only other Gothic writer worthy of praise is Matthew Lewis, though he is Radcliffe's inferior. Hazlitt also admires Inchbald's 'power over the springs of the heart' (6: 127), the 'imagination and passion' of the 'author of Waverley' (Scott's identity was unknown to Hazlitt when he wrote this essay) (6: 128), and the union of philosophy and romance in Godwin (6: 131–2). Maria Edgeworth's novels are pedantic, pert, and pretentious (6: 123).

'On the English Novelists' is a revised and slightly expanded version of Hazlitt's review of *The Wanderer* (1814) that first appeared in the *Edinburgh Review*. It was a hostile review, full of disappointment at Burney's departures from her earlier novels, novels that had won her 'a distinguished place' in the canon of British novelists. But not for their plots. 'The difficulties in which she involves her heroines' are always the 'Female Difficulties' that provide the subtitle of *The Wanderer*. 'They are difficulties created out of nothing' (6: 124). What Hazlitt had admired about Burney was that she was 'quite of the old school of novelists,' that is, 'a mere common observer of manners.' But she has an additional quality that distinguishes her novels from the 'masterpieces' of the age of George II: she is 'also a very woman,' a handicap with predictable results: 'She is a quick, lively, and accurate observer of persons and things; but she always looks at them with a consciousness of her sex, and in that point of view in which it is the particular business and interest of women to observe them. There is little in her works of passion or character, or even manners, in the most extended sense of the word, as implying the sum-total of our habits and pursuits; her *forte* is in describing the absurdities and affectations of external behavior, or *the manners of people in company*' (6: 123).

Insofar as *The Wanderer* fails to capitalize on Burney's proven strengths, it is treated harshly; Hazlitt finds nothing of value to compensate for what has been lost. The passages of severest condemnation are not, however, reprinted in 'On the English Novelists.' Instead, the more general discussion of Burney's first three, better novels stands largely on its own. As a result, the more general theory that informs the description of Burney's weaknesses becomes more central in the revised essay:

Women, in general, have a quicker perception of any oddity or singularity of character than men, and are more alive to every absurdity which arises from a violation of the rules of society, or a deviation from established custom. This partly arises from the restraints on their own behaviour, which turn their attention constantly on the subject, and partly from other causes. The surface of their minds, like that of their bodies, seems of a finer texture than ours; more soft, and susceptible of immediate impulses. They have less muscular strength; less power of continued voluntary attention – of reason, passion, and imagination: but they are more easily impressed with whatever appeals to their senses or habitual prejudices. The intuitive perception of their minds is less disturbed by any abstruse reasonings on causes or consequences. They learn the idiom of character and manners, as they acquire that of language, by rote, without troubling themselves about the principles. Their observation is not the less accurate on that account, as far as it goes; for it has been well said, that 'there is nothing so true as habit.' (124)

In linking his discussion of women novelists to a general theory of gender, and applying the result to the best women novelists, Hazlitt codifies and elevates an approach rarely made explicit and hitherto usually applied only to popular or disreputable women writers. Though he is too honest a critic to ignore the achievements of the Burneys, Inchbalds, and Radcliffes, his gendering of the novel assumes that women in his society cannot achieve the greatness of the best male writers because they are women. Hazlitt does not pursue this line to the levels of blatant misogyny of many subsequent critics, but he does pave the way either to a canon virtually free of women or to separate and unequal canons for men and women (which is not to suggest that he would have welcomed these developments, or have been proud of his contributions to them).[7] Hazlitt also anticipates two other lines that will recur in the subsequent criticism. He shares Scott's view of Fielding as 'thoroughly English' (6: 112), and extends this characterization by associating the triumphs of his favourite with the triumphs of English society, just as he follows Fielding himself in domesticating Cervantes and Lesage. (Edgeworth's only worthwhile novel, *Castle Rackrent*, is praised as a 'genuine, unsophisticated, national portrait' [6: 123]). The nationalistic component in Hazlitt's criticism will be developed and exploited by later critics. Finally, his treatment of Burney as the best of a bad lot of novelists between Smollett and Scott prepares the way for the later view of her as the transitional figure between Fielding and Austen that dominates so many late nineteenth- and twentieth-century narratives of the development of the novel.

**Francis Jeffrey (1773–1850)**

It is no mere coincidence that the original version of 'On the English Novelists' appeared in the *Edinburgh Review* (1802–1929). Its editor, Francis Jeffrey, shared Hazlitt's admiration for Scott and the early Burney, for many of the same reasons. His canon was also small, highly selective, well-informed through extensive novel reading, and dismissive of most of what was written in the last third of the eighteenth century. Jeffrey himself reviewed but a handful of novels, mainly by Scots (Scott, Galt, Wilson, and Lockhart), but also by the Irish Edgeworth. He welcomed the work of Edgeworth and Scott (and their imitators and successors) in part because of their patriotic representations of Scotland and Ireland[8] and in part because they embraced the new standards of realism. 'The writings of Miss Edgeworth,' Jeffrey declares in 1812, 'exhibit so singular an union of sober sense and inexhaustible invention – so minute a knowledge of all that distinguishes manners or touches on happiness in every condition of human fortune ... that it cannot be thought wonderful that we should separate her from the ordinary manufacturers of novels' (*Contributions to the Edinburgh Review*, 517). Two years later, Jeffrey welcomes the anonymously authored *Waverley* (1814) as the product of 'a man of Genius' with 'virtue enough to be true to Nature, ... even in the marvellous parts ... copying from actual existences, rather than the phantasms of his own imagination' (524).

One of Jeffrey's first reviews was of Barbauld's edition of the *Correspondence of Samuel Richardson* (1804). In it he suggests that it is not Richardson's 'knowledge of the human heart' or 'his powers of pathetic description' that will ensure his high reputation among novel readers, but rather his careful attention to detail. Anticipating Ian Watt, Jeffrey aligns Richardson with Defoe as the eighteenth-century masters of realistic detail, the main reason he is one of the few eighteenth-century novelists to pass the test of time. In an almost throw-away line Jeffrey refers to two writers who have not passed that test: 'The next series of letters is from Miss Fielding, who wrote *David Simple*; and Miss Collier, who assisted in writing *The Cry*. What modern reader knows any thing about the *Cry*, or *David Simple*? And if the elaborate performances of these ladies have not been thought worthy of public remembrance, what likelihood is there that their private and confidential letters should be entitled to any notice?' (126).

Jeffrey's sense of the novel is, then, as historicized as Barbauld's, Dunlop's, Scott's, and Hazlitt's. He recognizes that the novel has come a long way since the time of Richardson. One of his most interesting comments is made in the two-paragraph introduction to his reviews of 'novels, tales, and prose works of fiction' selected for publication in the *Contributions to the Edinburgh Review* (1843):

> As I perceive I have, in some of the following papers, made a sort of apology for seeking to direct the attention of my readers to things so insignificant as *Novels*, it may be worth while to inform the present generation that, *in my youth*, writings of this sort were rated very low with us – scarcely allowed indeed to pass as part of a nation's permanent literature – and generally deemed altogether unworthy of any grave critical notice. Nor, in truth – in spite of Cervantes and Le Sage – and Marivaux, Rousseau, and Voltaire abroad – and even our own Richardson and Fielding at home – would it have been easy to controvert that opinion in our England, at that time: For certainly a greater mass of trash and rubbish never disgraced the press of any country, than the ordinary Novels that filled and supported our circulating libraries, down nearly to the time of Miss Edgeworth's first appearance. There had been, the Vicar of Wakefield, to be sure, before; and Miss Burney's Evelina and Cecilia – and Mackenzie's Man of Feeling, and some bolder and more varied fictions of the Misses Lee. But the staple of our Novel market was, beyond imagination, despicable: and had consequently sunk and degraded the whole department of literature, of which it had usurped the name.
>
> All this, however, has since been signally, and happily changed; and that rabble rout of abominations driven from our confines forever. The *Novels* of Sir Walter Scott are, beyond all question, the most remarkable productions of the present age; ... In England ... they have imitators enough ... But the works most akin to them in excellence have rather, I think, been related as collaterals than as descendants. Miss Edgeworth, indeed, stands more in the line of their ancestry; and I take Miss Austen and Sir E.L. Bulwer to be as intrinsically original ... Among them, however, the honour of this branch of literature has at any rate been splendidly redeemed; – and now bids fair to maintain its place, at the head of all that is graceful and instructive in the productions of modern genius. (512)

Late Jeffrey provides a smooth transition to a Victorian canon, one the reviews played a significant role in forming. Jeffrey's is an early voice among the reviewers calling for the production of novels of moral realism, novels that reject both sensibility and the Gothic, the mainstays of the late eighteenth century and, in particular, of the women novelists who so thoroughly dominated the market.

## John Wilson Croker (1780–1857)

A second example, this time from the rival *Quarterly Review* (1809–1967), of a critic with a similar, though not identical, agenda is offered by John Wilson Croker. His similarity in approach to the novel is especially note-worthy since Croker shared so little else with Jeffrey or Hazlitt (who referred to Croker as a 'talking potatoe'). Croker joined Hazlitt as the other important reviewer of Burney's *The Wanderer*, and, like Hazlitt, found it a great disappointment, hard to distinguish from the popular women's novels they both contemned: 'We regret to say, that the Wanderer, which might be expected to finish and crown her literary labours, is not only inferior to its sister-works, but cannot in our judg-ment, claim any very decided superiority over the thousand-and-one vol-umes with which the Minerva Press inundates the shelves of the circulating libraries' (124). His review of *Melmoth the Wanderer* (1820) uses the occasion to condemn the Gothic and radical elements that were so popular at the turn of the century, in a typical blast of dismissive sarcasm: 'Compared with [*Melmoth*], Lady Morgan is almost intelligible – The Monk, decent – The Vampire, amiable – and Frankenstein, natural' (303).

Croker was also the *Quarterly*'s reviewer of *Waverley*, and he, like Jeffrey, welcomed it with enthusiasm. He used this review to present his version of the history of the novel, a version more sympathetic with eighteenth-century theories of literature (Croker was a life-long admirer of Pope and Johnson), but one which ultimately comes to the same conclusion: the novel has come a long way, and the end result is a great improvement.

> The earlier novelists wrote at periods when society was not perfectly formed, and we find that their picture of life was an embodying of their own conceptions of the *'beau idéal.'* – Heroes all generosity and ladies all chastity, exalted above the vulgarities of society and nature, maintain, through eternal folios, their visionary virtues, without the stain of any moral frailty, or the degradation of any human necessities. But this high-flown style went out of fashion as the great mass of mankind became more informed of each other's feelings and concerns, and as a nearer intercourse taught them that the real course of human life is a conflict of duty and desire, of virtue and passion, of right and wrong; in the description of which it is difficult to say whether uniform virtue or unredeemed vice would be in the greater degree tedious and absurd.
>
> The novelists next endeavoured to exhibit a general view of society. The characters in Gil Blas and Tom Jones are not individuals so much as

specimens of the human race; and these delightful works have been, are, and ever will be popular, because they present lively and accurate delineations of the workings of the human soul, and that every man who reads them is obliged to confess to himself, that in similar circumstance with the personages of Le Sage and Fielding, he would probably have acted in the way in which they are described to have done.

From this species the transition to a third was natural. The first class was theory – it was improved into a *generic* description, and that again led the way to a more particular classification – a copying not of man in general, but of men of a peculiar nation, profession, or temper, or, to go a step further – of *individuals*. (354–5)

There are few eighteenth-century novelists worth reading, and they are not women. With Croker, attitudes towards the eighteenth-century novelists that would dominate subsequent criticism are firmly in place. They never quite root out all memory of the early novel, but they come close.

Croker's reference to the Minerva Press points to the growing divide between popular novels and those held in high regard by the critics. Dorothy Blakey's study of the Minerva novels chronicles an enormous number of forgotten novels by forgotten novelists. She points out, for example, that only four of the Minerva's best-selling authors of 1798 are to be found in the *DNB* (Agnes Maria Bennett, Regina Maria Roche, Eliza Parsons, and Mary Meeke), and they were usually ignored by contemporary critics, just as they are now. The Minerva Press reprinted novels by Burney, Radcliffe, and Smith; it published novels by Bage, Brockden Brown, Fenwick, Genlis, Holcroft, Johnson, Lee, and Opie. But the vast majority of its publications were consumed by the circulating libraries and forgotten. These novels, largely supplied by women novelists, were not taken very seriously at the time and have never been given serious consideration in literary histories. Never candidates for anyone's canon, they were instead treated as confections. High-minded critics expressed opinions ranging from concern to outrage about the damage they might do their consumers, but not about the likelihood that they would displace better novels in the hearts and minds of the educated reading public.

### 'The Literary Spy' and Critical Survey in Magazines

The highest praise available to most Minerva novelists was recognition by a ladies' magazine. One of the most systematic surveys of the novel was published in six parts (January–July, excluding February 1808) by 'The Literary Spy' in *The Ladies Monthly Museum* (1798–1828). In order 'to correct the taste and improve the judgment of the fair readers,' the author offers 'an impartial review of female literature' in the form of a survey of 'modern authors.' These authors are all novelists, since it is novels that are 'universally read' ('however generally depreciated'), and since better novels, those 'written with elegance' and 'improved by purity of moral,' are 'likely to improve the manners, and awaken the sensibilities of the heart,' especially when pursued in moderation (June 1808, 19). 'The Literary Spy' adds with obvious pleasure that 'the greater number' of these modern authors are 'as commendable in their conduct in private life, as conspicuous for their genius and literary requirements' (20). The agenda here is clearly not canon formation in the sense of identifying a select list of the very best, but rather to provide a list of novels that will not embarrass the husbands and fathers of their intended readers, that is, an approved list of safe authors.

The survey covers forty-two novelists, thirty women and thirteen men.[9] Roughly a third of them are usually found on more elite canonical lists; about two-thirds had at least one work published by the Minerva Press. The survey is limited to 'modern' authors, more to appeal to its intended audience than to convey a sense of the superiority of recent fiction. The brief judgments offered range from effusive praise (Burney, Radcliffe) to generous praise (Hamilton, Inchbald), lukewarm praise (Gunning, Parsons), condescension (Gooch, Roche), and disapproval (Hunter). The vast majority of authors are praised, and very few are subjected to rigorous criticism. These articles were not written to encourage critical reading. Their importance lies in acknowledging and attempting to answer a need for guidance in choosing good popular novels regardless of canonical status.

'The Literary Spy' provides a useful survey of what was popular. Other magazines commissioned more critical surveys of the novel, from the very brief 'Thoughts on Novel Writing' in *Blackwood's* (1819) to the interesting set of parallel surveys in the *New Monthly Magazine* (1820). The *Blackwood's* article acknowledges that the novel now fills the social role once held by the epic, but laments that it has joined other literary and cultural forms in a spiralling decline. Scott is not seen here as a harbinger of better times. Rather, the article's author argues that English literature is in desperate need of regeneration of the kind that can be offered by German philosophy. A sense of decline and loss informs the proposed canon of great novelists: Cervantes, Fielding, Lesage, Smollett, Goethe, and Scott (394). The absence of reference to Richardson as one of the representatives of past greatness is startling in a critic who sees that greatness as having last been realized in the mid-eighteenth century. The total absence of women novelists, past and present, is still more startling and, I would argue, clearly related. It is another early indication of the strong correlation between assessments of Richardson and assessments of eighteenth-century women novelists.

More important is the two series of articles in the *New Monthly*, 'The Living Novelists' with an introductory essay 'On British Novels and Romances,' the other 'On the Female Literature of the Present Age.' Both offer unusually thoughtful criticism for a popular magazine. The series 'The Living Novelists' focuses on Mackenzie, Scott, Godwin, and Maturin. The introductory essay begins with praise for the novel as the form that has brought the benefits of literature to a wider audience than ever before. Early masters in the development of the novel are Richardson, Fielding, Smollett, Goldsmith, Defoe, Henry Brooke, Radcliffe, and Sterne (more or less in that order). The parallel series on women writers, sometimes in the same numbers, indicates a comfort with the separation of novelists by gender. 'There is no more delightful peculiarity in the literature of the present age than the work and brilliancy of its female genius. The full development of the intellect and imagination of women is the triumph of modern times' (271). This generalization is followed by a two-part survey documenting the case, in the form of a series of long paragraphs introducing and characterizing worthy woman writers. Novelists dominate the essays, though poets and others are also included. The novel canon emerges as Radcliffe, Smith, Hamilton, Brunton, More, Edgeworth, Opie, Lamb, the Porters, Inchbald, Burney, S.H. Burney, Morgan, Austen, and Frances Jacson, the then anonymous authors of *Rhoda* (1816) and *Things by their Right Names* (1812). It is clearly a list constructed by a critic with broad and catholic tastes. What is especially significant is that, however receptive this critic is to literature by women, there are no women writers worth mentioning before about 1790.

### Eaton Stannard Barrett (1786–1820)

Where critics like 'The Literary Spy' expressed concern about the moral well-being of novel readers, such efforts are at most damage control when compared either to the moral responses of the influential Evangelicals[10] or the satirical responses of the surprising number of parodists of popular fiction in the early nineteenth century. It was the latter group who, in the tradition of *Don Quixote* and *The Female Quixote*, expressed the most forceful concern about the well-being of the novel as a literary form and, for them a related issue, the dominance of women among novel writers. The most successful as well as the most excessive product of these concerns was Eaton Stannard Barrett's *The Heroine* (1813). Michael Sadleir considers only Beckford's *Modern Novel Writing* as a rival of its 'sheer lunacy of incident, but even Beckford does not brutally identify the particular works at which his mockery is aimed' ('Introduction,' 15). Barrett's list of targets is extensive and inclusive, ranging from Agnes Maria Bennett, Frances Burney, Sophia Lee, Madame de Genlis, Madame de Montolieu, and Hannah More to Edmund Burke (*Reflections*), Sir Francis Burdett (*Address to the Electors of Westminster*) and Napoleon (*To the Soldiers on Parade*), the poetry of Milton, Macpherson, and Scott, and the plays of Shakespeare and Sheridan. But his favourite targets are a much more limited and clearly defined group: Ann Radcliffe, Lady Morgan, Regina Maria Roche, Rousseau, Goethe, Sterne, Staël, that is, the leading writers of the Gothic and sentimental novels that were the most canonical novel texts of the age.

Gary Kelly is no doubt right to stress the conservative, Tory values informing *The Heroine*, solid, middle-class values that included a call for realism in fiction and a concern about overindulgence of the imagination. Barrett reveals little sympathy for progressive ideas, particularly on issues of class and gender.[11] Barrett's reformed heroine, having profited greatly from reading *Don Quixote*, concludes with the following, balanced view of novel reading:

> I do not protest against the perusal of fictitious biography altogether; for many works of this kind may be read without injury and some with advantage. Novels such as the Vicar of Wakefield, Cecilia, O'Donnel, The Fashionable Tales, and Cœlebs, which draw man as he is, imperfect, instead of man as he cannot be, superhuman, are both instructive and entertaining. Romances, such as the Mysteries of Udolpho, the Italian, and the Bravo of Venice, which address the imagination alone, are often captivating and seldom detrimental. But unfortunately, so seductive is the latter class of composition, that people are apt to become too fond of it, and to neglect more useful books. This, however, is not the only evil ... (349)

The predictable catalogue of dangers and concerns follows, with recommendations for a more balanced diet of pleasures. *The Heroine*, as Sadleir points out, comes late in the fashion for the Gothic and sentimental, though not too late to help push them out of fashion. So thorough was the subsequent rejection of Barrett's 'laughing-stocks' that they almost completely 'faded into the mists of the unknown' (Sadleir,

'Introduction,' 11), taking *The Heroine* with them as it became a signi-
fier which had lost its signified. The consequences for the next generation of histories of the novel form the subject of my next chapter.

## Conclusion

The critics of the Romantic period, then, were the major originators of
ideas about and approaches to the history of the English novel and its
canon. They established a progressive history of the novel that was to
remain Whiggish throughout the century and well into the next, a history
quite different from the histories of poetry and drama produced alongside
it. Where those histories looked back to an earlier, golden age of writers
like Homer and Shakespeare, histories of the novel had no need to apologize for the inability of recent writers to match the greatness of their predecessors. The Romantic critics occasionally praised eighteenth-century
novelists, particularly Richardson and Fielding, but for the most part, earlier novelists were valued largely for what they contributed to the development of an ever-improving genre. Since the perfection of the novel
(unlike poetry and drama) had yet to occur, there was no need to focus
unduly on the past. Later critics continued to apply a similar methodology
based on similar assumptions to their histories. The high points in those
histories continued to move forward with time; the presentist orientation
of the critics, their histories, and their canons remains constant.

The Romantic critics, like their predecessors and successors, disagreed
among themselves about specific titles to be included in a canon of the
novel. Most Romantic critics privileged realism in the novel, though
theirs was a realism that included elements of the Gothic and large doses
of sensibility, that is, a realism at odds with the Victorian realism that
heavily influenced standards and norms for twentieth-century critics.
There was an increasing preference for Fielding over Richardson, linked
to a growth of nationalism in the criticism, a devaluing of sensibility, and
an increasing gendering of the novel. Scott's view of Richardson as the
best novelist before Austen at representing women points to another reason why Richardson's reputation declined in the nineteenth century.
Once he had been surpassed in his area of greatest strength, his importance diminished for most of these presentist critics. Finally, with the
increasing respectability of the genre more men wrote novels, and the
predominantly male critics valorized a more masculine standard for
assessing them. These trends were established in the early nineteenth
century but not fully developed before the Victorians.

# 3 1840–1880

The critics and literary historians I discuss in the following three chapters are no longer writing about their contemporaries when they turn to the novel and the women novelists before Austen. Reviews of new novels were increasingly high-profile features of the most important and respected periodicals; even the most highly regarded men of letters frequently contributed these reviews. They are, of course, no longer immediately relevant to this study, but they point to the status and interest in the novel generated by Scott and his successors. That interest also resulted in an explosion of criticism of the novel and, of special relevance for my study, of interest in the history of the novel, so much so that I must now be more selective in my discussions of the criticism. The present chapter looks first at representative critics of the five major subgenres of literary history that consider early women novelists in the age of the high Victorian realist novel: general histories of British literature, histories of the British novel, literary encyclopedias, histories of literature by women, and belletristic essays about the novel. I then survey a wider range of critics on a number of specific, recurring questions related to the value and reputation of the early women novelists. The chapter ends before serious challenges to the hegemony of the critical axiom that Victorian realism marks the triumph of the British novel; it also ends just as academic criticism is about to join the subgenres listed above as a major formulator of ideas about the early novel and its canon. I argue that common questions and common assumptions dominate the critical discourse of the mid-nineteenth century, and that there are widely shared answers based on those assumptions, but I also include the full range of opinions found in the period, which saw increasing numbers of publications about the novel. Although dominant positions can be identified on most issues, no single, coherent narrative can encompass the positions of all the contributors to the debate. I believe it important to include the many discordant voices.

# I

## H.A. Taine (1828–1893)

The rise of the novel coincided with what René Wellek has termed the 'rise' of English literary history, a development that introduced historicist methods requiring critics to evaluate works and authors on their own terms rather than in the universalized, ahistorical terms of the critic. As the theoretical assumptions behind historicist criticism became increasingly sophisticated under the influence of German philosophy, so too did the resulting literary studies. The most influential nineteenth-century example is H.A. Taine's *History of English Literature* (first French edition, 1864, translated 1872). In it, Taine develops one of the most famous theories of literary history, that literature must always be seen as the product of three determining causes: race, milieu, and moment. Briefly, race is usually interpreted as the collective, innate, hereditary component in each individual, the *Volkgeist* or genius of the nation; milieu is made up of the external forces that determine the individual personality; moment refers to the impact of the particular age on the individual, that is, the *Zeitgeist*. These three factors determine all human activity, including literary activity, and Taine's analysis of English literature is predicated upon them.[1]

Taine's chapter on the novelists comes in Book 3, 'The Classic Age,' immediately following chapters on Addison and Swift. Like many of his contemporaries, Taine sees the novel as we know it as beginning with Defoe, though he recognizes that prose fiction is not an eighteenth-century invention. His opening paragraph reveals his approach:

> Amidst these finished and perfect writings a new kind makes its appearance, suited to the public tendencies and circumstances of the time, the anti-romantic novel, the work and the reading of positive minds, observers and moralists, not intended to exalt and amuse the imagination, like the novels of Spain and the middle ages, not to reproduce or embellish conversation, like the novels of France and the seventeenth century, but to depict real life, to describe characters, to suggest plans of conduct, and judge motives of

action. It was a strange apparition, and like the voice of a people buried underground, when, amidst the splendid corruption of high life, this severe emanation of the middle class welled up, and when the obscenities of Mrs. Aphra Behn, still the diversion of ladies of fashion, were found on the same table as De Foe's *Robinson Crusoe*. (3: 257)

Taine's outline is as deterministic as his theory: once-flourishing but now aging genres are described as 'old dried-up branches' whose energy is diverted to the 'unseen boughs' which suddenly 'grow and turn green ... The novel springs up everywhere, and shows the same spirit under all forms.' The English novel is a 'character novel,' since the English are 'more reflective than others, more inclined to the melancholy pleasure of concentrated attention and inner examination.' And the English novel depends on 'observation' and 'spring[s] from a moral design' (3: 268–9). Its moral centre vacillates between conscience and instinct; Taine's treatment of Richardson and Fielding is in terms of a dichotomy between 'rule and nature' (3: 270).

Rule, personified by Richardson, imposes its views on its audience with far too heavy a hand for Taine. 'By seeking to serve morality,' he tells Richardson, 'you prejudice it ... We are repelled ... We are not such fools as you take us for. There is no need that you should shout to make us afraid' (2: 287). Taine recognizes in Richardson the strengths of 'Christian casuistry,' those of the hard-working printer-bookseller who was 'delicate moreover, gentle, nervous, often ill, with a taste for the society of women, accustomed to correspond for and with them, of reserved and retired habits, whose only fault was a timid vanity' (3: 271).

Richardson's novels deserve the full treatment (seventeen pages) they receive: he is a major writer. Fielding rates fewer pages (eleven), and they are constructed in contrast: 'a robust, strongly built man, above six feet high, sanguine, with an excess of good humour and animal spirits, loyal, generous, affectionate, and brave, but imprudent, extravagant, a drinker, a roysterer' (3: 289). He, too, is 'eminently a moralist' (3: 296), but so true is he to nature (or opposed to rule) that he devotes far too much of his energy to the life of the senses, to the neglect of all that is decent, refined, poetic. 'You are so coarse yourself,' Taine tells Fielding, 'that you are insensible to what is atrocious ... Man, such as you conceive him, is a good buffalo; and perhaps he is the hero required by a people which gives itself the nickname "John Bull"' (3: 300).

Fielding and Richardson are followed by the 'mediocre' Smollett (five pages) and enigmatic Sterne (five pages), whose mixture of 'blindness and insight' reflects the 'sickly and eccentric humorist, a clergyman and a libertine, a fiddler and a philosopher' (3: 307–8). Taine has now dealt with the early novel, and his narrative moves forward to the moment 'when purified manners will, by purifying the novel, give it its final impress' by expelling 'the coarseness of Smollett and the indecencies of Sterne,' pausing only to pay tribute to that great favourite of the Victorians, *The Vicar of Wakefield* (four pages) before watching the novel fall 'into the almost prudish hands of Miss Burney' (3: 311–12).

Taine's discussion of the history of the novel resumes in Book 4, 'Modern Life,' where he asserts that 'modern man' is 'impelled by two sentiments, one democratic, the other philosophic,' the result of living in an age of challenges to established orders that have raised new aspirations in the common man. Wellek accurately describes this part of Taine's argument as 'a panegyric of the most unrestrained, passionate, emotional romanticism' (4: 52). The only novelist from the Romantic period to rate Taine's attention is Scott, 'the Homer of modern citizen life.' Taine has doubts about Scott's (or any other British novelist's) ability to come to terms with 'the historical novel,' but he is most impressed by Scott's representation of Scottish society and by his perfecting of 'the novel of manners.' His success led 'Miss Austen, Miss Brontë [*sic*], Mrs. Gaskell, George Eliot, Bulwer, Thackeray, Dickens, and many others [to] paint, especially or entirely in his style, contemporary life, as it is, unembellished, in all ranks, often amongst the people, more frequently among the middle class' (3: 440–4). These later novelists, treated in detail in subsequent chapters, realize the potential of the novel, one enabled by Scott.

Taine limits his discussion of the early novel to six novelists: Defoe, Richardson, Fielding, Smollett, Sterne, and Scott. Only two women before Austen, Behn and Burney, receive even passing reference, and both references are disparaging. Taine is important not for what he says directly about women novelists, but because of what his history of the novel implies about the novelists he does not mention. His handling of Richardson and Fielding is relatively even-handed, based as it is on serious reservations about each. But it is oppositional in ways that point to the growing preference (not Taine's own) for Fielding because he is more manly, more natural, the better artist and the more representative English writer (the novelist as John Bull). Taine's theory provides a greater impetus in this direction than he chooses to follow himself. As William VanderWolk points out, when Taine characterizes a writer, he 'is not a biographer'; his interest is 'not the individual author but the author as a representative of his race, surroundings, and epoch'

('Hippolyte Taine,' 901). It follows that an interest in the representative novelist limits Taine to the major novelists (invariably identified as the most representative by virtually every critic). And given his view of pre-Victorian English society, it is not surprising to find no women among his representative writers. Finally, given his belief in the recent perfection of the novel, there is little reason to pursue many novelists before Scott.

George Saintsbury anticipated Wellek's enthusiastic response to Taine. He considered the *History* 'one of the most brilliantly written of its class, one of the most interesting, perhaps *the* history of literature.' But he also anticipated one of the concomitant major weaknesses of Taine's approach: ignoring 'the minor writers who give the key of a literature much more surely than the greater ones.' The result is a study 'only valuable for qualities which are not of its own essence, and in qualities which are of its essence is very nearly valueless' (Saintsbury, *History of Criticism*, 3: 442). It would not be accurate to say that Taine was hostile to all women writers: many of his favourite writers in the nineteenth century are women. (Wellek expresses his disgust with Taine's 'high praise' for E.B. Browning's *Aurora Leigh* [*History of Modern Criticism*, 4: 57].) But both his theory and his taste militated against most novelists before Scott – and all women. Most of the lines of his thought about the novel are typical of the criticism of the period, and will recur in much of the criticism that follows.

### David Masson (1822–1907)

Fortunately, Taine's limited focus on major writers is also an extreme among the Victorian critics. Sharing many of his views does not limit other critics to the same short list of novelists. This is especially true for those who follow Dunlop in attempting histories of the novel. David Masson's *British Novelists and Their Styles* (1859), an expanded version of a series of lectures he delivered to the Philosophical Institution of Edinburgh in 1858, offers a prominent example. Masson begins by placing the novel as a prose branch of poetry (rather than history or philosophy), and more particularly the prose equivalent to narrative (rather than lyric or dramatic) poetry. (The similarity to Reeve is probably coincidental.) A long discussion of the similarities and differences between poetry and prose concludes by emphasizing the central value of each: just as for an epic poem, 'the measure of the value of any work of fiction … is the worth of the speculation, the philosophy, on which it rests ... No artist ... will, in the end, be found to be greater as an artist than ... thinker.' Of secondary but considerable importance to the critic is the way in which this philosophic speculation is realized through the handling of 'the incidents, the scenery, and the characters' (24). Masson's privileging of ideas in his construction of the novel as a genre informs his subsequent history.

Masson begins with a brief tour of the earliest works of prose fiction before settling into his subject proper, the history of the British novel, with the observation that 'in no country was the impulse to the narrative form of literature earlier or stronger than in Britain' (46). He surveys medieval and Elizabethan prose fiction, ending his discussion of early British prose fiction with Boyle, Bunyan, and Behn. He admires Bunyan; Behn is merely the representative novelist of the age of Dryden. Her 'place in the literature of her day was a slight one; and the fact that she alone is now usually named as representing the Novel of the Restoration shows how little of the real talent of the time took that particular direction.' It is only in the next generation, the generation of Swift and Defoe, that 'Prose Fiction shot up into vigour and importance' (78).

For Masson, the 'eighteenth century' (1688–1789) was 'a century bereft of certain high qualities of heroism, poetry, faith'; instead, it was 'distinguished chiefly by a critical and mocking spirit of literature' (82). One of the few benefits was the 'tide of prose unexampled in any former time' (87–8), with 'the new British prose fiction' one of its 'most notable manifestations' (89). The initial long catalogue of prose writers Masson provides to make his case for the special quality of eighteenth-century writing consists only of men. The more detailed discussion, that is, the bulk of the second 'lecture,' is only slightly more inclusive. Swift and Defoe are the early novelists of choice; among their contemporaries, Masson notes Addison and Steele, Pope and Arbuthnot, and finally 'those short novels of licentious incident by Mrs. Heywood [sic] and the other followers of Aphra Behn, which are to be found bound up in old volumes, four or five together, in the neglected shelves of large libraries' (98–9).

Little changes when Masson moves on to the novelists of mid-century. 'When we think of the British Novelists of the Eighteenth Century, we think of Richardson, Fielding, Smollett, and Sterne, and of the others as arranged round them. It is common ... to speak of them as the fathers of the present British Novel' (99). The fathers are then given full treatment. The latter three are humanists, writers of 'the comic prose epic of contemporary life' (130), the greatest strength of the period. Richardson is the exception, and Masson's reading of Richardson marks an important development of earlier trends. He plays the middle-class 'prosperous London printer, of a plump little figure and healthy complexion' (99) off against the aristocratic Fielding, 'tall, handsome, altogether magnificent fellow, with a face (if we may judge from his portrait by Hogarth) quite kingly in its aspect, and yet the very impersonation of reckless good-humour and abounding animal enjoyment' (101). As the rivalry between them unfolds, Richardson becomes 'the nervous, tea-drinking, pompous little printer, coddled as he was by a bevy of admiring women, who nursed his vanity, as Johnson thought, by keeping him all to themselves, and letting nothing but praise come near him' (103).

When Masson turns to the novels, it is with a similar ambivalence. 'We do not read Richardson's novels much now; and it cannot be helped that we do not.' They are 'written in the tedious form of letters' (107) and they move only 'inch by inch.' He reminds his Victorian readers that they were written at a time when there was more leisure, and fewer novelists of excellence available to satisfy the new class of eager consumers of novels. Johnson and Macaulay both consider Richardson a 'master,' and anyone who takes the trouble to read him must share their high opinion (108). Masson explains with care why Macaulay is wrong to consider Richardson a prose Shakespeare, but in the process points to the genuine strengths he admires in a long, careful analysis. He ends his account of Richardson with Coleridge's objection that Richardson's 'romances of love' are too 'limited.' Masson agrees, though he extends the point in a way that deflects some of its force: 'Now, though this is the practice, not of Richardson alone, but of the majority of modern novelists, and especially lady-novelists, it is worthy of consideration that the novel is thereby greatly contracted in its capabilities as a form of literature. Perhaps, however, we can well afford one eminent novelist, such as Richardson, to the exclusive literary service of so important an interest' (119).

Richardson is to be tolerated, but other writers who share his limited interests are thereby rendered redundant. Those other writers are, of course, the 'lady-novelists' of the eighteenth century. Richardson has, in short, become the synecdoche of choice for eighteenth-century women novelists – as well as their finest specimen.

Masson devotes the final four and a half pages of Lecture 2 to those remaining novelists of the period worth mentioning. The three important works in this group are *Rasselas*, *The Castle of Otranto* (1765) and that 'charming prose idyl [*sic*] of dear Irish Goldy' (151), *The Vicar of Wakefield.* 'To make the list ... complete,' Masson concludes with Johnstone, Mackenzie, Reeve, Burney, Beckford, Cumberland, Bage, and Moore. All of these novelists are talented, yet since all are derivative of 'some one or other of their recent predecessors,' Masson feels justified in denying them 'separate recognitions' (154). For Masson, then, Burney and Reeve are the only women novelists between Richardson and 1789 worthy of even a bare mention, a view increasingly dominant through the nineteenth century.

If one were to read no further, it would be easy to believe that Masson is another misogynist critic, his mind closed to any potential value in novels by women. Lecture 3, on the novelists of the Romantic period, qualifies any such conclusion. The hero of the chapter is clearly Scott, 'since Shakespeare, the man whose contribution of material to the hereditary British imagination has been the largest and the most various' (195). The lecture literally begins and ends with Scott, who receives more extensive coverage than any other novelist. Wedged in the middle is a retrospective review of Scott's immediate predecessors covering the period 1789–1814. Although this is the period of the 'Minerva-Press Novels,' dominant until Scott influenced tastes for the better, 1789 'as might be expected' also marks the appearance of 'novelists of a better class' (175) since it marks the beginning of the present age, an age that has profited from the philosophical and historical thinking sparked by the French Revolution. Nowhere is that benefit more apparent than in the revival of literature.

In the period 1789–1814 Masson counts 'twenty novelists of sufficient mark to be remembered individually in the history of British Prose Literature' (177). To the holdovers from the earlier period, Bage and Moore, he adds 'in order of their appearance ... Thomas Holcroft, Mrs. Charlotte Smith, Sophia and Harriet Lee, Mrs. Inchbald, Mrs. Radcliffe, Matthew Gregory Lewis, Mrs. Opie, William Godwin, Anna Maria Porter and Jane Porter, Miss Edgeworth, Miss Jane Austen, Mrs. Brunton, Mrs. Hamilton, Hannah More, Miss Owenson (afterwards Lady Morgan), and the Rev'd Charles Maturin' (178). A ten-page discussion of these novelists follows. The first part presents two significant 'facts': (1) that 'no fewer than fourteen out of the twenty novelists that have been named were women' (178), and (2) 'out of the entire twenty, *twelve* were of English, *six* of Irish, and only *two* of Scottish birth,' a point of special interest to the Scottish Masson, who returns to it later. Masson pauses to expand upon his first fact, noting that because men shifted their energies to other forms of literature, 'women took possession of the Novel' (179). He is not at all sure

why this happened, but the results are beyond dispute. His account, with
its echoes of Scott, is worth quoting at length:

> If the Novel or Prose Fiction was the first fortress in the territory of litera-
> ture which the women seized – nay, if they seized it all the more easily
> because the men, being absent elsewhere, had left it weakly garrisoned –
> it cannot be denied, at all events, that they manned it well. Not only were
> the women in the majority, but they also did the duty of the garrison bet-
> ter than the men who had been left in it. With the exception of Godwin, I
> do not know that any of the male novelists I have mentioned could be put
> in comparison, in respect to genuine merit, with such novelists of the
> other sex as Mrs. Radcliffe, Miss Edgeworth, and Miss Austen. Out of this
> fact, taken along with the fact that from that time to this there has been an
> uninterrupted succession of lady-novelists, and also the fact that, though
> the Novel was the first fortress into which the sex were admitted in any
> number, they have since found their way into other fortresses of the liter-
> ary domain, not excepting Poetry, nor even History, and have done excel-
> lent duty there too – out of these facts, I say, may we not derive a
> prognostication? ... It is obvious that we have already gained much by
> the representation which women have been able to make of their peculiar
> dispositions and modes of perception in the portion of the field of litera-
> ture which they have already occupied. Perhaps there was a special pro-
> priety in their selecting the Prose Fiction as the form of literature in which
> first to express themselves – the capabilities of that form of literature
> being such that we can conceive women conveying most easily through it
> those views and perceptions which, by presupposition, they were best
> qualified to contribute. (179–81)

Masson's welcoming of women to literary authorship was far from
universal. His acknowledgment of the contributions of women to the
novel during the Romantic period is not uncommon, but his embrac-
ing a world of equal opportunities is at odds with the reality of the literary world around him. Scott's success had given the novel sufficient
prestige to make it once again very inviting for male writers, who over
the next several generations transformed novel writing into a field in
which the most prominent, best-paid writers were largely male.

Finally, Masson concludes his discussion of Scott's predecessors by
turning to the novels, grouping them in 'three classes, each representing
a *tendency* of British prose fiction of the period' (183). The first class
comprises novels addressing the 'social speculations and aspirations'

that were raised by the French Revolution. Most prominent among these are the novels of Bage, Holcroft, and, notably, Godwin. The second group is 'the Gothic romance of the picturesque and the terrible' (185), the tradition begun by Walpole and Reeve. Its exemplars include Lewis, Maturin, the Porters, and Harriet Lee; its greatest master is Radcliffe. The majority of novelists have always belonged to the third class, the 'mere painters of life and manners' (188). This group includes Moore, the Lees, Inchbald, Smith, Opie, Brunton, Hamilton, More, and Owenson; its masters are Edgeworth and Austen, especially Austen, whose novels are 'not only better than anything else of the kind written in her day, but also among the most perfect and charming fictions in the language' (189). This is the subgenre of the 'lady-novelist' for Masson; it is interesting that he overlooks the contribution of women to his first class entirely. But it is also important that, like most critics of the previous generation or two, he includes large numbers of turn-of-the-century women novelists in his canon while continuing to exclude virtually all of their predecessors. It is worth noting, too, that when he turns his attention to his own contemporaries, he makes it clear that George Eliot is the greatest British novelist of all time.

## Robert Chambers (1802–1871)

Masson's *British Novelists* began as a series of lectures aimed at an educated general audience. Aimed at a broader audience still was Robert Chambers's *Cyclopædia of English Literature* (1843), the only study of literature to make it on to Richard Altick's list of Victorian best-sellers. Altick accepts Henry Curwen's estimation that Chambers's *Cyclopædia* sold 130,000 copies 'in a few years' (*The English Common Reader*, 389). Chambers's subtitle, *A Series of Specimens of British Writers in Prose and Verse. Connected by a Historical and Critical Narrative*, describes his volumes well. His intention is to extend 'the late efforts for the improvement of the popular mind ... to bury the belles lettres into the list of those agencies which are now operating for the mental advancement of the middle and humbler portions of society.' Chambers sees his work as an extension and updating of Knox's *Elegant Extracts* (1784), but the *Cyclopædia* is much more, for it is more comprehensive both in its selections and in the narrative provided to place them in a context intelligible to a broader readership than the one Knox addressed. The extraordinary success of Chambers's endeavour demonstrated how well he had anticipated the market for an encyclopedic treatment of British literature.

Chambers traces the history of prose fiction from Arthurian through pastoral to heroic romance, arguing that Scarron's 'ludicrous imitation' of the heroic romance 'became the first of a class of its own, and found followers in England long before we had any writers of the pure novel. Mrs. Aphra Behn amused the public during the reign of Charles II by writing tales of personal adventure similar to those of Scarron, which are almost the earliest specimen of prose fiction that we possess. She was followed by Mrs. Manley, whose works are equally humorous, and equally licentious' (2: 160). Lesage's contribution to the evolving new form is also noted. What remained necessary for the novel to emerge in its familiar form was realism, and Defoe is, predictably, credited with providing 'the first pictures of real life in prose fiction.' His weaknesses are also highlighted: 'of genuine humour or variety of character he had no conception; and he paid little attention to the arrangements of his plot.' Once these deficiencies are overcome, the modern novel is free to emerge triumphant a generation later, as Chambers reaches the climax of this portion of his narrative:

> The gradual improvement in the tone and manners of society, the complicated relations of life, the growing contrast between town and country manners, and all the artificial distinctions that crowd in with commerce, wealth, and luxury banished the heroic romance, and gave rise to the novel, in which the passion of love still maintained its place but was surrounded by events and characters, such as are witnessed in ordinary life, under various aspects and modifications. The three great founders of this improved species of composition – this new theatre of living and breathing characters – were Richardson, Fielding and Smollett, who even yet, after the lapse of more than a century, have had no superiors, and only one equal. (2: 160)

What follows is a remarkably balanced and thorough survey of the novel, beginning with the three founders. Chambers's preference is clearly for Fielding, 'the prince of novelists' (2: 162), but not at the expense of Richardson, who wrote a very different kind of novel, and wrote it very well. (Chambers finds comparing the two similar to comparing Lear and Falstaff.) He makes the now-standard observation about the feminized Richardson, that 'he was happiest in female characters. Much of his time had been spent with the gentler sex, and his own retired habits and nervous sensibility approximated to feminine softness.' But 'no man understood human nature better, or could draw with greater distinctness the minute shadow of feeling and sentiment, or the final results of our passions' (2: 161). For Chambers, the feminized Richardson is not a lesser novelist than the rakish, manly Fielding. Each has his strengths, and Chambers has no difficulty respecting both.

After Smollett Chambers moves to Sterne, 'next in order of time and genius' (2: 171), Johnson, Johnstone, Walpole, Goldsmith, Henry Brooke, Mackenzie, and Clara Reeve, by 1843 known only for *The Old English Baron*, a novel he finds an improvement on *The Castle of Otranto* in many ways. These are the only novelists he mentions in his 'sixth period,' 1727–80. For all his inclusiveness, Chambers follows the pattern of ignoring most mid-century novelists, and virtually all women novelists before Burney. He does not, however, denigrate everything from *Humphry Clinker* (1771) to *Waverley*. His is a far more generous and balanced view, even if one that has little use for the generation of Sarah Fielding, Charlotte Lennox, and Frances Brooke. The early masters remain unequalled until Scott, but Chamber's narrative freely acknowledges the many novelists in the interim worthy of honourable mention.

Chambers's account of his seventh and final period, 1780 to the present, is premised on his perception of the 'last forty years' as 'rich and prolific' for the novel. But before discussing the recent triumphs he returns to the late-century trough, this time to provide the missing link in his narrative. The great early masters produced a host of imitators, the best of whom, Mackenzie, Moore, Burney, and Cumberland, though 'greatly superior to the ordinary run,' nevertheless had 'little influence on the natural taste.' They did manage to support 'the dignity and respectability of the novel,' but since they 'did not extend its dominion,' they must be relegated to 'the head of the second class' (2: 533). With no first-rate novelist to take the lead, the novel fell on hard times. The void was quickly filled by the abundance of 'garbage' Chambers describes, which well sums up the standard interpretation:

> There was no lack of novels, but they were of a very inferior and even debased description. In place of natural incident, character, and dialogue, we had affected and ridiculous sentimentalism – plots utterly absurd or pernicious – and stories of love and honour so maudlin in conception and drivelling in execution, that it is surprising they could ever have been tolerated even by the most defective moral sense or taste. The circulating libraries in towns and country swarmed with these worthless productions (known from their place of publication by the misnomer of the 'Minerva Press' novels). (2: 533)

Having reached its nadir with the Minervas, the novel made a gradual and complete recovery. Chambers traces that recovery stage by stage:

The first successful inroad on this accumulating mass of absurdity was made by Charlotte Smith, whose works may be said to hold a middle status between the true and the sentimental in fictitious composition. Shortly afterwards succeeded the political tales of Holcroft and Godwin, the latter animated by the fire of genius, and possessing great intellectual power and energy. The romantic fables of Mrs Radcliffe were also, as literary productions, a vast improvement on the old novels; and in their moral effects they were less mischievous, for the extraordinary machinery employed by the authoress was so far removed from the common course of human affairs and experience, that no one could think of drawing it into a precedent in ordinary circumstances. At no distant interval Miss Edgeworth came forward with her moral lessons and satirical portraits, daily advancing in her powers as in her desire to increase the virtues, prudence, and substantial happiness of life; Mrs Opie told her pathetic and graceful domestic tales; and Miss Austen exhibited her exquisite delineations of every-day English society and character. To crown all, Sir Walter Scott commenced, in 1814, his brilliant gallery of portraits of all classes, living and historical, which completely exterminated the monstrosities of the Minerva press, and inconceivably extended the circle of novel readers. Fictitious composition was now again in the ascendant, and never, in its palmiest days of chivalrous romance or modern fashion, did it command more devoted admiration, or shine with greater lustre. (2: 533)

As had so often been the case with earlier nineteenth-century critics, the neglect of the first generations of women novelists does not mean that Chambers minimizes or ignores the contributions of subsequent generations. Chambers follows his earlier pattern of discussing individual writers and providing specimens from the work of most of those he considers of the greatest importance after the most general, summary narrative. Of the first twenty-seven he includes in his chronological survey, seventeen are women. The list reads: Burney, Sarah Harriet Burney, Beckford, Cumberland, Holcroft, Bage, the Lees, Moore, Inchbald, Smith, Radcliffe, Lewis, Opie, Godwin, the Porters, Edgeworth, Austen, Brunton, Hamilton, More, Morgan, Shelley, Maturin, Scott, and Galt. Chambers discussions run from a paragraph (S.H. Burney) to about four double-columned pages of small type (Scott).

In his accounts of individual novelists Chambers devotes most of his attention to their lives, but he also attempts to capture their strengths as novelists and points out weaknesses as part of his over-all effort to provide comparative evaluations for the uninitiated. Chambers's *Cyclopædia*, in other words, is very much a self-conscious attempt at canon formation. His judgments are rarely startling or original, but they are usually thoughtful and interesting as well as indicative of mainline early Victorian tastes and opinions. The survey described below reflects generally held perceptions of the most highly regarded post-1780 novelists. It is worth emphasizing, too, that Chambers is typical in considering the novel to have come of age since 1780, and especially with Scott. He anticipates later Victorian critics in believing that theirs was the time of the greatest novels and novelists.

Chambers begins his survey with Burney, 'the wonder and delight of the generation of novel readers succeeding Fielding and Smollett.' He notes the revival of interest in her work resulting from the recent publi-cation of her *Diary and Letters*, though even without this renewed attention, 'she has maintained her popularity better than most second-ary writers of fiction' (2: 535). Chambers prefers the early novels because he feels they best exhibit Burney's strengths as a novelist; she is 'quick in discernment, lively in invention, and inimitable, in her own way, in portraying the humours and oddities of English society.' Although longer on 'good sense and correct feeling' than 'passion,' she has 'rarely been equalled' at capturing 'the follies and absurdities that float on the surface of fashionable society ... Her sarcasm, drollery, and broad humour, must always be relished' (2: 536). Her half-sister, Sarah Harriet, is described briefly as an inferior imitator.

The sublimity and proto-Byronic romanticism of Beckford is very much to Chambers's taste and his enthusiasm for *Vathek* (1786) is unusually strong. He considers Cumberland unsuccessful as a novel-ist, a very pale imitator of Fielding. Despite some strengths, Holcroft is a second-rate Godwin, and Bage, with still fewer strengths, a third-rate Holcroft. Chambers cannot understand why Scott included him in his canon, and Chambers's judgment will soon prevail. Chambers next considers the Lees, and again his Byronic tastes inform his judgment of their 'striking and romantic fictions.' He respects Sophia Lee for *The Recess* (1783–5), but it is Harriet Lee, and particularly her contributions to *Canterbury Tales* (1798), that excites him, especially because of 'Kruitzner,' a story that inspired Byron. Chambers notes with interest that Byron's imitation, *Werner*, is generally held to be inferior to the original. Chambers then seems almost to surprise himself with the force of his overall evaluation:

> Indeed, thus led as we are to name Harriet Lee, we cannot allow the opportunity to pass without saying that we have always considered her works as standing on the verge of the very first rank of excellence; that is to say, as inferior to no English novels whatever, excepting those of Fielding, Sterne, Smollett, Richardson, Defoe, Radcliffe, Godwin, Edgeworth, and the author of Waverley. It would not, perhaps, be going too far to say, that the 'Canterbury Tales' exhibit more of that species of invention which, as we have already remarked, was never common in English literature, than any of the works even of those first-rate novelists we have named, with the single exception of Fielding. (2: 547)

He concludes with a generous extract.

Chambers has a sincere admiration for the novels of Moore, especially *Zeluco* (1786), though he considers them short of first-rate. Moore is treated as roughly equal to Burney and Mackenzie, but superior to Cumberland, the fourth on the earlier list of the best of the second-rate imitators of the early masters. Briefer discussions of Inchbald and Smith follow. The former has attained 'deserved celebrity' for her novels, which are 'sketches from nature' filled with 'striking and passionate scenes' (2: 553). The latter, though she was forced to work too quickly to do justice to her talents, was a novelist of 'superior merit,' of a 'more romantic cast than ... Miss Burney' and one who 'aimed more at delineating affections than manners' (2: 554). Ann Radcliffe, 'the Salvator Rosa of British novelists,' warrants much fuller coverage, in part for her powerful poetical description. (Chambers quotes Scott with approval here as elsewhere, though he also qualifies Scott's declaration that Radcliffe was the first to bring poetic description to the English novel.) For Chambers, Radcliffe's greatest strengths are 'her wonderful talent in producing scenes of mystery and surprise, aided by external phenomena and striking description,' along with her 'powerful delineation of passion.' When both are working effectively, her strength in narrative eclipses her weakness in characterization, and 'like the great painter with whom she has been compared,' she is able to 'haunt and thrill the imagination' (2: 554). Chambers argues that Radcliffe realized her powers most fully in her later novels, declaring for *The Mysteries of Udolpho* (1794) and *The Italian* (1797) over Barbauld's choice, *The*

*Romance of the Forest* (1791). M.G. Lewis is credited with being a particularly successful imitator of Radcliffe.

Amelia Opie is the object of some of Chambers's most gendered reflections on the novel and on the impact of Scott on earlier novelists: 'Without venturing out of ordinary life, Mrs. Opie invested her narrative with deep interest, by her genuine painting of nature and passion, her animated dialogues, and her feminine delicacy of feeling ... The tales of this lady have been thrown into the shade by the brilliant fictions of Scott, the stronger moral delineations of Miss Edgeworth, and the generally more masculine character of our more modern literature. She is, like Mackenzie, too uniformly pathetic and tender' (2: 560). Recent developments in the novel have relegated Opie to second-rate status, still high for Chambers, but they also point the way to the continued devaluation of her reputation as the century progresses.

Because of the impressive – even astonishing – contradictions that inform Godwin's career, Chambers considers him 'one of the most remarkable men of his times.' His 'plodding habits, his imperturbable temper, and the quiet obscure simplicity of his Life and manners' are strangely at odds with the 'startling and astounding theories [that] were propagated by him with undoubting confidence; and sentiments that, if reduced to action, would have overturned the whole framework of society' (2: 560). Chambers is repelled by Godwin's political philosophy but impressed with his power as a novelist, a power so 'poignant with thought and feeling' and so capable of reaching the 'higher sympathies and associations' that he ranks *Caleb Williams* (1794) above the fiction of Defoe and Swift (2: 562). Chambers's response to Godwin the novelist, then, is quite positive, but only after the rejection of Godwin's political philosophy. As Richardson is often the test case for a critic's attitude towards the feminine, Godwin is the test case for attitudes towards radical politics. Even the tolerant, inclusive Chambers is not well disposed; radical novels by women receive little attention in the *Cyclopædia*.

The Porter sisters are given a paragraph each; Anna Maria, Chambers's favourite of the two, wins the longer paragraph and is praised for a productive career and pious life. *Don Sebastian* (1809) is singled out as her best work. Jane Porter's *Thaddeus of Warsaw* (1803) is also given special mention, but her smaller output ensures a lesser place in Chambers's history. Far more important than either is Maria Edgeworth, 'one of our best painters of national manners,' whose importance is greatly enhanced by having 'stimulated the genius of Scott' (2: 568). Edgeworth is judged inferior to Scott, as usual the standard against which others are measured. Chambers's summary evaluation provides the basis for his judgment: 'Of poetical or romantic feeling she has exhibited scarcely a single instance. She is a strict utilitarian. Her knowledge of the world is extensive and correct, though in some of her representations of fashionable folly and dissipation she borders on caricature.' Though she follows Joanna Baillie's 'plan of confining a tale to the exposure and correction of one particular vice, or one erroneous line of conduct,' Edgeworth is able to succeed 'by the ease, spirit, and variety of her delineations, and the truly masculine freedom with which she exposes the crimes and follies of mankind. Her sentiments are so just and true, and her style so clear and forcible, that they compel an instant assent to her moral views,' despite her tendency to violate standards of consistency and probability. Chambers concludes his evaluations with the following, sustained comparisons reminiscent of Scott's own comparison of Fielding and Smollett:

> [Scott] excelled his model [Maria Edgeworth], because, with equal knowledge and practical sagacity, he possessed that higher order of imagination, and more extensive sympathy with man and nature, which is more powerful, even for moral uses and effects, than the most clear and irresistible reasoning. The object of Miss Edgeworth, to inculcate instruction, and the style of the preceptress, occasionally interfere with the cordial sympathies of the reader, even in her Irish descriptions; whereas in Scott this is never apparent. He deals more with passions and feelings than with mere manners and peculiarities, and by the aid of his poetical imagination and careless yet happy eloquence of expression, imparts the air of romance to ordinary incidents and characters. It must be admitted, however, that in originality and in fertility of invention Miss Edgeworth is inferior to none of her contemporary novelists. She never repeats her incidents, her characters, dialogues, or plots, and few novelists have written more. Her brief and rapid tales fill above twenty closely-printed volumes, and may be read one after the other without any feeling of satiety or sense of repetition. (2: 570)

To warrant such detailed, close comparison with Scott is no small praise from Chambers – or most of his contemporaries, so high was the critical reputation of Scott. Edgeworth avoids the more common traps that prevent most women novelists from attaining the heights she reached, heights unattainable by most novelists of either gender.

It is not surprising that a critic so receptive to Edgeworth and so greatly influenced by Scott, as critic as well as novelist, should also be drawn to Austen, 'a truly English novelist.' Chambers finds 'the great charm' of Austen's novels 'in their truth and simplicity. She gives us plain representations of English society in the middle and higher classes – sets us down, as it were, in the country-house, the villa, and cottage, and introduces us to various classes of persons, whose characters are displayed in ordinary intercourse and most life-like dialogues and conversation' (2: 571). Chambers, like Scott, regrets that she has not had the appreciation she deserves, seeing the neglect as a result of Austen's not writing in Scott's 'big *bow-wow* strain.' 'Ordinary readers,' he argues, 'have been apt to judge her as Partridge, in Fielding's novel, judged Garrick's acting. He could not see the merit of a man who merely behaved on the stage as anybody might be expected to behave under similar circumstances in real life.' But he does note that 'her works are now rising in public esteem' (2: 572), anticipating the growth in her reputation that will be fostered, at least in part, by those qualities Chambers admires in her work, its realism and its Englishness.

Chambers is also favourably impressed by the novels of Mary Brunton, whose *Self-Control* (1811) he considers 'a sort of Scottish Cœlebs, recommended by its moral and religious tendency, no less than by the talent it displays' (2: 572) and by Elizabeth Hamilton's 'one excellent little novel, or moral tale, *The Cottagers of Glenburnie*, which has probably been as effective in promoting domestic improvement among the rural population of Scotland as Johnson's Journey to the Hebrides was in encouraging the planting of trees' (2: 575). His praise for Hannah More and *Cœlebs* (1809) is more guarded, since she 'adopted fiction merely as a means of conveying religious instruction' (2: 578). Chambers's responses to these three writers anticipate the turn away from the overt didacticism so much encouraged by the Evangelicals in the first two decades of the nineteenth century.

Lady Morgan, too, earns praise for her 'clever lively national sketches and anecdotes.' Chambers doubts that 'any one book ... will become a standard portion of our literature' and acknowledges that she is deficient in 'taste' and 'delicacy, but he appreciates her 'satire and sarcasm' and her 'masculine disregard of common opinion or censure' (2: 580) even when in the service of an ill-considered liberal political program. Finally, what he sees as the typically Irish mixture of pathos and humour ensures that her better work still rewards its readers. Mary Shelley's *Frankenstein* (1818) is judged a powerful and original contribution to English prose fiction, one 'worthy of Godwin's daughter and Shelley's wife' (2: 581); Chambers considers Maturin an inferior imitator of Lewis, himself inferior to Radcliffe. Extended praise is reserved for Scott, whose 'immortal fictions can only be compared with the dramas of Shakespeare, as presenting an endless variety of original characters, scenes, historical situations, and adventures' (2: 585–6). Galt is also praised for his fine Scottish novels, second only to Scott. The chapter continues for an additional forty pages of fine print in double columns, concluding with Dickens, but, with the exception of Susan Ferrier, 'a Scottish Miss Edgeworth' (2: 602), the novelists covered are too late for inclusion in this study.

In his eighty-plus pages on the novel to Scott and Galt Chambers sums up many of the judgments and perceptions of his generation. He recognizes a large number of gifted novelists, the vast majority writing within the fifty years prior to the *Cyclopædia*. He characterizes the period as one when women not only dominated the novel, but were recognized as producing most of the best novels. He also recognizes some gender differences in some of his novelists, but they rarely affect his evaluative conclusions about their work. In fact, he follows Scott in his ability to judge without being influenced by issues of gender. His work is by definition encyclopedic, and his range and tastes are broad enough and catholic enough to produce an informed evaluative history of the novel; he is unable to appreciate fully the achievements of all but the best of the early novelists.

It is interesting, then, to turn to the revisions of the *Cyclopædia*, to see what changes are made by the time of the third edition (1876). Both the second and third editions were undertaken by Robert Carruthers (1799–1878) and consist primarily of additions rather than alterations. Few pre-1843 authors are added; none are removed. But in the third edition, Carruthers includes entries on Manley, Robert Paltock, Sarah Fielding, Frances Sheridan, and Charles Brockden Brown. 'De La Riviere Manley,' we learn, was 'a female novelist, dramatist, and political writer [who] enjoyed some celebrity among the wits of the Queen Anne period. Neither her life nor her writings will bear a close scrutiny.' The other new entries are of a piece, offering minimal comment and evaluation. Sheridan's novels, for example, 'evince fine imaginative powers and correct moral taste' (2: 248). But the addition of three early novelists is noteworthy, as are the minor readjustments made to already-existing entries. Johnstone, Mackenzie, Brunton, and Hamilton are cut, while entries on Sterne, Inchbald, Edgeworth, Austen, Morgan, and Scott are all expanded. Moreover, while Scott is given more space, his reputation is no longer quite what it was: the 'three great founders' still 'have had no superiors,' but they no longer have had an equal (1: 731). Carruthers has also removed Johnson and More from the section on novelists and rewritten extensively the entry on Defoe. Most of his effort, however, went into providing new entries on more recent authors, and updating those on authors still living in 1843 (e.g., Beckford, Harriet Lee, Opie, Jane Porter, Edgeworth, Morgan, and Shelley). The *Cyclopædia* received major revisions in 1901, and again in 1925–7; I shall return to it in my final chapter.

## Julia Kavanagh (1824–1877)

It should probably not be surprising that the period that saw the gendering of the novel on a large scale should also be the period that produced a considerable body of gendered criticism; most relevant are a number of studies and compilations of women writers in Britain. Julia Kavanagh's *English Women of Letters: Biographical Sketches* (1862) was neither the first nor the only one to be devoted exclusively to novelists, but it is the first book-length study of English women novelists, and the best to appear in the period. Kavanagh brings to her study considerable experience both as a critic (her *French Women of Letters* appeared earlier in 1862) and as a prolific and successful novelist herself. Her purpose is 'to show how far, for the last two centuries, and more, women have contributed to the formation of the modern novel'; her focus is limited to those women who are long dead or those who have 'already stood the test of all merit – time.' Unlike the more encyclopedic Chambers, Kavanagh wishes to include only the best women novelists. This limits her to ten in a 330-page study. Her canon consists of Behn, Fielding, Burney, Smith, Radcliffe, Inchbald, Edgeworth, Austen, Opie, and Morgan. Only Behn and Fielding are even slightly surprising, and they receive the briefest and most guarded treatment: Kavanagh's study entrenches the increasingly dominant view that novels by women before Burney are of little value.

Kavanagh describes the novel in 1862 as dominated by women. As a result, it has overcome 'the repelling coarseness' of eighteenth-century fiction but at the price of endangering 'its manliness and its truth' (2). The new 'delicacy' is welcome, but not the accompanying tendency to present 'a world too sweet, too fair, too good … Let fiction teach noble lessons, let it avoid debasing coarseness, let it show human greatness and virtue; but neither in good nor in evil let it belie truth, if it wishes to live.' This view of the threats to the novel in the 1860s provides the backdrop to Kavanagh's study. When she turns to her history, she quickly points out that it has not always been thus: 'Too much delicacy or refinement was not the sin of poor Aphra Behn, or of the times when she wrote,' and it is Behn, for Kavanagh, who 'opens the line of English novelists' (3). The 'disgrace of Aphra Behn and of her pupils,' in contrast to the French women novelists such as Scudéry and Lafayette, 'is that, instead of raising man to woman's moral standard, they sank woman to the level of man's coarseness' (11).

Kavanagh's first chapter on Behn is largely biographical. Her second, after noting (not for the first time) that 'the novels and histories of Mrs. Behn have long ceased to be read' (14), proceeds to discuss *Oroonoko* (ca. 1688), 'the only one of her tales that, spite all its defects, can still be read with entertainment' (15). An extended plot summary is followed by reflections on how Scudéry or Lafayette would have handled this fine, powerful story, much to the improvement of its delicacy. But Kavanagh is able to salvage *Oroonoko* by stressing Behn's importance to the development of the English novel:

> Though Mrs. Behn's indelicacy was useless, and worse than useless, the superfluous addition of a corrupt mind and vitiated taste – though her style was negligent, incorrect, and often awkward, and she had no claim to the rank of a good or a great writer, she had two gifts in which she excelled either of the French ladies – freshness and truth. 'Oroonoko' is not a good book, but it is a vigorous, dramatic, and true story. True in every sense. The descriptions are bright, luxuriant, and picturesque; the characters are rudely sketched, but with great power; the conversations are full of life and spirit. Its rude and careless strength made it worthy to be one of the first great works of English fiction. In some of the nobler attributes of all fiction it failed, but enough remained to mark the dawning of that great English school of passion and nature, of dramatic and pathetic incident, which, though last arisen and slowly developed, has borrowed least and taught most. (23)

There is little new in Kavanagh's response to Behn, except, perhaps, that she recognizes some of Behn's strengths at a time when very few did. Somewhat more surprising is her version of the next sixty or so years of the history of the novel, as she contributes to the Victorian consensus. She sees little progress in the development of the genre until Richardson: Swift and Defoe 'produced wonderful books, but assuredly not novels' (24). Far more novelistic is Addison's Sir Roger de Coverley, and Kavanagh is dismayed that this fine model of 'delicacy,' 'tenderness,' 'grace,' and 'quiet though clear power' was not again realized until Goldsmith; even Richardson was guilty of the 'coarseness' and 'rudeness' characteristic of the 1740s and 1750s.

Though Behn had been 'a feminine prodigy during the days of the Restoration,' Kavanagh notes that 'such another even the fertile reign of Queen Anne could not yield' (24). Nor did women contribute much to the eventual reemergence of the novel, an absence Kavanagh attributes to passivity. The one bright spot at mid-century, the only 'very significant work' (albeit not influential) was Sarah Fielding's 'long forgotten' *David Simple* (25). Fielding's name is still known to those interested in the literary history of the eighteenth century, but 'she was a popular authoress in her own day – she was a friend of Richardson, and the sister of England's greatest novelist.' *David Simple* was still read at the turn of the nineteenth century, but, Kavanagh asks, 'Who reads it now? – who even has read it?' The answer is that it is virtually unread, though 'it is not without merit.' In fact, 'parts of it can still be read with amusement,' and if Fielding was not 'an excellent novelist,' she was certainly 'a woman of remarkable abilities' (25). Kavanagh takes her reader through the plot, pointing out its several strengths, before reaching her not unexpected conclusion: no critical analysis is going to restore *David Simple* to the canon of favourite novels. Time and changing manners have set their 'fatal seal on all that Sarah Fielding wrote' (38).

Having exhausted the early contributions of women to the novel with Behn and Fielding, Kavanagh next moves to Burney, 'the first English authoress of real celebrity' (39). She continues her pattern of following a biographical sketch complete with observations about the literary career and works of her subjects with analyses of individual novels. For Burney, this means chapters on *Evelina* and *Cecilia* (1782), with a few pages at the end of the *Cecilia* chapter on *Camilla* (1796) and *The Wanderer*. Kavanagh opens her discussion of *Evelina* by reasserting Burney's importance as a woman novelist, clearly placing her in the history of the English novel:

> More than a hundred and thirty years after the fame of Mademoiselle de Scudéry had reached its acme, the name of Frances Burney redeemed English literature from the reproach of having produced no woman of genius sufficient to rule, for a time at least, the world of fiction. For some years Miss Burney was certainly the greatest of living English novelists.

Her 'Evelina' and 'Cecilia' had, in their day, as much power and importance as the 'Great Cyrus' and the 'Princess of Clèves' in another. They were
the books which everyone had read, or must read, of which the appearance created delighted surprise or impatient expectation. Goldsmith was
dead, and Walter Scott was not yet in his teens. Miss Burney long stood
first. Godwin never had her popularity – Mrs. Inchbald, though more original, and far more pathetic, failed in too many essentials to win an equal
position – Mrs. Radcliffe appealed to a lower class of readers – moral teaching spoiled Miss Edgeworth as a novelist. Miss Austin [sic] was not popular in her lifetime. We find Sir Walter Scott talking of her to Miss Baillie, not
long after her death, as the authoress 'of some novels,' &c. – neither he nor
anyone else could have spoken so of the authoress of 'Cecilia' and 'Evelina.'
Her fame was rapid, solid, and widely-spread. It reached Germany and
France, and may have extended farther. From the appearance of 'Evelina,'
in 1778, to that of 'Waverley,' in 1814, no English novel or romance had the
good-fortune of equal success. (58)

Kavanagh then explains Burney's high stature in a critical overview
sensitive both to strengths and weaknesses, summarizing most prior
Burney criticism and bringing it up to date in a thoughtful and incisive
manner:

Miss Burney lived in the very heart of the world of her day. She saw,
she heard, and she painted. Her vision was keen, her hand unerring. She
was too genuine a woman of her times to appeal to the feelings or to the
imagination. No presentiment of a new school – of still undisclosed hori-
zons – of regions fair and fruitful – disturbed her quick sense of the
present. Sufficient for her were the men and women whom she saw, and
their manners, their oddities, their vulgarity, their coarseness, insolence,
and pride. The refinement of Addison, the pseudo-tenderness of Sterne,
the exquisite delicacy of Goldsmith, were foreign to her. The spirit of
Fielding and Smollett animated all she wrote. Her delicacy was that of a
woman, – it made her works pure, and gave them great finish – but it was
not intellectual delicacy. She reveled especially in pictures of high-born or
middle-class vulgarity. Her sense of the humourous and the ludicrous was
keen – too keen for geniality. Her works are cold – hence, we think, the great
falling off in their popularity. Cold, with all their errors, the great novelists of
the last age were not. They were coarse, offensive, but their coarseness is like
the outpouring of a broad and genial nature. They wrote like happy epi-
cures, whose good humour and mirth efface a thousand sins. (58–9)

It is from the position staked out in these passages that Kavanagh proceeds to read Burney's novels in chronological order: *Evelina* is her greatest triumph, with *Cecilia* a close second; though it lacks 'the charm and seduction' of *Evelina* (71), it is 'well-nigh equal as a novel.' *Camilla*, however, is a 'falling off' and *The Wanderer* 'a failure.' These judgments, occasionally challenged, are still common today, often for the reasons Kavanagh offers. Burney's strength is the realistic presentation of fashionable society, and especially of its follies. When she shifts her attention to the problems women face in society, she abandons her strength. Unlike Staël, who shared her concerns, Burney is unable to maintain sympathy for her heroines, 'so inexorable is she to the least dereliction from the right part of prudence – for virtue is never questioned – that she is ready to inflict every sorrow and every humiliation upon them if they take a step beyond its narrow limits. The world is right, and always right – if they suffer, let them thank their own folly for their sorrows' (86). Though it was certainly not Kavanagh's intention to undermine Burney's reputation, one she thought deservedly secure, she provides several lines of criticism in her analyses that will be pursued by later critics who do not share her high opinion of this novelist.

Kavanagh's account of Charlotte Smith provides another example of her ability to present readings that in large part accept Victorian consensus without sacrificing her own judgment. Like most of the better critics in this study, she is a generous reader with a wide-ranging, catholic taste, and an honest, candid reader with a commitment to providing balanced judgments about the novelists she discusses. Her account of Smith's life as 'one long sorrow' dominated by 'sadness and disappointment' repeats the standard view of earlier biographers, as does the obvious conclusion that follows: Smith's 'great talent – she was one of the best novelists of the day' was hopelessly compromised by the 'haste' forced upon her by financial pressures and by 'the gloom that overshadowed her life' (91). Her unhappy life limited her to the 'middle region' among novelists. Though that status was, in a sense, 'great good fortune' for her during her lifetime, it does little for her subsequent reputation: 'she but helps to fill the vacant space between Miss Burney and Mrs. Radcliffe' and 'will leave no lasting trace in the literature of her country' (91).

When she turns to the novels Kavanagh selects *Emmeline* (1788), *Ethelinde* (1789), and *The Old Manor House* (1793) as 'three of her best and most agreeable.' The critical overview is again interesting and balanced. Smith is a good storyteller, a shrewd creator of character, a writer of feeling and

judgment, and an accomplished descriptive writer, yet even her best stories are 'tinged with a sort of mediocrity,' in part because of hasty composition, but also because her modest competence in all areas produced
excellence in none: 'It is not moderation, but excess that strikes the public,
and even posterity. Miss Burney verged on caricature, yet she holds a far
higher place than Mrs. Smith; Mrs. Radcliffe was natural in nothing, her
terror, her landscapes, are utterly beyond all truth, yet she can still charm
the imagination and win forgiveness for her sins. It is Mrs. Smith's fault
that she has none, and yet is not perfect' (94–5). Smith's principal claim to
fame becomes historical. She is 'a connecting link between opposite
schools, and the most characteristic representative of the modern domestic novel,' the combination providing her claim to the 'originality' so
strongly valued by Kavanagh.

Smith's contribution to fostering a new understanding of the didactic responsibility of the novelist also earns Kavanagh's praise.
Kavanagh believes that 'novels have a double character – they reflect
an age, and they influence it. They are a mirror and a model.' It is difficult to improve a coarse age, but refined books can make a difference;
it is hard 'to conceive a coarse book being written in a refined age' (98).
Coarseness in what is spoken, the coarseness she has already noted in
Burney, Edgeworth, Opie, and Inchbald, was not the only kind of coarseness that 'revolted the female mind.' To it, Kavanagh adds 'one which
women of any refinement must by instinct have detested – the delineation of woman as mere woman – as the embodiment of beauty and the
object of passion' (96). Unlike France, with its long succession of important women novelists, England was dominated by male novelists in the
eighteenth century, and among their early ranks only Richardson was
able to do women greater justice. The English women who did write
were unable or unwilling to match the lofty heights of the French:
'Aphra Behn's ideal of womanhood was coarse and low; Miss Fielding's
was uncertain.' Burney's heroines thus 'indicate the great change'; they
play important, central roles in their society. Smith's, though 'generally
poor, and in depressed circumstances' represent another progressive
step. They too are important, and their importance is 'that of intellect
and refined manners.' They form 'the most perfect prototype of the lady
in the modern novels of to-day' (97). Smith's fresh conception of how
women should be represented in the novel gives her pride of place in
bringing about an essential corrective.

When Kavanagh turns to Radcliffe she commits herself to a cyclical
model of the history of the British novel based on a binary opposition

between novels and romances: 'Romance stories and tales, that profess to deal with the truths of life, rarely flourish side by side. The regularity with which they sink and rise in public favour is one of the most curious features in the history of fiction' (114). Thus does she introduce the development of the Gothic novel on the heels of the success of Richardson, Fielding, and Smollett. What follows is an account that differs from most of its predecessors in that it comes at a time and from a critic no longer strongly under the influence of the genre. Kavanagh briefly rehearses Walpole's innovations in *The Castle of Otranto*, before turning to its progeny. She spends a couple of pages on Clara Reeve and *The Old English Baron*, not because she admires this 'very cold and commonplace production' with 'neither poetry not imagination,' but rather because it is of historical importance; because it is an ongoing 'favourite of the young' (116); and, most of all, because it allows her to demonstrate the fundamental errors of the Gothic enterprise. Reeve, like Walpole before her and Scott after her – Kavanagh's resistance to Scott is a tell-tale sign of a change in attitudes – limited herself to the 'romantic customs' of the Middle Ages without daring to present their accompanying 'rudeness and with it the breadth and geniality of those wonderful times.' Reeve's errors were, however, inevitable since 'modern delicacy and refinement' would not have allowed a realistic portrayal of medieval society. The result, nevertheless, is that these 'pseudo Middle Ages tales … give us the falsest impressions. We have been told of great cruelty, and we have not felt that it was the inevitable result of great coarseness … The Knight has been clothed in modern gentleness, politeness, and refinement, and in that smoothing down of features offensive to modern taste, the largeness, that great characteristic of the Middle Ages, and perhaps the greatest, the manly and noble frankness, have been irremediably lost' (117).

With the early history of the Gothic novel established as context, Kavanagh next addresses Radcliffe's innovations. Radcliffe avoided the historical errors of her predecessors by setting her novels so vaguely in the past as to make them virtually ahistorical. She gave the Gothic a 'thoroughly original' turn, 'not a good one … but one so fertile in interest and beauty, spite its faults,' that she remained a great favourite for 'more than two generations' (117). By the 1860s, however, 'it is not easy to appreciate the great merit of these well nigh forgotten productions' since it consists largely in their historical importance as the bridge between Reeve and Scott. Radcliffe deserves high marks for changing the direction of the Gothic, and, finally, 'great though her faults are, in terror and description she is still unequalled' (122).

Two chapters on Radcliffe's novels then follow, the first mainly devoted to *The Sicilian Romance* (1790) and *The Romance of the Forest*, the second to *The Mysteries of Udolpho* and *The Italian*. Typically, they emphasize what Kavanagh most admires in her subject, though without avoiding acknowledgment of the accompanying weaknesses. Those weaknesses stem from the lack of education and knowledge that limits so many women writers, compounded in Radcliffe's case by her limited experience in the world. She could draw only on 'Nature, which she loved tenderly and painted with extraordinary power, and Terror, which she knew wonderfully how to waken.' The corollary is that 'in character, in penetration, in historical Knowledge, in all the minutiæ that prove reading, skill, and cultivated taste, she failed. She was never vulgar, because her nature was delicate and refined, but she was awkward and ignorant' (123).

The analyses themselves detail Radcliffe's strengths. A long discussion of the development of landscape painting, both on canvas and in words, leads to the familiar praise of Radcliffe as one who 'wrote landscapes, and wrote them well, though ideally' (126), that is, her landscapes remind Kavanagh far more of those of the old masters than those of the recent masters of a more realistic, detailed landscape. Kavanagh is with the majority of critics in preferring *Udolpho* to Radcliffe's other works, and the description she offers of its glories summarizes her tribute well: 'We are led through scenery soft, splendid and grand, such as we may have imagined, but have never seen; through a sublime world, peopled with beings real enough to arrest attention, sufficiently unreal not to harrow; beings that seem called forth from nothing to yield us a sense of freshness and repose in the very midst of terror, so unlike all we know are both that terror and they' (139). Kavanagh ends her discussion by emphasizing the enormous influence Radcliffe had both on novelists and on poets of the calibre of Byron, Wordsworth, and Hemans. Their recognition of her power is not to be taken lightly.

Having paid tribute to Ann Radcliffe, Kavanagh is able to return to the more congenial main line of British novels with her chapters on Elizabeth Inchbald. The biographical chapter emphasizes that for Inchbald, unlike Radcliffe or Smith, the novel played a very small part in her life. She wrote only two: the justly acclaimed *A Simple Story* (1791) and the much inferior *Nature and Art* (1796). Since novel writing was nowhere near so lucrative as playwriting, it is not surprising that Inchbald preferred to write plays. Like most women writers, she wrote for money, a fact she used to justify her shortcomings. These are many, though not quite enough to negate her strengths. Her novels 'display wonderful talent, more than talent, genius, and great ignorance, great want of delicate refinement which is the offspring of a cultivated mind.' She is the 'least literary' of women writers, lacking 'the graces of style, of thought, of imagery.' Kavanagh endorses received opinion in arguing that Inchbald's great strength, a strength that was possibly intensified by her deficiencies, was her 'irresistible' ability to evoke pathos (182).

Inchbald is a writer of wonderful economy. 'She had a story to tell,' and did so 'in the simplest and the plainest way.' In *A Simple Story* 'every word tells and goes home' (183). Kavanagh is not impressed by the link between the two stories that make up Inchbald's novel, and she considers Lady Elmwood's affair with Lord Frederick literally unbelievable, the product of that 'most dangerous syren' for novelists, 'theory' (in this case the need to prove that a 'bad education' inevitably leads to an unhappy ending) (192–3). Fortunately, Inchbald does not dwell on the point, turning instead to her second, equally powerful tale. Her characters are moving because their imperfections make them seem real (Kavanagh contrasts Inchbald to Edgeworth on this point, criticizing the latter for failing to recognize 'the great art' in drawing imperfect characters) (198). The imperfect character, especially 'a new woman, a true one, a very faulty one,' is Inchbald's contribution to the novel (199).

Kavanagh ends her discussion of Inchbald with a few pages on *Nature and Art*, a novel that contains some passages of great dramatic power and much pathos, but one far too heavily influenced by 'the French Revolution, social theories, and foregone conclusions' (199) to hold the interest of a reader. Here Kavanagh's general dislike (unlike Masson) for novels structured on ideas is reinforced by her distaste for the radical politics of so many of the novels of the 1790s, a dislike hinted at in her chapters on Smith and now made more explicit. The critical fortunes of most of the radical writers of the 1790s suffered by virtue of the fact that their support for the French Revolution was for the losing side. Later critics do not always address the issue openly, but a commitment to radical principles rarely did much for the subsequent reputation of an author. Smith and Inchbald were not as guilty as Godwin, Holcroft, or Wollstonecraft in this regard; had they been, they probably would have shared the obscurity of Mary Hays and Helen Maria Williams. Nevertheless, a certain reserve often descends on descriptions of their work, while their admirers try to ignore their unfortunate political views.

Kavanagh opens her discussion of Maria Edgeworth by affirming that it takes more than natural ability to be a great writer. Talent, 'even genius,' comes from both nature and nurture, and it is the superior nurture that the French provide for women that explains their superiority as writers. Edgeworth's unusual upbringing served an analogous function for her. 'What the actual business of life has done for them, without depriving them of one feminine charm or folly, the contact of a strong, active mind seems to have done for Maria Edgeworth, the most vigorous though the least masculine of female writers, in that great touchstone of temper and genius – style' (203). Kavanagh identifies Edgeworth's father, Richard Lovell Edgeworth, as the dominant influence on her for both good and bad. So strong was that influence that when he died, some thirty years before his daughter, she was unable to continue in her literary career.

The two chapters on the novels, the first on *Castle Rackrent* and *Belinda* (1801), the second on the *Tales of Fashionable Life* (1812), document Edgeworth's perceived strengths and weaknesses, both of which stem primarily from a didactic theory of fiction:

> Amongst the women who have won celebrity in fiction, three will long remain pre-eminent for a thoroughly feminine quality – that of teaching. This natural gift, which will may perfect, but cannot bestow, has never been possessed more completely, and exercised more successfully, by man or woman, than by Mademoiselle de Scudéry, Madame de Genlis, and Miss Edgeworth. With the three, teaching was the first object, literature came next. They wrote to improve their readers, not by actual scientific knowledge, but by advice, by lessons kind, delicate, and persuasive. Mademoiselle de Scudéry wished to make society and women more polished, more refined, more virtuous. Madame de Genlis devoted herself to childhood and to youth; to inculcate knowledge, practical and theoretical, was her object. Miss Edgeworth's aim was similar, but less educational; and her method was essentially different ... She attacked the passions by denying them. She stripped them of their false greatness, and showed them in their baseness. She preached virtue and wisdom by painting vice and folly, and these she covered with immortal ridicule. (216)

The association with Scudéry and Genlis points to one of the main critical problems for Edgeworth's reputation in the nineteenth century. Scudéry had been out of fashion for many years, and Genlis was the model of the woman novelist devoted to instruction at the expense of art and entertainment. As Edgeworth increasingly became known for her teaching, her status as a novelist would inevitably suffer.

But for Kavanagh, Edgeworth has a compensating strength she shares with the greatest geniuses: the power to make truth visible. It is the strength of Shakespeare, and one in which she is rivalled among women writers only by Lafayette and Austen. 'The candour of her nature enlightened Madame de La Fayette; she transferred her own sincerity to her pages. Marvellous perception of character was Miss Austen's gift. Miss Edgeworth had not the heart knowledge of the one, or the penetrating power of the other. But, better than either, she perceived moral truths as shown in character – a noble domain, in which her reign was long and supreme' (218).

For Kavanagh, the conflict between teaching and truth runs throughout Edgeworth's writing. When the latter is sacrificed to the former, as it often is in Edgeworth's novels, the writing suffers. But there is enough truth remaining, aided by 'style, power of character, and humour,' to ensure her a place among the best writers. In addition, Edgeworth counts among the short list of novelists who are honoured with being 'suggestive.' Finally, she joins Kavanagh's favourites because of her originality: she was the first to introduce 'the national novel' (219), that is, the novel that depends on treating 'national peculiarities, customs, and feelings' with respect rather than ridicule. This aspect of Edgeworth's writing was developed by Scott, and continues to contribute to the British novel in the 1860s.

Kavanagh also shares the commonly held critical view that *Castle Rackrent* is Edgeworth's best book (she does not consider it a 'novel'), because it profits most from her 'talent for truth' (225). The novels tend to sacrifice that truth for a moral. *Belinda*, with its analysis of fashionable society, is an accomplished novel, but also a good example of truth sacrificed to morality. *Tales of Fashionable Life* is more successful at providing 'entertaining lessons of morality deducted from the lives of the vain and frivolous' (233). The gravity is also extreme, but it is tempered by the introduction of humorous sketches of Irish character. Kavanagh considers *The Absentee* (first published in the *Tales*) to be Edgeworth's triumph as a novelist. When she was no longer able to write as well, and her readers turned instead to the newer 'school of wild adventure and dangerous tenderness,' she stopped writing: 'Her decorous teaching had grown old-fashioned, and her plain speech had become offensive' (247). Kavanagh sees no need to challenge the judgment of Edgeworth's readers or to offer additional comment.

From Edgeworth, one of the best-known, most highly respected novelists during her own lifetime, Kavanagh moves to Austen, virtually unknown during hers. The transition provides an occasion to spell out Kavanagh's sense of a female tradition of the novel:

> The writings of women are betrayed by their merits as well as by their faults. If weakness and vagueness often characterize them, they also possess when excellent, or simply good, three great redeeming qualities, which have frequently betrayed anonymous female writers. These qualities are: Delicacy, Tenderness, and Sympathy. We do not know if there exists, for instance, a novel of any merit written by a woman, which fails in one of these three attributes. Delicacy is the most common – delicacy in its broadest sense, not in its conventional meaning. Where that fails, which is a rare case, one of the other qualities assuredly steps in. Aphra Behn had no delicacy of intellect or of heart, but she had sympathy. Perhaps only a woman could have written 'Oroonoko,' as only another woman could have written 'Uncle Tom's Cabin' two hundred years later. Man has the sense of injustice, but woman has essentially pity for suffering and sorrow. Her side is the vanquished side, amongst men or nations, and when she violates that law of her nature she rarely fails to exceed man in cruelty and revenge. (251)

Kavanagh's account of Austen is largely positive, though not without reservations. Its importance for this study lies in its eloquent testimony to the reputation Austen had secured by the 1860s. In her emphasis on the representation of ordinary life with near-perfect accuracy as a central skill for a woman novelist to master, Kavanagh points the way – one she herself does not follow – to using Austen as a standard that her female contemporaries and predecessors are unable to match. The implications for the canon will become clear in my final two chapters.

The contrast between Austen, about whom she knew so little, and Amelia Opie is apparent in the much richer biography Kavanagh is able to provide for Opie. Kavanagh is impressed by the purity of Opie's life, and by the pleasure she took in society. But she finds her good qualities linked to 'a want of a will of her own.' Though Opie is not as great 'in mind and temper' as many other women, it is hard to find 'any more pure or more tender' (288–9). That purity and tenderness become the key to Kavanagh's brief chapter on *The Father and Daughter* (1801) and *Adeline Mowbray* (1804):

> Of all the women who have written, Mrs. Opie is the one who succeeded most by qualities distinct from those generally called literary, or,

better still, intellectual. She was not much of a thinker, still less of a writer. Her style is careless, and often incorrect; her pictures of life are not such as we can value. Strong character she neither conceived nor painted. Yet she succeeded in an age where men and women, far beyond her in power and attainments, might have made the public fastidious; and that success, a matter of fact, not of assertion, entitles her to consideration. Great though her deficiencies were, it was merited. Mrs. Opie had but one gift – a great one, a beautiful one, a woman's gift – a gift which won and ruled hearts amenable to no other power; better than any in her generation she knew how to appeal to the heart. (289)

It is 'the pathos of everyday life,' and that pathos alone, that Opie conveys better than other novelists, even better than her friend Inchbald. Like Inchbald and Smith, Opie travelled in radical circles in the 1790s and Kavanagh details these connections in the biographical chapter, but she presents an Opie entirely immune to ideas or thought in the critical chapter. 'Her talent was remote from art, and suffered from any thing approaching premeditation.' And when she attempted to extend her use of pathos in aid of religion in her late novels she was out of her depth, unable to succeed in what was Hannah More's realm. 'It was by pathos that she taught, as Miss Edgeworth taught by wit and wisdom' (296). Opie, Kavanagh concludes, is not a 'great writer ... She had few of the mental qualities that win a lasting name in literature; but those which she had were very sweet and true' (297). Such an assessment is hardly one to capture the attention or promote the admiration of later critics. It would have taken a far stronger case to ensure Opie a secure place in the canon.

Kavanagh ends her study with the recently deceased Lady Morgan, a woman like Staël, who was a 'two-fold' celebrity, 'personal and literary.' Her death was too recent to allow a judgment to be made with full confidence, but Kavanagh feels that 'her genius is not of that commanding order over which Time has no power' (297). The biographical chapter focuses on Morgan's very public career, and the many controversies and disputes surrounding it. Kavanagh's response is largely sympathetic, and her survey of the novels in the final chapter is balanced as always, but her enthusiasm for Lady Morgan as novelist is clearly limited.

Kavanagh begins with the sensational early success of *The Wild Irish Girl* (1806 – written when Morgan was still Miss Owenson), a success she attributes more to its youthful freshness, lively, romantic manner, fervour, and sincerity than to originality or fine writing. 'If Miss Owenson had not the merit of being, in date and ability, the first of Irish writers who have made their country the theme of their writings; if Miss Edgeworth came before her, and showed a higher power; yet to none did she yield in ardour for the cause of Ireland, in enthusiasm and generous desire to serve it, or to avenge its unmerited obloquy' (308). The success of *The Wild Irish Girl* remained unsurpassed by Morgan's next several novels, all in the same mode. But with *O'Donnel* (1814), she turned to 'the flat realities of life' and achieved what for Kavanagh was her greatest artistic success. Kavanagh also admires its successors, *Florence Macarthy* (1818) and *The O'Briens and the O'Flahertys* (1826), written in the same, more realistic style, though she observes that the latter was greatly influenced by Scott (who, she points out earlier in the chapter, had himself been influenced by Morgan's pre-Waverley novels). The comparison does not work in Morgan's favour. Scott's 'consummate art' was unmatched by Morgan or any other member of his 'short-lived but brilliant school of fiction' (327), a judgment less surprising in its evaluation of Morgan and Scott as novelists than in its bald recognition that Scott's kind of romances were long out of fashion.

Kavanagh reserves her overview of Morgan for the end of the chapter. She finds this novelist first and foremost a political writer; Irish nationalism is her favourite cause, but she is also at home attacking repressive governments in France and Italy. 'Attack is the meaning of all she wrote. She knew not how to build. There is no calmness and no peace in any of her books. Restless, brilliant, good-humoured, very witty, and often eloquent, she dazzled and subdued more than she really won over her contemporaries.' Her final placement of Morgan is one of unrealized greatness:

> As a writer, she had far more vigour, and especially originality than women usually show. This is her superiority. Her Irish novels are bold, energetic conceptions. In execution she was weak. That something which we miss in the tone of her writings failed her when she came to the fulfillment of what she had conceived. She had no control over her faculties; she did not appreciate what was excellent in them, and knew not how to conquer what was bad. They procured her great but passing celebrity, money, and popularity; but had she known how to rule and develop them, they would have secured her one of the very highest places ever held by woman in literature. (329)

Kavanagh concludes her study with two paragraphs on the twenty women she has covered in this volume and in the earlier companion volume on French women novelists. She acknowledges that few of the books by her authors are still read, but is nonetheless able to find an alternative kind of immortality in their contribution to a most vital, thriving form of literature. Kavanagh's is by far the most intensive and thorough study (330 pages) of British women novelists in the nineteenth century. She is a sophisticated critic, with a clear sense of the history of the novel, and an effective representative of the attitudes to the novel and to novels by women that dominated Victorian criticism.

## George Henry Lewes (1817–1878)

Unlike the first four critics discussed in this chapter, George Henry Lewes wrote neither a history of English literature nor a book-length study of the novel. He was a frequent contributor of essays and reviews in the periodicals; author of a highly influential history of philosophy, the first biography of Goethe, and numerous other works on science and philosophy; and a moderately successful dramatist and novelist. Best-known in the twentieth century for his long relationship with George Eliot, one which helped shape his developing view of the novel after the mid-1850s, he was a highly respected man of letters during his lifetime and still holds an important place in the history of criticism. R.L. Brett, for example, endorses 'his claim to rank as the most important critic between Coleridge and Arnold' ('George Henry Lewes,' 120), and René Wellek singles him out as 'the first English exponent of the theory of realism in the novel' (*History*, 4: 150). Lewes was also the first English critic to pay serious attention to *Jane Eyre* and *Moby Dick*. His single most important piece on women novelists appeared in the *Westminster Review* not long after he first met Marian Evans (Ashton, *The German Idea*, 132–8). A thirteen-page review article purportedly devoted to (1) George Sand's *Œuvres Complètes*, (2) 'The Novels of Miss Austen, Mrs. Gore, Mrs. Marsh, Mrs. Trollope, Mrs. Jewsbury, and Miss Lynn,' (3) *Jane Eyre* (1847), and (4) *Mary Barton* (1848), 'The Lady Novelists' is in fact a general discussion of the phenomenon of the woman novelist. In many of his other reviews (those of *Jane Eyre* and *Shirley* offer good examples), Lewes engages closely with the novels under consideration, but his interest here is in more general, theoretical questions. Brief as this essay is, he nonetheless begins with first principles, in this case definitions of literature and the novel. Literature is distinguished from philosophy and science as 'the expression of the forms and order of human life,' as measured in 'experiences and emotions.' When these expressions assume 'the forms of universal truths, of facts common to all nations or appreciable by the intellects,' the results are 'permanently good and true. Hence the universality and immortality of Homer, Shakspeare [sic], Cervantes, Molière.' Lewes's humanism takes its specific realistic turn in what is for him the corollary of his definition of literature: 'only *that* literature is effective, and to be prized accordingly, which has *reality for its basis*' (Olmsted, ed., *Victorian Art of Fiction*, 2: 40).

Having established his definition of literature, Lewes then addresses the real issue of this essay: 'What does the literature of women mean?' An answer is now possible. 'It means this: while it is impossible for men to express life otherwise than as they know it – and they can only know it profoundly according to their own experience – the advent of female literature promises woman's view of life, woman's experience' (2: 41). Lewes's realism thus forces him to gender literature in order to defend the appropriateness – even the necessity – of literary women. Though he considers women (potentially) intellectually equal to men, he also recognizes that equality does not mean identity. There are differences that seem to be mental as well as physical. 'The Masculine mind is characterized by the predominance of the intellect, and the Feminine by the predominance of the emotions' (2: 41–2). The implications of this commonplace distinction for other critics rarely work to the advantage of women writers. But for Lewes, what follows is that 'according to this rough division the regions of philosophy would be assigned to men, those of literature to women' (2: 42).

Why, then, have so few women realized their potential as writers? Their problem is imitation. 'To write as men write, is the aim and besetting sin of women; to write as women, is the real office they have to perform' (2: 42). Given Lewes's definition of literature, it follows that if women are to write realistically about what they know, 'of all departments of literature, Fiction is the one to which by nature and circumstance, women are best adapted' (2: 43). He then spells out some of the implications of his gender casting:

The domestic experiences which form the bulk of woman's knowledge finds an appropriate form in novels; while the very nature of fiction calls for that predominance of Sentiment which we have already attributed to the feminine mind. Love is the staple of fiction, for it 'forms the story of a woman's life.' The joys and sorrows of affection, the incidents of domestic life, the aspirations and fluctuations of domestic life, assume typical forms in the novel. Hence we may be prepared to find women succeeding better in *finesse* of detail, in pathos and sentiment, while men generally succeed better in the construction of plots and the delineation of character. Such a novel as 'Tom Jones' or 'Vanity Fair,' we shall not get from a woman; nor such an effort of imaginative history as 'Ivanhoe' or 'Old Mortality;' but Fielding, Thackeray, and Scott are equally excluded from such perfection in its kind as 'Pride and Prejudice,' 'Indiana,' or 'Jane Eyre:' as an artist, Miss Austen surpasses all the male novelists that ever lived; and for eloquence and depth of feeling, no man approaches George Sand. (2: 43)

Lewes points out that 'exceptional women' will not follow this predictable pattern, but exceptions never threaten the rule.

Having determined the place of women novelists in the realm of literature Lewes is prepared to survey that corner of the realm. His survey is necessarily brief and highly selective, but all the more telling for that. The canon, for Lewes, consists of only the very best writers: 'first and foremost let Jane Austen be named, the greatest artist that has ever written, using the term to signify the most perfect mastery over the means to her end.' Lewes acknowledges the familiar limitations to Austen's art: 'There are heights and depths in human nature Miss Austen has never scaled.' But for him, unlike many others, this does not lessen her claim to a prominent place among English writers. 'Her circle may be restricted, but it is complete. Her world is a perfect orb, and vital. Life, as it presents itself to an English gentlewoman peacefully yet actively engaged in her quiet village, is mirrored in her works with a purity and fidelity that must endow them with interest for all time' (2: 44). Lewes exaggerates when he claims in 1852 that he merely echoes 'an universal note of praise,' but it will not be long before the praise will be universal. As the doctrines of realism become entrenched, others will share his sense that 'of all imaginative writers [Austen] is most *real*.' And the fact that her novels are 'written by a woman, and Englishwoman, a gentlewoman' who keeps to a 'womanly point of view' reinforces the 'durable' nature of her work. Finally, 'there is nothing of the *doctrinaire* in Jane Austen; not a trace of woman's "mission;"' but as the most truthful, charming, humorous, pure-minded, quick-witted, and unexaggerated of writers, female literature has reason to be proud of her' (2: 45). Lewes anticipates well most of the reasons critics for the next several generations will favour Austen of all women novelists.

Lewes's decision to review *Jane Eyre* resulted in a well-known exchange of letters with Charlotte Brontë preceding and following publication of the review itself. Brontë focuses on Lewes's warning to 'beware of Melodrame' and 'adhere to the real,' expressing her concern about the implied additional warning to turn her back on her 'imagination' in favour of 'real experience' (Letter of 6 November 1847; 1: 559). She fears that this can only lead to limitation, repetition, and egotism. When Lewes's review proves 'generous' and 'lenient,' Brontë playfully revisits his earlier strictures and advice: 'If I ever *do* write another book, I think I will have nothing of what you call 'melodrame'; I *think* so, but I am not sure. I *think* too I will endeavour to follow the counsel which shines out of Miss Austen's 'mild eyes'; 'to finish more, and to be more subdued'; but neither am I sure of that. When authors write best, or at least, when they write most fluently, an influence seems to waken in them which becomes their master' (Letter of 12 January 1848; 2: 9–10).

Lewes demonstrates his range by his second choice among women novelists. No Austen clone, George Sand is seen as a writer 'of greater genius, and incomparably deeper experience'; she 'represents women's literature more illustriously and more obviously' (2: 45). No one could be fooled by her masculine pen name. His next choice, 'by a whimsical transition,' is Lady Morgan, 'the "Wild Irish Girl" who delighted our fathers' (2: 46–7). Then comes Edgeworth, who is strong in 'observation' but at the expense of 'sentiment,' the other quality 'which distinguishes female writers.' The best have both. Those without sentiment are limited to 'humour and satire'; those without observation to 'rhetoric and long-drawn lachrymosity' (2: 47). Burney is an example of the former, L.E.L. of the latter. The only other women he can mention who unite these necessary components of the best women's novels are Charlotte Brontë and Elizabeth Gaskell; Geraldine Jewsbury, Eliza Lynn, and Dinah Mulock earn honourable mentions.

Some of Lewes's views alter in his later criticism. His enthusiasm for both Austen and Fielding diminishes in favour of his all-consuming dedication to the work of George Eliot. Eighteenth-century fiction had little appeal for him, and eighteenth-century fiction by women still less. The earliest woman novelist he considers, though not very seriously, is Burney, and the only novel he mentions by name is *The Wanderer*, contemporary with the work of Austen, Morgan, and Edgeworth. Lewes again anticipates later criticism with his Victorian version of the lack of interest in the earlier women novelists; they did not fulfil his expectations for the kinds of novels women should write. As critics became both more prescriptive and narrower in their taste, they would increasingly reject Lewes's more general claims for women as novelists. That rejection would add force to their evaluation – shared by Lewes – of early women novelists as beneath notice.

## II

The five critics discussed above demonstrate much of the range of Victorian novel criticism as well as many of its commonly held assumptions and evaluations. There is of course some predictable variation in both theory and taste that accompanies the shared assumptions and evaluations. The particular subgenre of criticism is always relevant: an encyclopedia like Chambers's will necessarily be more inclusive than an essay like Lewes's, even if the critics have identical methods and goals. As the nineteenth century progresses, the ever-increasing numbers of new novelists inevitably compete with and assume places in the canon once held by their predecessors. Serious reconsideration of the eighteenth-century novel that raises it in critical esteem still lies some time in the future.

Having established the large issues that determined the place of the early women novelists for Victorian critics, I now turn to some specific responses to these issues from a fuller range of Victorian critics. I begin with criticism of writers who are reliable indicators of critical trends: the female wits, Richardson, Burney, and, increasingly, Austen. Opinion about Behn changes little after Scott documents her eighteenth-century loss of favour. Taine's one-sentence dismissal and Lewes's complete neglect form one pole; the other, represented by Chambers and Kavanagh, recognizes her historical importance for the novel while endorsing the well-established position that, like most of the literature of the reign of Charles II, Behn's novels are too indecent for respectable Victorian readers. She continues to be noticed by any historian with pretensions to thorough coverage, but her inclusion always requires justification if not apology. Sarah Josepha Hale (1788–1879) limits her account of Behn to a brief biography, avoiding the problem of her work entirely. Jane Williams (1806–85) offers the standard line that Behn had to be licentious in order to please her audience, but finds that apology insufficient to keep her work in print. She adds that the only reason she has included Behn is for understanding 'the true state of female literature at this period,' granting Behn the dubious distinction of being 'the first English authoress upon record whose life was openly wrong, and whose writings were obscene' (*Literary Women of England*, 128). Williams joins Kavanagh and others in identifying Behn's denunciation of the slave trade in *Oroonoko* as one of the few good things to be said about her, a line pursued enthusiastically by J. Cordy Jeaffreson (1831–1901), who turns her into a proto-abolitionist who anticipated the work of Harriet Beecher Stowe.[2] Jeaffreson credits Behn with being one of those rare women to succeed as a professional writer before acknowledging that 'no man of common respectability would, in our days, permit these works to be on the table of his drawing-room' (*Novels and Novelists*, 1: 57–8). Unlike many of his contemporaries, he concludes that since she is no worse than her male contemporaries, she should not suffer stronger condemnation through the invocation of a critical double standard. William Forsyth (1812–99) claims Behn is the first to approach 'in idea the modern novel,' but only after declaring it 'remarkable that some of the most immoral novels in the English language should have been written by women,' that is, by Behn, Manley, and Haywood (*Novels and Novelists*, 174–5). Anthony Trollope (1815–82) anticipates a later approach to Restoration drama in characterizing the novels of Behn as much by their 'terrible dulness' ('On English Prose Fiction,' 100) as by their indecency,[3] though he grants that the novels are not so bad as the plays.

It is not surprising that Manley and Haywood fare even worse, for as imitators of Behn (according to most of the critics), they lack her historical importance and her originality. *The New Atalantis* (1709), for Forsyth, is 'one of the worst books I know – the worst in style and worst in morals' (*Novels and Novelists*, 196). Jeaffreson is perhaps the only critic to find value in Manley's work, seeing her as a great innovator with important contributions to the epistolary, the satirical, and the political novel. But his praise comes in the context of his declaration that 'it would be difficult to find in the whole course of English literature, Lord Rochester and his fraternity not excepted, an author so immodest, and so delighting in voluptuous license' (*Novels and Novelists*, 88). Williams notes that Manley's 'popularity was great in its day' before expressing her approval that 'none of her productions have lived' since none 'deserved to live' (*Literary Women*, 128). Haywood receives still less attention, though Sarah Hale retells the story of her post-Richardson reform, and Forsyth pays tribute to *Betsy Thoughtless* as 'rather a clever work and interesting' as well as 'the first really domestic novel according to modern ideas, that exists in the language.' He also notes Haywood's major claim to fame, that *Betsy Thoughtless* is the model for Burney's *Evelina* (*Novels and Novelists*, 203). The criticism of the female wits, then, is dominated by familiar cultural clichés, but even they are rarely expressed. Few critics talk about these novelists at all.

Though most critics recognize the historical importance of the fathers of the novel, they tend to be unenthusiastic about eighteenth-century fiction in general. Frederic Blanchard's complaint that '*all* the eighteenth-century novelists (save, perhaps, Goldsmith) ceased by degrees to be generally read except by those inclined to literature' (*Fielding the Novelist*, 368) is justified. Nor did the kind of general hostility to the century so evident in Taine and Masson help the novelists maintain their place in the literary hierarchy. Richardson and Fielding remain at the head of the list, frequently played off each other. Richardson's admirers and detractors alike continue to comment on his feminization, often as part of the dialectic which places him in opposition to the masculine Fielding.

William Francis Collier (fl. 1850–75) praises Richardson as the 'first parent of ... the modern novel,' crediting *Pamela* for 'turning the tide' against 'the affectation and deep depravity' of earlier fiction. The key to his success was a 'quiet, womanly nature' which 'made him love the society of the gentler sex' (*History of English Literature*, 306–8). Thomas B. Shaw (1813–62) also credits Richardson with important advances in prose fiction, particularly in the representation of character. His explanation for Richardson's success is similar, though developed in a more interesting way: 'There appears to have been, whether derived from nature or only resulting from circumstances, something *feminine* in his mental organisation; for his works show not only a good deal of that sensitive or rather sentimental melancholy which characterizes the female mind, but much of the female timidity of taste, the female appreciation of minute peculiarities, and also, it is but just to say, the female penetration, and the female purity of moral sentiment' (*Outlines*, 258). For Leslie Stephen (1832–1904), Richardson is one of the few original writers to add 'a new type to the fictitious world,' a 'man of true genius,' but a genius with obvious, major faults. His 'special characteristic it was to be a milksop; ... his most obvious merits and defects resulted from his feminine characteristics' ('Richardson's Novels,' 2: 600). His female characters rival even Austen's, but without her 'feminine sensitiveness and closeness of observation' (2: 620). For Trollope, Richardson and Fielding were the first novelists to represent lived experience, though because they do so in descriptions of 'coarse things' and in 'coarse language,' they are no longer read. 'Richardson was, as it were, a saint among novelists – and Fielding a sinner. Richardson laid himself out to support high-toned feminine virtue. The praise of strict matrons and of severe elders was the very breath of his nostrils' ('On English Prose Fiction,' 101). It is hardly surprising that Trollope admits to preferring the sinner to the saint. Trollope's saint becomes Forsyth's 'sentimental little prig,' the author of books once thought fit guides for young women but now recognized as mere 'twaddle.' For Forsyth, this testifies to the 'perverted state of the public taste, not to say public morals' of the mid-eighteenth century (*Novels and Novelists*, 216–19, 256). The most extreme and the most influential portrait of Richardson came from Thackeray (1811–63). The context is Thackeray's case for the unjustly neglected and maligned Henry Fielding; Richardson is used to further Fielding's cause by contrast. In the process, Thackeray's famous vignette draws out the misogynistic implication of the feminized Richardson:

> Fielding, no doubt, began to write [*Joseph Andrews*] in ridicule of 'Pamela,' for which work one can understand the hearty contempt and antipathy which such an athletic and boisterous genius as Fielding's must have entertained. He couldn't do otherwise than laugh at the puny cockney bookseller, pouring out endless volumes of sentimental twaddle, and hold him up to scorn as a mollcoddle and a milksop. *His* genius had been nursed on sackposset, and not on dishes of tea. *His* muse had sung loudest in tavern choruses, had seen the daylight streaming in over thousands of emptied bowls, and reeled home to chambers on the shoulders of the watchman. Richardson's goddess was attended by old maids and dowagers, and fed on muffins and bohea. 'Milksop!' roars Harry Fielding, clattering at the timid shop-shutters. 'Wretch! Monster! Mohock!' shrieks the sentimental author of 'Pamela;' and all the ladies of his court cackle out an affrighted chorus. (*The English Humourists*, 317–18)

There are, of course, no women writers among *The English Humourists* (1853).

Frances Burney, the greatest humourist among the eighteenth-century women novelists, wrote too late to be included in Thackeray's study, but she figured in almost all other Victorian studies of the early novel. Taine and Kavanagh represent the extreme differences of opinion about Burney. Jeaffreson summarizes the case against her in arguing that she is derivative of Richardson and Fielding to a fault, as well as too unpleasant for more refined tastes. *Evelina*, her best work, reveals her gift for satirizing those beneath her, a gift unworthy of a great writer. His conclusion is that 'as a novelist, Madame D'Arblay does not merit a second-rate, or even a third-rate place' (*Novels and Novelists*, 1: 337–8). James Hannay (1827–73) is barely more positive in describing Burney as filling up 'the interval' between the fathers of the novel and Sir Walter Scott. 'While so much of our old light literature lies neglected,' he concludes, 'we cannot urge our students the perusal of her works' (*Course of English Literature*, 248–9). Critics more favourably disposed give her stop-gap function a far more positive turn. Henry Coppée (1821–95) finds her novels the 'intermediate step between the novels of Richardson, Fielding, and Smollett and the Waverley novels of Walter Scott. They are entirely free from any taint of immorality and they were among the first feminine efforts that were received with enthusiasm: Thus it is that, without being of the first order of merit, they mark a distinct era in English letters' (*English Literature*, 369). More enthusiastic and far more influential is Lord Macaulay (1800–59), who argues that *Evelina* was 'the first tale written by a woman, and purporting to be a picture of life and manners, that lived or deserved to live.' Burney succeeded in writing a novel fit for ladies to read. In doing so, she 'did for the English novel what Jeremy Collier did for the English drama.' Her 'honourable mention' in literary history comes in part from her skill as a writer of humours and in part from her enabling others to write great novels (*Critical, Historical, and Miscellaneous Essays*, 5: 319–20). Without Burney, Macaulay suggests, there would be no Austen or Edgeworth, a claim later maintained by Jerom Murch (1807–95), who credits Burney with 'not only Evelina, Cecilia, and Camilla, but also Miss Austen's Mansfield Park and Miss Edgeworth's Absentee' (*Mrs Barbauld and Her Contemporaries*, 95). Murch sees Burney as the founder of the main line of English women's fiction, one he extends well into the nineteenth century. If Burney falls short of first-rate in the Victorian criticism she remains an important novelist with a central place in the history of the novel, whether the history of a line that begins with Richardson and/or Fielding or a line solely of women novelists. Her status as the first important, creditable woman novelist implies the lack of status of her predecessors.

Fuelling the Victorian neglect of all but a handful of eighteenth-century women novelists was the transformation of Austen from little-known favourite of the few like Scott who recognized her value to a major writer. Macaulay set the tune early in the period, suggesting that Austen comes close to approaching 'the manner of the great master,' Shakespeare. She is 'a woman of whom England is justly proud' (*Critical, Historical, and Miscellaneous Essays*, 5: 307). Not many share Macaulay's virtually boundless admiration for Austen – although Lewes does – but a more qualified admiration becomes increasingly commonplace. Forsyth considers it 'wonderful' that Austen, 'by the intuitive force of genius' could produce novels 'which in a knowledge of the anatomy of the human heart and gracefulness of style, and in individuality of character, have never been surpassed' (*Novels and Novelists*, 330). Jeaffreson laments her neglect by the majority of readers looking for more sensational fiction, but takes comfort in recognizing that 'wiser and more intelligent minds' appreciate her novels as 'the best specimens of one department of the fictive art in literature.' He feels certain that they will be 'much studied five hundred years hence by scholars curious to obtain a true insight into the family life, and form a correct estimate, of the simple, gently-bred women, of the nineteenth century.' He urges men who wish to understand women better to consult Jane Austen (*Novels and Novelists*, 2: 84–7). Trollope captures the critical consensus as well as anyone: 'Miss Austen was surely a great novelist. I do not know how far I may presume that you are acquainted with her works, but I recommend such of you as may not be so, to lose no time in mending the fault. What she did, she did perfectly. Her work, as far as it goes, is faultless. She wrote of the times in which she lived, of the class of people with which she is associated, and in the language which was usual to her as an educated lady' ('On English Prose Fiction,' 105). However qualified the praise, however condescending the tone, as Austen eclipsed all predecessors – even Burney – earlier fiction by women became unnecessary or irrelevant. If you can enjoy perfection, why settle for anything else?

The Victorian reassessment of women novelists accompanied the continuing, unhesitating, nearly universal recognition of Scott as the greatest novelist, perhaps the most frequently shared assumption informing the criticism of the period. Scott's place in the history of the novel was unprecedented. Archibald Alison (1792–1867) pulls out all the stops in presenting his version of a narrative frequently told after Scott's death. Alison, a lover of classical literature, recognized Cervantes, Shakespeare, and very few others as worthy of praise. But Scott's 'historical romance' deserves a 'place beside the plays of Shakespeare': 'The prodigious addition which the happy idea of the historical romance has made to the stories of elevated literature, and through it to the happiness and improvement of the human race, will not be properly appreciated, unless the novels most in vogue before the immortal creations of Scott appeared are considered. If we take up even the most celebrated of them, and in which the most unequivocal marks of genius are to be discerned, it seems hardly possible to conceive how their authors could have acquired the reputation which they so long enjoyed' ('The Historical Romance,' 65–6).

That kind of praise, approaching worship, tends to dwarf the strongest of rivals. And Alison is not alone in his excess. For Robert Plumer Ward (1765–1846), Scott led the development of the novel to the 'pitch of perfection' (*De Vere*, i); only Shakespeare 'surpasses him' (*De Vere*, v).

'No writer since the days of Shakespeare has created so many fine, healthy, life-like, and original characters ... He stands without a rival at the head of Prose Fiction,' declares Allan Cunningham (1784–1842) ('British Novels,' 1: 152–3). Thomas B. Shaw argues that 'no author in the whole range of literature, ancient or modern, ... exhibit[s] so perfect an embodiment of united power and activity as is found in Walter Scott' (*Outlines*, 315). 'All the novels of such a man ought to be read by everybody who cares for novels,' James Hannay informs his readers (*Course of English Literature*, 250). Stopford Brooke's (1832–1916) 'primer' covers the history of the novel in just over three pages; about 20 per cent is devoted to Scott, 'the great Enchanter.' Men are still alive, Brooke notes, 'who remember well the wonder and the delight of the land when *Waverley* (1814) was published.' Scott's art is of such a magnitude that 'since Shakespeare there is nothing we can compare to it ... He raised the whole of the literature of the novel into one of the greatest influences that bear on the human mind' (*English Literature*, 130). The effect of Scott's reputation on other novelists was like that of Shakespeare on other dramatists. The early masters were relegated to the status of minor writers; the rest are reduced to footnotes if they are not entirely forgotten.

The rewriting of the history of the novel after Scott is consolidated into a version which typically portrays him, as Charles D. Cleveland (1802–69) puts it, not only as 'the head of fictitious writers,' but 'the inventor of a new class of fictitious writings' (*English Letters*, 232). Even at the end of this period Trollope sees Scott as the foundation of all the novel has become: it was Scott who is credited with making novels respectable ('mothers allowed their daughters to read them' ['On English Prose Fiction,' 114]), and it is Scott who ushered in the age of the realistic novel:

> I have said that this æra divides our Prose Fiction into two epochs. But he himself belongs to both. He partook of that unreal romance which was the very base on which Prose Fiction was first founded. There is still the touch of the Paladin and the Princess about his men and women; but he wove them into stories of such vital interest, and threw such movement and passion and mirth into the telling of these stories, that he created a new system of Fiction. If he was not always life-like himself, he produced a love for such likeness which has imposed an obligation on all English novelists coming after him. In parting with his name I must again repeat my belief that from the reading of his novels nothing but good has come to the people for whom he wrote. (117)

Trollope's view that before Scott the novel was both morally and artistically unacceptable is a widely shared Victorian view. The implications for writers before Scott are, again, obvious.

The axiom that great novels begin with Scott points to two other aspects of Victorian responses to early novels, the widely held belief that the novel was a form just beginning to realize its potential, and its corollary, the belief that the novel would continue to improve, along with the society that produced it. Anne Elwood (1796–1873) incorporates both aspects of this progressive history in her apology for Mary Brunton, an author she admires for 'interesting narratives pleasingly told and pervaded by a high tone of moral feeling,' yet cannot call 'first-rate' because her works have 'too many palpable improbabilities.' She is able to excuse Brunton since she wrote at a time before 'the taste of the public' was 'raised' by Scott (*Memoirs*, 2: 221). The only reason Forsyth can offer for looking at eighteenth-century fiction is to find out about the society represented in it. With few exceptions, the stories are 'deplorably dull,' the plots 'contemptible,' the style 'detestable.' The process is sure to be unpleasant, but not without its rewards:

> We have to face an amount of coarseness which is in the highest degree repulsive. It is like raking a dust heap to discover grains of gold. And herein lies the specialty of the case. It is because the novels reflect, as in a mirror, the tone of the thought and language of the age in which they were written, that the perusal of them even now is useful ... That 'Roderick Random,' 'Peregrine Pickle,' 'Tom Jones,' and 'Tristram Shandy' could have been written and become popular, not only amongst men but amongst women proves that society was accustomed to actions and language which would not be tolerated now. (*Novels and Novelists*, 3, 5–6)

Even the end of the eighteenth century is not free from the 'vulgar' and the 'indecorous.' Forsyth must add Inchbald, Burney, and Edgeworth to Defoe, Swift, Richardson, Fielding, and Smollett, offering the usual apology for including the highly regarded Edgeworth: 'Nobody can think higher of the last-named authoress than myself, and I attribute whatever faults of this kind she has committed to the manners of the age' (162–3). If Edgeworth could not meet Victorian expectations, what chance did her predecessors have? Cunningham offers the same excuse for Burney: 'No doubt the fault lies in society rather than in Madame D'Arblay: she paints what she sees, and she paints it vividly' (*British Novels*, 149).

Other Victorian critics adopt the argument that eighteenth-century fiction was hopelessly coarse and indelicate in variant versions of the history of the novel. Charles Duke Yonge (1812–91), Regius Professor at Queen's College, Belfast, is typical, an advocate of the novel whose history mixes defence with celebration of one of the greatest 'triumphs of the British genius ... above all competition' (*Three Centuries of English Literature*, 569). The novel, for Yonge, begins with Defoe and Swift and matures very quickly: 'the middle of the last century produced writers of novels of the very first class as men of ability and artistic skill.' But, Yonge must add, their works 'are almost equally proscribed by the modern taste, which in this case cannot be pronounced needlessly delicate and fastidious' given that 'the indelicacy and coarseness of the age in which they lived' are only 'too faithfully reproduced in their writings' (595). It follows that a more refined age should be able to close the gap between art and its subject matter; to Yonge's delight, this is in fact the case. It was 'reserved for the present century to produce a writer who could unite all the good qualities of his predecessors, wit, humour, and invention, with a learning to which they made no claim, and a poetic fire' (595). That writer was, of course, Scott. Edgeworth is given an honourable mention, in part for her contribution to Scott's development, but also because 'her own powers were of a very high class' (598). Yonge brings to his history another increasingly common critical position, that students should focus only on 'the most perfect specimens,' and that general readers have time only for the best (608). Once the novel reaches the perfection of Scott, there is no point in looking back. He eagerly moves on to Scott's successors: Marryat, Cooper, Dickens, and Thackeray.

An anonymous 1853 omnibus review of Heliodorus, *Amadis of Gaul*, the novels of Richardson, Fielding, Smollett, Radcliffe, Austen, Burney, Scott, and new novels by Collins, Kavanagh, and Kingsley in the *Westminster Review* offers a similar history, with implications still more damaging to the status of eighteenth-century fiction. The reviewer, identified by Robert Colby as George Eliot (1819–80) (25), begins by affirming the universal 'love of fiction' ('Progress of Fiction,' 2: 73) in its varying manifestations reflecting the changing societies and times that produce it, and by observing with satisfaction the current domination of realistic fiction as a sign of the progress of the novel as a form. Her brief survey of novelists before 1700 reveals deep disappointment at how little they reveal about their societies. She has some regard for Sidney's *Arcadia* (1590–3), and she considers *The Pilgrim's*

*Progress* (1678–84) not without cause 'the most universally popular fiction ever written.' But she is no lover of the Stuart monarchs, especially 'the licentious Charles II,' who is responsible for 'the questionable productions of Aphra Behn' (2: 85). Fiction becomes an 'art' and the novelist a 'moralist' and 'philosopher' (2: 86) only with Richardson.

Richardson was the first to present 'the feelings and passions common to human nature in all ages,' however much 'the greater refinement of manners in modern days may render Richardson's pictures of life revolting to our more fastidious tastes.' He is still far preferable to contemporaries like Fielding and Smollett, whose 'studied coarseness' seems deliberately 'to pander to the evil passions of human nature' (2: 86). Eliot continues the familiar narrative with her description of the reaction that took place at century's end: 'Lady authors become more numerous – the Minerva press looms heavily in the distance, and the new school makes up for its inferiority in power and nature, by irreproachable modesty and propriety of tone' (2: 88). Fashions come and go. The current vogue for 'morbid *feelings* and over-wrought *sensibilities*' is but the latest of many 'fashions,' like the Gothic before it, 'which contradict nature' and will therefore necessarily 'pass away.'

Though unnatural novels of fashion continue, the dialectic between 'prose and nature' and 'modesty and propriety' (2: 88) is resolved in the nineteenth century. Austen and Burney each proved that 'a high reputation' and an 'enduring name' will be the reward of an author who 'dares to be natural.' But even Austen and Burney 'must be classed in the lower division': 'As pictures of manners, they are interesting and amusing, but they want the broader foundation, the firm granite substratum, which the great masters who have followed them have taught us to expect ... They fall short of fulfilling the objects, and satisfying the necessities of Fiction in its highest aspect – as the art whose office it is "to interest, to please, and sportively to elevate – to take man from the low passions and miserable troubles of life into a higher region ..."' (2: 89).

Eliot's endorsement of Bulwer Lytton's call for an elevated novel anticipates an Arnoldian call for 'high seriousness' in literature generally. The dialectic is here described in terms of art and morality (rather than Yonge's art and its subject matter) but the process of resolution sounds very much the same:

It was a happy opening of a rich and unworked mine when Miss Edgeworth gave her humourously descriptive tales of Irish life to the world – most happy if, as Sir Walter Scott declares, they had the merit of first suggesting to him the idea of a series of stories illustrative of the character and manners of his own country, and we owe the Waverley novels to that idea. Of those world-known fictions, eulogy seems superfluous, and criticism almost impertinent ... In the whole range of fiction it would be impossible to mention any author, the tone of whose works is so thoroughly healthy and pure as Sir Walter Scott's. (2: 90–1)

Eliot then proceeds to more recent fiction, having established the moral tone of the account of the novel with Scott as the first master. She recognizes Richardson and Fielding as the best that could be expected from a less refined culture, and has little time for lesser novelists before Scott.

Eliot's raising of the moral stakes and tying them to the doctrine of realism implies the exclusion from critical favour of two kinds of fiction that had been dominated by women novelists, the overtly didactic, often Evangelical, and the Gothic. Ann H. Jones points out that not long after the publication of Hannah More's *Cœlebs in Search of a Wife*, 'the most popular novel of the first two decades of the nineteenth century, going through twelve editions in the first year, ... there rose a growing demand for the morality, while remaining present, to be less obtrusive' (*Ideas and Innovations*, 10, 14). Jones sees the assimilation of the morality of the Evangelicals into more entertaining works of art as the key to the triumphs of Victorian fiction, and the Victorian critics appear to share her judgment. Where the young Macaulay cited *Cœlebs* as his favorite example of 'religious novels which ought to be read' (*Christian Observer*, December 1816, quoted in Jones, *Ideas and Innovations*, 12), later critics are increasingly unsympathetic with More as a novelist, though they are often reluctant to criticize her openly. T.H. Lister (1800–42), for example, anticipates the response behind the revision to Chambers's *Cyclopædia* in presenting his reservations about *Cœlebs* in terms of a problem of genre: 'Mrs Hannah More hung some good moral discourses upon the frame-work of a story; but we can hardly call her a novelist' (1: 59–60). Allan Cunningham tackles the More problem more candidly: 'Of Hannah More it is not easy to speak: the sentiments which she utters have a scriptural source, and the aim of her writings is the eternal welfare of mankind ... In religious romance, no one has come near the inventor and maker, honest John Bunyan ... We are no admirers of religious romances; we are content with the New Testament, and prefer the simple language of our Saviour to all the glosses of the learned and the speculations of the ingenuous' ('British Novels,' 1: 153–4). It is the rare critic who, like John Eagles (1783–1855), admits that he 'abominate[s] everything Hannah

More wrote.' *Cœlebs* is the produce of 'unwomanly dishonesty,' built around a plot that represents the central character as 'converted,' most improbably, 'through his vice,' and More is 'the precursor to a worse set ... [the] wickedly religious' ('A Few Words About Novels,' 1: 583). As More's reputation as a novelist declined and the overtly Evangelical novels went out of fashion, critical rhetoric could be more comfortably restrained – the restraint of victory. Forsyth dismisses *Cœlebs* as 'a dramatic sermon' (340); Henry Coppée describes More as a woman of 'pure morals and religion' whose 'merits are indulgently exaggerated' (*English Literature*, 365). The gradual removal from the canon of the Evangelical, religious, didactic novels so popular at the turn of the century meant the removal of one more kind of early novel dominated by women writers. Critics who looked for moral antecedents of the Victorian novel looked back to Goldsmith and Addison, erasing from their histories the contribution of these writers of more overtly didactic fiction.

As the Gothic novel went out of fashion it also lost critical favour, though never to the point of being written out of literary history. Instead, the number of Gothic novels worth mentioning was kept to a minimum and the subgenre increasingly dismissed for failing to fulfil the requirements of the advocates of high realism. Women novelists were again the major losers on both counts. George Moir (1800–70) is typical in presenting a trimmed-down canon of Gothic novelists that runs from Walpole and Reeve through the 'perfection' of 'the species of romance writing' in Radcliffe to her only two followers worth mentioning, Lewis and Maturin. Moir clearly enjoys the Gothic, and especially Radcliffe, but feels the need to apologize for devoting eight pages (of 112) to so flawed a form of fiction ('Modern Romance and the Novel,' 194–202). Jeaffreson also keeps to a minimum the number of Gothic novelists in his more comprehensive history. He too admires Radcliffe, and in order to distinguish her from the mass of her imitators, emphasizes the way in which she is a proto-Victorian realist: 'It has been the fashion of late years to speak of Mrs. Radcliffe with contempt, and to point to her works as the best possible representatives of stupidity.' But it is not her fault that 'the excellence of her works' encouraged inferior imitators. And what is too frequently forgotten is that 'the condemned authoress introduced a new element into fictitious literature perfectly distinct from the growls and groans and ridiculous horrors with which her name is associated in the popular mind.' She was the 'first to adorn the "English Novel" with what has ever since been regarded as necessary to a fiction of any pretensions to excellence, – *truthful, graphic, attractive description of scenery'* (*Novels and Novelists*, 2: 4). His plea, however, persuaded few; Radcliffe is mentioned in most histories, but she is no longer considered worth reading. Typical of the brief comments offered by most critics is Trollope's declaration that because Radcliffe's novels are 'unreal and unlife-like,' readers find them 'very dull and very long' ('On English Prose Fiction,' 104). Forsyth generalizes the point to encompass the Gothic as a genre: 'They are too unreal to be of any service ... and it is enough to say that no young gentleman or young lady at the present day is likely to be frightened at night and disturbed in sleep by reading their shadowy horrors' (*Novels and Novelists*, 313). The loss of stature of the Gothic, like that of didactic fiction, both casualties of Victorian tastes and doctrines, eliminated large numbers of once-successful women novelists from the canon.

Most Victorian critics subscribed to a progressive history of the novel that looked to the early novel for its contributions to the triumph of Victorian realism. Critics increasingly funnel the novel through Austen as she becomes the most important early woman novelist, and, next to Scott, the most important pre-Victorian novelist. Thus partisans of both Richardson and Fielding, however violent their disagreements about the relative merits of their respective champions, see the novel moving from their hero to Austen. And increasingly Austen is seen as superior to either. Leslie Stephen points to her 'feminine sensitiveness and closeness of observation' as what was needed 'to complete Richardson' (Richardson's Novels,' 2:620). Lewes traces an important line of the novel from Fielding to Austen to Thackeray. He subsequently argues that Fielding is 'quite unworthy to rank beside Scott or Miss Austen' ('The Novels,' 2: 449; 'A Word,' 2: 657). Other critics, of course, trace the line of the novel from Richardson and/or Fielding to Scott. Both Collier and Coppée comment on Richardson being, in Coppée's words, 'driven from our shelves' by much greater masters, beginning with Scott (Coppée, *English Literature*, 287; Collier, *History of English Literature*, 309).

Changing tastes and Whiggish histories both reinforce the trend to a more selective, smaller canon, especially for earlier novels. After over a hundred years of active novel publication, most early novels, that is, most novels before Scott and Austen, were no longer read. Or, as Leslie Stephen put it, 'How many English authors between Shakespeare and Scott are still alive, in the sense of being familiar, not merely to students, but to the ordinary bulk of conventionally "educated persons"?' (*Hours* 1: 220). Stephen points to one of the main resources for maintaining the reputations, however diminished, of eighteenth-century writers, texts for students. They will play an increasingly central role in this history. Another increasingly important resource for retaining some early women novelists in the critical consciousness is the gendering of the novel during the middle of the nineteenth century in the form of histories and encyclopedias of women novelists or writers. At a time when accounts of the novel once again minimized or even excluded women novelists, the kind of study best represented by Kavanagh provided a place for these otherwise neglected writers and their works.[4]

Specialized histories and compilations, like textbooks for students, kept information about many earlier novelists available. They did not, however, keep novelists in the canon any more than they kept their novels in print. It is impossible to provide a definitive list of Victorian reprints of eighteenth-and early nineteenth-century fiction. The most thorough bibliographical record of all novels published in the nineteenth century remains Michael Sadleir's *XIX Century Fiction: A Bibliographical Record Based on His Own Collection* (1951). Sadleir records the contents of a number of reprint series, and they probably offer the best indication of the relative value of earlier novelists to Victorian publishers. The following lists extract the novels by men and women from the period of this study:

1 Bentley's Standard novels (first series); 126 titles (1831–54): *Caleb Williams, Thaddeus of Warsaw, St Leon, The Scottish Chiefs, Frankenstein, Edgar Huntly, The Hungarian Brothers, Canterbury Tales, Self-Control, Discipline, The Pastor's Fire-Side, Fleetwood, Sense and Sensibility, Corinne, Emma, A Simple Story, Nature and Art, Mansfield Park, Northanger Abbey, Persuasion, Pride and Prejudice, Vathek, The Castle of Otranto, The Bravo of Venice, Helen, Marriage, Inheritance, Destiny.* (Sadleir 2: 100–2)

2 Roscoe's Novelist's Library; 19 vols. (1831–3): *Robinson Crusoe, Humphry Clinker, Roderick Random, Peregrine Pickle, Tom Jones, Joseph Andrews, Amelia, The Vicar of Wakefield, Sir Launcelot Greaves, Tristram Shandy, A Sentimental Journey, Don Quixote, Gil Blas.* (Sadleir 2: 109–10)

3 The Novel Newspaper; 12 vols. (1839–42): *The Hungarian Brothers, Don Sebastian, Peregrine Pickle, Ormond, Manfroné, The Old Manor House, The Ransom, The Recess, Wieland, Caleb Williams, Canterbury Tales.* (Sadleir 2: 143–4)

4 The Parlour Library; 14 vols. (1846–7): *Mansfield Park.* (Sadleir 2: 148–9)

5 The Parlour Library; 279 vols. (1847–63): *Emma, Northanger Abbey, Persuasion, Mansfield Park, Discipline, A Simple Story, Inheritance, Frankenstein, Marriage, The Hungarian Brothers, Edgar Huntly.* (Sadleir 2: 152–60)

6 The Romanticist, and Novelist's Library, new series; 4 vols. (1839–40):
   *The Bravo of Venice, Mistrust, The Anaconda, Amorassan, The Castle of
   Otranto, The Misanthrope Corrected, The Shepherdess of the Alps, Lauretta,
   Friendship Put to the Test, The Castles of Athlin and Dunbayne, The Sicil-
   ian Romance, The Romance of the Forest, The Italian, The Story of LaRoche,
   Louisa Venoni, The Man of Feeling, Lazarillo de Tormes, A Love Tale,
   Antonelli, The Old English Baron, Paul and Virginia, The Indian Cottage,
   The Vampyre, Captain Singleton, The Vicar of Wakefield, Nourjahad,
   Nature and Art, Castle of Wolfenbach, A Simple Story, Annigait and Ajut,
   La Gitana, The Wild Irish Boy, The Ghost Seer, The Sport of Destiny, Walsh
   Colville, The Children of the Abbey, Longsword, A Tale of the Passions,
   St Irvyne, Zastrozzi, Edgar Huntly.* (Sadleir 2: 164–5)
7 The Romanticist, and Novelist's Library, new series; 6 vols. (1841–2):
   *The Fatal Revenge, Raymond and Agnes, Zadig, The Women's Revenge,
   Criminal.* (Sadleir 2: 165–7)
8 Routledge's Standard Novels; 14 vols. (1851–3): *Pride and Prejudice,
   Sense and Sensibility, The Recluse of Norway, The Knight of St John,
   Self-Control, Discipline.* (Sadleir 2: 169)

Two additional series are also of interest:

9 The Bohn Libraries; 536 titles (1846–1921): *Joseph Andrews, Tom Jones,
   Amelia, Roderick Random, Peregrine Pickle, Humphry Clinker, Evelina,
   Cecilia, Corinne.* (Todd and Bowden)
10 Tauchnitz International Editions in English; 3068 titles (1841–95):
   *The Vicar of Wakefield, Tom Jones, Gulliver's Travels, Robinson Crusoe,
   Roderick Random, Humphry Clinker, Tristram Shandy, Evelina, The
   Pilgrim's Progress, A Sentimental Journey, Clarissa, Sense and Sensibility,
   Mansfield Park, Peregrine Pickle, Pride and Prejudice, Northanger Abbey,
   Persuasion, Emma, Moral Tales, Popular Tales.* (Cordasco)

What these various collections point to is the absence of a single
rigid canon, and the relatively small group of early novelists the publishers regularly turn to for likely sales. They also confirm the high
profile of the small number of late eighteenth- and early nineteenth-
century women novelists who dominate the critical studies and the
lack of attention given to other, especially earlier, women novelists.

None of the other accounts of women writers match Kavanagh
for thorough and thoughtful insights. But, at the very least, they
provide a list of those thought most worthy, and they usually provide

much more. Sarah Josepha Hale's *Woman's Record* (1853) is an encyclopedic compilation, in this case of hundreds of brief entries about women writers with extracts from the most important. What criticism she offers is taken from other critics, usually quoted without acknowledgment. But anyone interested in women novelists could find out about Burney, Austen, Brunton, Edgeworth, Lafayette, Ferrier, Genlis, Hamilton, More, Morgan, Newcastle, Opie, Jane Porter, Radcliffe, Rowe, Shelley, Smith, Staël, and Williams with extracts of their work, and Behn, Brooke, Fielding, Fouqué, Wollstonecraft, Grafigny, Griffith, Hays, Haywood, Inchbald, Sophia Lee, Lennox, Manley, Anna Maria Porter, Reeve, Roche, and Sheridan without extracts. Anne Elwood's *Memoirs of the Literary Ladies of England* (1843) provides biographical accounts with minimal criticism of Sheridan, More, Smith, Inchbald, Burney, Hamilton, Wollstonecraft (though not as novelist), Radcliffe, Austen, Brunton, and the Porters. Jerom Murch's *Mrs Barbauld and her Contemporaries* (1877) is limited to the period (roughly) 1775–1825. He includes among the novelists More, Edgeworth, Austen, Jane Porter, Burney, Opie, Inchbald, Radcliffe, the Lees, Hamilton, and Morgan.

Jane Williams begins her *Literary Women of England* (1861) by establishing the need for a single volume that collects basic biographical information about women writers. She modestly offers the following rationale: 'In both "Cyclopaedia" [Chambers] and the "Sketches" [Craik, *Sketches*] the authoresses are doubtless reduced to their true relative properties when contrasted with authors, but the peculiarly valuable and most attractive attributes of the female mind are obscured' (7). As her full title points out, her entries include biographical information, some criticism, and extracts. Among the novelists she includes Behn, Manley, Rowe, Smith, Williams, and More.

Is it possible, then, to determine a Victorian canon? I would argue that it is as long as the ever-present minority opinions and exceptions are not forgotten. A very good core is to be found in the entry on 'Modern Romance and the Novel' written by George Moir at the beginning of Victoria's reign. Moir's is an interesting article, full of intelligent comments and evaluations. His canon is two-tiered. The major novelists are Defoe (only for *Robinson Crusoe*), Richardson (mainly for *Clarissa*), Fielding, Smollett (to a lesser extent than Fielding), Goldsmith, Sterne (with concern over a reputation in decline), Walpole, Radcliffe (also with concern over a reputation in decline), Godwin (with concern over a reputation in decline), Edgeworth, Austen (with a still-growing reputation), and Scott. The minor novelists are Cumberland, Johnstone, Mackenzie, Johnson, Reeve, Lewis, Maturin, Moore, Bage, Shelley, Inchbald, Burney, Smith, the Lees, and the Porters.

Minor novelists are, not unexpectedly, a more fluid category, and I would add some noted by other critics to make the list more representative. From Thomas Shaw's *Outlines of English Literature* (1846), Sarah Fielding, Lennox, Sheridan, Opie, Beckford, Holcroft, Brunton and Hamilton; from William Forsyth's *The Novel and Novelists of the Eighteenth Century* (1871), Coventry, Henry Brooke, Graves, and Ferrier; from George L. Craik's (1798–1866) *Compendious History* (1878), Frances Brooke, Jane Marshall, Helen Maria Williams, More. The major novelists recognized by the Victorians are few (twelve). The list of minor writers (thirty-five) is much larger and more fluid, but always marginal. The canon in the most common sense of the term is probably best seen as the major writers only. It is a small list; a quarter is female. It is also clear, however, that the Victorians did a respectable job of not forgetting minor novelists, and that more than half of them (twenty) are women. Things would get worse for early women novelists before they got better.

# 4 1880–1920

I began chapter 3 with reference to the explosion of writing about the novel in the Victorian period. That explosion continued to grow exponentially during the second half of Victoria's reign and for the first decades of the new century. In addition to the growing production of popular literary histories and encyclopedias, there is an increased interest in histories of the novel and a developing interest in more general studies of it. This is also the period that sees the introduction of English studies to the curricula of many universities, and, with it, the production of the first considerable body of academic criticism. Much of the early academic criticism attempts to capture two groups of readers at once: critics and their publishers attempted and often succeeded in reaching the new student audience without losing their more traditional audience of general readers.

Histories of the novel remain progressive, and they retain their nationalistic overtones, especially as the critics themselves are increasingly multinational. A significant number of influential studies are produced and published in the United States, often with an American audience as principal readership. These American contributions often focus on the novel as the most progressive and democratic of literary forms. Two additional trends inform the canon-making instincts of many of the writers: there is a more self-conscious insistence on the value of originality in determining canonical status, and an increasing insistence that the canon be highly selective, that is, that only the very best survive. Finally, changing times and their changing values, along with the more specialized concerns of academic critics, make this a period somewhat more open to the early novel and its writers.

My chapters continue to lengthen as I attempt to account for an ever-increasing number of studies. I have had to be more selective, limiting myself to a diminishing proportion of the work being done. I have tried to compensate by choosing a representative group of texts and critics, beginning with general histories of literature and encyclopedias and moving on to histories of the novel and the more specialized studies of women writers. I conclude this chapter with two academic studies that include lengthy discussion of women novelists. In each section, I note the distinction between academic work and work aimed at a general readership, though, as indicated above, the distinction is anything but clear or firm in practice in this period.

## Histories of English Literature

### Edmund Gosse (1849–1928)

Taine's *History* had little room for the early novel and less for early women novelists. Edmund Gosse begins his survey of late seventeenth-century prose in *A History of Eighteenth-Century Literature (1660–1780)* with a similar disdain: 'It is eminently pedestrian in character, unimaginative, level, neutral. It has neither the disordered beauties of the age that preceded it, nor the limpid graces of that which followed it' (73). When he traces the development of the English novel, he recognizes the importance of Elizabethan and French romances in preparing 'the way for the exact opposite to the heroic romance, namely, the realistic story of everyday life' (242). For Gosse, the English novel begins with *Pamela*. He recognizes as forerunners a line that includes Bunyan, Richard Head, Behn, Defoe, *Gulliver's Travels*, the *Spectator* (1711–14), and Marivaux. But the forerunners fall short of meeting Gosse's two main criteria for the novel, 'careful analysis of character' and 'profound delineation of emotion' (244). (Behn comes closest, but she captures these qualities in but 'some very slight and imperfect degree.) The novel flourishes for twenty-five years, long enough to see the publication of *Pamela*, *Joseph Andrews* (1742), *David Simple, Jonathan Wild* (1743), *Clarissa, Roderick Random* (1748), *Tom Jones, Peregrine Pickle* (1751), *Amelia* (1751), *Sir Charles Grandison* (1753–4), *Tristram Shandy* (1759–67), *Rasselas, Chrysal* (1760–5), *The Castle of Otranto*, and *The Vicar of Wakefield*. Then, with the exception of *Humphry Clinker*, *Evelina*, and *Caleb Williams*, 'no great novel appeared again in England for forty years' (244), that is, until *Sense and Sensibility* (1811).

Richardson is, for Gosse, the first English novelist and 'a man of unquestionable genius,' whose greatest gift is his 'extraordinary insight into female character' (250). But 'the greatest of English novelists' (251) is

Henry Fielding, because 'he knew men ten times better ... and his place in the fiction of manners is broader as well as higher than Richardson's can ever be' (258). Gosse's ability to appreciate both Richardson and Fielding is indicative of the balance found in his study; his preference for Fielding points to the biases he reveals in his choice of other novelists to discuss. Predictably, Smollett and Sterne receive full treatment. Gosse's second-tier novelists are Robert Paltock (with the disclaimer that *Peter Wilkins* is not really a novel), Sarah Fielding, Charles Johnstone, Walpole, Henry Brooke, Johnson, Goldsmith, Frances Sheridan, Burney, and Mackenzie. He notes that *David Simple* deserves recognition for being the third novel to appear in English. It is as much for historical reasons as literary merit that he provides his one-paragraph analysis of Sarah Fielding's strengths. She is 'the pale moon who attended' (264) Richardson, Fielding, and Smollett. Gosse sees *David Simple* as holding 'a place midway between the work of Richardson and that of her brother, less morbid than the former, less gutsy than the latter, and of course much feebler than either' (265). He regrets that she 'made no further serious effort in fiction' since 'she had a genuine talent of her own.'

Sheridan's *Sidney Bidulph* gets two sentences. Gosse seconds Johnson's well-known objection to the excessive suffering that dominates the novel, a quality he likes still less in Mackenzie's novels. Burney produced 'the one great comic novel between Smollett and Jane Austen.' Her focus in *Evelina* on 'the droll and farcical side of life' (361) is, for Gosse, the perfect antidote to the novel of sensibility he finds so distasteful. Gosse's regret is that she continued to write novels: 'Her *Cecilia* is only read because it is by the creator of *Evelina*, and her *Camilla* is never read at all' (362). (Gosse does not even mention *The Wanderer*.) Here in embryo is the view of Burney as novelist that held sway throughout most of the twentieth century. Although he ends his study in 1780, Gosse provides an indication of the novelists from the end of the century he would have included had his study extended that far, 'a whole group of lively novelists, all tinged with the new spirit of romance ... "Zeluco" Moore, Beckford, Bage, Holcroft, Sophia Lee, Ann Radcliffe' (361). Regrettably, he provides no commentary on their respective merits. What is clear is that Gosse's canon is broad and catholic if slightly daring in his willingness to overlook traditional moral objections to many of the novelists of the eighteenth century. He has read widely, and he includes a relatively large number of women, especially for a work aimed at the general reader. He was surprised that his study was as well-received as it was by the critics, and no doubt pleased that it remained in print for the rest of his long life.

## William Vaughn Moody (1869–1910) and Robert Morss Lovett (1870–1956)

Gosse's *History* represents one kind of literary history of the period. A very different kind is represented by William Vaughn Moody and Robert Morss Lovett's popular textbook for American university students, *A History of English Literature* (1902), a book that remained in print over eight editions through the late 1960s. Moody and Lovett describe their text as 'an elementary history of literature' (v). In trying to provide the essentials for their readers they necessarily delineate a clear vision of the major and minor writers every student should know about. For Moody and Lovett: 'the novel has been the prevailing type of popular literature in the last two centuries' (229). They trace it back to medieval fiction and provide a quick survey of its developments in the sixteenth and seventeenth centuries. The only writers they mention by name are Malory, Chaucer, Boccaccio, Lyly, Sidney, Greene, Lodge, Nashe, and Bunyan. Bunyan is the most important precursor of the English novel; Defoe signals its 'real beginning.' Defoe was able to master two of the key components for the novel as understood by Moody and Lovett: the 'authoritative' presentation of the 'personality' of a fictional 'character' and the 'perfect illusion of reality' (233). The remaining missing ingredient, 'plot,' was first provided by Richardson. Moody and Lovett respect Richardson's middle-class morality, but find him limited by his focus on women, both in his life and in his novels:

> As a mature writer he worked in close connection with the female part of his audience ... They petted him, flattered him, and debauched him with tea; until the good Richardson lost himself in the Avalon which they provided, and forgot the world of action outside. So secluded did he become that at last he would communicate even with the foreman of his printing-house only by letter. Because of this seclusion Richardson's novels lack depth and freshness. They deal with a petty world, a world of trifles and scruples, of Puritan niceties of conscience, of feminine niceties of sentiment and casuistries of deportment. (237)

Given this reading of Richardson, it is not surprising that Moody and Lovett have little time for eighteenth-century novels by women.

It is also not surprising that, although they have reservations about him, they prefer Fielding to Richardson. They note Fielding's preference for viewing his characters from the 'outside,' and his consequent lack of interest in 'the problems of motive and influence.' They admire his 'simple, epic manner,' his knowledge of 'natural human needs,' and his 'physical vigor,' even though the price for these qualities was a 'coarse realism' and 'moral indifference, his acceptance of things as they are.' They prefer his 'inborn sympathy' and 'tolerant way of looking at things' to 'the smug prudish morality that the eighteenth century accepted for literary purposes' (241).

Moody and Lovett are, then, neither particularly friendly nor hostile to eighteenth-century novelists. Their preference for Fielding's realism over Richardson's predicts their taste in subsequent eighteenth-century fiction. Smollett and Sterne get full treatment; Mackenzie, with his 'morbid emotion' (246) rates only a brief mention. They share the widespread Victorian fondness for *The Vicar of Wakefield* and its 'more wholesome view of life.' Their discussion of Burney begins with the following observation: 'With the possible exception of lyric poetry, the novel is the form of literature which has been most successfully practised by women. In the period before Defoe, the most popular writers of romance were women, Mrs. Behn and Mrs. Manley. Miss Sarah Fielding, sister of the novelist, wrote a story, *David Simple*, which both Richardson and Fielding praised' (248). So much for previous women novelists. Burney herself is valued for her representation of contemporary life, that is, for her 'social history' (249). Her satire compensates for her 'prudish, over-scrupulous, over-sensitive' heroines (248–9); only *Evelina* and *Cecilia* merit mention.

Moody and Lovett look to the late eighteenth century for the 'revival' of Romanticism and celebrate its 'triumph' at century's end. Romanticism allows for a healthy trifurcating of the novel, with 'romance' (representing 'the purely emotional interest in nature and the past') and the 'humanitarian' novel (undertaking 'to right the wrongs sustained by the individual at the hands of society') joining the 'realistic' novel (dealing with 'life and manners') as the three streams that run through the nineteenth century (249–50). These three schools of fiction are best represented by Scott, Godwin, and Austen. The other Romance writers worth mentioning are Walpole, Beckford, Lewis, and Radcliffe. They consider Radcliffe 'the most successful producer of gothic stories' (251) but are critical of her desire to provide rational explanations for the events in her novels, of her inaccurate 'local color' and history, and of her weak characterization. The only late eighteenth-century works by the humanitarians (or 'revolutionary romanticists') they mention are *Caleb Williams* and Thomas Day's *Sandford and Merton* (1783–9).

The novel canon expands greatly in the nineteenth century, becoming 'broader and more complex ... by virtue of the greater breadth and complexity of the life' represented in each of the three kinds of fiction. A whole host of factors contribute to the superiority of later novels: 'the increase in knowledge of the past and of strange lands'; 'the extension of the reading public'; 'the growth in curiosity concerning the circumstances of man's life under varying conditions'; an expanded world beyond that of the 'leisure class'; and the 'deeper thought of the century' (353). The early nineteenth-century writers who provide the first examples of the new, improved novel are Edgeworth, Austen, and Scott. Edgeworth is seen as a follower of Burney; her importance in no small part derives from having anticipated some of the directions Scott would follow. Austen is treasured for her mastery within a very narrow range. Judging by allocated space, Scott is the most important novelist of the period under discussion, and no other novelists from the first two decades of the nineteenth century warrant inclusion. Moody and Lovett's canon is a small one, and their view of the novel is entirely progressive. They are both conservative and catholic in their taste, as is appropriate for a basic introductory history for students.

### Alfred H. Welsh (1850–1889)

Alfred H. Welsh's *Development of English Literature and Language* (1882) offers a particularly clear example of a history determined largely by a nationalist agenda. Welsh's dedication to Charles Foster, the governor of Ohio, and his prologue make clear that for him the study of English literature and language is important for Americans because it provides the historical background and context for the literature and language of the United States. American authors are increasingly included as the history approaches Welsh's own time. His audience is the educable public, including students (the reprint I used is the 'University Edition'); his format is to provide a historical overview of a period followed by an overview of its literature and studies of its representative authors. Each author is discussed in terms of biography, writings, style, rank, character, and influence.

Welsh sees 'romantic or fanciful fiction' as beginning with Lyly (1: 321). The only other Elizabethan writer of prose fiction he includes is Sidney, one of the representative authors of the period. Bunyan is the sole seventeenth-century writer of fiction to merit inclusion, and another representative author, but Welsh's interest in him is not as a fiction writer. The novel, for Welsh, begins in the eighteenth century with the demand for a fiction that was 'domestic and practical, telling the story of common life only.' Its 'precursor' was Defoe (2: 75); he and Swift are the only writers of prose fiction among the representative authors of the early eighteenth century. Discussion of the novel proper begins at mid-century. Welsh sees prose fiction as divided into the usual poles of romance and the novel. Novels in turn are historical or ethical, and ethical novels explicitly or implicitly didactic. The last distinction separates Richardson from Fielding, the writers of the first great novels in English. Their novels are the 'freshest feature of the period, and the most interesting' (2: 137). They are the only novelists among the representative authors of the period, though *Rasselas* is mentioned in passing when Welsh turns to Johnson. Richardson created 'the first epic of real life – the novel of character' (2: 148). Though vain, long-winded, overly self-conscious, and subject to 'the flattery of female friends,' Richardson 'possessed original genius' and, as a successful 'ethical novelist' was a genuine public 'benefactor' (2: 149–50). Fielding is a finer stylist with a command of a far greater range of human experience and character. 'He is the novelist of the lower million; Richardson, of the upper ten thousand' (2: 155). Fielding may surpass Richardson as a writer of humour and satire, and as a craftsman, but Richardson's ethical superiority earns him 'the seat of honor' (2: 156).

Welsh's discussion of the novel between Fielding and Scott is remarkably brief and, for its time, dated. His general description reads in full:

> It is doubtful whether the best novels of the preceding reign could be read aloud in any family circle, they contain so many passages of needless and offensive coarseness. The heroes are often profane and gross. The heroines take part in conversations which no modest woman would consent to hear. Yet these novels were the delight of their generation, not so much because that generation was less chaste, as because it was less delicate and refined. Words now considered indecent were then in common and daily use. But the moment approaches when the novel becomes natural without being indelicate. Purified manners give to it its final impress and character. In the noble hands of Goldsmith, it becomes in every respect moral. (2: 182)

Goldsmith is the only novelist among the representative authors in this chapter.

Welsh's final chapter relevant to this study covers the Romantic period. Given his view of the eighteenth-century novel his account of this period is entirely predictable: after a period of long decline, the novel at last achieved 'an unprecedented lustre in the masterpieces of Scott' (2: 307). Welsh mentions a few other novels of the period, *Caleb Williams*, *Persuasion*, Porter's *Scottish Chiefs* (1810), and, 'in particular, the Irish tales of Miss Edgeworth' as, like Scott, 'directed in one way or another to utility, all seeking the amelioration of man, all realistic and moral' (2: 308). Welsh's is among the most restrictive of canons. His list of representative authors is very small, and his general discussions cover few writers in any period. Most women writers are ignored; George Eliot is the only woman named a representative author in the entire history. The absence of reference to Smollett, Sterne, and Walpole lends some perspective, but not enough to allay suspicion that gender is an important if unspoken factor in Welsh's selection process. It is noteworthy that his history went through many editions and reached a readership larger than that of many better studies.

### Thomas Seccombe (1866–1923)

Thomas Seccombe's *The Age of Johnson (1748–1798)* (1900) was written for the publisher George Bell's very popular series of 'Handbooks of English Literature.' The introduction makes clear that Seccombe is trying to overcome the Romantic (and Victorian) reading of eighteenth-century literature as ugly, brutal, and dull. His goal is one of advocacy, of challenging a reading he considers inaccurate and outdated. Two of his ten chapters are devoted to the novel: a long chapter (thirty-five pages), 'The Great Novelists,' is followed by the much shorter (ten pages) 'Minor Novelists.' The great novelists are Richardson, Fielding, Smollett, and Sterne, and Seccombe first briefly surveys their prehistory. He notes that there has always been prose fiction but finds most of it tedious, especially early English prose fiction. He acknowledges Behn's role in domesticating the French romance, and the unique contribution of Bunyan. Defoe is more the climactic figure of the old romance than the originator of the new novel, but he is credited as the most important figure in the transition. For Seccombe, the novel begins with *Pamela*: 'Samuel Richardson's contribution to the development of the novel was almost what Harvey's discovery of the heart's action was to the study of medicine' (156).

Richardson's 'sentimental romance' (157) combined the picaresque with the old heroic romance to produce a form superior to either.

Seccombe is impressed both by Richardson's enormous impact on his eighteenth-century readers, in Britain and on the Continent, and by his subsequent neglect. He sees Richardson as central in improving the status of the novel to the point that it is 'admitted to the select partnership of imaginative literature,' soon to become 'the predominant partner' (162–3). No matter that the 'demure little printer' had a 'feminine instinct' for narrative (157), *Clarissa* is a great novel. Fielding is, predictably, defined as Richardson's opposite, though the division is not merely gendered. Instead, Seccombe contrasts the two in terms of class, politics, and religion before mentioning the 'strong masculine common sense' (167) he so admires in Fielding. Though not considered as great as either Richardson or Fielding, Smollett also attracts considerable admiration. (In a footnote to his discussion of Smollett's translation of *Don Quixote* Seccombe cites *The Female Quixote*, a novel he sees as informed by a promising concept, but 'worked out in a sadly monotonous manner' and now 'almost forgotten'; the same note also mentions *The Spiritual Quixote*, for Seccombe, as for Saintsbury, a far superior novel [174].) Sterne develops the novel well beyond the first three masters and earns his place among them. The four collectively, for Seccombe, represent the greatest literary achievement of eighteenth-century Britain, Swift excepted.

Seccombe discussed *Rasselas* and *The Vicar of Wakefield* in an earlier chapter. The former is 'less a novel than an excursion in imaginative ethics'; the latter is a 'story *sui generis.*' The discussion of the 'subordinate fiction' of the period is brief since it is largely of interest only to the 'literary archæologist' (189), but Seccombe mentions a considerable number of writers and novels in that brief space: Amory, *William Bingfield*, *John Daniel*, Paltock, Rudolf Eric Raspe, Burney, Henry Brooke, Mackenzie, Walpole, Reeve, Moore, Radcliffe, Beckford, Strutt, and, as writers for children, Day and More. Burney is 'the *doyenne* of an unrivalled series of novelists of a sex to which English imaginative literature had (before her) owed remarkably little' (191). (It is rare for a critic to state so baldly this commonplace, which informs so many of the accounts of the place of women novelists in the history of the genre.) He acknowledges *Betsy Thoughtless* as the source of the 'plan' of *Evelina*, but adds that 'it cannot be said that any great merit resides in the plan' (191). Instead, *Evelina*'s importance comes from Burney's contribution to the development of the realist novel and from her 'youthful daring' and 'wonderful powers of fresh observation.' Seccombe seconds Saintsbury's view that the balance of Burney's career as a novelist is one of steady decline. He considers her *Diaries and Letters* (1842–6) 'interesting, though too voluminous' (192).

Seccombe finds much charm in *The Castle of Otranto*, stemming from readers' uncertainty about whether or not Walpole is serious. He has no doubt about the seriousness of Reeve and Radcliffe, both of whom contributed to the production of the abundance of 'inferior imaginative textiles' of century's end. He admires Radcliffe's 'skill and ingenuity' if not her choice of the Gothic form (195). He considers More a 'good woman' but one whose 'views of education were not quite of the modern type.' Her success as a writer is attributed to her ability to provide 'orthodox didactic works' (198). Overall, Seccombe fails to mention a number of women novelists cited by many of his contemporaries (some of the most obvious were excluded by the plan of the 'Handbooks' series).

### C.H. Herford (1853–1931)

C.H. Herford's volume on *The Age of Wordsworth* (1889) continues the story of the novel at century's end – and well beyond. Herford assumes that the great novelists of the period are Austen and Scott: 'If we set aside the totally alien masterpieces of Jane Austen, almost all that was richest and soundest in contemporary English imagination found expression in Scott.' He also follows earlier critics in considering 1774–1814 a 'period of anarchy' (91), a time of transition between the early masters and Austen and Scott. Herford notes that 'Godwin was almost the only man of high distinction who wrote novels in his generation' (100), a generation of novelists dominated by women (some of whom had close personal connections to Godwin). The novelists of the turn of the century worthy of (in many cases very brief) mention are Bage, Holcroft, Radcliffe, Lewis, Maturin, Mary Shelley, Godwin, Inchbald, Opie, More, Morgan, Edgeworth, the Porters, the Lees, Hamilton, and Brunton. This list is clearly determined largely by those who can be seen as paving the way for Scott, and with him the triumph of the Romantic novel.

Herford sees the end of the century as producing new variations on the previously established novels of manners, sentiment, and terror. Novels of manners, including those by Inchbald and Edgeworth, become 'doctrinaire' if not 'revolutionary.' The novel of terror (Radcliffe) becomes sentimental, set within a 'tender emotional landscape' (92). Meanwhile, the Lees, the Porters, and a host of still less impressive writers attempted historical fiction, and Edgeworth pioneered national fiction. Scott was then able to unite the two and achieve a major breakthrough in the development of the novel. Mary Shelley is faulted for 'the inaptitude for history which marked the Godwinian and Radcliffian schools alike,' an inaptitude that ultimately undermined her considerable 'descriptive and analytic talent' (98). Opie is of interest exclusively for the Godwin connection; her works 'show spasmodic symptoms of her interest in his ideas and personality.' Inchbald is 'far abler' (100), and *A Simple Story* is praised as a powerful forerunner of *Jane Eyre*. More, on the other hand, is noted for her 'well-remembered contribution to the rational education of young women, *Cœlebs in Search of a Wife*' (101).

Herford takes Edgeworth, Morgan, and Austen far more seriously than any of the other women novelists of the period. Edgeworth is first and foremost an educational writer, but she explored the possibilities for educational writing with such invention that 'she became, in some sense, both a doctrinaire Miss Austen and an Irish, yet prosaic, Sir Walter' (101). Her corrections both of Rousseau and of Wollstonecraft are impressive if equally programmatic. Her greatest success is *Castle Rackrent*, where in 'a less pretentious form, she attains a far greater result.' Above all, 'her sense of the defects of the Irish character was so blended with warm-hearted delight in it, that the dreary tale of follies, seen through the medium of the old Irish servant's mind, gathers an atmosphere of pathetic charm' (102). Morgan similarly merits attention primarily as an Irish novelist, another of the path-breakers for Scott.

All of these turn-of-the-century writers are eclipsed by the two great originals of the new century. Austen and Scott are the great writers who transcend their predecessors as the novel becomes a more impressive form in the nineteenth century. Like Seccombe, Herford continues the progressive line in historians of the novel. Their narratives, both separate and shared, fit well within the standard account of the novel as it existed at the beginning of the twentieth century.

## William Henry Hudson (1862–1918)

William Henry Hudson's one-volume survey, *An Outline History of English Literature* (1913), is intended for his extension students at the University of London as well as other readers in need of a brief overview. His goal is to provide a chronological history that places the great works in their larger context. Hudson believes that literature is a reflection of its time; he also believes that the study of great literature is the study of genius, which for him means essentially 'strength of personality and, as a consequence, what we call originality' (2). Such geniuses are also the 'most characteristic and representative' (9) writers of their time; in fact, because of their enormous influence, they create the schools that define Hudson's periods of English literature. They are exclusively male writers.

Hudson includes a section on prose fiction in the age of Shakespeare. The writers are, in order of importance, Lyly, Sidney, Lodge, Greene, and Nashe. He skips the prose fiction of the age of Milton entirely; the age of Dryden adds Bunyan to the brief list. In the age of Pope, Defoe and Swift make significant contributions to prose fiction and to the pre-history of the novel, but it is with the age of Johnson that the novel arrives in its modern form, and here Hudson provides his first (sixteen-page) discussion of the novel from its origins. He refers back to the Elizabethans (already covered, but not in this context), and notes the influence of French romances in the seventeenth century. Their popularity led to an inevitable reaction. Behn and 'several other women-writers' are credited with cultivating 'a form of story which was marked by brevity and concentration of treatment, and which, while still radically conventional in matter and method, showed by contrast a certain desire to get back to truth and nature' (175). Character writers, periodical essayists, Bunyan, and Defoe then make their contributions to the development of prose fiction, preparing the way for the major breakthrough that comes with Richardson.

Before discussing Richardson Hudson pauses to consider the 'historical significance of the novel.' He notes that it appears at a time of increased literacy, when women were assuming a more important role in society; he sees the novel as the key to breaking the stranglehold of classicism on eighteenth-century writers; he considers the novel the most democratic of literary forms; and he is interested in the formative process of 'the typical art-form of the introspective and analytical modern world' (176–7). Richardson deserves pride of place for writing the first modern novel, and for writing the first masterpiece in the genre, *Clarissa*. He is long-winded to a fault, with a genius 'rather feminine than masculine,' a moralizing tendency 'apt to sink into worrisome twaddle,' and a need for sentiment that is too often 'overstrained and mawkish' (180). But 'for patient, microscopic analysis of motive and passion,' he remains 'pre-eminent' (179). It comes as no surprise, given his view of Richardson, that Hudson finds Fielding a far greater novelist, 'virile' and 'vigorous' if 'somewhat coarse,' and with 'a strength and a breadth in his work for which we look in vain in that of his elder contemporary' (180). Fielding's masterpiece, *Tom Jones*, is 'the greatest novel of the eighteenth century' (181).

Smollett is probably the best of the rest, but a very distant third. Others worthy of mention are Goldsmith, Sterne, Mackenzie, Godwin, Burney, Walpole, Reeve, Radcliffe, and Lewis. *Evelina* is credited with laying 'the real foundations of the woman's novel.' Hudson finds Burney's 'second book, *Camilla*' [*sic*], more 'ambitious' but less successful (188), and her final two novels failures. Reeve and Radcliffe are noted for their part in the revival of romance; neither has much intrinsic interest, but they retain a special importance for what they did to 'stimulate and fertilise the genius of Scott' (190). Hudson completes his account of the novelists of the period in his chapter on the novel in the age of Wordsworth. The important writers here are Scott and Austen, but Edgeworth and Ferrier are also mentioned, primarily for their influence on Scott. Hudson's canon is again a small one, a fact explained largely by the nature of his outline history. His taste is catholic; he offers few if any surprises or challenges.

## William Minto (1845–1893)

William Minto's *The Literature of the Georgian Era* (1895), like Sidney Lanier's *The English Novel and the Principle of Its Development* (1883, rev. ed. 1897), is a series of posthumously edited lectures originally addressed to an audience more general in its make-up than the usual advanced students Minto taught at the University of Aberdeen. Minto, one of the finest historical critics of the late nineteenth century, devotes three lectures to the Georgian novel. The novel, for Minto, is one of the new entertainments that replaced poetry as the literature of choice in English society. Richardson is given pride of place, though Minto recognizes that earlier prose fiction and periodical essays made important contributions to the form Richardson was able to realize, the 'novel of manners.' The novel of manners requires two components: 'there is a description of ordinary character, and there is a plot-interest – *i.e.*, there is a story. Both of these elements were found in the generation before Richardson, but not in combination' (104). Minto's Richardson is the 'pet' of society ladies and, though 'a master of his art,' so long-winded it is now rare for anyone to 'read any of his novels through' (107).

Richardson's partner in establishing the modern novel was, of course, Fielding, 'a much more brilliant writer' (108). Minto provides a brief description of Fielding, largely as Richardson's opposite, and passes over their immediate successors, Smollett, Sterne, and Goldsmith, to conclude his first lecture with Horace Walpole and his founding of the other 'new school of fiction' of the eighteenth century, the 'Gothic Romance' (111), a form that united the old-fashioned romance with the new novel. Having established his outline view of the development of the novel, he fills in a number of the missing pieces in the remaining two lectures. The second begins with a reiteration of his sense of the need to recognize the originality of the great innovators in fiction along with the fact that new developments do not spring from nothing. He mentions *Longsword* (1762), a novel he has never been able to find, as an important precursor of Scott. But before discussing Scott he turns to the intervening period: 'In the fifty-five years between Sterne's "Tristram Shandy" and Scott's "Waverley" the chief honors in novel-writing were carried off by women – Miss Burney, Mrs. Radcliffe, Miss Edgeworth, and Miss Austen. The names that became classic during this interval were all names of women' (116).

Minto begins his account of these women with Burney, 'the first woman to achieve first-rate distinction in the modern novel' (116). Burney's success, however, depended in part on the contributions of Lennox, Sarah Fielding, Sheridan, and Frances Brooke; his accounts of them are as full as his account of Henry Fielding, and far fuller than those of most male novelists of the period. Burney remains the first master among women novelists, though he corrects Macaulay's claim that Burney was also the first woman novelist of respectable morality, pointing to the above four predecessors as thoroughly unobjectionable on moral grounds. (He assumes that Macaulay is thinking about Behn, Manley, and Haywood.) What makes Burney more important than her predecessors is her originality: 'It was the masterly natural freshness of the character-drawing, the clear, unencumbered vivacity of the incidents, the frankness of the humour, – in a word, the originality, the absence of literary artificiality, – that signalized "Evelina" as a work of genius, and set every-body talking about the new writer. Miss Burney was not the first woman novelist, but she was the first with a distinct vein of her own who wrote with her eyes on the subject, and not on any established model of approved style' (120). Minto finds that distinct vein in Burney's characters, especially the middle-class characters who are the objects of her finest comic writing, *Evelina* and *Cecilia* (for him, her only novels of distinction). He disputes claims that Burney is overrated, arguing that she is the pre-eminent writer of this kind of comedy. He refuses to mark her down for failing to write a different kind of novel.

Minto next turns to Radcliffe, the writer who realized most fully the aims of Walpole's Gothic romance. He considers her the master of the genre, though he also recognizes the contribution made by Reeve. He defends Radcliffe at length from the common objection that she should not have provided rational explanations for things apparently supernatural; for Minto, this objection is mere 'affectation' (127), even when voiced by Scott. Following Moir, he considers most other objections as projections backwards from the weaknesses and excesses of her successors. She is immune from such misguided complaints.

Minto's third lecture returns to the remaining women novelists who 'stand out above the crowd as being not imitators, but writers of sufficient original genius and sufficiently fortunate in the novelty of their subjects to be ranked as leaders, as founders of schools or epochs in a small way' (275). He considers *Castle Rackrent* the first novel to explore the Irish national character; for all practical purposes, Edgeworth created 'the sly, ready-witted, fluent, faithful and generous Paddy' (276), a character type soon imitated by countless others. He differs from many of his contemporaries in denying Edgeworth credit for inventing 'the novel with a purpose'; that he takes to be more generally 'the invention of the age,' in the same spirit as the moral tales for children written by the likes of Edgeworth and Hannah More (277–8). Minto then moves on to Austen. He recognizes her genius and reputation, but confesses a personal lack of enthusiasm for the kind of novel at which she excels. He briefly discusses Lady Morgan (whose novels he admires) and Maturin before reaching the giant of the period, Scott. He closes his account with Ferrier and Shelley, the latest of his Georgians who are within the range of this study. Minto is among the literary historians highly selective in their coverage of writers. He is typical of many in holding originality to be the most important requirement for inclusion in his history (though it is insufficient without literary excellence as well). His canon is thus a small one, with women novelists doing as well in it as men.

## The Cambridge History of English Literature (1907–16)

The most prestigious and influential literary history of the period was the fifteen-volume *Cambridge History of English Literature*. Unlike most of the histories under discussion in this chapter, the *Cambridge History* was the product of many critics, each assigned specific authors or genres within specified periods by the general editors, Sir A.W. Ward (1837–1924) and A.R. Waller (1867–1922). There is considerable discrepancy among the contributors about the appropriate degree of inclusiveness. Some try to survey the field broadly; others limit their discussion to the best. Volume 4 has a chapter by J.W.H. Atkins (1874–1951) on Elizabethan prose fiction, covering the work of Lyly, Greene, Sidney, Lodge, Ford, Breton, Munday, Nashe, and Deloney; volume 7 includes a chapter on Bunyan by the Rev. John Brown (1830–1922); volume 8, 'The Age of Dryden,' allots no space at all to prose fiction. Felix Schelling's (1858–1945) chapter on early Restoration drama notes that Behn's novels are important forerunners to Defoe, but he does not expand on them. Volume 9, on the early eighteenth century, contains the chapter 'Defoe – The Newspaper and the Novel' by W.P. Trent (1862–1939). Trent has two goals in this chapter, describing the development of journalism and tracing the novel in the period. Each stream leads to Defoe, the central figure in Trent's history of the two genres. When he turns to *Robinson Crusoe*, Trent speculates about the range of fiction likely to have influenced Defoe. This includes Elizabethan romances, heroic romances, satiric anti-romances, criminal literature, Bunyan, periodical essays, and 'the stories of intrigue by Aphra Behn, the highly coloured pictures of the court and the aristocracy by Mrs Manley, and the attempts at domestic fiction by Mrs Eliza Haywood and other more or less forgotten women' (18). Trent feels certain that *The New Atalantis* had some direct influence. He then ends the chapter with a survey of Defoe's novels. G.A. Aitken (1860–1917) includes *Gulliver's Travels* in his chapter on Swift; no other prose fiction is discussed in this volume.

Volume 10, *The Age of Johnson*, begins with three chapters on the novel (as well as a chapter on Johnson and Boswell and one on Goldsmith). Louis Cazamian's (1877–1965) chapter on Richardson begins where Trent left off. Cazamian cites Bunyan, Addison, and Defoe as predecessors to the 'graphic realism' (2) that for him characterizes the novel. Richardson's strong moral purpose is the determining quality of his writing. Cazamian finds ongoing and 'enduring worth' in Richardson and regrets that current interest in him is 'largely historical.' Richardson's popularity had begun to decline in the early nineteenth century and is 'now, mainly, a thing of the past.' Cazamian attributes this decline to the length of his novels, to their epistolary form, to his sentimentality, and to his psychology and morality (12–13). He ends the chapter with a discussion of Richardson's enormous influence on the development of the novel in England and on the Continent.

Cazamian's chapter is followed by Harold Child's (1869–1945) on Fielding and Smollett. Child sets them up as opposites in their novel writing: 'Fielding was humane, genial, sweet-tempered; Smollett rancorous and impatient' (20). He extends the comparison of these greatest of eighteenth-century novelists over the course of the chapter, grounding their greatness in their influence on the still greater novelists of the nineteenth century. Richardson he considers of secondary importance, which has implications for the status of the women novelists in this study: they are at best footnotes to a less than major writer.

The third chapter on the novel in this volume is C.E. Vaughan's (1854–1922) 'Sterne and the Novel of his Times.' Vaughan focuses on the novel between roughly 1760 and 1780, seeking what was new and of lasting value in providing an account of the very best novelists of the period. He finds Sterne unique, 'the sole novelist of first-rate importance'; his nearest rival, Burney, 'inventive and sparkling though she is, can hardly lay claim to that description' (46). The novels of the period are divided into three groups: novels of sentiment, novels of home life, and romantic novels. The first group, Sterne's 'alleged disciples' (55), includes two worthy of mention, Mackenzie and Henry Brooke. Vaughan sees Sterne's use of sentiment as enabling for these writers, but he also finds them limited in their range, unable to benefit fully from Sterne's many innovations. The romantic novel here means the novel of terror as initiated by Walpole and Reeve. Walpole's historical importance is asserted; Reeve's attempt to unite his medievalism with the eighteenth-century novel is seen as a watering down of the limited power of *The Castle of Otranto*. Vaughan is eager to minimize the importance of either for Scott except in providing him with negative examples. Vaughan's chapter ends with his discussion of Burney. It is with her novels that 'we pass into another world. They stand far nearer to the novel as we know it than anything which had yet appeared. The picaresque scaffolding, the obtrusive moral, the deliberate sentiment – much more the marvellous and the medievalism – of the writers who had immediately gone before her are thrown to the winds. She sets herself to tell a plain story – enlivened, doubtless, with strange adventures, with characters still stranger – and that is all' (63). For Vaughan, Burney's simplicity marks a major development in the novel. Removing the tragic from the Richardsonian formula while lacing the story with eccentric characters and behaviour and leavening it with a dose of sentiment creates the 'novel of home life ... a landmark in the history of fiction.' Vaughan attributes her success to two gifts, 'talent' and 'a power in which she is surpassed by Dickens only – of giving flesh and blood to caricature' (64). Vaughan is unusually effusive in his long discussion of Burney's many triumphs. He considers *Evelina* and *Cecilia* her best work, but he also defends *Camilla* and even *The Wanderer* as unjustly neglected works of significant merit. No other novelist of home life is mentioned.

Taken together, these three chapters on the novel offer a severely limited canon (Day and Paltock are added to the bibliography at the end of volume 10), and an overview of the eighteenth-century novel which implies that it has little to offer to twentieth-century readers. The downgrading of Richardson is especially important; it has the predictable result of minimizing the significance of the novelists that could be seen as his followers, many of the better women novelists of the period. Once again, the likelihood of women before Burney receiving much critical attention remains small.

The chapter 'The Growth of the Later Novel' in volume 11, *The Period of the French Revolution*, is by George Saintsbury, whose views on the novel are discussed in detail below. He describes his chapter, one of the most inclusive in the *Cambridge History*, as looking like a 'badly assorted omnibus-box.' But he defends his wide-ranging choices as representing both an immature period in the novel and a time of transition from the great novels of the middle of the eighteenth century to the great novels of Austen and Scott (285). It is, for Saintsbury, a period of experimentation and of a number of false starts (like the Gothic), and though a period of great interest, it lacks novelists of great genius. The novelists Saintsbury discusses are Amory, Beckford, Godwin, Holcroft, Inchbald, Bage, Edgeworth, Radcliffe, Lewis, Maturin, the Porters, the Lees, Hope, and Peacock. The bibliography adds Barrett, Brunton, Coventry, Cumberland, Hamilton, Henley, Johnstone, Lennox, Moore, Opie, Reeve, Roche, Smith, and Walpole, as if Saintsbury felt the need to address the omissions of other critics of the novel in the *Cambridge History*. Volume 11 also includes Mrs H.G. Aldis's (fl. 1900–15) chapter 'The Bluestockings,' but its extended discussion of Hannah More does not include her work as a novelist. The volume ends with F.J. Harvey Darton's (1878–1936) chapter 'Children's Books.' Darton's discussion provides a brief, inclusive survey of the field throughout the eighteenth century and into the nineteenth. His bibliography includes Bunyan, Day, Edgeworth, and Sarah Fielding.

Scott and Austen each receive chapters of their own in volume 12, *The Nineteenth Century I*. This volume also includes Harold Child's brief chapter 'Lesser Novelists.' Most of the writers included here are too late for this study, but Child does discuss Ferrier and Shelley. He admires each, Ferrier as 'a novelist of power, whose work is still fresh and interesting' (245), and Shelley as an underrated novelist of 'strong imagination and no little power of emotional writing' (248). His bibliography includes Lady Morgan.

The *Cambridge History* remains uncommitted to a single set of historiographical principles, just as it is uncommitted to a single canon or approach to canon making. There was clearly no consensus among its contributors. Most prefer to focus on the best only, an approach guaranteed to minimize inclusion of women novelists before Austen. There are few surprising judgments or revaluations in it.

### Andrew Lang (1844–1912)

Andrew Lang's widely read *History of English Literature from 'Beowulf' to Swinburne* (1912), intended as a selective history, is addressed more directly to a general readership than those discussed above (which have at least one eye on the new student audience). Lang would have preferred to focus exclusively on the masters of 'pure literature,' but acknowledges that they each spring from an 'underwood,' and that the occupants of the underwood deserve some recognition (v). He notes the current of prose fiction from medieval romances to Sidney, Lyly, Nashe, and Greene. He discusses Bunyan's 'religious and moral novels' with other prose writers, and he treats Defoe and Swift in a similar fashion. He is aware of Behn writing 'short novels of love which do not quite deserve the bad reputation conferred on them by an anecdote told by Sir Walter Scott' (a curious interpretation), and that Haywood was 'prolific in prose tales.' But the 'novel of modern life, manners, and sentiment,' for Lang the real novel, does not begin until Richardson and fails to achieve full respectability until Scott (458).

Lang finds Richardson's popularity difficult to fathom. His Richardson 'neither sought nor was sought by men,' and his circle of female admirers failed to correct his portrayal of 'well-bred people' (459). Yet despite his 'living in a kind of moral and sentimental hothouse,' and despite his 'more than feminine liking for accumulated minutenesses of details and a more than mediaeval prolixity,' he managed to attract huge numbers of readers both in England and on the Continent (460). Lang's reading of

Richardson is predictably unsympathetic to eighteenth-century women novelists. None are mentioned between Haywood and Burney. He is better disposed to Fielding and Smollett, the remaining early 'great novelists,' in no small part for their influence on Thackeray (Fielding), Burney, and Dickens (Smollett).

Lang's following chapter, 'Georgian Prose,' includes among the novelists Johnson, Goldsmith (a favourite; *The Vicar of Wakefield* should be read annually), Walpole (important for begetting Radcliffe, in turn important for begetting Scott; 'from the mustard seed of "Otranto" grew "a tree with birds in all its boughs"' [485]), and Sterne (not a novelist, for Lang, though a good writer in the Addisonian tradition). The chapter on 'Later Georgian Novelists' begins with the commonplace assertion that after Sterne, the 'novel expired for the time.' Lang knows that many novels were written, but notes that 'experience proves that nobody need waste his time over the tales of Clara Reeve' (530). Henry Brooke and Beckford are dismissed by name with Reeve; others are not mentioned at all. The first important novelist to appear after Sterne was Burney. Lang admires both *Evelina* and *Cecilia* but thinks less well of *Camilla* and 'that lucrative failure' *The Wanderer* (532). Radcliffe is 'the grandmother' of 'the Romantic school of fiction' (532). Her importance is largely historical, but Lang does consider her undervalued 'merely because she is not read. The student who gives her a fair chance is carried away by the spell of this "great enchantress"; and "The Italian" is by far the best romantic novel that ever was written before Scott.' Lang even forgives her for explaining away the supernatural in her novels, attributing the blame to 'the stupid "common sense" of her age' (533).

Lang also admires Edgeworth. He follows most others in considering *Castle Rackrent*, though not a novel, her best work of fiction – because neither her father nor his friend Thomas Day had a hand in it. He notes that his great favourite, Austen, did not meet with the success of either Burney or Edgeworth in her lifetime; he rejoices in the slow but steady subsequent recognition of a writer whose genius can now be named alongside Shakespeare's. Austen and Scott are the great novelists of late Georgian period; Brockden Brown also deserves mention, as do Mary Shelley, Susan Ferrier, and John Galt discussed in the chapter 'Latest Georgian and Victorian Novelists.'

Lang produces another small and conservative canon. It largely reflects the standard judgments of his time, and the growing tendency to limit discussion as much as possible to major writers. It is a canon friendly to women, though not particularly friendly to the early novel.

The novelists of most value are those who prepare the way for Austen, Scott, and the great Victorians.

## Arthur Compton-Rickett (1869–1937)

One of the most interesting of the popular histories is Arthur Compton-Rickett's one-volume *A History of English Literature* (1918). Compton-Rickett's primary goal in this history is to establish the connection between 'Art and Life.' As a result, he provides summaries of important political and social events for each period to help his readers understand that 'literature is viewed not as a mere academic product, but as one expression of the many-sided activities of national growth' (vii). He traces the origins of the novel back to Chaucer, noting the contributions of Lyly, Greene, Lodge, Nashe, and Sidney. Bunyan is, for Compton-Rickett, the 'pioneer of the modern novel'; he and Defoe share the honour of being its founders (174).

The novel becomes far more central in Compton-Rickett's chapter covering 1740–1780, what he calls 'the age of Johnson and Fielding.' He mentions *Rasselas* and *The Vicar of Wakefield* (the latter with clear approval), but not in the section of the chapter devoted to the novel. That section is divided in two parts. The first is devoted to the 'great novelists,' Richardson, Fielding, Smollett, and Sterne. Richardson's novels are noted for their sentimentality and their portrayal of character; he is 'not only our first novelist of character, but our first novelist of feminine character' (249). His treatment of feminine character is also credited with stirring women into writing novels; without Richardson, Compton-Rickett argues, no Burney or Austen. It is for his originality and influence that Richardson 'deserves some measure of praise from posterity' (250), despite his overt moralizing, tedious length, and obvious absurdities. Fielding, by contrast, concentrated on manners over morals. His strengths are in satiric humour and commonsense morality; his range is wider than Richardson's, and his most successful characters are male, not female. Fielding is also the greatest novelist of his age. Compton-Rickett considers Smollett an inferior artist to Richardson and Fielding, though an undervalued one. Sterne is praised for adding subtlety of humour and characterization laced with sentimentality to the novel. He is an important if quirky novelist for Compton-Rickett.

The next section of this chapter, 'The Rise of the Woman Novelist (from Aphra Behn to Jane Austen),' is especially interesting for my study. Compton-Rickett begins by expounding on his views about the differences between men and women, differences not strictly physical. He observes that for a mixture of historical and psychological reasons women have achieved inferior results in poetry, history, and philosophy, but that they can claim equality as writers of fiction because 'as a rule,' they have brought feminine qualities to the novel in which men are 'deficient.' He includes the phrase 'as a rule' because 'every man has something of the woman in him, every woman something of the man.' Some men 'are more feminine than masculine,' he continues, and 'some women more masculine than feminine.' He concludes from these observations that the best results in literature come from an equal mixture of masculine and feminine qualities, for 'genius is bi-sexual' (259).

When he turns to women novelists, Compton-Rickett argues that it took some time for women to realize their distinctive qualities as writers. Behn is important for anticipating Defoe, but she would have been a far better writer had she been able to draw on the 'woman's point of view' more effectively: 'she had nothing of Defoe's genius for actualising her material, and could not escape the "high-falutin" style of the elder Romanticism.' Manley and Haywood also suffer from the artificiality of the old romances, though the late, post-*Pamela* Haywood reveals 'traces of that aptitude for detailed effects, and little subtleties of observation' that would be the hallmarks of later women novelists. All that was necessary was the influence of the 'dumpy Fairy Prince' Richardson to show women how to write like women (259). The initial beneficiaries were Sarah Fielding and Frances Sheridan, the only two women of their generation to merit even a brief mention.

By the end of the century there are 'greater signs of promise,' particularly in the enormous impact of Ann Radcliffe, 'despite her crudeness and absurdities.' Radcliffe is a model, however, for a false turn in fiction by women: 'Romanticism to be effective demands a broad, massive treatment rather than a subtle, detailed one. It was not in romance that woman was to gain her laurels' (259–60). Fortunately, the refinement of manners in the late eighteenth century produced a society more receptive to novels that documented female experience than the cruder, more brutal world of Richardson and Fielding. The resulting improvement in the woman's novel can be seen in the work of More, Burney, Edgeworth, Ferrier, and Austen. More's *Cœlebs in Search of a Wife* shows the 'satirical bent' that was to characterize the best fiction by women in the near future, but *Evelina* was 'the first book of distinctive literary power in this direction.' It is 'an admirable picture of the manners of the time, from the woman's point of view,' with some humour if little characterization or sentiment. (Compton-Rickett credits Frances Brooke's *The Excursion*, a novel otherwise 'devoid of merit,' as a possible source.) No matter that the heroine is dull; ample compensation comes from the more broadly represented spirit of the age. The rest of Burney's career receives the standard treatment: *Cecilia* lacks the 'freshness' of *Evelina*; *Camilla* and *The Wanderer* are 'very feeble productions' because Burney leaves the realm of her own experience (260).

Compton-Rickett again repeats the established line when he turns to Edgeworth: 'Maria Edgeworth shows greater vivacity, and a more genial breadth than Fanny Burney, but less delicacy of touch, though her education theories, largely inspired by Thomas Day and by her father, hindered her as a literary artist.' Her 'real power' was in her 'delineation of Irish peasant characters' (260). The importance and impact of that power was, of course, realized by Scott. Ferrier is the Scottish counterpart to Edgeworth, and her connection to Scott still more central. Her work 'shows greater variety' than Edgeworth's, and Compton-Rickett seems to prefer her (261). The chapter ends with a full treatment of Austen, the first woman novelist of 'genius' (260).

Compton-Rickett subsequently includes a parallel chapter on Victorian women novelists, but he integrates men and women in his chapter on 'Romanticism in English Fiction.' This chapter opens with the usual tale of the rise of the Gothic novel. It begins with *The Castle of Otranto*, and moves next to *The Old English Baron*, characterized as an attempt on Reeve's part to 'improve upon the original,' though the result only repeats 'most of [Walpole's] absurdities' while 'showing even less acquaintance with mediæval life' (355). (Compton-Rickett credits Leland's *Longsword* as 'the first historical *romance* in our fiction'; he finds it 'more interesting' than either of the pioneer works of Gothic fiction.) The Gothic comes of age with Radcliffe. Despite her well-known shortcomings, Radcliffe commands 'power and charm' in her writing. Her use of sentiment and of 'scenic surroundings' effectively blends the 'Thomsonian school of verse' with the 'emotional expression' and 'moral impeccability' of Richardson (356). The other Gothic novelists worth mentioning are Beckford and Lewis.

The discussion of writers of different kinds of novels of the period begins with Godwin. He is the best of the didactic writers of the revolutionary period, although Opie and Inchbald are also mentioned, along with Day. Compton-Rickett ends this chapter with a brief discussion of the historical novel between Leland and Scott. The writers he considers important predecessors of Scott are Sophia Lee, James White, Jane Porter, and Joseph Strutt. Porter is the 'most able' (358) of the lot. Scott, a major writer, is given a chapter to himself.

Compton-Rickett adds little to the discourse surrounding the history of the novel, aside from his unusual sensitivity to the gender of the writers and his attention to the development of the woman novelist. His taste is largely catholic, and he follows the trend towards minimal coverage of most novelists. Women novelists are central to his narrative, but they are seen in terms of his particular sense of the kind of novel best produced by women and Compton-Rickett has little time for the majority of eighteenth-century women novelists.

### The Encyclopædia Britannica (1911)

The most important general reference volume of this period is the eleventh edition of *The Encyclopædia Britannica* (1911), which includes a four-and-a-half-page entry on the novel by Edmund Gosse. The novel, for Gosse, remains realistic, a story that might be true. Of the six paragraphs devoted specifically to the English novel the first provides its pre-history from Malory through the Elizabethans (Lyly, Munday, Greene, Dickenson, Riche, Lodge, Nashe), the heroic romances (Orrery), the anti-romances of Congreve and Behn, the periodical essay, and Defoe. The next traces the first genuine novels through the works of Richardson, Fielding, and Smollett. A paragraph on Sterne, Johnson, Johnstone, Walpole, and Goldsmith follows. The fourth paragraph covers the balance of the eighteenth century, particularly Burney, Radcliffe, Godwin, and Beckford. His paragraph on Austen and Scott also discusses Edgeworth. (The final paragraph covers the Victorian novel.) Gosse's is necessarily a barebones account of the novel, with a limited number of writers mentioned by name. Johnstone is perhaps the only surprising inclusion: that Behn, Burney, Radcliffe, and Edgeworth are the only women mentioned before Austen is significant. Individual entries in the *Britannica*, however, are far more inclusive. Among the women novelists with individual entries (though some are not included for their novels) are Behn, Manley, Haywood, Lennox, Sheridan, Frances Brooke, Reeve, Burney, Radcliffe, Inchbald, Opie, Smith, Wollstonecraft, Sophia Lee, Jane Porter, More, Brunton, Hamilton, Edgeworth, Austen, Morgan, Ferrier, and Shelley.

## Histories of the Novel

### J.J. Jusserand (1855–1932)

A generation after Taine, J.J. Jusserand, for whom Taine had been an intellectual mentor, produced his revisionist study, *The English Novel in the Time of Shakespeare* (1890), arguing that the origins of the realist novel are to be found not in Defoe, but rather in Nashe and the Elizabethan writers of prose fiction. He is not impressed generally by the fiction of the seventeenth century, 'a long period of semi-stagnation' (417), but he considers it essential, nevertheless, to include a chapter on the French romance and its impact on English fiction. Two of the most important contributors are women, the Duchess of Newcastle, who is 'credited with having anticipated Richardson in her "Sociable Letters," in which she tries to imitate real life, to describe scenes, very nearly to write an actual novel' (378), and Aphra Behn, whose *Oroonoko* is the only work of its time to include 'an original thought' and thus serves as the first 'philosophical novel … Rousseau before Rousseau' (414). Neither Newcastle nor Behn receives anything like Jusserand's highest praise, but it is significant that he can write about both of them with minimal biographical commentary, and, especially, that he can write about Behn without feeling the need for an apology or a caveat.

### George Saintsbury (1845–1933)

René Wellek describes George Saintsbury, professor of English literature in the University of Edinburgh from 1895 to 1915, as 'by far the most influential academic literary critic of the early 20$^{th}$ century' (4: 416). Though not intended primarily for university students, his *The English Novel* ([EN] 1913) and *The Peace of the Augustans: A Survey of Eighteenth Century Literature as a Place of Rest and Refreshment* ([PA] 1916) aim to meet the 'strictest scholarly if not scholastic purposes' while remaining 'attractive to the general reader' (PA v). Saintsbury claims that *The English Novel* is the first study of its kind, a full survey of the novel in English, more focused than Dunlop's and more comprehensive than Raleigh's or Lanier's. For Saintsbury, novel and romance share more similarities than differences; it follows that 'the separation of novel and romance – of the story of incident and the story of character and motive – is a mistake logically and psychologically,' for 'when you have excogitated two or more human beings out of your own head and have set them to work in the narrative ... you have made the novel *in posse*, if not *in esse*' (*EN* 8).

Saintsbury traces the novel in English back to its earliest, medieval exemplars. He pays special attention to Lyly's *Euphues* (1578–80) and Sidney's *Arcadia* among texts before the Restoration, though he also discusses Elizabethan picaresque narratives and early seventeenth-century heroic romances. When he turns to the Restoration, he acknowledges the continuing popularity of heroic romance, the appearance of Bunyan, Richard Head, and Aphra Behn, the latter 'a woman of very great ability, with a suspicion of genius' (*EN* 48). Saintsbury devotes two and a half pages to Behn's novels (about half of what he gives to Bunyan). He has clearly read most, if not all, of the works of 'the illustrious Afra' (50), and Saintsbury is one of the first critics to celebrate the end of 'the fashion merely to dismiss her with a "fie-fie!"' He is a close enough reader to recognize that the *Oroonoko* of the mid-eighteenth century and the Romantics is far from the novel she actually wrote: 'To see at once Rousseau and Byron in it, Chateaubriand and Wilberforce and I know not what else, is rather in the "lunatic, lover, and poet" order of vision' (51; see also Spencer, *Aphra Behn's Afterlife*, chap. 6). Saintsbury is eager to place *Oroonoko* in its historical context in order to appreciate Behn's important contributions to the development of the English novel: 'To say it wants either contraction or expansion; less "talk about it" and more actual conversation; a stronger projection of character and other things; is merely to say that it is an experiment in the infancy of the novel, not a following out of secrets already divulged. It certainly is the first prose story in English which can be ranked with things that already existed in foreign languages. Nor is it the only one of the batch [of Behn's novels] in which advance is seen' (51–2). Saintsbury singles out *The King of Bantam* (1698), *The Adventure of the Black Lady* (1684), *The Lucky Mistake* (1689), and *The Fair Jilt* (1688) from 'the batch' to support his contention that Behn was one of the earliest English writers with 'an awakened conscience' (52), that is, with an awareness of the literary potential of prose fiction. His appreciation would not be shared by many for some time to come.

Bunyan, Neville's *The Isle of Pines* (1668), Congreve's *Incognita* (1691), the 'Coverley Papers' in the *Spectator*, Defoe, and Swift are also mentioned in Saintsbury's chapter on the formative years of the English novel, the years in which writers came to recognize the four essential 'Elements of the novel ... Plot, Character, Description, and Dialogue' (68). These authors and texts prepared the way for the breakthroughs of mid-century in the work of Richardson, Fielding, Smollett, and Sterne, the writers who established the novel as an important literary form in England. Saintsbury devotes a full chapter of *The English Novel* to these four novelists. (Few new judgments appear in the briefer account of the novel in the eighteenth century in *The Peace of the Augustans*, published a mere three years later. The later work covers a far more limited time span, and adds no new texts to those already covered in *The English Novel*.) Although Saintsbury sees the novels of the eighteenth-century as ultimately paving the way for the still greater triumphs of the nineteenth century, his enthusiasm for the early novel is genuine, and it is not limited to the four 'great names' who 'overshadowed ten times their number of writers.' In fact, Saintsbury wishes to convince his readers that these unknown writers 'deserve more or less to be read, not merely for purposes of study' (*PA* 144). What follows is an unusually thorough survey, complete with full descriptions of the pleasures offered by the many novels under consideration, since, for Saintsbury, the first obligation of criticism is to encourage the development of well-educated literary sensibilities.

While Saintsbury clearly prefers Fielding, he also recognizes many of Richardson's strengths as well as his importance for the development of the novel. He accepts the gendering that so often accompanied discussions of the two: 'Richardson seems to have been a respectable person of rather feminine temperament and, though good-natured to his friends, endowed with a feminine spitefulness' (*EN* 81). His preference of *Pamela* to Richardson's other novels suggests, however, that his appreciation of Richardson is severely limited; and the reasons for his partiality prove this to be the case (though they recognize an aspect of Richardson often overlooked or denied by more sympathetic critics):

> We have not ourselves been very severe on the faults of *Pamela*, the reason of lenity being, among other things, that it in a manner produced Fielding, and all the herd of his successors down to the present day. But those faults are glaring: and they are of a kind specially likely to attract the notice and the censure of a genial, wholesome, and, above all, masculine taste and intellect like Fielding's. Even at that time, libertine as it was in some ways, and sentimental as it was in others, people had not failed to notice that Pamela's virtue is not quite what was then called 'neat' wine – the pure and unadulterated fruit of the grape. (99)

Despite his preference for Fielding Saintsbury is open to the full range of novelists of the period. He has read a remarkable number of them, and he does a remarkably good job of capturing their strengths – as well as their weaknesses. Richardson's immediate predecessors are not of the greatest interest. Saintsbury covers only three: Manley, Haywood, and Simon Berington. *The New Atalantis* is a 'key-novel,' and it is of interest primarily for the key; as such, it is of minimal importance to the development of the novel. (Again, Saintsbury says nothing about the morality or lack thereof of one of the female wits. This from a critic who declares that 'moral intention – the most dangerous misleaders of the novelist, except immoral intention – led Richardson and many others astray' [*PA* 175].) More interesting to Saintsbury are the novels of Haywood. Like most of Haywood's earlier critics he divides them into two groups, the early 'Behnesque' *nouvelles* like *Idalia* and the later novels like *Betsy Thoughtless* and *Jemmy and Jenny Jessamy*. His explanation for the radical difference between them is familiar: the appearance of the novels of Richardson and Fielding. Saintsbury considers the early works 'not bad books to read for mere amusement' (*EN* 136), but he greatly prefers the later novels, giving Haywood full marks for "opportunism" of craftsmanship' (137), that is, for learning from technical developments of others. Haywood also points the way to Burney, the novelist in the next generation to bring her narrative technique to the next level.

The generation of novelists contemporary with the 'big four' receive far more attention. Saintsbury includes Sarah Fielding, Lennox, Frances Sheridan, John Shebbeare, Thomas Amory, Richard Graves, Francis Coventry, Robert Paltock, Charles Johnstone, Henry Brooke, Johnson, Goldsmith, and Walpole. Sarah Fielding is no favourite; 'one of Richardson's seraglio,' she lacks her brother's 'constructive grasp of life.' Still more fatal, 'one looks up for interest, and is not fed.' That Saintsbury finds this Fielding uninteresting is hardly uncommon in the early twentieth century, but his explanation for her shortcomings as a novelist is engaging: 'It was, in fact, too early or too late for a *lady* to write a thoroughly good novel. It had been possible in the days of Madeleine de Scudèry, and it became possible in the days of Frances Burney: but for some time before, in the days of Sarah Fielding, it was only possible in the ways of Afra and of Mrs. Haywood, who, without any unjust stigma on them, can hardly be said to fulfil the idea of ladyhood, as no doubt Miss Fielding did' (*EN* 138). *The Female Quixote* is far more to Saintsbury's taste. Overly long and a bit too earnest, 'it is very far from contemptible.' Ultimately, however, he prefers Graves's *The Spiritual Quixote* (1773), both as an imitation of Cervantes and as an independent work.

Like Lennox, Frances Sheridan is a one-novel author for Saintsbury. He finds *Sidney Bidulph* too long, yet a powerful novel of the Richardsonian kind. Its main fault is the expected one, although Saintsbury introduces something of a twist in his criticism. He begins with Johnson's familiar observation

> that he 'did not know whether she had a right on moral principles, to make her readers suffer so much.' Substitute 'aesthetic' for 'moral' and 'heroine' for 'readers,' and the remark retains its truth on another scheme of criticism, which Johnson was not ostensibly employing, and which he might have violently denounced ... Miss Biddulph ... is too persistently unlucky and ill-treated, without the smallest fault of her own, for anything but really, not fictitiously, real life. Her misfortunes spring from obeying her mother ... and husbands, lovers, rivals, relations, connections – everybody – conspire to afflict her. Poetical justice has been much abused in both senses of that verb: *Sydney Biddulph* shows cause for it in the very act of neglect. (143)

Saintsbury endorses the view that the final quarter of the eighteenth century (and he extends this period several years into the nineteenth) was a period of decline for the novel, that is, that no novelist appeared to rival Richardson, Fielding, Smollett, and Sterne until the appearance of Austen and Scott. That said, he nevertheless turns his attention to a considerable number of novelists: Burney, Reeve, Radcliffe, Lewis, Holcroft, Godwin, Inchbald, Mackenzie, Moore, Wollstonecraft (an especially rare inclusion), Bage, Thomas Day, Cumberland, Opie, Smith, Beckford, Bennett, Byrne, Sarah Wilkinson, Henrietta Mosse-Rouvière, Harriet and Sophia Lee, Jane (but not Anna Maria) Porter, Regina Maria Roche, Brunton, Lady Morgan, Sarah Green, Barrett, Edgeworth, and the Minerva novels. He has his clear favourites as well as those dismissed as 'small fry' (173), and the proportion of women novelists covered is again considerable, roughly two-thirds. This is not because Saintsbury believed that the majority of eighteenth-century novelists were women; on the contrary, he asserts that the 'larger number' were men (139), although no evidence is offered to support this assertion. If relative importance is determined by length of treatment, Burney, Radcliffe, and Edgeworth are in a class of their own among this group. The others range in importance from third-rate to very minor indeed (just important enough to be noticed).

Saintsbury's response to Burney is complex: he considers her of great historical importance despite her mediocre literary talent. She gets full marks for being the first after Fielding to advance the course of the novel on its destined path of primacy in holding up the mirror to nature. Her life and her *Diary* (which Saintsbury considers her greatest work) have attracted enormous attention, yet, he observes, 'actual critical evaluations of the novel-values of Miss Burney's four attempts in novel-writing are very rare. I dare say there are other people who have read *The Wanderer* through: but I never met any one who had done so except (to quote Rossetti) myself: and I could not bring myself, even on this occasion, to read it again. I doubt whether very many now living have read *Camilla*. Even *Cecilia* requires an effort, and does not repay that effort very well. Only *Evelina* itself is legible and relegible' (151).

Why, Saintsbury asks, was it possible for a writer without 'fine understanding,' with less 'sense' than 'sensibility,' with little education and less taste who, at best, wrote with a 'tolerable style of the kind that has no style,' to have earned a 'secure and distinguished place in the great torch-race of English fiction-writers' (152–3)? His answer is that 'Miss Burney had a quite marvellous faculty of taking expressions of actual speech, manners, and to a certain extent character: that she had, at any rate for a time, a corresponding faculty of expressing, or at least reporting, her impressions. Next (and perhaps most of all) that she had the luck to come at a moment when speech and manners were turning to the modern; and lastly, that she was content, in parts of her work at any rate, to let her faculty of expression work, automatically and uninterfered with, on the impressions: and thereby give us a record of them for all time' (153). Saintsbury believes that the progress of the novel had been impeded by its early focus on 'exceptional interests and incidents.' What Burney 'had hit upon – stumbled upon one may almost say' was 'the real principle and essence of the novel as distinguished from the romance – its connection with actual ordinary life' (154). Saintsbury expands Burney's importance from the oft-noted bringing together of the lines of Fielding and Richardson to point the way to Austen to a more explicitly central role in the development of the novel as a form. Regardless of her worthiness for the task, he concludes, 'all glory ... be to Frances Burney' (155).

When Saintsbury turns to the Gothic, he notes *The Old English Baron* only to dismiss it as dull. He cannot match Scott's enthusiasm for the 'positive genius' (161) of Radcliffe, but he holds her in high regard, largely for three advances: her propriety ('a point in which the novel had always been a little peccant'), her determination to explain what at first seemed supernatural (160), and her 'elaborate' often 'picturesque' descriptions of natural landscapes (162). Radcliffe may seem less than exciting to readers of Saintsbury's contemporaries. Her plots may even seem mechanical. But she still has the power to capture her readers' attention, and she has a historical importance not unlike Burney's in that she helped to revive and modernize the romance in ways that prepared for the far greater achievements of Scott, just as Burney prepared the way for Austen.

Inchbald is lumped with Bage, Holcroft, and Godwin as part of the 'revolutionary school' of the novel, a group whose politics are not at all to Saintsbury's Tory tastes. His forthright disapproval, however, does not extend to all aspects of their novel writing. He recognizes the Richardsonian '"human-heart"-mongering' power of the central scenes in *A Simple Story* and *Nature and Art*. He sees Inchbald's style as derived from the French, particularly Marivaux; in fact, he goes so far as to describe her as 'very much of an English Madame Riccoboni.' Her strength remains primarily in 'the dramatic or melodramatic quality which attracts people in "decadent" periods,' a quality that leads to this summary overview:

> There seems, indeed, to have been a certain decadent charm about Mrs. Inchbald herself – with her beauty, her stage skill, her strict virtue combined with any amount of 'sensibility,' her affectation of nature, and her benevolence not in the least sham but distinctly posing. And something of this rococo relish may no doubt, with a little good will and sympathy, be detected in her books. But of the genuine life and the natural language which occasionally inspirit the much more unequal and more generally commonplace work of Miss Burney, she has practically nothing. And she thus falls out of the main line of development, merely exemplifying the revolutionary and sentimental episode. (170–1)

No passage better illustrates Saintsbury's evaluative principles in *The English Novel*. Each novelist is read for his or her own merits, but each is placed in a historically determined canon, a canon for eighteenth-century novelists determined by reading backward to find how earlier novelists contributed to the greater achievements of subsequent novelists. Saintsbury is an attentive and sensitive reader of eighteenth-century fiction, but despite his Tory politics, he is a hardline Whig when it comes to the history of the novel.

After Inchbald, Saintsbury turns to a large group of 'minor' figures, the 'small fry' of century's end, before concluding his chapter with the two remaining authors of importance before Austen and Scott, Edgeworth and Maturin. He compares Agnes Maria Bennett's *Anna* (1785) and Amelia Opie's *Adeline Mowbray* as representative bookends of a twenty-year period of 'rapid growth of the novel ... when nothing of the first class appeared.' The former is dismissed as a bad imitation of Burney; the latter is a better book if too strongly influenced by 'Godwinian theories of life' (173). Mrs Byrne (Charlotte Dacre) is Saintsbury's designated representative of the 'pure (or not-pure) rubbish' produced by the Minerva Press.

Smith and the Lees are much superior to Bennett and Opie, as they are to Wilkinson and Mosse-Rouvière (the former is one of the worst of the imitators of Radcliffe and Lewis, her style 'very nearly consummate – in badness'; the latter equally abysmal in her attempts to write historical fiction [175]). Smith, 'tolerably expert in verse as well as prose,' is faulted because 'she neither innovates nor does old things consummately.' Saintsbury similarly dismisses the claims to innovation made for the Lees and for Jane Porter: for him, all historical fiction before Scott lacks 'real historical spirit' (174), and therefore deserves minimal recognition. Roche, a writer best read by the young, likewise fails the innovation test. Her work is 'a curious sort of watered-down Richardson, passed through successive filtering beds of Mackenzie, and even of Mrs. Radcliffe.' Saintsbury concludes his paragraph on Roche with a statement that well summarizes his approach to most of the late eighteenth-century novelists he covers: 'Regina is a document of the demands of readers and the faculty of writers: and so she "standeth," if not exactly "crowned," yet ticketed' (176–7).

*The English Novel* includes treatment of four women novelists among the early nineteenth-century writers mentioned at the end of the chapter, that is, the end of the lean period preceding Austen and Scott. A long paragraph on Mary Brunton suggests that her importance is as a faint prototype for Scott in her treatment of Scottish society. Saintsbury is unusually reticent about offering a clear assessment of her work. More typical are the two paragraphs given to her Irish counterpart, Lady Morgan, who gains Saintsbury's sympathy for being one of the victims of the 'Reviewers ... discreditably savage' response to 'women-writers.' But, he adds, 'it must be said that nothing she wrote can really be ranked as literature, save on the most indiscriminate and uncritical estimate. It is, however, difficult to see much harm in her' (178). Sarah

Green, like Eaton Stannard Barrett, is of interest to Saintsbury for her fictional critique of late-century romances and their excesses. He notes that like Barrett, she is hard on women novelists, especially Lady Morgan.

Very different is Saintsbury's response to another female Irish novelist: 'There are few more curious and interesting personages in the history of the English Novel than Maria Edgeworth. The variety of her accomplishment in the kind was extraordinary: and in more than one of its species she went very near perfection' (181). He divides Edgeworth's work into three types – stories largely for children, novels, and Irish fiction – and he considers her novels the weakest of the three. *Belinda* is the best of the lot, especially because of its early date (again, the innovation factor is what gives it special status): 'It preceded Miss Austen's work in publication, and is specially cited by her as a capital example of novel in connection with the work of Miss Burney: and it is evidently founded on study of the latter, of which, indeed, it is the first really worthy continuation. Maria has nothing as good as Fanny's Smiths and Branghtons: but the whole book is far superior to *Evelina*' (182).

Saintsbury faults Edgeworth for excess didacticism and sentimentality (he cites Marmontel as the probable source) in all her work, but finds it least inappropriate in her work for children. The '"national" element' (183) is credited with making up for these shortcomings in the Irish novels and this aspect of her work makes Edgeworth an important predecessor and influence on Scott. As the most important immediate influence on Austen as well she must be forgiven the 'platitudes and crotchets' of her father, the source of many of the more unfortunate aspects of her work. No one better represents this 'imperfect stage' of the development of the novel (184). No one better prepares Saintsbury's readers for the realization of the full potential of the novel that finally came with his twin-heroes of the new century, Austen and Scott.

Saintsbury has often been criticized, and sometimes even dismissed, as a belletristic impressionist, not 'a fully paid up professional scholar.' According to John Gross, 'his ultimate philosophy was a simple one: first read all the books, and then recommend whatever you have enjoyed as forthrightly as possible' (142). I would not dispute the centrality for Saintsbury of pleasure as a criterion for determining literary excellence, but his account of the English novel is structured around a clear sense of its development as it struggles to find its way as a form until the triumphs of the early nineteenth century. (For Saintsbury these triumphs continue with the century; there is no greater novelist than Thackeray.) Saintsbury's history of the novel can well be criticized for its teleological overview, and the consequences of that overview for eighteenth-century novels. The ability of the early novelists to intuit later realizations of the form determines most of his evaluations of individual novels and novelists. But neither the gender of the writer nor his or her subject matter carries much weight. Saintsbury is remarkably open to all kinds of novelists, and his canon is based on the kind of omnivorous reading that Gross describes.

## Walter Raleigh (1861–1922)

Walter Raleigh, one of the early professors of English, and one of the first to hold that position at Oxford, was also one of the first academics to write a history of the novel. His *The English Novel: Being A Short Sketch of Its History from the Earliest Times to the Appearance of 'Waverley'* was published in 1894, when he was appointed at University College, Liverpool. It is a 'sketch' of nearly three hundred pages, but Raleigh is right nonetheless to point out that it is too brief to be inclusive or even to do full justice to the novels he considers major. He does begin at the beginning, and he covers, far more succinctly, roughly the same period covered by Dunlop, though his focus is entirely on the English novel. The first three chapters examine the classical, medieval, and Elizabethan periods. For Raleigh, the Italian novel displaced the medieval romances, and it in turn inspired the Elizabethans. Lyly's *Euphues* is 'strictly speaking, the first original prose novel written in English' (29). The other important Elizabethans are Sidney and Nashe, Sidney for his influence on Richardson and on 'the second birth of the novel in England' ('Paméla, her name shortened to Paméla, came to life again, no longer a princess, but a servant-girl … Richardson is the direct inheritor of the analytic and sentimental method in romance which Sidney had developed' [63]), Nashe as 'the direct forerunner of Defoe' (85).

Raleigh's chapter on the heroic romances briefly mentions Lady Mary Wroth's *Urania* (1621) as a work in the Sidney tradition. He credits the many seventeenth-century imitations of French romances with creating an audience with the patience to read long novels – and little else. Improvement finally comes at the end of the seventeenth century with Congreve's *Incognita*, and with the more sustained efforts of Aphra Behn. Behn the novelist, for Raleigh, has been unjustly neglected because she 'trod the stage loosely.' But she has very real merit as a novelist 'for making use of incidents of real life in the service of fiction at a time when the heroic romance was at the height of its vogue' (107). Raleigh limits his discussion to the two novels he considers her best, *Oroonoko* and *The Fair Jilt*. He finds neither successful in overcoming the stilted language of the romances, and he considers *The Fair Jilt* morally suspect as well. *Oroonoko* is read as a prototype of the fiction of Rousseau. Behn's achievement is thus limited to a 'faint and ineffective' attempt 'to bring romance into closer relation with contemporary life' (109). That is the highest praise Raleigh has to offer to any seventeenth-century writer of prose fiction.

Raleigh anticipates by nearly a hundred years recent views of the origin of the novel as being found not in romance but rather in a wide range of other literary forms. Addison and Steele, Swift, Defoe, and more generally the essayists and political writers of the early eighteenth century are credited with preparing the way for Richardson and Fielding. But unlike many more recent accounts, Raleigh minimizes contributions by early women writers of fiction. Newcastle is mentioned briefly for her autobiographical writings (Bunyan is also presented largely as a life-writer), and equally briefly in a list of writers of imaginary travels. Raleigh ends his discussion of the early eighteenth century with a page and a half on Manley and Haywood, 'imitators of Mrs. Aphra Behn' (138). *The New Atalantis* and *Memoirs of a Certain Island Adjacent to Utopia* (1725) are dismissed as artless scandal romances. Their short fictions are 'akin to the comedies of the Restoration, but destitute of the glitter and life of the Restoration stage.' Haywood's *Betsy Thoughtless* and *Jemmy and Jenny Jessamy* are, of course, much better, thanks to the influence of Richardson, Fielding, and Smollett, an observation that leads to his overall view of Haywood: 'Mrs. Haywood is a good specimen of that third-rate kind of author that multiplies the faint echoes of a literary success, and writes novels, as an oriental tailor makes garments, to a ready-made pattern, with dexterity and despatch. Her pre-Richardsonian work deserves mention, but it could teach nothing at all to the new novel that was so soon to supplant it' (139).

The 'first modern novel,' for Raleigh, is *Pamela* (143), though he considers *Clarissa* to be Richardson's masterpiece. He sees Richardson as a middle-class, moralistic writer, and as the founder of the novelistic school of sensibility. Raleigh clearly has reservations about Richardson, but he is restrained in expressing them. He prefers Fielding, for him a more natural writer with standards of morality that avoid Richardson's pedantic formality. To his credit, he is one of the few critics of his generation to resist the temptation to gender their differences.

When Raleigh turns to 'the novels of the eighteenth century' (chapter 7), he begins with 1740 and saves late-century romances and domestic satires for subsequent chapters. His final, climactic chapter is devoted to Scott. Raleigh has read widely, and he provides several lists of anonymous eighteenth-century novels of various kinds to illustrate the explosion of novel writing after 1740 and to register his disdain for virtually all of it. The only novelists of real import in chapter 7 are Smollett, Sterne, Johnson, and Goldsmith; the minor writers who merit mention are Sarah Fielding, Amory, Paltock, Henry Brooke, Coventry, Johnstone, Moore, Mackenzie, Cumberland, Bage, and Frances Sheridan. Women of this period are clearly of minimal interest to Raleigh. Among the very early followers of Richardson and Fielding he considers Sarah Fielding the 'only imitator of any note' (180) and her novels are described as a curious, unsuccessful mixture of 'sentiment and characters' (her main strengths) and 'picaresque romance of incident,' further limited by her 'slight knowledge of the world' (181). Sheridan's *Sidney Bidulph* is important as an early example of a novel that refuses the happy ending that most novelists provided.

'The revival of romance' is, for Raleigh, part of and central to the Romantic revival. There is no question about credit for originality in promoting romances in the late eighteenth century: Walpole gets full marks. The renewed romance then quickly divides into two groups, the school of terror and the school of theory. The major writers of terror are Radcliffe and Lewis, with Reeve and Maturin also worthy of notice. Reeve's desire to make her romance more probable than Walpole's is, however, condemned as reactionary. Radcliffe also failed to conquer 'her fear of the supernatural,' but because she 'exercised so enormous a power on the new generation, and displayed so many decisive advances on previous romantic essays,' she has earned 'a foremost place among the early apostles of Romanticism' (227). With little experience of the real world, Radcliffe is credited with creating from within everything from the famous landscapes of places she never saw to 'a type of character that subsequently passed from art into life. The man that Lord Byron tried to be was the invention of Mrs. Radcliffe'. (228). For Raleigh, Radcliffe's imaginative power and originality compensate for her many flaws: timid, formulaic plots; simple-minded, rational solutions to anything apparently supernatural; gross ignorance of the historical contexts of the period settings of her novels; a limited cast of stock characters. These faults have become more prominent with time as Radcliffe's remarkable contributions were gradually absorbed into the literary conventions of Romanticism.

Raleigh credits her with ushering the 'Romantic School' into 'maturity' (231). 'Prose like hers,' he claims, 'could not hope to remain prose long' (233). Her influence is strong on both lyrical and narrative poets of the next generations, as well as on novelists from Lewis and Maturin to Scott, Hawthorne, and Stevenson.

When Raleigh turns to what he calls the School of Theory, he is dealing with something he recognizes as a much less coherent group of novels. He finds its origins more easy to define than its practice; they are clearly found in Rousseau, with precursors in such English writers as Behn (via John Shebbeare), Locke, and Richardson, the latter two clearly influences on Rousseau. It was from Rousseau, and such French followers as Bernardin de St Pierre and Genlis, that English writers caught up in the issues of the French Revolution learned to use the novel to speculate on 'politics, religion, marriage, and education' (238). (For Raleigh this is not a good thing. Fiction is not improved by forcing characters to demonstrate the laws of political economy, and those laws in turn do not profit from having their scientific purity violated through novelistic presentation.) The diverse group Raleigh considers here includes Godwin, Holcroft, Bage, Henry Brooke, Day, Opie, and Inchbald. Raleigh considers *Adeline Mowbray* one of the best of the novels written under Godwin's influence, a mixed compliment. And Inchbald deserves 'a very high place among the novelists proper of her day' despite 'the prevalent ideas on education and social convention spoiling the outlines of the work of a real artist' (248–9).

Women novelists played prominent roles for Raleigh in both the Gothic and theory schools. It is hardly surprising that they are still more prominent in his final group, the writers of novels of 'domestic satire.' These novelists play an important role in Raleigh's history even though they represent a genre of severe limitation. As Raleigh sees it, the early women novelists such as Behn and Haywood 'attempted pictures of life as it is seen through the eyes of men.' Radcliffe, while she centred her plots on pathetic heroines, did not attempt to capture the passions from within. When he fast-forwards to Charlotte Brontë, he finds 'passion represented as it could only have been conceived by a woman.' The novelists of domestic satire bridge the path from the early, masculine women novelists to 'the greatest of woman romancers.' Their historical importance, again based on the originality of the contribution, justifies the inclusion of novels that show the world through the eyes of very young heroines, characterized as 'intensely self-conscious,' with no higher goal in life than pleasing the male guardians who have trained them to do just that. This kind of novel required little 'power' or 'daring,' rather 'much skill' if 'little courage' (253–4). Burney is credited with founding the new school with *Evelina*. It is a school with three important early members, Burney, Austen, and Edgeworth, and a great many members of lesser consequence.

Raleigh sees the novel of domestic satire as the natural outcome of the transformation of British society in the eighteenth century from brutality and coarseness to excessive refinement. Swift and Fielding were no longer able to please an audience who looked to domestic life as the proper subject matter for the novel. That life, he claims, 'was adorned with a complete literature of its own by the talents of Miss Burney and Miss Edgeworth and the genius of Jane Austen. The thirty years or so before the appearance of *Waverley*, in 1814, were the years of the triumph of woman, creator and created in the novel; they were the years also during which Miss Edgeworth and Lady Morgan struck out those first attempts in the portrayal of national character which may claim the merit of having suggested his most brilliant successes to Sir Walter Scott' (255). Raleigh rejects the contemptuous dismissal of these novels as romances of the tea-table, while he also considers them far too narrow in focus for the more general term social satire. Domestic satire is the compromise, one that also captures the somewhat reserved endorsement that accompanies it.

Burney's great success with *Evelina* was never matched in the inferior, later novels. *Cecilia* shows a modest decline, but by the time of *Camilla*, Burney had abandoned both the 'simplicity of theme' and the 'simplicity of style' so central to the success of her first two novels. Raleigh is especially vehement in his denunciation of the Johnsonian period that characterizes her later style, since, without 'a familiar knowledge of the Latin tongue,' Burney was attempting 'to practise diving before learning to swim.' Yet, despite the decline he finds in the later work, Raleigh still asserts that 'her brilliant, shrewd satire and close observation were unmatched in her own time, and she prepared the way for Miss Austen' (260).

Where Burney, like Austen, produced fine work early in her career, Maria Edgeworth is praised for overcoming the kind of work her father encouraged her to undertake early in hers, work of the kind endorsed by the 'school of theory' in the branch that focused on the education of the young. Raleigh considers *Castle Rackrent* and *Belinda* her greatest triumphs, primarily for introducing 'serious' fictional treatment of the Irishman and the Scot (267). That treatment is especially important for its

influence on Scott, for it was Scott who was able to transcend the limitations imposed on Edgeworth's work by the need to use the novel first
and foremost as a pedagogical tool:

> Miss Edgeworth's world, let it be admitted, is a dull place; for human
> character, although it repelled, attracted, and at times amused, never puz-
> zled her in the least. Even complexity of badness is disallowed, and the
> errors, faults, and foibles that she excelled in depicting are distributed
> parsimoniously, one to each person, for clearness' sake. In the gay world
> of fashion she shakes off something of her pedantry, and her worldly
> women are among her best sketches. It is difficult to say what she might
> have done had she ever succeeded in getting clear of her fetters. The mar-
> vel is that so spirited and humorous a series of portraits should have been
> produced as illustrations to the text of an educational hand-book – for so
> she conceived of her work. (269)

The only followers of Burney that Raleigh mentions are Mary Brunton
and Susan Ferrier (whom he calls Mary). There is just enough real life in
Brunton to make her interesting, despite her strong religious, pedagogical mandate. Ferrier is mentioned for having eclipsed her countrywoman
Brunton. Because Raleigh considers the novel of everyday life harder to
write than the romance, he is not surprised that relatively few second-
rate women novelists followed in the Burney line. The majority were
romancers, usually associated with the Minerva Press. His list includes
Charlotte Dacre, Sarah Wilkinson, Mary Charlton, Agnes Musgrave,
Agnes Maria Bennett, and Regina Maria Roche. 'Literature has no concern with these works, which fulfilled the utmost end of their being when
they found a purchaser' (271). For Raleigh, Lady Morgan also belongs in
this group, with the partial exception of *The Wild Irish Girl*, with its 'spir-
ited sketches of Irish life.' He thinks Morgan's 'social celebrity and great
personal charm' had more to do with what lasting reputation she has
achieved than her merit as a writer (272). Raleigh concludes this chapter
by noting S.G. [Sarah Green]'s *Romance Readers and Romance Writers*
(1810) and Eaton Stannard Barrett's *The Heroine*, books that helped laugh
away the turn-of-the-century Minerva romances.

*The English Novel* is highly determined by Raleigh's progressive
reading of the history of British prose fiction. He knows where it is
going, and he most values the triumphs that postdate the period he
discusses. Originality is his highest value, as defined by contributions
towards the perfection of the novel he finds in the nineteenth century.

Women play a prominent role in his history, but those who count are chosen for their influence on the development of the novel. Raleigh's sense of progress as applied to the novel was shared widely, and it remained a significant factor in determining which early women novelists received critical attention.

### Sidney Lanier (1842–1881)

George Saintsbury dismisses Sidney Lanier's *The English Novel: A Study in the Development of Personality* (1897) as little more than an excuse for extended praise of George Eliot (*EN* v). There is some justice in this objection, but it fails to convey accurately what is a far more complex argument. Lanier's study was first delivered to his students at Johns Hopkins University as a series of lectures shortly before his early death. It is an early first example of the kind of academic criticism that would become commonplace in the twentieth century, one which develops and affirms an already entrenched hypothesis. Lanier's argument pursues four parallel lines of interest: 'the enormous growth in the personality of man which our own time reveals' (5); 'Physical Science, Music, and the Novel all take their rise at the same time' (9); 'the increase of personalities' rendered 'older forms of expression ... inadequate' (10), producing, among other things, the novel; and 'copious readings from some of the most characteristic modern novels in illustration of the general principles thus brought forward' (10). More recent criticism is rarely as candid in revealing its agendas, though it often explores the same interests.

For Lanier, the novel is linked to a clear sense of inevitable progress, at least until its triumphant moment in the work of George Eliot (he has nothing good to say about Henry James or Émile Zola). He is happy to accept the 'customary' date of 1740 as the point of origin; he considers Newton, Bach, and Richardson the seminal figures in the development of the modern personality as manifested in science, music, and the novel. Lanier devotes half of his book to his theory before turning to the novelists. *Pamela* is 'the first revolutionary departure from the wild and complex romances – such as Sir Philip Sidney's *Arcadia* – which had formed the nearest approach to the modern novel until then' (176). It is hard to imagine a sentence that would more clearly reveal the narrow limits of Lanier's interests, and perhaps of his knowledge of the history of the novel, yet the temptation to ignore a work of such gross deficiencies should be resisted. It was very influential, and important in stimulating others in the next few generations.

Richardson's importance for Lanier is in formulating a new species of writing. He welcomes Richardson's 'perfectly clear and conscious moral mission.' But when he turns to 'this wonderful first English novel' he is horrified by its 'silly and hideous realization' (178). Lanier thinks no more highly of Fielding, Smollett, or Sterne: the four 'so-called' masters of the early novel all leave him 'feeling as if my soul had been in the rain, draggled, muddy, and miserable.' In fact, he concludes, 'if I had my way with these classic books I would blot them from the face of the earth' (187–8). There is no great novel in English before *Waverley*, and only a few of Scott's predecessors merit even the briefest mention. The best of the lot is *The Vicar of Wakefield*, the one 'snowdrop springing from this muck of the classics' (189). The others are 'the society novels of Miss Burney, *Evelina* and *Cecilia*, the dark and romantic stories of Mrs. Radcliffe, the *Caleb Williams* of William Godwin – with which he believed he was making an epoch because it was a novel without love as a motive – Miss Edgeworth's moral tales and the quiet elegant narratives of Jane Austen' (190).

Far more interesting than even any of these for Lanier is Erasmus Darwin's *The Loves of the Plants* (1789), 'practically a series of little novels' (191) and far better equipped to satisfy Lanier's standards of excellence. With Scott, the way to the true novel is established, and Lanier is free to devote the final hundred pages of his study to the greatest novelist in the language, George Eliot. According to Lanier, the only value of the eighteenth-century novel is historical; without it, no George Eliot. He sees no reason to provide a thorough survey, since that is not the kind of history he is writing. Early women novelists fare badly, but hardly worse than the early men: Lanier's bias, like Masson's before him, is strong but not based on gender. He knows what he is looking for in the novel, and he cannot find it in the eighteenth century. His overbearing moral vision of what the novel should be and do represents an extreme to be sure, but it is also a model for a kind of criticism that would inform many of the responses to the early novel through the twentieth century.

### Richard Burton (1861–1940)

One very successful popularizer of Lanier's approach to the novel was Richard Burton. His *Masters of the English Novel: A Study of Principles and Personalities* is aimed at a general readership, and he clearly found his market (the copy I looked at was the eleventh printing [1932] of his 1909 study). Like Lanier, Burton begins with a set of assertions about the novel to be demonstrated over the course of his study. Less rigorous than Lanier's, they are also far less contentious. He begins with a dialectical view of the novel: there are two ways to look at 'life in fiction, which have led to the so-called realistic and romantic movements' (vi). Prose fiction in English begins with Lyly, Nashe, Lodge, and Defoe. The essay had a great influence on its development, as did seventeenth-century French romances. But it is not until the realization of its social function that the novel emerges in the mid-eighteenth century:

> The Novel in its treatment of personality began to teach that the stone thrown into the water makes circles to the uttermost bounds of the lake; that the little rift within the lute makes the whole music mute; that we are all members of the one body. This germinal principle was at root a profoundly true and noble one; it serves to distinguish modern fiction philosophically from all that is earlier, and it led the late Sidney Lanier, in the well-known book on the subject, to base the entire development upon the working out of the idea of personality. The Novel seems to have been the special literary instrument in the eighteenth century for the propagation of altruism; herein lies its deepest significance. It was a baptism which promised great things for the lusty young form. (9)

Burton refers earlier to the novel as the literary form that is most 'truly reflective of the *zeitgeist*' in modern times (1). Having established that *zeitgeist*, he turns to the ways in which novelists chose to embody it in their fiction. Theirs was a progressive form, one calculated to 'introduce a more truthful representation of human life' (12). Realism was the obvious way to achieve their goal. Two other progressive strands essential to the new novel also require attention. The novel was, from its outset, a 'democratic' form, and its 'democratic ideal' has only increased with time so that it has clearly established itself as the 'most democratic' of literary forms (15). It was also the form to recognize, again from the outset, 'the increasing importance of woman as a central factor in society,' above and beyond the importance of women as readers and writers of novels (20–1). One final methodological decision on Burton's part is not to attempt a history of the novel, but rather to focus on the 'indubitable masters,' leaving the 'secondary personalities' to others (vii). With these principles in place, Burton is ready to turn to the novels themselves.

The novel proper for Burton begins with Richardson. Defoe and Swift anticipated Richardson in writing prose fiction full of realistic detail, but it is only with Richardson that 'the psychologic method' becomes 'paramount' (47). Richardson's middle-class focus and commitment to sentiment also contribute significantly to his designation as the first English novelist. Though little read in 1909 (largely, Burton speculates, because of the length of his novels), he remains a writer of the greatest importance for preparing the way for the great novelists of the next century – Austen, Dickens, Thackeray, Trollope, and Eliot – and his genius earns him a full chapter. Fielding, who possessed the 'larger' genius, is given the same space (70). Burton structures his discussion of Fielding around an extended comparison with Richardson. He notes that 'Richardson's way was more modern, and did more to set a seal upon fiction'; the novel of the early twentieth century is 'psychologic and serious' (53). But he suggests that a combination of the respective strengths of both fathers of the novel made the greater achievements of the next century possible. Fielding's comic observations of everyday life, though reflecting the more primitive moral standards of his age (making his novels unsuitable for all but the most sophisticated readers), add the broad sweep of society by a more comprehensive genius to the inventory of the realist novel.

Burton's next chapter sets out to bridge the gap between Richardson and Fielding and Austen. He credits Richardson and Fielding with establishing the novel as a viable product in the literary marketplace. In the next quarter-century the novel quickly reaches 'independence and maturity' (72), but Burton limits his discussion to 'a few of the most important' (73) novelists who contributed to this remarkably rapid maturation. It is a short list, beginning with Smollett, the best of the lot, followed by a discussion of three books important to the development of the novel but not themselves novels proper: *Tristram Shandy*, *Gulliver's Travels* (deliberately out of chronological sequence), and *The Vicar of Wakefield*. Burton then ends this chapter with eight pages on the less important novelists: Johnson, Mackenzie, Godwin, Day, Walpole, Radcliffe, Beckford, Lewis, and Brockden Brown. The final three pages of this discussion turn to the late-century trend (contemporary with the Gothic) towards the social novel, a form dominated by women: 'It is a remarkable fact for the fifty years between Sterne and Scott, the leading novelists were of that sex, four of whom at least, Burney, Radcliffe, Edgeworth and Austen were of importance' (98–9). Burney is the 'prophet' for the group. Burton does not think her work lives up to its eighteenth-century reputation, but he considers *Evelina* and *Cecilia* full of a 'fresh spirit' and 'lively humor' that compensates for their lack of more

serious substance. He also considers Burney the master among eighteenth-century writers of realistic dialogue (99). Edgeworth is a better
writer, noteworthy for 'a wider scope and a more incisive satire.' Her
representations of 'English high society' and 'Irish types' add to her
importance, the latter preparing the way for Susan Ferrier and Scott
(100). Collectively, these women laid the foundations for future women
novelists, and for the time when women were to become equal players
as writers of fiction. But none of them – and none of their eighteenth-
century male counterparts – could equal the triumphs of the early nineteenth century in the work of Austen and Scott. Burton's account of the
eighteenth-century novel partakes strongly of the growing tendency not
to linger over many of the secondary players in its development.

### Wilbur Cross (1862–1948)

Wilbur Cross, professor of English at Yale and later governor of Connect-
icut, produced *The Development of the English Novel* (1899) as a guide to
the novel from Arthurian romance to Stevenson for both students and
general readers. He sees his study as building on Dunlop and Raleigh,
upon whom he depended largely for his narrative up to Scott. His most
original contributions, as he sees them, consist of his discussions of the
novel after Scott. The development of the early novel, for Cross, is dialectical, since 'all literary development' is determined by the 'principle
of action and reaction' (xi). The terms of this dialectic are romance and
the novel. (Cross quotes Clara Reeve's formulation of the basic opposition between the two forms in *The Progress of Romance*.) Both are always
present, but successive generations prefer one and then the other, until
the two are united in the work of Scott.

   Cross begins his history with a brief survey of medieval romances,
Elizabethan fiction, and the French romance, always with an eye to what
each contributed to the development of the English novel, before he
turns to the fiction of the Restoration. He sees the romances of the 1660s
as emerging from the 'groups of platonic lovers' who 'hovered about
Katherine Philips and Margaret Duchess of Newcastle' (18). The results
were 'inexpressibly dull' and tired imitations of the French by the likes of
Roger Boyle, Nathaniel Ingelo, George Mackenzie, and John Crowne
(19). Nearly as unimpressive and unoriginal is such realistic fiction as *The
English Rogue* (1665–71); its sole utility is helping prepare the way for
Defoe. Better, because 'more original,' is the fiction of Behn, particularly
*Oroonoko*, a novel Cross finds noteworthy as 'the first humanitarian novel

in English.' Behn is unable to realize the success of *Uncle Tom's Cabin* (1851–2), but Cross believes that she was motivated by the desire to 'awaken Christendom to the horrors of slavery,' the familiar reading of Behn based on eighteenth-century adaptations. Behn's other novels are of interest as versions of 'her own tender experiences' (20). Manley and the early Haywood are less interesting; though their scandal chronicles were 'piquantly immoral' at the time they were produced, 'to later times, they are not so amusing.' But they retain some importance for their contribution to the development of the novel: 'They represent a conscious effort to attain to the real, in reaction from French romance. They are specimens, too, of precisely what was meant in England by the novel in distinction from the romance, just before Richardson: a short story of from one hundred to two hundred pages, assumed to be founded on fact, and published in a duodecimo volume' (21). Cross concludes his discussion of Restoration fiction with a brief encomium on Bunyan, whose contribution to later fiction he considers the most significant in the period.

Other literary forms that contributed to the development of the novel – diaries, journals, lives, letters (real and imaginary) and character sketches – all receive mention, although the Duchess of Newcastle is one of the few authors singled out by name. The major leap forward towards the modern novel does not come until Defoe and Richardson. Cross likens their predecessors to the Elizabethan playwrights before Shakespeare. Defoe's realistic 'novel of incident,' written for a middle-class audience, brought fiction 'home to the Englishman' (27–8). Swift, Defoe, and Bunyan are the 'three writers who usher in a new era for the novel,' and who remain 'the source to which romance has returned again and again for instruction, from Scott to Stevenson' (30).

Cross follows his introductory chapter with two more on the novel before Scott. The first is devoted to the 'eighteenth-century realists,' with sections on Richardson, Fielding, Smollett, Sterne, and the 'minor' novelists of the period, Sarah Fielding, Johnson, and Goldsmith. Defoe had made 'fictitious adventure seem real'; Richardson made 'equally real his men and women, and the scenes in which he placed them.' Where Defoe, in other words, had 'discovered the art of the novel of incident,' Richardson had discovered 'the art of the novel of character' (33). Cross admires Richardson's work, and he considers *Clarissa* a masterpiece, but he also notes some serious limitations. Richardson's thought is that of the Protestant casuist (lacking philosophical depth); he is a self-indulgent sentimentalist; his language is tainted by the old romances; his understanding did not extend into social circles beyond the middle class. Cross then moves to Fielding, his favourite eighteenth-century novelist and the subject of his 1918 three-volume biography (which remained the standard biography for seventy-five years). While resisting the trend to feminize Richardson, Cross makes much of the manly wholesomeness of Fielding. In terms of the development of the novel, dialectic again rules: one of Fielding's great triumphs was in uniting the novel of incident with the novel of character in his masterpiece *Tom Jones*. Smollett's importance is similarly found in his contributions to the developing novel, in particular the introduction of national types and of many elements of the Gothic romance; Sterne contributes by refining the sentimental into a mode that removes the melancholy of Richardson and Rousseau. Cross sees the achievement of the four mid-century masters as lying in their moving the subject matter of the novel firmly to the human heart, each adding his own special twist to a commonly shared 'ethical motive.' 'Richardson makes the novel a medium for Biblical teaching as it is understood by a Protestant precisian; Fielding pins his faith on human nature; Smollett cries for justice to the oppressed; Sterne spiritualizes sensation, addressing "Dear Sensibility" as the Divinity whom he adores.' A few minor writers merit attention as followers who produced work of 'excellence' (76). Sarah Fielding combines elements of both Richardson and her brother, and she pays special attention to the analysis of friendship in *David Simple*, the only one of her novels cited by Cross. No other mid-century woman novelist is seen to have made a contribution of sufficient originality or excellence to merit inclusion.

Cross shares the common conviction that the period between *Humphry Clinker* and *Waverley* was a low point in the development of the novel. The only genuinely important writer was Austen, and the vast majority of the novels of this period deserve the neglect they have received. A few merit ongoing attention 'for their art, their humor, or their keen perception'; others are noteworthy as 'literary curiosities' or for 'their very great historical interest.' Cross is more programmatic than most in explaining why his minor writers are second rate: they lack originality. 'In form, though not in content, all the fiction of this period is in immediate descent from our first school of novelists' (82). That is, each writer can be seen as an imitator of at least one of the 'big four' of mid-century. Cumberland is the best of Fielding's imitators. Most of Sterne's many imitators (Richard Griffith is provided as an example) are 'inexpressibly dull.' Mackenzie's *The Man of Feeling* 'enjoys the distinction of being the most sentimental of all English novels' (83).

Richardson, with help from Rousseau, is given credit for fathering what Cross calls 'the novel of purpose' (84). He classifies Henry Brooke, Thomas Day, Inchbald, Holcroft, Godwin, Opie, Smith, and Bage as the important writers of these didactic, pedagogical, and often revolutionary novels. *A Simple Story* traces the impact of early education on the moral values of a young woman, a typical theme for these novels. Another popular subject is marriage and relations between men and women. Smith's *Desmond* (1792) and Opie's *Adeline Mowbray* are prime examples. A third consists of variations on the earthly paradise; Smith's *The Old Manor House* is cited as an example here. A fourth is the impact of upper-class villains on their innocent, sensitive victims; Inchbald's *Nature and Art* is representative of this group. Still another follows Behn's lead in using outsiders, often from the New World, to comment on British society. Cross finds the novelists of purpose hopelessly naïve as a group (he describes but does not evaluate them individually). They are credited with inventing the didactic novel, but lacked the ability 'to embody their ideas in high and enduring art' (93).

Cross then considers less overtly didactic writers, novelists of manners who differed from Richardson and Fielding by reflecting the changes in English society after mid-century. The key text in this regard is *Evelina*. Cross's reading of Burney is not, however, the standard reading of his time. The characters in *Evelina* are 'mere humors'; it is only with *Cecilia* that they are 'moulded into types' (94). (Cross mentions neither *Camilla* nor *The Wanderer*.) He concludes his discussion of Burney with a paragraph that explains her importance to the development of the novel, again emphasizing originality:

'Cecilia' is the best caricature we have of English society just before the French Revolution. Before the appearance of Miss Burney, the novel of manners had been cultivated almost exclusively by men. The absurdities of society had been viewed from the standpoint of the man of the world, the preacher, the recluse, and the rogue. Richardson alone had gained the reputation of interpreting the feminine mind with any degree of success. The outlook is now completely reversed. The world is presented in fiction as it appears to a woman. Man falls from the pedestal that he had erected for himself. Young ladies are the centres around which young men gyrate. The question ever kept before us concerning the character of a man is, Does he promise well as a husband? Feminine dress is described in painstaking minutiae, and sensations are recorded which were never dreamed of by men. Moreover, the novel had been written not only by men, but for men. Frances Burney created for it a wholesome moral atmosphere. (95)

There are a number of remarkable assertions in this paragraph, driven by Cross's search for Burney's originality. The resulting history of the novel before *Evelina* will soon be incorporated by most critics, adding a new level of complacency to the general neglect of women novelists before Burney.

One consequence for his study is entirely predictable. Burney inspires Edgeworth, 'the popularizer of the society novel,' as well as 'the creator of the international novel' (97). Cross is unusual in acknowledging favourably aspects of Edgeworth's work beyond its Irish quality. He admires her as a social critic of sound morality able to expose 'false sentiment and sophistry' in *Belinda* and in *Fashionable Tales* (96). And he sees her developing a strand he finds in Smollett into the first recognizable 'international novel,' in anticipation of a form to be perfected by Henry James. Finally, Cross does not fail to praise Edgeworth's formative contribution to the national novel, singling out her achievement in freeing the novel from 'traditional characters' by introducing 'the most specialized portrait of manners' (98) yet to be seen. The characters in *Castle Rackrent* were all new, and they were imitated for at least the next fifty years. Few of Cross's contemporaries share his level of enthusiasm for Edgeworth.

The next group of novelists are the writers of Gothic, Oriental, and historical romance. Cross sees romance's return as a result of the epic strain inherent in the novels of Fielding and Richardson becoming dominant for a new generation of novelists. In formal terms, 'the epistolary and dramatic analogies employed by Richardson and Fielding were to be displaced by the epic narrative; for the content of the novel, it meant the abandonment of analysis and ridicule, and a return to magic, mystery, and chivalry' (99). This process begins with Smollett's pushing realism beyond its limits, but it is not fully realized until, in the case of the Gothic romance, Walpole; in the case of the Oriental romance, Beckford; and in the case of the historical romance, Thomas Leland's *Longsword, Earl of Salisbury*. The romancers who merit mention for Cross are: among the Gothic, Reeve, Radcliffe, Lewis, Godwin (Cross recognizes that a novel can be both didactic and Gothic), Brockden Brown, P.B. Shelley, Mary Shelley; among the historical, Sophia Lee, James White, Reeve (for *Roger de Clarendon*), Jane Porter, and Joseph Strutt (whose unfinished *Queenhoo Hall* was completed by Scott). No other writers of Oriental romance are mentioned.

Reeve's *The Old English Baron* is credited with blending Walpole's Gothic with the novel of manners and with uniting the historical and the Gothic strains of romance. The subsequent triumph of the Gothic among the romances of this period is attributed to the remarkable popularity and influence of Ann Radcliffe. 'In the redundancy of her style, her passion for music and wild scenery, and her ability to awaken wonder and awe,' she achieved 'the most complete expression of romanticism in English fiction before Scott.' To her many progressive qualities Radcliffe added 'considerable literary merit' (104). She is treated as a writer of near first-rate status, and one who was highly influential in ensuring that the novel was not reduced to mere utilitarian realism. The historical romancers of late century developed the heroic French romance, already modified by Behn and Manley, as well as Prévost, and further influenced by the renewed interest in Shakespeare's history plays. It began to be a 'distinct species' with the publication of Sophia Lee's *The Recess*, the first of a 'steady flow of historical romances down to Scott' (111). Reeve contributed to that flow, and Jane Porter is credited with 'a great improvement over any imaginative treatment of history that had yet appeared' (112). Cross's account of the late-century novel ends with an encomium on the greatest novelist since Fielding: Jane Austen. He then moves to Scott and beyond. Cross's historicist agenda is both simple and clear, as are the bases of his taste in novels. He is highly selective in his choice of novelists to include in his history, but consistently open to the inclusion of women novelists when they demonstrate a central role in the development of the novel.

### William Lyon Phelps (1865–1943)

William Lyon Phelps, Lampson Professor of English at Yale, wrote *The Advance of the English Novel* (1916) with the general reader in mind. In this compilation of previously published essays from the *Bookman*, (with one added from the *Yale Review*) Phelps attempts to explain how the novel came to realize its dominance in the early twentieth century. His taste is catholic. He favours works of fiction over works of religion, politics, or sociology pretending to be fiction. He defines a 'high-class novel' as '*a good story well told*' (12), a class he then divides into stories that emphasize events (romances) and stories that emphasize the development of character (true novels). (He considers himself to be the first to bring this important corrective to the definitions of novel and romance that go back to Clara Reeve.) The model for the first is *Quentin Durward*

(1823); the model for the second is *The Mill on the Floss* (1860). He considers *Henry Esmond* (1852) the greatest work of fiction in English, in part for its success in fusing the two (17).

Phelps also considers himself among the vanguard of turn-of-the-century critics reassessing the judgments of the Victorians. The eighteenth century, he observes, is being rehabilitated, largely in recognition of its success at representing the real world in clear and simple prose. The clarity of 'the men of Queen Anne' may result from their avoidance of 'difficult themes' in favour of confining 'themselves to subjects entirely within the range of limited minds' (27–8). But that did not prevent unprecedented success. With the exception of *Morte d'Arthur* (1485), Phelps can find no work of prose fiction to recommend to a general reader before Defoe. In his view, 'there is no early development from crudity to perfection, from simple to complex' in the English novel. Rather, 'the thing began with an immortal masterpiece' (29). Phelps notes the importance of character books and periodical essays to the development of the novel over earlier prose fiction. If it were not a religious tract, Bunyan's *The Life and Death of Mr. Badman* (1680) could have qualified as the first English novel; instead, that honour goes to *Robinson Crusoe*.

Phelps is committed to the realist novel and opposed to anything that compromises the integrity of that realism. Turning to Raleigh's analysis of modes of narration, he points out that many novelists combine all three. He agrees with Raleigh that omniscient narration offers a level of sophistication that cannot be equalled with either epistolary or first-person narration, but he also recognizes the danger of introducing didacticism or sentimentalism, both enemies of realism, as inherent in omniscient narration. He considers Fielding far more culpable of abandoning his realist mandate than either Defoe or Richardson, despite, or perhaps because of his sophistication. Phelps feels compelled to apologize for Richardson's prefaces, but he considers the novels themselves, especially *Clarissa*, masterpieces. Richardson is 'the originator of the psychological novel' (52), and as such a central figure in its development.

Phelps's next chapter focuses on Fielding, Smollett, and Sterne. His praise for Fielding is high, though not as high as might be expected from a critic who measures the novel against Thackeray. His comparison of Fielding to Richardson is even-handed; gender emerges only in his praise for Fielding's success with male characters and Richardson's with female characters. Smollett is described as a naturalist as well as the hardest-hearted of novelists, whose work rarely appeals to women;

Sterne is a sentimentalist of very questionable morality. Phelps does not care for either of them. He enjoys *The Vicar of Wakefield*, but considers *Rasselas* an 'embalmed corpse': 'it is much easier to listen with credulity to the whispers of fancy, than it is to listen at all to the history of Rasselas' (71).

Phelps's final chapter on the pre-Victorian novel focuses on romances. He begins with the commonplace that 'the forty years that elapsed from the publication of *Humphry Clinker* to *Sense and Sensibility* are notable for the absence of good fiction,' though Austen has now pushed the end date forward three years from *Waverley*. Burney and Edgeworth rate mention for mirroring and satirizing English manners, 'but both these irreproachable novelists are faint in comparison with the great geniuses of English fiction and growing fainter in the process of years' (79). Phelps attributes the decline in novel writing to pale imitations of Richardson and to the rise of romance which produced little of value before Scott. (Phelps considers the English prone to romance by nature; it takes a great genius, like Richardson or Fielding, to control the urge to romance; it also takes a genius of substance not to sacrifice good English prose to romantic excess.) He traces the history of late eighteenth-century romance, beginning with Leland's *Longsword*, the first historical novel, and credits Reeve as one of the few critics to have been aware of Leland's originality. But it is Walpole who initiates the most successful romance of the period, the Gothic, with *The Castle of Otranto*. Other Gothic novels worthy of mention are *The Old English Baron*, *The Mysteries of Udolpho*, and *The Monk* (1796), 'although not one of these books is worth reading for its own sake' (87). Much of their importance derives from their paving the way for Austen and Scott. Austen was stimulated by the Gothic novels to parody, and then to an alternative form; Scott realized the potential of the romantic novel, though it is not surprising that Phelps prefers the 'absolute realist' Austen (91) to the often 'unreadable' Scott (101).

Phelps's history is notable for two significant departures from most of his predecessors. The increased privileging of realism has reached the point where Scott's achievement and reputation can be called into question, and the consequences for the canonical position of other writers of the end of the eighteenth century are obvious. Phelps also takes the growing tendency towards selectivity to its extreme. He is interested almost exclusively in novels he considers of the highest quality, and his history incorporates far fewer titles than most of his predecessors. He believes that the general reader should bother only with the best; most novelists don't make the cut, and only a few women before Austen are even worthy of mention. The result is a very small canon, and one heavily skewed towards the realistic novel.

## Ernest A. Baker (1869–1941)

One of the most remarkable accounts of fiction ever produced is Ernest A. Baker's *A Guide to the Best Fiction in English* (1903). The future writer of the most thorough history of the novel (see chapter 5) prepared himself for his magnum opus by producing a comprehensive catalogue of 'best' fiction, including works translated into English. It is anything but selective. One of Baker's aims was to provide an annotated guide for librarians; another was to encourage reprints of neglected novels. He sometimes lists inferior titles by authors whose best work merits inclusion, and the *Guide* is deliberately skewed in favour of more recent fiction. It nonetheless remains one of the most inclusive treatments of early fiction ever produced.

Baker begins with eight medieval and twenty-five sixteenth-century listings. Some are collections, the majority works by single authors, some with several titles. None of the authors are women. Sixteen listings are provided for the seventeenth century, including Behn and Lady Mary Wroth. (The others are: *The Adventures of Covent Garden*, Bacon, *The Famous Historie of Fryar Bacon*, Barclay, Bunyan [three titles], Congreve, Crowne, Francis Godwin, Harrington, Head, Ingelo, *Nova Solyma*, and Orrery [two titles].) Baker had recently edited Behn's novels for his Routledge series, the 'Library of Early Novelists.' His annotation of his edition reads: 'Mrs. Behn wrote a large number of licentious plays, one novel of singular merit, *Oroonoko*, and some indifferent novelettes which are collected here. These last are negligible effusions, poor in plot, false in sentiment, unreal in method, all on variations of the one theme – the omnipotence of love. *Oroonoko* has a truth and power unexampled in these. It is the story of an heroic Negro who is kidnapped and sold into slavery in Surinam, where Aphra perhaps witnessed his sufferings and magnanimity. As a glorification of the natural man, this book anticipated Rousseau, and as an emancipation novel, Mrs. Stowe' (10). This note is among the longer of those Baker provides, in a collection in which length has some correlation with importance. The Wroth entry is one of the shorter: 'An imitation of Sidney's *Arcadia* by a niece of his, daughter of Robert, Earl of Leicester. A mixture of Sidneian prose and verse, with the conventional shepherd-princes and royal shepherdesses herding their flocks and making love in Greece and the isles' (12).

Baker divides the eighteenth century in half and lists nine writers from the first half: Addison, Captain George Carleton, Defoe, both Fieldings, Haywood, Manley, Richardson, and Swift. He does not define his terms with precision, but it becomes clear in this section that Baker shares the common view that what distinguishes the novel is its realism. The earlier writers in this group are included in part as important precursors; the novel proper is realized by Richardson and Fielding. *Pamela* is described as 'epoch-making in literature as a study of the female heart' (16). Baker has so little good to say about Manley that the reason for her inclusion is unclear. *The Secret History of Queen Zarah and the Zarazians* (1705), her best effort, is 'a romance made up of disguised scandal of political and fashionable life.' *The New Atalantis* is 'a more impudent miscellany of slanderous stories.' The rest are 'pretentious romances of intrigue, illicit passion, and unreal sentiment, as conventional and vapid as the poorer of Mrs. Behn's' (15). Haywood's early novels are imitations of Behn and Manley, with no value added. *Betsy Thoughtless* is more important for its influence on Burney's *Evelina*. Baker considers *David Simple* 'a moralizing novel, inspired by Richardson's *Pamela*' (15).

With the second half of the eighteenth century the list begins to grow, though it is worth noting that the entire eighteenth century is allotted eleven pages while the 'present day,' a period covering roughly 1890 to 1912, gets 228. The late eighteenth-century list includes Amory, Bage, Beckford, Henry Brooke, Burney, Day, Godwin, Goldsmith, Graves, *Hartly House* (1789), Holcroft, Inchbald, Johnson, Johnstone, Sophia Lee, Leland, Lennox, Lewis, Mackenzie, Moore, Paltock, Radcliffe, Reeve, Roche, Sheridan, Smith, Smollett, Sterne, Walpole, and James White; nine of thirty authors are women. *The Female Quixote* is described as a light imitation of Cervantes, *Sidney Bidulph* as 'written in opposition to the theory of poetic justice' (22). Baker considers Burney 'a sharp-eyed girl,' who observed 'the surface things of London – its people and pleasures, life in theatre and ballroom, at Marylebone Gardens, The Pantheon, etc.; and of the people of fashion, the eccentrics, the conceited, and the vulgar; the last in particular being sharply satirized' (17). *Cecilia* is a 'more studied and elaborate work' without being better; *Camilla* and *The Wanderer* reveal 'a complete falling off' (18).

*The Old English Baron* is a 'very early and crude attempt to give a real historical setting to the Gothic romance'; Reeve's *Roger de Clarendon* (1793) is 'a dull novel' also from historical sources (22). Sophia Lee's *The Recess* is 'one of the earliest historical novels, interesting now as a curious relic of literary history' (20). Smith's *Ethelinde* (1789) and *The Old Manor House* are summarized briefly and described as 'sentimental' and 'without satire' (22). *A Simple Story* is 'a pleasing example of the novel of sensibility.' He notes that 'Mrs. Inchbald wrote bad plays for the stage, and there is a theatrical manner about this one successful novel of hers that is curious but not unpleasing' (19). Baker also describes *Nature and Art*, but without evaluation. Radcliffe 'is of great importance in the history of romantic literature. She laid her plots in remote periods, and in countries she had never seen, thus avoiding any responsibility to fact. Picturesque ruins, distant mountains, forest-shrouded landscapes are described with rich but monotonous colour, in a semi-lyrical style. The scenic glamour prepares the reader for sensational occurrences that conjure up feelings of awe and terror; but in the sequel she invariably dispels our apprehensions by some commonplace explanation of her ghosts and other mysteries' (21). He describes five of her novels and identifies Roche's *The Children of the Abbey* (1796) as a famous example of an end-of-century imitation of Radcliffe's romances.

The nineteenth century is divided into quarters, the first of which includes sixteen writers in this study. Only five are men: Strutt, Barrett, Peacock, Maturin, and Scott. Twelve of Edgeworth's titles are described; Baker considers her a moralist, prone to didacticism, yet strong on character portraits from Irish life. Opie's *The Father and Daughter* is 'a somewhat conventional novel characterized by deep and harrowing pathos.' *Adeline Mowbray*, 'the earliest treatment of the now hackneyed theme of the "Woman Who Did" – embodies not only the teaching of Mary Wollstonecraft, but the main incidents of her life and her connexion with Godwin ... An early problem novel, as acutely pathetic as [*The Father and the Daughter*]' (30). Jane Porter's *Thaddeus of Warsaw* is a 'sentimental idyll suggested by the exploits and tragic after-life of Kosciusko'; her *The Scottish Chiefs* is a 'better story though not so famous.' Anna Maria Porter's *The Hungarian Brothers* (1809) is an 'early and very old fashioned historical romance' (31).

Baker describes four of Lady Morgan's novels with minimal evaluation. Hannah More's *Cœlebs in Search of a Wife* is 'the only readable survivor of a series of didactic stories having little of the art of Miss Edgeworth' (29). Elizabeth Hamilton's *The Cottagers of Glenburnie* (1808) is 'a homely tale, didactic in aim, portraying the lowly life and character of rural Scotland' (28). Baker considers Ferrier a good portrayer of Scottish manners if not a skilful constructor of plots. *Frankenstein* is a 'ghastly extravaganza,' though better than those Percy Shelley and Byron wrote in competition with it (35). Scott and Austen are clearly major writers. All of their works are described, most with evident approval.

Baker's volume is more an encyclopaedic dictionary than a history of the novel. He offers few judgments, and still fewer fresh opinions. But his *Guide* is clearly intended to expand the list of novels read: Baker himself seems to have read every novel ever written. His coverage of English fiction is followed by a full discussion of its American counterpart (including Brockden Brown from the early period), and representative fiction originally published in other languages from the ancient Greeks to modern European and non-European. Baker's selection criteria appear to be free of any critical principle: this study is so inclusive that it is hard to see canon formation as part of his mandate.

## Studies of Women Novelists

### A.M. Williams (b. 1858)

Although critical work dedicated exclusively to women novelists does not increase at the same rate as more general literary histories and histories of the novel, there is ongoing activity. The title essay in A.M. Williams's collection, *Our Early Female Novelists and Other Essays* (1904), first appeared in the *Cornhill Magazine*. Williams, the principal of the Church of Scotland Training College in Glasgow, begins with Chaucer and his reliance on incorporating real life into his narratives as key to his greatness. Writers of prose fiction were much slower in making the transition from romance and allegory to nature, a transition crucial to the development of the modern novel. Seventeenth-century romances like Boyle's *Parthenissa* (1651–6) provide the negative example, but it is also in the seventeenth century that the first glimmers of better things occur. Williams gives pride of place to Newcastle, though Behn is 'a much more important figure' (6). Writing when the heroic romance was still the fashion, Behn 'went for her characters and incidents to real life' (8). *Oroonoko* is, of course, her greatest work; it reveals 'instinct with real feeling and womanly sympathy' (9) sufficient to excuse her many lapses of morality and delicacy (he cites Kavanagh in support of this approach to Behn). Williams isolates Behn's worst lapses in her plays, where 'she certainly did her best to add to the iridescent filth of the Restoration drama.' The novels, however, though 'indelicate and coarse ... possess the merit of lively narrative, and make some attempt to portray distinct characters and to analyse emotion' (10–11). Williams sees Behn's novels as the origin of the realist novel that developed over the next hundred years until the revival of romance at the end of the eighteenth century. Aside from *Oroonoko,* he singles out *The Adventure of the Black Lady* and *The Fair Jilt* from the Behn corpus.

Manley was, for Williams, the next writer who 'floated high on the rising tide of realism' (11). In her case, though, he has 'little good to say: her life was vicious, and so are her books' (13). He considers *The New Atalantis* gross and immoral, full of cruel and merciless satire. The only thing that makes the *Power of Love* (1720) somewhat better is the absence of satire. Nonetheless, Williams concludes that Manley 'may not be lightly passed by in a review of what women have done to develop the novel' (14). Where Haywood is concerned, Williams is impressed by the quantity of her writing but laments that she did not use 'her pen to any good purpose' (15). Her realism focuses on the nasty side of human behaviour. Even *Betsy Thoughtless,* written after the novel was realized by Richardson and Fielding and important for its influence on Burney, is distasteful because of its realistic representation of eighteenth-century attitudes towards women.

Sarah Fielding's *David Simple* shares Haywood's approach to a 'purely physical estimate of women' (16), though she is a more important and better novelist in other respects. (Charlotte Smith is credited with being the first to demand that women be judged by 'intellectual and moral qualities' [17]). Fielding is praised for her analyses of characters but criticized for poor, that is, overly picaresque, plot construction. She is also praised as an effective satirist, a quality she shares with the next woman novelist considered, Charlotte Lennox. Williams notes her contemporary fame in a number of literary genres, observing that she is now all but forgotten. Posterity has been far kinder to Burney, a writer who also had 'a keen eye for the ridiculous and a considerable gift of satire.' To this she added the ability to describe 'contemporary manners ... free from unnecessary coarseness' (20). That said, Williams turns to her shortcomings and is far more severe in his judgment than most: 'Madame D'Arblay is not entitled to any high place as a novelist; her constructive skill is small, and her characters are for the most part what Jonson would have called "humourists," that is, they are the incarnation of qualities rather than flesh and blood individuals. Moreover, the author herself is a "humourist," her ruling passion is a morbid craving to be "genteel"; she has no mercy for vulgarity or the vulgar, but she fails to see that her own worship of society conventions is itself vulgar' (21). Even the approval of Samuel Johnson does not excuse her fundamental priggishness. The only one of Burney's novels to merit mention is *Evelina.*

Smith is far more to Williams's taste. He prefers her as a person and as a writer. Aside from her depiction of women, he singles out Smith's use of natural description to enrich her novels. He considers *The Old Manor House* her best, a novel 'which may still be read with pleasure' (22). Still more important and more successful is Inchbald, the master of 'pure, unsophisticated nature' which she applied to the new problem novel (23). Williams blames a limited education for many of Inchbald's faults, from clumsy plot construction to an inability to make admirable characters credible. These faults, however, do not undermine the readability of either *A Simple Story* or *Nature and Art*.

Williams concludes his account with the return of romance in the school of terror. He credits Walpole as the originator, notes his many weaknesses, and then turns to Reeve and Radcliffe. Reeve corrects Walpole's excesses, but *The Old English Baron* is nevertheless not a success. Excellence in this school of writing was not achieved until Radcliffe: *The Mysteries of Udolpho* is the greatest of the novels of terror, despite Radcliffe's insistence on offering rational explanations. The final authors in Williams's survey are the Lees. He admires Harriet for her contributions to the *Canterbury Tales*, especially 'Kruitzner'; he also notes the importance of Sophia's *The Recess* as 'one of the very earliest,' but, 'it must be added, very worst of our historical novels' (30). Soon after the Lees the public was able to read Scott, and the novel reached 'its most flourishing days' (31).

Williams's goal in *Our Early Female Novelists* had been to establish the role of women in the development of the novel. In the process, he provides a basic canon, one still recognizable to critics in the field. He is willing to bring the female wits back into the discussion, and with the exception of his surprisingly low view of Burney, he offers an overview very much in the spirit of the more general histories of the period.

## R. Brimley Johnson (1867–1932)

A far more influential study was R. Brimley Johnson's *The Women Novelists* (1918), a book given the highest praise by Virginia Woolf, in the *TLS*, for its thorough knowledge of the subject and non-partisan balance. For Johnson, 'although women wrote novels before Defoe, the father of English fiction, or Richardson, the founder of the modern novel, we cannot detect any peculiarly feminine elements in their work, or profitably consider it apart from the general development of prose' (1). Johnson's brief, introductory chapter is thus a pre-history to the appearance of those he considers women novelists proper. He begins with Behn, the first woman in England to write a novel equal to what was being produced on the Continent. That novel is, of course, *Oroonoko*, for Johnson, a novel that anticipates Rousseau in its presentation of the state of nature, and a novel unlike her others in that it contains almost 'nothing peculiarly objectionable' (3). The two other novelists 'of that generation' who deserve mention are Manley and Haywood, both of whom produced 'vile libels' and 'novels of some vigour, but deservedly forgotten.' Johnson notes that the best of their efforts 'were written after *Pamela*, and bear striking witness to the influence of Richardson' (5). Sarah Fielding and Lennox are acknowledged as making genuine progress towards the true novel.

Johnson considers Burney 'the first woman novelist.' The novel itself came into being with Richardson and Fielding and was developed by Smollett, Sterne, and Goldsmith. What distinguished it from its fictional predecessors was its realism and its reliance on middle-class characters. Burney was clearly influenced by 'the fathers of fiction,' especially Richardson, but *Evelina* 'inaugurated a new departure – the expression of a feminine outlook on life. It was, frankly and obviously, written by a woman for women, though it captivated men of the highest intellect' (12). Even in *Cecilia*, 'partially disfigured by Johnson's advice' about form and correct style, what comes through is 'the manipulation of [Burney's] own experience of life, and her own comments thereon' (13). To appreciate Burney's achievement Johnson compares her to Richardson. Although the acknowledged master of the representation of women, Richardson's view remains that of an outsider. 'Our *consciousness* of his skill proves it is conscious.' He is clearly 'pulling the strings,' and 'they are man-made' (15). Nothing could be farther from the case in a Burney novel. Burney was able to project the naturalness of what she represented, its credible authenticity.

Burney was also able to develop Richardson's realism in more 'strictly *domestic*' (17) directions (Austen would subsequently perfect this development). Johnson notes her use of 'the revelation of *sensibility*, that most elusive of female graces on which our grandmothers were wont to pride themselves' (18). Twentieth-century readers have difficulty comprehending the demands the cult of sensibility made on young women; the result is an inability to respond with the degree of sympathy he assumes in Burney's first readers. To the in-depth presentation of her heroines Burney adds a large number of humours characters that broaden the range and variety of life captured in her novels.

This range, and her ear for female wit, round out the picture of Burney's many strengths. Her major weakness is structural, the sign of her amateur status as an author. 'Genius and experience' (31), not craft, were key to her success. Johnson closes his discussion of Burney with a long and approving quotation from Hazlitt. Hazlitt was able to capture Burney's essential quality as a writer – her femininity – but where for him it is a fault, for Johnson it is the source of her major contribution as a woman novelist.

Given Johnson's by-now standard account of *Evelina*, his reader is ill-prepared for the following chapter, a defence of the much-maligned and little-read *Camilla*. He acknowledges the standard complaint that the sentiments in *Camilla* are 'palpably strained, absurdly high-flown, and singularly unbalanced,' but insists that we place the novel in its historical context, a context in which 'the ideals for women, and for all intercourse between the sexes, differ in nearly every particular from those of our own day,' and in which characters considering love and marriage were 'almost ridiculously young,' often as young as fifteen (36–7). Johnson provides a full account of the novel, noting its tendency towards melodrama and artificiality. He insists, however, that even Burney's most extravagant moments are *'founded on* nature' (as opposed to 'imagination'); 'experience and observation' remain the hallmark of her fiction (50). Burney's presentation of the 'greater purity and refinement, the superior moral standard' of women is also essential to her achievement, for although these areas of superiority had been 'practically assumed without comment' by male novelists, her emphasis on them established an important core set of issues for subsequent women novelists. 'Here, as elsewhere, Miss Burney was almost the first to teach us what women actually thought and felt: in marked contrast to what had been hitherto considered becoming for them to express. She was, always, and everywhere, the mouthpiece of her sex' (52). Johnson concludes his discussion of *Camilla* with a return to the problem of her 'grandiloquent style,' Burney's major 'drawback' as a writer. Again, he attributes the problem to her amateur status and the resulting undue influence of the 'Dictator,' Samuel Johnson: 'Miss Burney wrote Johnsonese fluently, and thereby ruined her natural powers' (52–3).

Burney's importance is considerably enhanced by her influence on future women novelists, most notably Austen, for it is with Austen that the 'Woman's School' reaches maturity. One of Johnson's three chapters on Austen (the most allotted to any of his writers) is an extended comparison of her work with that of Burney, demonstrating how thoroughly Austen was versed in Burney's novels, and thus adding weight to his claim for Burney's importance as a woman novelist. In considering those who wrote between Burney and Austen he begins with Radcliffe and the return of romance. As Johnson is no fan of romance, his defence of Radcliffe emphasizes the realistic qualities he can identify, her use and development of sensibility, the poetic quality of her writing, and her sympathetic descriptions of nature; he also credits her with making *Northanger Abbey* possible. Inchbald, by contrast, remains in the more purely realistic camp, though 'she produced little more than a pale imitation of *The Man of Feeling*, by Henry Mackenzie, the only masculine exponent of "sensibility."' Still, he grants 'a certain melodramatic, and almost decadent, charm in her work' (59–60).

The most important writer of this period is Edgeworth, who was a significant force in the establishment of four new kinds of fiction: juvenile fiction with clear didactic lessons, in Edgeworth's case resulting in 'nursery classics deserving of immortality' (61); Burney-like social satire of turn-of-the-century society; the short story; and the national novel. Edgeworth is credited with extending Burney's women's novel to the 'discussion of social and political problems' and with being 'the first to make fiction a picture not only of life but of its meaning.' He recognizes that she was nowhere in her voluminous work able 'to reveal genius,' but still considers Edgeworth an unjustly neglected writer of humour, pathos, knowledge of the world, and, above all, common sense that should win her a more secure place in the canon (62–3). He ends this chapter with Hannah More, a writer whose work in other genres surpasses her achievement in her one novel, *Cœlebs in Search of a Wife*. Johnson considers *Cœlebs* 'no more than a "dramatic sermon,"' and a sermon, moreover, in support of 'narrow-minded sectarianism' (64).

Once Johnson has completed his survey of women novelists he provides a chapter comparing his 'great four': Burney, Austen, Charlotte Brontë, and George Eliot. He reiterates Richardson's centrality in establishing the domestic, middle-class novel that each of these writers develops. Burney is distinguished from the others by her focus on London, her reliance on sensibility, and her eye for comedy. A chapter on 'the woman's man' follows, again citing Richardson as the point of origin. Johnson sees Sir Charles Grandison as the first man created to satisfy female desire for male perfection. Burney's Lord Orville is based on Grandison, but more credible, and the type is then developed by Austen and her successors. Johnson's penultimate chapter explores how the individual personalities of his four greats are manifested in

their works. He concludes by reasserting and developing his contention that 'women developed – and perfected – the domestic novel.' In
establishing their right to write novels, they developed the middle-
class novel of Richardson and Fielding; in the process, 'they made novels a reflection, and a criticism, of life' (282). The novel continues to
develop and improve throughout its history, mirroring the development of the power of the middle class it represents.

The other major achievement of the women novelists is in 'their own
particular sphere, – the revelation of Woman.' The nature of woman
develops over time, with the novelists themselves playing an important role: 'By teaching us what was "going on" *in women*, they taught
women to be themselves. They opened the doors of Liberty towards
Progress' (285). Finally, Johnson provides as an appendix a brief list of
minor women novelists, with thumbnail descriptions of one to three
sentences. The novelists from the period of this study are: Newcastle,
Sheridan, Reeve, Smith, the Lees, Bennett, Roche, Opie, the Porters,
Brunton, and Morgan.

Johnson's is the first systematic study of a dedicated line of women
novelists, and it makes a strong case for the centrality of women in the
development of the novel. Since his focus is on the 'greats', his is not a
very inclusive history, but Johnson's appendix gives some indication of
how he would flesh out a fuller history if one were necessary. His
choices are not new, but his advocacy of the woman novelist gives this
study a special importance.

## William Dean Howells (1837–1920)

A curious but related study is William Dean Howells's two-volume
*Heroines of Fiction* (1901). It is in fact a study of nineteenth-century heroines, but Howells makes the case for beginning with the eighteenth
century, arguing that chronological divisions by century are too arbi-
trary for strict observance. He would have liked to begin with Defoe, a
writer of 'nobler morality' than Fielding, every bit as 'well intentioned
as Richardson,' and 'a greater, a more modern artist than either.' But
because of Defoe's subject matter, 'his heroines must remain under
lock and key, and cannot be so much as named in mixed companies'
(1: 2–3). Since *Robinson Crusoe*, the only one of his novels acceptable for
all readers, has no heroine, Howells must look elsewhere to begin. He
considers Richardson, and although Clarissa Harlowe is 'a masterpiece
in the portraiture of that Ever-Womanly which is of all times and

places' (1: 3), her environment is too similar to Defoe's. In searching for the first modern heroine Howells turns to 'a greater artist.' 'It is not going much too far,' Howells argues, 'to say that the nineteenth-century English novel, as we understand it now, with its admirable limitations, was invented by Oliver Goldsmith. The novel that respects the right of innocence to pleasure in a true picture of manners, and honors the claim of inexperience to be amused and edified without being abashed, was his creation' (1: 5). With Howells, the Victorian history of the novel, complete with Goldsmith's central place in it, enters the twentieth century virtually unchallenged. When he turns to women novelists Howells looks to Burney, Edgeworth, and Austen to find the women who 'fixed the ideal of Anglo-Saxon heroines ... In some sort Richardson served them as a model, and Goldsmith as an inspiration, but it was they who characterized the modern Anglo-Saxon novel which these masters had perhaps invented' (1: 11). The remainder of Howells's study devotes chapters to specific heroines.

The first of these chapters considers Burney's Evelina. Evelina is of special importance because before her, 'the heart of girlhood had never been so fully opened in literature' (1: 15). Howells takes his readers through Burney's novel, apologizing for her 'quaint and obsolete' novelistic techniques as well as 'the manners of the outdated world to which she was born.' The character of Evelina herself remains 'a masterpiece, and she could not be spared from the group of great and real heroines' (1: 22). Howells finds the secret of Evelina's success in her closeness to her author: 'Fanny Burney *was* Evelina' (1: 24). He considers *Cecilia* a greater novel, but its title character is not as fine as Evelina. (*Camilla* is deemed inferior in both areas.)

Before he moves to the near 'ideal perfection' (1: 26) of Austen, Howells spends a chapter examining Edgeworth. His goal in discussing her work is to reverse 'the popular superstition which still prevails that she was all precept, all principle, all preaching' (1: 26). Had this been so, he argues, she would not have been an important influence on so consummate an artist as Turgenev. What follows is an account of the two heroines, Belinda Portman and Lady Delacour, of his favourite Edgeworth novel, *Belinda*.

Howells's focus on heroines leads him to study the novels by women he considers writers of merit. While his nineteenth-century focus does not encourage him to explore the eighteenth century with much care, it is easy to infer the strong prejudices against both the century and its novels that inform his study. There are no women before

Burney and only two before Austen worthy of serious attention. This attitude dominates the first half of the twentieth century.

### Catherine J. Hamilton (b. 1841)

Catherine J. Hamilton's two-volume *Women Writers: Their Works and Their Ways* (1892–3) collected two series of magazine articles on women writers. Aimed at a popular audience, they are far more biographical than critical and premised on a sense that Swift's account of the trivial nature of most women's lives was accurate for his time. Only at the end of the eighteenth century do women finally attend to serious intellectual pursuits, including writing. The writers in the first series are the pioneers. Their earliest member is Burney, and among the novelists she is followed by Inchbald, More, Radcliffe, Edgeworth, Opie, Morgan, and Ferrier. Hamilton's canon is small and select, and her interests do not extend back before the late eighteenth century. But she is a useful source for understanding what was valued from received opinion for a popular account of women writers. (Lucy B. Walford's [1845–1915] *Twelve English Authoresses* [1893] is a similar collection of periodical essays, in this case from the American magazine *Far and Near*; the writers she selected include More, Burney, and Edgeworth.)

Hamilton notes in her Preface that she wrote her articles before the appearance of the 'Eminent Women' series. This series, in the manner of the better-known 'English Men of Letters,' consists of nineteen diverse volumes published by W.H. Allen in the final two decades of the nineteenth century; the writers considered include Mary Wollstonecraft, Mary Shelley, Hannah More, and Maria Edgeworth (see Pennell, Rossetti, Yonge, and Zimmern). The series seems to be based on a view of women writers similar to Hamilton's, so it is not surprising that she feels the need to place her own work in a similar context. But the 'Eminent Women' volumes provide far more thorough accounts of their subjects, generally by more interesting critics, such as Julia Ward Howe (1819–1910), Violet Paget (1856–1935), and Charlotte M. Yonge (1823–1901).

### Specialized, Academic Studies

### Clara Linklater Thomson (fl. 1900–1929)

Clara Linklater Thomson's *Samuel Richardson: A Biographical and Critical Study* (1900) presents itself as the first work of its kind since Barbauld. It should not be necessary by now to justify the inclusion of a work on Richardson in this study, and its relevance is only increased by Thomson's chapters on the development of the novel before him, and on Richardson's influence on its subsequent development. The chapter on the early development of the novel provides a standard survey beginning with medieval romances and fabliaux and working through Elizabethan prose fiction (Lyly, Sidney, Greene, and Nashe), French romances of the seventeenth century, Cervantes, Scarron, Bunyan, character writing, periodical essays, memoirs, Defoe, Swift, and French and English letter writers of the seventeenth and eighteenth centuries. This last group includes a number of women; otherwise, for Thomson, women play no part in the development of the early novel. The same need not be said of her account of writers influenced by Richardson, whose followers she divides into three groups. The largest group is Continental novelists; consequently, they receive the fullest account. Next are the novelists of sentiment, represented by Sterne, Mackenzie, and Henry Brooke. The third group is women novelists, who turned to him because he established in English fiction 'those topics which are most familiar to women, and which will never lose their attraction as themes for the lady novelist.' Richardson attracted his large readership of women 'not only because he possessed so much knowledge of feminine psychology, but also because he limited himself to topics which were well within the comprehension of an ordinary woman of the eighteenth century' (269). Burney acknowledged his importance for her, especially with *Sir Charles Grandison*, and 'Miss Burney's mantle fell on Miss Austen' (270). The line of women novelists is thus clearly established – without the need for others before Austen. Thomson has little to add to the history of the novel she inherited. What is telling about her work is that, even in a discussion focused on Richardson, she finds no need to include the numerous eighteenth-century women novelists who would so greatly have enriched her account of the context for Richardson's own achievements.

### Allene Gregory (1887–1947)

Allene Gregory's *The French Revolution and the English Novel* (1914) offers a specialized, academic account of a group of novelists important for my study. Gregory provides considerable historical and philosophic background and an account of a number of male novelists before turning to the chapter 'Some Typical Lady Novelists of the Revolution.' She begins with the observation that 'one of the literary features of the later eighteenth century in England was the large crop of Lady Novelists. A Lady Novelist, be it observed, is altogether a different thing from a woman who writes novels. The latter may sometimes allow us to forget her sex; the former, never' (191). The Lady Novelist is sentimental, didactic, domestic, devout, and proper. The model Lady Novelist is Austen. 'There was,' she observes, 'little natural affinity between the Lady Novelists and the Revolution.' It is all the more surprising, then, that 'there were some few gentle feminine souls who through their humanitarian sympathies, the influence of Rousseau, or a personal association with the leaders of English Revolutionism, were swept into the heterodox currents of the time' (192–3). The most important of these women are Inchbald, Opie, and Smith; less important, but still noteworthy, are Mary J. Hanaway, Mary Hays, Eliza Kirkham Mathews, Eliza Fenwick, Anne Plumptre, Mary Shelley, and Lady Caroline Lamb.

Related to the novels of the Revolution are a group Gregory calls the 'Rights of Women' novels. She provides a brief introduction tracing the history of feminist thought in England up to the end of the eighteenth century before turning to the novelists themselves, and begins with the following observation: 'It can hardly have failed to occur to us how few of the novelists we have considered so far are living figures in the world of literature. A few volumes gathering dust on the shelves of libraries and special collections, occasional perfunctory notices in histories of the novel; these are all that remain of the little group who echoed in the fiction of their time the splendid audacities that so inspired the poets of the Revolution' (239–40). This is by way of preparation for the exception, the one writer able to remain a living force a century later, Mary Wollstonecraft. Gregory must acknowledge that 'we are concerned here primarily with her novels, which formed a very insignificant part of her work' (240). The subsequent discussion is largely biographical, descriptive, and thematic; Gregory is not attempting a case for Wollstonecraft as a major *novelist*. The other 'Rights of Women' novelists she mentions include Mrs West, who, under the name 'Prudentia Homespun' wrote 'a rather stupid narrative sermon' (259), *The Advantages of Education, or, The History of Maria Williams* (1793). The other novels in this group are either anonymous or too late for this study.

## Conclusion

The end of the nineteenth and beginning of the twentieth century brought a considerable softening of much of the entrenched hostility to eighteenth-century prose fiction. It was still a time of progressive histories of the novel – the last period when such views were dominant. But it was also a time of comprehensive histories, many written by critics well-read in the history of the novel, and increasingly written by ones unencumbered by values that required them to reject the early novel on moral grounds. It witnessed early indications of a renewed openness to the novels of Richardson, always a good indicator of potential openness to early women novelists. This was not, however, a time of radical canon change, and this period did not contribute to any significant improvement in the standing of early women novelists in the years around mid-century, the years of my final chapter.

# 5 1920–1957

The final period considered in this study, 1920–57, sees a further explosion of academic scholarship and critical attention to the novel. The shortest period covered in any of my chapters becomes the longest chapter, since it discusses the largest number of publications. This is also the chapter in which I have had to be most selective in my choice of critics. The chapter is divided along the same lines as chapter 4, with the addition of a section devoted to critical studies of the novel. There is relatively less activity in the area of histories aimed at the general reader or the student, but that is only because of the increased activity in more specialized scholarly studies, particularly those devoted to the novel. This is the period of literary modernism and the attendant rise of formalist criticism, a development that influenced how critics read earlier literatures, including the fiction of the eighteenth and early nineteenth centuries.

## Histories of English Literature

### Oliver Elton (1861–1945)

The transition from the belletristic criticism of the Victorians and Edwardians to the more formalistic and academic approaches of the twentieth century is well represented by Oliver Elton's influential *A Survey of English Literature* (six volumes), covering the period from 1730 to 1880. It was published in two-volume units, each covering a fifty-year period, over sixteen years, beginning with *1780–1830* in 1912 and ending with *1730–1780* in 1928 (the *1830–1880* volumes are not relevant for this study). Elton's work, then, straddles the 1920 boundary dividing this chapter from the previous one. It is also transitional in that Elton was directly influenced by historians from the earlier period (he mentions Seccombe, Gosse, and Saintsbury as especially important to him). He calls his work a 'survey' rather than a history to signal that his primary concern is evaluating literary texts as works of art. Brief 'sketches' at the beginning and end of his chapters cover many of the more conventional historical topics, though always with the confession that these topics deserve more focused attention and considerably more space than he gives them (vii).

The *1730–1780* volumes begin with a recognition that 'the literature of our eighteenth century has come back into its own.' The reason, he suggests, is that 'it expresses, better perhaps than that of any other time, the permanent average temper of our race, as it is found in Johnson, in Fielding, and in Captain Cook' (1: vii). Elton speculates that the greater interest in the eighteenth century is a reaction against the Victorian age. The former is now safe and comfortable, while the latter remains something of a threat to the current generation of writers and critics. Elton's approach, like that of his mentor Saintsbury's, is inclusive. He covers a wide range of writers.

When Elton turns to the novel, he begins with the premise that it emerges from 'lower forms' in 1740 'to express far better than the poetry could do, the temper of the age and the race. A Briton will always feel more at home with Fielding and even with Sterne than with Gray or Thomson.' Elton marvels at how quickly the 'four masters,' Richardson, Fielding, Smollett, and Sterne, established 'the true, the lasting pattern of the novel.' He also marvels at the gap between them and their nearest rivals. Those rivals often produced enjoyable reading; there remains, however, 'a sharp descent from *Joseph Andrews* or *Peregrine Pickle* to the *Female Quixote* and *David Simple*' (160).

Before turning to Richardson Elton devotes a few pages to the 'graveyards of fiction' (1: 160), Richardson's predecessors. His brief survey of them is remarkably inclusive for a critic who thinks so little of their work. He credits Richardson with eclipsing earlier writers of prose fiction, most notably the Continental romance writers so popular in translation and a number of 'fashionable women novelists, only one of whom is now more than a shadow.' That one is Manley, and Elton feels that she is one too many. Aubin is 'another hack romancer,' Barker 'another copious authoress' of 'moral essays sprinkled with tales of the disagreeable kind that may be termed the mawkish-realistic.' A cut above is Haywood, who, after an undistinguished but productive early career 'mended her ways' and produced two novels, *Jemmy and Jenny Jessamy* and *Betsy Thoughtless*, that are 'curious and sprightly' as well as 'virtuous' (1: 161). Others who contributed to the development of the novel include Defoe and Swift and Addison and Steele. But it was Richardson who put together the modern novel from this diverse body of predecessors: 'He was to design a real plot, based on real life and on a large scale; to steep it in sentiment, and in a kind of passion, and yet to moralise everything; to transplant the analytic habit into the bourgeois world; and to throw in much sinister and squalid episode. He was also to build up a crowd of characters whose fortunes were followed by his readers like those of personal acquaintance' (1: 164). With the background established and Richardson's breakthrough defined, Elton can now turn his attention to the novel proper.

Elton takes Richardson seriously enough to devote sixteen pages to him, despite his unpromising origins, his timidity and 'nervous vanity,' and the 'extraordinary smugness' that pervaded his circle, a circle chiefly made up of women. A thirty-four-page chapter on Fielding and Smollett follows, then fourteen pages on Sterne before Elton returns to those he considers the minor novelists. It is worth noting that Elton admires all four of his masters and does an even-handed job of presenting their strengths and weaknesses. He is not an advocate of one at the expense of another.

Johnson and Goldsmith are treated in separate chapters. Elton maintains the Victorian commitment to *The Vicar of Wakefield* as a great novel: it is the only novel between Defoe and Burney still widely read aside from some of those by the four giants. He considers the judgment of the general reader a significant indicator of merit, though he recognizes the implications for a large number of early novelists. He chooses to limit himself to a small, representative selection and begins with three works of fantasy, *Gaudentio di Lucca*, *Peter Wilkins*, and *John Buncle* (1756–66). From them, he moves to *The Fool of Quality* and *David Simple*. The latter 'would hardly have been named so often in the literary histories but for the surname of the writer,' he claims, though he acknowledges that 'Miss Fielding has a thread of talent' (1: 241).

Elton considers Sheridan a vastly better writer. *Sidney Bidulph* has much of the tragic power of *Clarissa*; it is 'a good specimen of the dexterous fiction which can be found, and which was applauded, while the great performers were at work' (1: 244). He regrets the need to provide a long plot summary owing to the general unavailability of the text. *Nourjahad* he considers similarly successful. *Chrysal, Pompey the*

*Little* (1751), *The Man of Feeling*, and *Julia de Roubigné* are the next to join the canon of also-rans, followed by a discussion of Quixote literature beginning with *The Female Quixote*, a work Elton finds one of the weaker examples of the subgenre (he quotes Barbauld, expressing complete agreement with her evaluation). He then moves to *The Spiritual Quixote*, and Graves's *Columella* (1779) before ending his discussion of the novel with hints at how it develops in the next period, that is, in the volume he had published many years earlier.

The *Survey* for 1780–1830 has four chapters on the novel, extending beyond the limit of this study. The first is 'The Novel of Manners and Jane Austen.' Elton repeats the commonplace that the period between *A Sentimental Journey* (1768) and *Humphry Clinker* and *Sense and Sensibility* and *Waverley* was not a high point in the history of the novel, though he adds that there were a number of late-century novelists still worth reading. Most of the imitators of the four early masters produced singularly unimpressive work; Cumberland and Mackenzie provide examples. Instead, the realistic novel of manners takes a new turn as it is suddenly dominated by women writers: by Burney, Inchbald, Opie, Edgeworth, and Austen. 'For the first time in England, women are nicely depicted by their own sex, sometimes with heart and sympathy, but oftener with that cool, intimate veracity which is so salutary, but which omits so much of the essence of women as men see them. This instinct, in any case, lies near the heart of the *counter-romance*, the passion for realism, which will meet us so constantly in the age of romance, and which may be thought of as the spirit of the eighteenth century living on and asserting itself against the rebels' (1: 174). Realism is not entirely limited to women any more than its opposite, what Elton calls the 'novel of suspense' (rather than the more familiar 'novel of terror') is produced entirely by men. These forms themselves overlap considerably, most notably in their tendency towards the 'didactic and doctrinal,' their frequency of historical setting, and their increased emphasis on the natural landscape (1: 175).

Elton begins his survey of the novel of manners with *Evelina*, in which 'the gay photographic comedy of the male novelists assumes a feminine sharpness and lightness of touch.' But not too light. Elton, like many of Burney's admirers, focuses on the character sketches that so effectively avoid excess sentiment. Burney is for him, as for so many of his predecessors, 'less a novelist than a reporter, or an ideal maker of memoirs.' Her strength is in characters and manners, not plot. He finds *Cecilia* in many ways a more mature novel, but Burney's gains are balanced by the losses she suffered in succumbing to a more Johnsonian style. He considers *Camilla* inferior to both, and excludes mention of *The Wanderer* entirely.

A paragraph on Charlotte Smith describes her in phrases of the faintest praise: *The Old Manor House* 'is a not incongruous or ungraceful mixture of the story of manners and the story of suspense.' Smith's 'old once-fashionable stories are now thin and pale,' but they are 'at least recited without rhetoric' (1: 179). Elton segues from here into a lament about the decline of the 'edifying tale of real life' as it moved from the hands of Fielding and Hogarth to the 'more dubious' hands, 'or aprons,' of late-century women novelists, where it 'takes on the character of sampler-work,' that is, 'story-telling, while seasoned with more or less of wit and observation, becomes a means of preaching the reader into virtue and good sense. Fiction becomes a spinster, or elderly wedded relation, of *The Alchemist* and *The Spectator*' (1: 179). Elton's adoption of a modernist approach to showing rather than telling is not surprising, but his tying his preference so closely to gender seems strangely unsupported by his evidence.

Elton then turns to Inchbald, declaring her 'more daring, and with not a little vigour of observant wit,' despite the gross improbability of her plots. Two pages of discussion clearly indicate that he considers her one of the best of the minor novelists, and if coverage is an indicator, he prefers her novels to those of Bage, Holcroft, and Cumberland, all of whom suffer from 'the same awkward compound of theory and horse-play' (1: 183). He considers Opie, 'now little read,' to be 'undervalued' (1: 184) in a survey of all her work, not just *Adeline Mowbray*, and he has a special fondness for *A Wife's Duty* (1828). He finds Opie 'most herself when she is working out the embroilments caused by some minor vice or foible, in a witty moral tract. Her knowledge of the world is generally sufficient to make her narrative water-tight, and she excels in the slightly formal dialogue of persons of quality, ironically presented' (1: 185).

Better than any of these is Edgeworth, who warrants three pages. Elton notes her 'impulse to preach' but finds it mixed, like Addison's, with a desire 'to laugh men into good behaviour.' He is impressed by the range of her characters; she does not limit herself to 'sheep and goats,' but rather focuses especially on the middling types – her specialty. He prefers the full-length novels to the stories, since they tend to be less heavy-handed in their didacticism. *Castle Rackrent* 'reveals her larger purpose: it is to paint a portion of the Irish people as they really were, for the enlightenment of English readers' (1: 187). He respects her craft, but still more he respects her 'national service' and her creation of a new kind of fiction (1: 189). A paragraph on Edgeworth's father's friend Thomas Day reveals his sympathy with the pedagogical idealism that was central to Edgeworth's own education.

The focus on educational theory quite naturally leads Elton to Hannah More, whom he admires thoroughly as a person and as a witty opponent of radical political writers. He is, however, unable to extend his admiration to *Cœlebs in Search of a Wife*. Literature was not her vocation, nor should it have been. Elizabeth Hamilton he describes as 'a forerunner of Galt and the chroniclers of Scottish country manners,' and 'a northern sister of Mrs. Opie and her company, writing with an innocent and avowed moral purpose' (1: 190). The chapter then concludes with over ten pages on the master of the genre, Austen.

'The Novel of Suspense' is the subject of the following chapter. Elton argues that these novels are best understood in opposition to novels of manners. They return to the earliest form of prose fiction, the romance, accommodating the ever-present need for the fantastic or the supernatural. 'The perfection of that fine and feminine skill,' realism, for Elton, produces a movement in the opposite direction. Realism means 'contraction'; the novel of suspense is the novel of 'expansion': 'The windows are opened, the horizon is enlarged, the wings are fledged, and, in spite of all zigzag flights and absurdities, the earth is left behind. The writers of this group, in the nature of the case, are more unlike one another than the lively describers of manners, but they have traits in common, and some genius amongst them, and their vices are full of instruction' (1: 203). He of course begins with Walpole, acknowledging the influence of *The Castle of Otranto*, but dismissing the novel itself as 'unbearable' (1: 203).

Reeve develops the suspense tradition, though Elton is disappointed that *The Old English Baron* is merely a 'domestic tale' in disguise with its 'good boy of the didactic novel, Edmund, dispossessed of his inheritance, the wicked rival, the benevolent priest, and the sampler heroine' (1: 205). He is similarly reserved in his discussion of *The Progress of Romance*, a text he finds too ladylike and deferential as well as too programmatic in its support of romance at the expense of the novel. Elton moves from Reeve to a brief account of the Oriental tale, and a full account of his admiration for Beckford. From *Vathek* he turns to Godwin, as 'the doctrinaire succeeds the fantast' (1: 209). Elton sees in Godwin 'the makings of an artist' never quite realized because of the prior commitment to a political agenda. He respects *Caleb Williams*, but none of Godwin's other novels. A paragraph on Moore and his *Zeluco* bridges the way to Radcliffe.

Radcliffe merits but two pages from Elton, an indication of her declining status. He considers her an able story-teller with a gift for 'the rhetoric of landscape' (she was unfamiliar with the genuine landscapes she described in her novels) and for melodrama (1: 214–15); he prefers her work to the sensational novels of the late nineteenth century. But she does not emerge as significantly more important than Lewis (whose work he contemns), Shelley, or Maturin (the latter two earn his respect). Maturin, in fact, gets more than double the coverage of Radcliffe. The chapter then covers writers too late for this study before ending with Barrett, Austen, and Raspe, writers who mocked or parodied the novel of suspense.

Elton's thirty-six-page chapter on the Waverley novels indicates by coverage alone his sense of the relative value of prose fiction before Scott. He is one of the last critics of the twentieth century to evaluate Scott so highly. Wedged in the middle of this chapter is a page on the historical novel before Scott, that is, on Scott's 'scanty and futile precedents' (1: 335). The four writers he considers worthy of mention are Sophia Lee, Jane Porter, Strutt, and Cumberland. Porter is the only one of the four he is at all positive about, and even she is not credited with a contribution of the order of Edgeworth's.

The chapter on Scott is followed by 'The Other Novelists,' most of whom are too late for inclusion in this study (Elton's volume covers the period through 1830). Elton does devote over three pages on the 'lively, free-spirited' Ferrier, a writer he clearly enjoys: 'Miss Ferrier has a sense of surface absurdities hardly matched among women novelists, and though she has little subtlety, and her pure brisk English is without Miss Austen's verbal cunning, she has one point of contact with the greater artist. Both writers love to depict persons who are all surface and gesture, light and null existences, fops and praters about whom there is no more to say than what they say themselves' (1: 366). The final writer Elton mentions relevant for my study is Morgan; in just over a page he praises her development of Irish fiction after Edgeworth, making clear in the process that he does not consider her a great writer.

Elton, then, is a transitional critic, retaining much of the canon he inherited while applying a more modernist aesthetic that rejects the didacticism and doctrinaire quality he finds in so much of the fiction before Austen and Scott. Like many of his predecessors, he regards Austen and Scott as the great writers who brought the novel to new levels of sophistication and artistic excellence. His interest in much of the earlier fiction is genuine, and his taste quite broad and tolerant, but the novel of the eighteenth century remains, for him, an early stage in the development of the form and one burdened with considerable baggage that prevents it from reaching the grander heights that were yet to come.

### Émile Legouis (1861–1937) and Louis Cazamian (1877–1965)

One of the earlier and most successful general literary histories of the period is *A History of English Literature* by Émile Legouis and Louis Cazamian, the English translation of their successful 1924 French text. This history is in two volumes, breaking at the Restoration, the first by Legouis, the second by Cazamian. They share some common principles, but Cazamian's, the more important for this study, is informed by a more complex and systematic theory of literary history. The authors begin by placing themselves in relation to Taine, their major French predecessor. They find him too rigid, too much infused with what Cazamian calls 'the spirit of a dogmatic philosophy.' Legouis criticizes Taine's work for its inadequate attention to aesthetic issues. Cazamian is more interested in refining Taine's historicism; he wishes to focus not merely on 'the physical or social agents' but also, especially, on the 'moral.' This, for Cazamian, is the key to the 'development of the national mind itself.' The English national mind, he argues, reached 'full growth' during the Renaissance. His task becomes the working out of a 'genetic order' for modern literature, one that allows him to divide it into periods 'each of which really corresponds with a broad phase in the moral history of England' (vii). His secondary goal is to take into account the originality and singular qualities of each of the writers he discusses so that their individuality is not sacrificed to the grand history.

Legouis's volume contains a section on the Elizabethan novelists, Greene, Lodge, Nashe, Deloney, and Dekker. Cazamian's volume covers the period from the Restoration to 1914. The first five 'books' deal with the periods up to 1832. In the book on the Restoration (1660–1702), the chapter on Restoration prose excludes prose fiction. The chapter on 'dissident' writers includes Bunyan. The book on classicism (1702–40) has no chapter or section on the novel, though Swift and Defoe are discussed and Cazamian establishes a link between classicism and the rising middle class. 'De Foe, Steele, and Addison,' he argues, 'are psychologically connected with Richardson, in line with whom they already find themselves; and after Richardson, middle-class literature, of which they mark the advent, will gradually become one of the indirect causes of Romanticism' (116). (That sentence reveals the nature of Cazamian's historicism.)

It is in his next chapter, 'The Survival of Classicism,' that Cazamian finally turns his attention to the novel. He begins with 'the novel of sentiment.' Though the origins of the novel are in the distant past, it is only with Richardson that it appears in its mature form. That form is realistic, and its realism is driven by the nature and needs of the middle class. A realistic picture of life pushes all of the buttons dearest to the middle class audience: 'it will beget a mood of reflectiveness applied to conduct, and will tell upon the resolution to behave well; it will be animated by moralizing intentions; and in order to set these working, it will have recourse to feelings' (164). And what writer was better qualified to represent the middle class than Richardson? Cazamian sees him as coming from the Puritan tradition of Bunyan and the middle-class tradition of Defoe, Addison, and Steele. To their mix he adds the new sentimentalism, and the result is the modern novel of sentiment. Richardson's influence is 'deep and lasting,' but not in a direct or immediate line:

> His influence is mixed with a spirit rather different from his in the work of the sister of his great rival, Sarah Fielding, whose *David Simple* is the naïve and moralizing account, at once realistic and emotional, of the journey of an upright soul through life. The *Peter Wilkins* of Robert Paltock inclines sentimentalism strangely in the direction of a fanciful liberty of imagination.
>
> With brilliant success the novel of Goldsmith, *The Vicar of Wakefield*, renews the inspiration of sentiment, by bringing it nearer to the average human being, and by delivering it from a Puritan tension against which many temperaments will remain rebellious. (168–9)

From Goldsmith, the sentimental novel reaches its limit in Sterne, the writer who liberated it from its ethical origin and thus pointed the way to Romanticism.

Cazamian's next chapter turns to realism proper, and to Fielding and Smollett. The relationship between realism and sentiment is not antithetical for him. Rather, Fielding's realism integrates Richardson's extreme sentiment into a 'more normal and sound' middle-class spirit, a moderation that makes Fielding rather than Richardson truly representative and 'one of the most profoundly national' English writers (175). Smollett goes too far the other way and serves Cazamian as Richardson's opposite. These are the only seven novelists Cazamian includes from his late classical period.

Book 4 covers 'The Pre-Romantic Period' (1770–98) and includes a chapter on the pre-Romantic novel. The obvious focal point for this chapter is 'the novel of terror,' and the obvious approach, given Cazamian's characterization of the period, is to look for its contributions to the development of Romanticism. It was the novel, he argues, that first allowed 'all the latent possibilities of the coming Romantic revival to combine in a union so complete, that it would be difficult not to recognize in it an immediate forerunner and a fully developed example of Romantic literature.' Radcliffe's novels represent the realization of early Romanticism, however 'inferior both in the moral substance and in the artistic value of the contents.' Cazamian offers the following explanation for why Radcliffe's novel of terror worked:

The reason is that it adds to the elements already in evidence a new resource of inspiration rich in powerful and subtle effects; the search for terror and, on a wider scale, the probing of the mysterious. And here we have a case of natural sequence in moral evolution. A feeling of wonder mingled with terror provides a new thrill which, in reality, owes its origin to the cultivation of certain other emotions; the need for it is naturally created by the merging of sentimentalism and fancy. The basis for the novel of terror is a mood in which the power of imagining is brought to bear most closely on that feeling, after the latter has been led by frequent exercise to crave for refined satisfaction. (224)

Cazamian's is the most thoughtful account of the Gothic in some time, and he values it more highly than virtually any critic since Dunlop. Victorian realism no longer dominates the criticism of the 1920s in the way it had done a generation earlier. Cazamian is able to get past the Victorians to value the Gothic for its contribution to the Romanticism he so clearly treasures.

Having made the case for the importance of the novel of terror, he seeks its origins, finding them in Mackenzie, Walpole, and Reeve. Mackenzie is the surprise here, but Cazamian argues that the intense cultivation of feeling, especially suffering, exemplified by *The Man of Feeling*, prepares the way for the more creative, original, and sensational use of feeling Walpole first attempted in *The Castle of Otranto*. Mackenzie, himself a singularly unoriginal writer, was largely writing in the Richardsonian tradition, heavily influenced by Sterne (a Richardsonian, too); his extension of sentimentalism, however, points the way to the new manipulation of feeling so triumphant in Radcliffe. Walpole's contribution was of imme-diate importance, enabling others to develop an important line of the English novel. But Cazamian finds *The Castle of Otranto* a 'lifeless' work of little artistic value. He considers the 'decidedly mediocre' *The Old English Baron* a more important book, because Reeve brought to the Gothic a solid, Richardsonian, middle-class sensibility. This enabled the new form to 'strike root in great general needs of the soul, which con-science accepts, or regards as normal and necessary for its well-being. Then only does it take its legitimate place among the recognised literary kinds' (226).

Cazamian ends this chapter with three pages on Radcliffe and Lewis. He notes that Radcliffe's name is now 'as good as forgotten' (226) and attributes the decline in her reputation to her long and repetitive novels; her conventional, uninteresting characters (except Schedoni in *The Ital-ian*); and her insistence on explaining away the supernatural. Yet he still admires her 'feeling for nature' and the wonderful descriptive passages it enables in her work (228). Lewis, on the other hand, fed only the 'dark-est aspect of Romanticism' with his Satanism; Cazamian has nothing to offer in defence of his many artistic deficiencies and lack of 'all moral depth' (229).

Cazamian's following chapter, on the 'Classical Temperaments' in the pre-Romantic period, also includes a section on the novel. Here he turns to writers whose work remains under the influence of classicism, that is, those who resisted the force of the paradigm shift to Romanticism. His examples are Burney and Austen. He sees Burney as developing her own distinctive version of the novel from Richardson, Fielding, Smollett, and Sterne. Elements of each of the early masters are evident in her work. Burney brings spontaneity and a 'fresh new touch' to the novel with *Evelina*. Cazamian praises the powers of observation and judgment that are revealed so effectively in 'satire and realism,' Burney's preferred modes of expression. He also sees in her work the 'first tentative revela-tion of the feminine self in the novel, if we leave aside the bold freedom of a Mrs. Behn or a Mrs. Manley' (242). Cazamian considers *Cecilia* a more polished but less fresh and lively novel; he also, of course, consid-ers Austen the greater writer.

His next chapter is 'The French Revolution and English Literature,' and it includes a short section on the novelists. Godwin is the most forceful and successful of the lot, the only one to be mentioned in the text. He describes the others as overly propagandistic or didactic, citing Holcroft, Smith, Bage, Inchbald, Opie, and Edgeworth in footnotes (he notes that Edgeworth is not a perfect fit here, and that she earned considerable importance by paving the way to Scott). The final book relevant to this study is 'The Romantic Period.' It includes a long section on Scott which includes brief references to Edgeworth and Shelley.

Cazamian is also something of a transitional figure. He retains a number of the commonplaces from the earlier historians while softening the theoretical determinism of Taine (though remaining far more committed to a theoretical methodology than his contemporary English critics). His canon is highly selective, and he looks to aesthetic judgment for the last word in evaluation. Inclusion in his history, however, remains strongly influenced by originality and influence. R.S. Crane noted that 1660–1800 was not the period most familiar to Cazamian, while granting that he still 'knows it far better than many specialists.' He considered Cazamian's 'the most satisfactory synthesis of the period that has yet appeared' (1: 95).

## Chambers Revised

Among the more popular histories in this period is the last edition of *Chambers's Cyclopædia of English Literature*, now subtitled *A History Critical and Biographical of Authors in the English Tongue from the Earliest Times Till the Present Day with Specimens of their Writing*, a 1925–7 revision by J. Liddell Geddie (b. 1881) of the 1901 edition by David Patrick (1849–1914). The *Cyclopædia* has been expanded to three volumes; it includes a far larger number of early writers, especially medieval writers; it incorporates articles on writers who appeared after the original edition; the entries have been rewritten by a range of critics, largely specialists in specific periods and genres; and the structure is now by author rather than genre. Lost entirely is Chambers's narrative of the history of the novel in favour of more traditional, encyclopedia-style entries arranged by author. While far more inclusive than the original, the new *Chambers* is also far less interesting as a literary history or as an attempt at canon formation. Entries range from twenty-three pages with many specimens (Swift) to brief paragraphs without specimens (Sarah Fielding). Medieval and Renaissance romances receive more attention than they did in the first edition. In volume 1, which covers literature through the Restoration, the only woman writer of prose fiction mentioned is Newcastle.

Behn is the first novelist in volume 2, the volume on the eighteenth century. She is now 'the female Wycherley,' as well as 'the first English professional authoress.' Best known as a playwright, Behn's novels are also considered of interest and of similarly questionable propriety. Two are mentioned by name, *Oroonoko*, her best, and *The Nun* (1689), a story with 'a clever satire on town-fops' (68). Scott's anecdote about Mrs Keith of Ravelston is recounted, and Swinburne's comment about Behn and *Oroonoko* endorsed: 'This improper woman of genius was the first literary abolitionist – the first champion of the slave on record in the history of fiction.' 'Thus Mrs Behn,' the writer continues, 'is brought into strange companionship with Mrs Beecher Stowe' (69).

Another forty-four novelists follow in this volume, nineteen of whom are women. Carruthers's take on Manley is repeated; she was a celebrity in her time, but 'neither her life nor writings will bear a close scrutiny.' She was best known during her lifetime for the *New Atalantis*. 'All her works, however, have sunk into oblivion. Her novels are worthless, extravagant productions' (96–7). Defoe is credited with being 'the father of Richardson and partly of Fielding.' The full range of his novels is mentioned, and *Moll Flanders* (1722) and *A Journal of the Plague Year* (1722) are described respectively as 'a marvel of the novelistic art' and 'a fresh masterpiece of verisimilitude' (151). Richardson and Fielding each have full entries with minimal evaluation. Sarah Fielding is described as a novelist eminent in her lifetime; Richardson's view of her as having 'a more perfect knowledge of the human heart than her great brother' (417) is dismissed with contempt. No specimen is provided. Lennox is given a longer paragraph and a specimen with no evaluation. Reeve, like Fielding, has a single paragraph and no specimen. She fails to retain the modest prominence given her by Chambers, though *The Old English Baron* continues to 'assure her a place in the history of the Romantic movement in our literature; she was Mrs Radcliffe's literary godmother' (420). None of Reeve's other novels are deemed worthy of attention.

Chambers's successors are far more attentive to novelists of the end of the eighteenth century. Hannah More's *Cœlebs* receives fuller coverage than it did in the original; its 'fine vein of delicate irony and sarcasm' (577) is noted, but the original judgment that it is too didactic is endorsed. Inchbald has a full biographical entry with specimens, though only the briefest mention is made of her novels. The entry on Burney retains Chambers's sentences of high praise and his overall evaluation of her novels, without his enthusiasm for her letters and diaries. Despite the generous provision of specimens, the entry fails to convey the sense of genuine appreciation so prominent in the original. Smith is no longer seen as the novelist to break the dominance of the Minervas; her sympathy for the French Revolution is noted as problematic, but a problem overcome in her best novel, *The Old Manor House*. The entry on Radcliffe is more positive but again lacks the enthusiasm of Chambers's original. Like so many of the entries, it has no new critical views to add; the emphasis instead is on accurate biographical summary and judicious quotation from the best authorities, in this case Scott and Raleigh.

The new edition repeats in reduced form Chambers's appreciation of Opie's strengths as a novelist as well as his critique from the perspective of 'the more masculine temper of our modern literature' (598). Chambers's view of the Lees is similarly retained. Wollstonecraft's *The Rights of Woman* (1792) is 'a work of genius' (706), but her novels rate only the barest mention and no specimens are provided (the first such example since Reeve). The entry on Edgeworth offers a severe revision of the earlier assessments of Chambers and Carruthers. Scott's praise is declared 'extravagant,' though Turgenev's acknowledgment of her influence is duly noted. The summary judgment is balanced and favourable for a writer no longer considered of the first importance: 'Her novels are doubtless too didactic; the plots may be poor, the *dramatis personæ* sometimes wooden; but for wit and pathos, for lively dialogue and simple directness, for bright vivacity and healthy realism, and for their vivid presentation of their times … they well deserve still to be read' (735). Brunton, too, is downgraded, and denied a specimen, but the Porters are given more equal treatment; Chambers's high opinion of Anna Maria is balanced by an equally high regard for Jane, perhaps the favourite of the revisers. The new focus is on *The Scottish Chiefs*, which gets more attention than *Thaddeus of Warsaw*. Lady Morgan is reassessed in a way that does little to change her status, but with time and distance, her 'strength' is found 'in describing the broad characteristics of her nation, their boundless mirth, their old customs, their love of frolic, and their wild grief under calamity or in bewailing the death of friends and neighbours' (781). Chambers's appreciation of Elizabeth Hamilton remains much as in the original. An entry on Susan Ferrier is added to volume 3, and the entry on Austen has been expanded in testimony of the accuracy of Chambers's original estimation of her importance.

## Albert C. Baugh (1891–1981)

The most important one-volume history in this period is *A Literary History of England* (1948), edited by Albert C. Baugh. It was conceived and largely written in the early years of the Second World War, though the war delayed its publication until 1948. Intended for 'mature students' as well as 'cultivated readers,' the volume is divided chronologically into five parts, each written by an expert in the literature of the period. The first two parts, on literature in Old and Middle English, by Kemp Malone (1889–1971) and Baugh, survey the early romances. Tucker Brooke's (1883–1946) section on the Renaissance includes two chapters on prose fiction. The first, 'Lyly and His Predecessors,' covers jest books, Bullein, Painter, Fenton, Pettie, Grange, Melbancke, Gascoigne, and Lyly. The second, 'Greene and His Followers,' covers Greene, Rowlands, Chettle, Riche, Dickenson, Lodge, Forde [*sic*], Dekker, Nashe, and Deloney. Sidney is given a chapter of his own. The comprehensiveness of the coverage of early English fiction is indicative of the kind of literary history Baugh and his colleagues provide.

The central section of their *History* for this study is George Sherburn's (1884–1962) on the Restoration and eighteenth century. Sherburn dedicates three chapters to prose fiction, as well as making additional references in discussions of authors singled out for extensive treatment. 'Types of Prose Fiction' is the chapter on the novel in the Restoration. He begins with the French romances, emphasizing their enormous popularity, before moving to the English romances of John Reynolds, Crowne, Boyle, Sir George Mackenzie, Newcastle, and Ingelo. He is dismissive of all of them, considering them inferior to Continental models which are themselves not worthy of imitation. Another Continental form imitated by English writers was the fictitious letter. The writers he mentions in this group include Newcastle (for her 'curious' *CCXI Sociable Letters*), Charles Gildon, Tom Brown, several translations, and, as examples of 'English genius,' Behn's *Love Letters* (1684) and Manley's *Letters* (1696). Sherburn is critical of the form for 'making love lurid rather than tender' and for its mixture of 'at times a sentimental tone and at times the cynical mood of Restoration gentlefolk' (795–6), but he recognizes its English masters.

Sherburn proceeds to the rogue literature of the Restoration ('less depraved but equally bleak' [796]) before concluding with over six pages on Bunyan, an introduction to the late-century 'novel,' a 'type of short story' (802), and two pages on 'the most praised and condemned single writer of such novels,' Behn. Sherburn notes her successful confusion of biography and fiction in these stories, a confusion that aided their popularity. He describes the stories as 'lively intrigues – chiefly amorous – handled without too much tact or care, but still lively and interesting' (803–4). Behn's rather off-handed gestures towards authenticity 'achieve an admirable illusion of reality, though she clearly has no high sense of duty to truthfulness or even to plausibility, unless one compares her work with the supernatural episodes of romance.' Sherburn notes that with the exception of Agnes de Castro and Oroonoko her protagonists are not sympathetic, but he considers *Oroonoko* both impressive and important: 'It is easy to point out flaws in this brief tragic romance, but Mrs. Behn by some accident of genius has made real for us the noble aborigine as no one else had done. It is a great achievement in a period in which idealized persons are practically always artificial. It makes one realize that while the prose fiction of the Restoration is as a whole neither important nor greatly significant, a period that produced masterpieces as diverse as those of the righteous Bunyan and the unrighteous Mrs. Behn has much to its credit' (805). Sherburn is clearly not an unqualified Behnite, but he is far more receptive than most if not all of the historians of the previous 150 years. Some of the credit for his more receptive response should no doubt go to the critics who had presented her as a writer worthy of serious consideration (see, for example, Baker, *Novels*, Sackville-West, and Summers).

The section on the first half of the eighteenth century includes chapters on Defoe and journalism, on Swift, and on the essay before Sherburn reaches his chapter on the mid-century novel. His approach is very much at one with the twentieth-century emphasis on the great masters. His thesis is that there were 'three great novelists who permanently modified the art of English fiction: of these Richardson dilated the short story or "novel," as it was called before his day, by means of psychological or sentimental detail; Fielding added structure, style, and a realistic attitude toward life; and Smollett excelled in the invention and crisp presentation of unforgettably vivid burlesque episode' (950).

Two paragraphs in this chapter summarize the predecessors of these masters and their contributions. They include Defoe and other writers of fictional biography and autobiography; Manley, Haywood and the 'scandal chronicle'; and Continental fiction, from the romances of Scudéry to the comic fiction of Marivaux and the sentimental fiction of Prévost. The scandal chronicles are daring if limited in interest; Manley is the master of this minor genre. Haywood 'learned much from her betters' and produced better novels later in life, if 'verging towards pathos and melodrama' (951). Sherburn's account of the novel is so selective that no other novelist is mentioned in this chapter, male or female.

Sherburn's third chapter on the novel takes it from 1760 to 1789. (He has separate chapters on Johnson and Goldsmith, including their prose fiction.) The popularity of the new novel attracted many imitators, and with time led to new developments: 'The function of the novel remained the study of man and his manners and morals. The most notable developments are those due to emphasis on the emotions or sentiments of men – and of women! – rather than on their rational endowments' (1021). Sherburn sees the novels of this period as focused on sentiment or manners; in either case he finds an emphasis on universal qualities· rather than individual idiosyncrasies. This did not preclude experimenting with structure or introducing exotic or more poetic settings, and it occurred at a time when a 'surprising number' of novelists were women. With women novelists, Sherburn argues, came 'the incurably sentimental tone of most novels of this period.' He mentions eight examples, dividing them into two groups: Lennox, Scott, Frances Sheridan, and Brooke; Griffith, Reeve, Smith, and Inchbald. What distinguishes the groups is that the second is 'somewhat too sentimental for long popularity' (1022), but no explanation is offered for this assertion. The paragraph on these women is followed by four pages on Sterne, one on Mackenzie, and one on Henry Brooke. This survey of the novelists of sentiment is extended to the early Gothic romances and Oriental tales; Walpole gets a page; Hawkesworth, Frances Sheridan, Johnstone, Bage, and Johnson share a paragraph; and Beckford is granted a paragraph of his own.

Sherburn concludes with novels of manners, novels that 'escaped the drug of sentimentalism, and preserved, if not a high sense of human comedy, at least a satiric attitude.' They remained, much to his delight, the dominant form in the period. He notes *Betsy Thoughtless* and Sarah Fielding's *Countess of Dellwyn* (1759) as novels able to 'maintain a generally critical attitude towards female difficulties and dangers.' He also notes the more picaresque satires of Coventry, Johnstone, Lennox, Graves, and Amory, all authors of rather old-fashioned novels, before turning to the best writer of 'true comedy' in the period, Burney (1031). The chapter ends with three pages on her. Sherburn considers Burney fortunate to have published *Evelina* 'at an auspicious moment when little or no coolly decorous and elegant fiction – in contrast to sentimental ardors – was being produced' (1032). He takes special pleasure in the comic characters, and seems especially approving that she 'forgets "universality" in the face of an original character' (1033). Sherburn considers Burney's mastery of the epistolary novel surpassed only by Smollett's in *Humphry Clinker*. He also admires *Cecilia*, which he finds more melodramatic and sentimental but 'equally thrilling' and more dramatic. Burney's final two novels, however, sacrifice story and character to social instruction; they read like tedious courtesy books. But her early triumphs had opened up a new

form of the novel, one that 'through manipulation of accidental misun-
derstanding or unseasonable coincidence, delineated "female difficulties"
thrillingly' (1034). Finally, this form was crucial in preparing the way for
Austen. Sherburn is clearly out of sympathy with the kinds of fiction
most women wrote in the mid-to-late eighteenth century. Burney is
important for him for breaking that mould and opening up alternatives
he considers far superior to those favoured in the generation before her.

The period from 1789 to the time of Austen is covered by Samuel
Chew (1886–1960). The important chapter for this study is 'Gothic
Romance and the Novel of Doctrine.' Chew offers this polarity as a way
to characterize the novel for the first twenty or so years after the beginning of the French Revolution, only to observe that few novelists in this
period respected generic boundaries. Rather, 'fiction at this time seems
to be at once sentimental, doctrinal, historical, and Gothic.' Chew considers the 'flood of extravagant fiction' (1192) to have been stimulated by
the late-century discovery of German literature, as well as by early British experiments in both terror and historical Gothic. For Chew, the key
players for the development of the historical novel are the Lees and Jane
Porter, the latter the better historian though 'lifeless' as a novelist (1193).
His paragraph on Smith presents her as the typical novelist of the period
in terms of combining material from different novelistic genres, adding
Gothic trappings to the domestic novel, mixing sentiment with satire,
and each with radical and philosophic doctrine.

Chew's page on Radcliffe offers a balanced if deflated view of her
achievement and status, reflecting the general decline in her reputation
through most of the twentieth century. He focuses on Radcliffe's descriptive powers and her ability to achieve effects of terror through them, and
he also notes the anti-Catholic, anti-sacerdotal bias that informs her villains. Her well-known avoidance of the supernatural leads to the following summary: 'A basic rationalism forbade her to do more than touch
the marvelous. The compromise adopted is never quite satisfactory, for
her mysteries are often held so long in suspense that the rational explanations, when they come, fail to satisfy a curiosity which is no longer
alert. It was beyond her ability, and aside from her purpose, to people
her stage with convincing human beings; the dialogue put into the
mouth of her characters is of a stiltedness that must be sampled to be
imagined. But there is no denying the effectiveness of her tenebrous
landscapes and atmosphere' (1194). Chew ends his survey of the Gothic
with Lewis, Shelley, and Maturin. *Frankenstein*, he observes, is the only
novel of terror from this period that still commands a readership. He is

aware of the multitude of minor imitators, but sees no need to descend into these 'noisome fastnesses' (1196). Chew's pattern, like Sherburn's, is to focus on important writers only. Like Sherburn, he covers the second-rate, but he too is reluctant to waste space on anything he considers more minor.

Chew concludes this chapter with just over a page on the novel of doctrine and a page on Edgeworth. The novel of doctrine is traced back to Rousseau, Henry Brooke, and Thomas Day, and its three important exponents are Inchbald, Bage, and Godwin, each of whom is allotted a paragraph. All three novelists score points as social critics, but they are less adept as novelists. *Caleb Williams* is the only novel of doctrine he considers successful as a novel.

The anti-didactic bias of most twentieth-century critics strongly informs the evaluative criticism of both Sherburn and Chew. The page Chew devotes to Edgeworth is indicative of his judgment that she was able to harness her didacticism far more effectively than most of her contemporaries. She is, in other words, sufficiently closer to Austen and Scott to deserve higher praise, especially for *Castle Rackrent* and *The Absentee*. She also falls too short of them, largely because of her excessive didacticism, to be considered in their league. Each merits a dedicated chapter, an honorific reserved only for the most important writers in the entire volume. When Chew returns to the novel, it is to the novel after Scott, though brief mention is made of Hogg, Galt, and Ferrier among the list of second-rate Scottish novelists.

### William J. Entwistle (1895–1952) and Eric Gillett (1893–1978)

A very different kind of history from Baugh's is represented by William J. Entwistle and Eric Gillett's *The Literature of England A.D. 500–1942: A Survey of British Literature from the Beginnings to the Present Day*, the second edition of which appeared the same year as Baugh's history (the first edition, 1943, was updated to include the most contemporary literature). Entwistle and Gillett provide a small, 300-page volume, aimed at British and foreign general readers who seek an accessible overview. Their method is to introduce earlier literature from a self-consciously contemporary point of view. Roughly half the volume covers the literature from the beginning through the Victorians. This part of the survey is by Entwistle.

The early chapters mention prose fiction by Sidney, Lyly, and Bunyan. The chapter 'Augustan Prose' presents Defoe, Addison, and Swift as the important precursors of the novel, a form that first appears with Richardson. Entwistle credits Richardson with 'some curious divination of feminine psychology' that allowed him 'to follow the emotions of his heroine in more subtle detail than had ever been done; perhaps in more subtle detail than anyone since has achieved.' But Richardson's weaknesses outweigh his strengths: he is unable to create a 'corresponding' male character; 'there is a wealth of sentiment with but little real life in his writing'; 'there is a conventional, calculating element in Pamela's too conspicuous virtue that offended the spirit of a far greater writer, Henry Fielding.' Fielding is credited with saving the novel from 'degenerating into a new kind of sentimental romance' (92).

Entwistle sees the next hundred years of novels as either following Richardson or Fielding, 'either psychological with a minimum of happenings, or primarily representational' (93). There is no union until George Eliot. Neither Smollett nor Sterne is as good as the first two masters of the novel. Johnson and Goldsmith each get a sentence as novelists; Goldsmith's is positive. The Gothic 'craze' exemplified by Walpole is soon eclipsed by Scott (97). The Oriental 'extravagance' of Beckford is interesting as a precursor of Romanticism, but not as a contribution to the novel. No other novelist warrants a mention before Austen and Scott; from them, Entwistle moves to the Victorians, 'the Golden Age of the English Novel' (131). Entwistle's, then, is the most highly selective history to date, and one which reveals a common approach at mid-century: The novel does not reach maturity until the Victorians, so there is little point wasting much time on what came before. He is presenting a guide for general readers, and his message is that they should not read many early novels. One corollary is that not a single novel by a woman before Austen is worthy of his readers' attention.

### Histories of the Novel

### Robert Morss Lovett (1870–1956) and Helen Sard Hughes (1882–1955)

One of the most influential one-volume histories of the novel was Robert Morss Lovett and Helen Sard Hughes's *The History of the Novel in England* (1932). The focus in this volume, unlike that in Lovett's earlier collaboration with William Vaughn Moody, is on 'the relation of the novel to the interests and attitudes of successive ages,' a focus that encourages the inclusion of 'many minor novelists' (iii). What is noteworthy is that Lovett and Hughes feel the need to justify the inclusion of minor writers in a history of the novel. They expand Moody's focus on plot, character, and realism to a much broader, three-part methodology: 'A novel, then, is to be approached, first, historically, as a social document; second, technically, as a work of conscious art, the result of workmanlike manipulation of the technical element of his story in accordance with the author's special purpose, artistic or moral; and third, personally, as a record, conscious or unconscious, of the author's experience, and of his reaction to it' (2). That reaction will determine the quality of the work and provide a key to the genius of the author. They argue that by applying their method, 'the objective reader may watch the English novel grow in power and complexity century after century' (2–3). The novel arrived as a form with 'artistic dignity' (3) in the eighteenth century, after earlier experimentation, and that dignity was the precondition for the far greater triumphs of the one which followed.

Lovett and Hughes begin with Elizabethan fiction. They find that it divides into three kinds: romance (Sidney, Lodge, Greene), prototypes of the novel of manners (Lyly), and the picaresque (Nashe). They argue that the oft-neglected fiction of the seventeenth century provided new forms that would contribute significantly to the development of the novel: character writing (Hall, Overbury, Earle); heroic romance, first in translations from the French and then the English imitations (Boyle); and *histoire véritable* ('which employed characters and incidents of past epochs, to be sure, but with all the psychological realism of which the author was capable' [23]) via Lafayette and native 'secret histories.' The first important novelist of the seventeenth century is Behn. Lovett and Hughes focus primarily on the heroic *Oroonoko*, but they also recognize Behn's other short fiction with its 'scenes and characters' of 'ordinary life,' its realistic presentation in the manner of the Italian *novelle*, and its stories of 'crossed love' in the manner of the French and Spanish, such as Cervantes' *Exemplary Novels* (24). They rightly debunk the claims for *Oroonoko* as the prototype for *Uncle Tom's Cabin*, instead seeing Behn (and Congreve) as promoters of a more realistic prose fiction. If *Oroonoko* anticipates later fiction, it is much more the early verisimilitude of Defoe.

Manley is presented as a follower of Behn who, to Behn's love novels, added the new element of the application of characters and events to prominent people in the England of her day. The resulting scandal chronicles are decadent representations of a corrupt society, hardly a formula for great art. But they were very popular and highly influential; their influence includes the backlash and subsequent demand for didacticism in the novel exemplified by the *Spectator*. Lovett and Hughes end their chapter on the seventeenth century with two more developments towards realistic fiction: the work of Bunyan and the continuation of the picaresque narrative by the likes of Head and Kirkman.

The novel for Lovett and Hughes is not an eighteenth-century invention, but it is only with the twin developments of English prose and of a reading public that it reaches maturity. The important figures in these 'sudden' developments are Defoe, Richardson, and Fielding (36). They were able to respond to the new reading public in ways that met its religious, moral and social needs and demands by representing the 'vices and virtues of the average man, the dangers that beset him and his sons, and especially his daughters; together with the opportunities which might reward his benevolence and industry' (38–9). Journalists and satirists, notably Swift, responded to many of these same needs, but it is with Defoe that the novel first fully responds, and he, consequently, is for Lovett and Hughes the first great English novelist. Their account of Defoe is followed by a brief discussion of the minor novelists published between Defoe and Richardson. The most important of these is Haywood, whose career is traced in three parts: Behn-like romances, followed by Manley-like scandal chronicles, followed by Richardson-like novels, the last being her best works of fiction. Haywood moved with the times, and was successful in whatever form pleased her public. This chapter concludes with a one-sentence reference to other women novelists (only Barker and Aubin are mentioned by name); their importance lies in 'blazing a trail for Fanny Burney and Jane Austen, and slowly winning the rights and privileges by which modern women novelists have so ably profited' (51).

The next chapter focuses on the novel at mid-century, and primarily on Richardson and Fielding. Lovett and Hughes are far more even-handed than Moody and Lovett in dealing with them. They are both seen as moralists eager to reform the novel, but they differ in tactics. Richardson focuses on models of virtue for emulation, Fielding on models of vice for avoidance. The chapter ends with an extensive discussion of Hogarth as an artist who combined the methods of the two. The next chapter is on Smollett and Sterne, 'a step down' (76), but the best of their contemporaries. Each receives full treatment, while a number of minor writers – Coventry, Johnstone, George Brewer, Lennox, Graves, Paltock, and Amory – are merely mentioned in passing.

The following chapter, 'The New Romantic Fiction,' moves on to fiction written in response to changes in society as well as in literary taste. An extended section on the influence of French fiction is followed by a discussion of a number of women novelists. Lovett and Hughes devote a lengthy paragraph to Sarah Fielding, a short one to Frances Sheridan, and two long paragraphs to Frances Brooke; their accounts of each are largely descriptive, yet the extent of each discussion implies evaluative judgment. They then acknowledge that 'many other women novelists of less individual distinction were simultaneously writing novels of domestic manners or romantic adventure. These works are touched, in different proportions, with Richardson's morality, the psychology of Marivaux, and the sensibility of Rousseau and Prévost' (102). The two who warrant mention by name are Sarah Scott and Elizabeth Griffith.

Lovett and Hughes see the Gothic novel as part of the 'sentimental movement,' a response to the realism of Richardson and Fielding (103). It was also a sign of renewed interest in pre-modern history. They cite Leland's *Longsword* as an early fictional pioneer before moving on to Walpole and the Gothic proper. They consider *The Castle of Otranto* of enormous importance in the history of the novel, the first in a line of novels continued by Reeve, Sophia Lee, Radcliffe, Lewis, and many more. Two paragraphs on *The Old English Baron* concentrate largely on its divergence from Walpole's model in favour of one in which events have rational explanations, the model developed soon after by Radcliffe. Sophia Lee is seen more as a follower of Prévost than Walpole in creating *The Recess*, a tale of 'thrilling adventure and all-pervading sentiment' (114). They agree with those who consider Harriet Lee's 'Kruitzner' (in *Canterbury Tales*) as containing the prototype for the Byronic hero. They note Charlotte Smith's combination of revolutionary politics, Gothic landscapes, and French sensibility before moving to 'the most famous and influential of the writers of Gothic romance,' Radcliffe (116). Five pages are devoted to summarizing her work; the pattern of offering minimal evaluation continues, though they make it clear that they prefer *The Italian* among her novels. The section on the Gothic ends with Lewis, and the chapter concludes with a discussion of the Oriental tale, which Lovett and Hughes see as a cousin of the Gothic romance, both being 'vehicles of the romantic escape' (122). The Oriental tale is traced to its French sources, the heroic romances and, especially, the *Arabian Nights*. The English tale comes in two versions, the moral apologue exemplified by *Rasselas* and the *conte philosophique* exemplified by *Vathek*. Each is described in detail, and as the chapter closes mention is made of three other Oriental tales: Hawkesworth's *Almoran and Hamet*, John Langhorne's *Solyman and Almena* (1762), and Sheridan's *Nourjahad*.

Lovett and Hughes's final chapter covering the period of this study is 'The Fiction of the Revolutionary Era.' They see the writers of this period responding to new philosophies, particularly Rousseau's, to the extent that the realistic portrayal of plot and character that defined the work of Richardson and Fielding was sacrificed for 'the popularization of theories – social, political, and educational – the novel seemed an instrument delivered providentially into the hands of the propagandist – and little more.' They further divide the novels of theory into those of 'benevolent feeling' and those of 'purpose' (134). The model for the novelist of feeling is, of course, Mackenzie. The novel of educational purpose finds its model in Day's *Sandford and Merton*. Other prominent examples are Henry Brooke's *The Fool of Quality* and Inchbald's *Nature and Art*. The political novel of purpose promotes the ideas behind the French Revolution; its greatest example is *Caleb Williams*. Other prominent examples include Godwin's other novels, the novels of Bage and Holcroft, and the more minor contributions of Opie, Smith, and Wollstonecraft (one of the relatively rare acknowledgments of her work as a novelist). Lovett and Hughes consider the importance of Wollstonecraft's two novels to be largely biographical.

The chapter ends with a return to the novels of manners written during this period of the dominance of the newer forms. The best known of these is Goldsmith's 'masterpiece' (152) *The Vicar of Wakefield* (though published earlier than any of the other novels in the chapter, Lovett and Hughes include it here as 'a sentimental novel of reform' [154]). 'Most distinguished among the exponents of the novel of manners at the end of the eighteenth century was Fanny Burney,' who unites the strains of Richardson and Fielding (155). Their approach to Burney is by now standard: the youthful *Evelina* and the more complex *Cecilia* are the great novels; *Camilla*, perhaps because of Johnson's influence, seems an 'incredibly stilted novel of feeling' (160), and *The Wanderer* is 'an even greater artistic failure' (161). The late eighteenth century is not, for Lovett and Hughes any more than for most of their predecessors, a period of great fiction. They do, however, consider it important for providing the ideas and methods that would be put to use more effectively and with greater genius in the following century.

The chapter on the early nineteenth century is largely devoted to Austen and Scott, the major representatives of the realistic and Romantic novels written at the end of the eighteenth century. They also discuss Edgeworth, seeing her as developing both the realistic and the Romantic strains, as well as the novel of reform. *Castle Rackrent* and *The Absentee* are singled out for special attention, 'but it is as a recognized pioneer in more than one field that she deserves a place in the history of fiction' (182). Other, minor novelists who earn at least a mention in this chapter are Jane Porter (as an early exponent of the historical novel); Ferrier (a realistic Scott, influenced by Burney and Edgeworth); Galt, Maturin, and Shelley (important historically for *Frankenstein*, but weak and naïve as an artist).

## Ernest Baker (1869–1941)

The major history of the novel of the last century was Ernest Baker's ten-volume *The History of the English Novel* (1924–39). It remains the most comprehensive account of the English novel ever written, and a standard reference work in most libraries. Baker has never had a reputation as an important literary critic, but as a reader and promoter of the novel, and one committed to evaluative criticism, he has few equals. To be excluded from Baker's *History* speaks volumes about the reputation of any work of prose fiction. And while Baker is comprehensive in covering the novel, he always offers his view of the importance of any work he discusses.

Baker considers the modern novel an eighteenth-century invention. It is only with Richardson and Fielding that the form reaches its maturity as 'a prose story, picturing real life, or something corresponding thereto, and having the unity and coherence due to a plot or scheme of some kind or to a definite intention or attitude of mind on the part of the author' (1: 11). A history of the novel, for Baker, however, does not begin with the mature form. Rather, he traces the evolution of the form from its originary precursors (the Darwinian metaphor is Baker's own). He believes that prose fiction evolves in cycles associated with times of decadence. Decadence, for him, follows a period of 'imaginative creativeness,' a period of high achievement in poetry. The novel is more the product of 'intellect' and 'reason,' appearing after a burst of creativity. (It is hardly surprising that Baker has not made much impact as a theorist of the novel.) This evolutionary theory determines Baker's approach to many of the texts he discusses, and he develops it at great length. Most of that narrative is marginal for this study.

English fiction (as opposed to the novel), begins, for Baker, with medieval translations from the French. Little significant development occurs until the Elizabethans. Baker credits Malory with bringing the Romance to an end. What follows, in a period dominated by fine poetry and drama, is influential experimentation in prose, largely without lasting impact. The only 'classic' is *The Pilgrim's Progress*. Even the next-best works, *Euphues* and the *Arcadia*, 'cannot be graced with that dignity' (2: 11). Experimentation at this time also brought in early realism, particularly in the form of rogue narratives and fictional biographies and autobiographies. The important figures are Nashe, Greene, and Deloney; Baker's preference is for Deloney as a writer who represented a more normal, less sordid range of experience. He continues to trace forms free from a clear sense of the divide between fact and fiction: the essay, the character, and the utopian narrative. The discussion of the latter includes reference to Newcastle.

Baker's third volume begins with his 'tentative' definition of the novel as 'the interpretation of human life by means of fictitious narrative in prose.' He points out that the fictions covered in the first two volumes are 'defective as stories or as interpretations of life' (3: 5). This volume deals with writers who come much closer to realizing the novel. It was during the seventeenth century that it became possible to make a living writing fiction, and different kinds of fiction were demanded by increasingly diverse groups of readers. Popular romances retained their audience, as did imitations of Sidney (Lady Mary Wroth earns a mention here). Religious allegory had its market throughout the century. A new form with a significant impact was the heroic romance, and Baker devotes considerable attention to d'Urfé, Gomberville, La Calprenède, and Scudéry, along with their English imitators (Barclay, Ingelo, Orrery, Newcastle, Mackenzie) and translators (including Katherine Philips). Restoration comedy developed alongside the heroic romance; Baker considers it an important influence on prose fiction. Congreve pointed the way in his plays (not in *Incognita*): 'Only a genius of Congreve's power could vie with Congreve, and till the advent of Fielding no such rival was to appear' (3: 37).

Baker moves naturally from romance to anti-romance, again beginning with foreign models before discussing native criminal and rogue literature, particularly Kirkman and Head. Next is a chapter on Bunyan; Baker considers his contribution to the development of realistic characters and dialogue significant. The following chapter continues the discussion of the anti-romances with a focus on Behn. Baker sees her as gifted with 'a mediocre allowance of talent,' but because of her need 'to write for bread,' as someone who was able to put her limited talent to good use through 'mere energy and ordinary intelligence.' Her career was one of learning 'what there was to learn from other writers,' and handing 'it on with all the improvements gained in her own practice' (3: 79). Despite his reservations, he devotes twenty-one pages to her novels.

Baker considers *Oroonoko, The Fair Jilt,* and *Agnes de Castro* (1688) Behn's best fiction (he has read all of her work, including *Love-Letters,* and he had edited the short fiction for Routledge twenty-five years earlier). He argues that she worked from the tradition of the French heroic romance, one that sees the 'world through romantic spectacles' (3: 89), and used the conventions of romance to create dramatic effect through 'elaborate setting.' And she knew the taste of her audience well enough to accommodate their desire for authenticity, that is, however 'sensational' and 'far-fetched' (3: 90), they were happy as long as the improbable was accompanied by a claim that it actually happened. Here he sees her anticipating Defoe. Behn is, in short, a romantic novelist who tried to impose verisimilitude on the novel. Her failure lay in her inability to evoke 'for an instant the illusion of real life' (3: 99). Baker reveals occasional concerns and discomfort with the moral values he finds in Behn's fiction, but he is one of the earliest critics of the novel to argue that her morality is a secondary matter in evaluating her achievement as a novelist. Behn's major problem remains her inability to anticipate the requirements of formalist critics of the twentieth century.

Baker then turns to Behn's followers, and here he lumps together (and segregates) most of the women novelists of the early eighteenth century as 'a regular school,' developing Behn's initiatives in sentimental, pseudo-historical and domestic fiction. The most important are Manley and Haywood, writers who kept up with developments on the Continent and responded to them with home-grown versions of the new scandal chronicles. Still more limited, yet worthy of mention, are Barker, Davys, Aubin, and Rowe. Collectively,

> the service they rendered was to have kept up a large supply of novels and stories, which habituated a larger and larger public to find their amusement in the reading of fiction, and which, poor in quality as they were, provided the original form for the eighteenth-century novel of manners. Defoe, for the most part, took a line of his own; yet he was not entirely out of their debt. Richardson and Fielding were less innovators than is usually supposed; in turning to novel-writing, they entered upon an established and thriving business, and they adopted many tricks of the trade from these humble precursors. (3: 107)

Here Baker is (rightly) at odds with virtually all his contemporaries. What is curious is his need to form a female school in order to recognize the continuities between Richardson and Fielding and their predecessors.

A seven-page summary of Manley's fiction describes the workings of her scandal chronicles in detail. Baker is hardly an admirer, though he credits her with inspiring *Gulliver's Travels*. But again his reservations are not largely moral. His sharpest criticism stems from Manley's inability to represent convincing, realistic characters: 'We know what her characters want and what they do; but we know them as interests, not as interesting personalities' (3: 114). The same objection holds for Haywood, except, of course, for her final two novels, 'written after Defoe and Richardson had given her a lesson in the art of drawing from life' (3: 114). The early works are seen as love stories modelled on Behn's and scandal chronicles modelled on Manley's. Eight pages summarize her novels. As with Manley, Baker is highly critical of Haywood's artistry, her inability to draw convincing character or to subordinate the letters she includes to her plot. He also has doubts about the means by which she achieves her self-declared moral ends.

Baker's 'followers' of Manley and Haywood are more committed to morality in their work. Rowe is clearly a pious writer, but she shares with Manley and Haywood the inability to draw character and a reliance on 'the shallowest sentimentalism' to explain motive. She is 'on a lower plane,' as moralist and novelist, 'than her literary descendant Hannah More' (3: 124). It is challenging to grasp the curious line Baker is drawing from the female wits through Rowe to More. Barker and her edifying love stories (which also prepare the way for Richardson) do not fit comfortably. The same holds for Aubin, seen by Baker as a religious and moral writer whose love stories were influenced by the adventure novel as represented by *Robinson Crusoe*. Davys is the closest to the female wits among this group, but her return to the picaresque and her purer morality call even her connections to the proposed lineage into question. Baker considers Arabella Plantin's return to the Sidneian pastoral novel and Elizabeth Boyd's return to fiction in the manner of Behn before concluding with a summary of the contributions novelists were making towards realizing the novel as he knows it. None of the women novelists discussed in this chapter is for him a major writer. Their only quality in common is gender. What distinguishes Baker's account is that he has taken these pre-Richardson novelists sufficiently seriously to provide extended accounts of their work. His is not a work which rethinks the canon, but once it became the standard reference, the best of the women novelists before Richardson could no longer be forgotten, at least by academic specialists.

Volume 3 ends with a hundred pages on Defoe and twenty on Swift. Defoe marks 'the turning-point in the history of the English novel' (3: 130); hence the full and detailed account. Baker has some reservations about Defoe: though his contribution to realism is beyond dispute, 'he overdid the thing, and took it upon him to hoodwink his readers' (3: 227), that is, he refused to recognize the difference between fact and fiction. For Baker, such recognition is an important component of the modern novel. Defoe is also deficient in his drawing of characters and in his representation of dialogue. But he is clearly the most important figure in the history of the English novel to date. Swift, a far greater writer, is a much smaller player in this tale, because his works 'are not novels and were never meant to be' (3: 230).

Volume 4 is central to Baker's account of the establishment of the novel, but since it is devoted to Richardson, Fielding, Smollett and Sterne it has less value for this study. Passing references are made to women novelists, but their main entries are contained in other volumes. This volume, Baker declares, 'deals with the most decisive period in the history of the English novel.' The implications for the canon are clear, and they are spelled out precisely when Baker asserts that 'the cardinal achievement of the period was the establishment of what I have called at a venture, intellectual realism, which is synonymous with the novels of Henry Fielding' (4: 5). Fielding receives 120 pages of coverage, compared to Richardson's 64, Smollett's 43, and Sterne's 37.

Baker sees Richardson as 'the feminine counterpart' to Defoe: 'The one produced a close likeness of the world as we see it by the steady accumulation of hard, tangible facts; the other, preoccupied with the inner world of feeling and motive, was as thorough and exhaustive in the registration of mental facts' (4: 35). The explanation Baker offers for Richardson's inwardness is his limited experience in the world, an ever-present handicap in his writing. Given his limitations, Baker is impressed by how well Richardson was able to perform. His enormous influence is responsible for the dominance of sentimental fiction throughout much of the remainder of the century, a theme Baker will develop in the following volume.

Baker's gendering of excellence in the novel is spelled out still more clearly in the opening paragraph of the section on Fielding:

> The man who counts more votes than Richardson for the title of father of the English novel was a son of the upper classes, and in almost every lineament of person and fortune the very opposite of his rival. Fielding's

was an open, full-blooded, hearty nature, that disposed him to warm sympathy with all classes of Englishmen and a thoughtful delight in every idiosyncrasy and vagary of the human mind. He was the outdoor man, roaming the woods and hills and farming the broad fields of life, whilst Richardson applied intensive cultivation to his human garden and hothouse. (4: 77)

The novel, for Baker, is defined by realism; realism, in turn, was defined by Fielding. Baker asserts that 'Tom Jones is the most important landmark in the whole history of English fiction; Fielding's, in that one book, was the most important work ever done for the development of the novel' (4: 189). A page later he argues that 'his novels contain the germs of every kind of fiction that has come to maturity since' (4: 190). One of Baker's goals in the following six and a half volumes is to demonstrate the truth of these contentions, and he ends his chapter on Fielding with a discussion of his influence. He sees the finest work of Burney, Austen, and Edgeworth as stemming from Fielding's 'comic realism.' Austen's is the closest parallel, matched only by Meredith many years later. Burney and Edgeworth reveal his influence in spite of themselves. Baker considers Burney a poor reader of Fielding, parroting the hostile criticism of Richardson and Johnson. Edgeworth, he claims, 'thought herself a Richardsonian, and was in truth such in her didactic hours; but when she let her genius have its own way it speedily led her into the region opened up by Fielding' (4: 194). The Romantics and the Victorians increasingly appreciated Fielding's superiority, and 'George Eliot was the first eminent novelist to declare in unequivocal terms the supremacy of Fielding' (4: 195). Thus, just as Baker appears inexorably on a path to a deeply misogynistic history of the English novel, he finds a way to include numerous women novelists by showing them to be in perfect harmony with all that Fielding represents. Though no chapters are dedicated to women novelists in this volume, they enter through association with Fielding.

Baker's long chapters on Smollett and Sterne add little to my study, but his opening sentence on Sterne is worth repeating: 'No sooner was fiction provided with a structural form and a set of canons firmly coordinated, than the form began to be knocked to pieces and the canons flouted' (4: 240). His immediate reference is to Sterne, though he also includes Henry Brooke and Amory among the challengers of the newly stabilized form. Baker welcomes the challenges, however, and makes it clear that they represent a recurring theme in the history to follow.

Baker's fifth volume, *The Novel of Sentiment and the Gothic Romance*, includes most of the women novelists central to this study. His response to them should be seen from two angles. His is a comprehensive history of the English novel, so he feels compelled to account for the increased activity among novel writers. As a historian, he finds that the period between the 'great four' and Edgeworth and Austen 'teems with interest.' But Baker is also an evaluative critic, and as such he finds the period 'dull'; it is a period 'when one writer alone, Fanny Burney, achieved anything notably creative on the lines that had now been laid down' (5: 11). Baker is surprised that the lessons provided by Fielding were heeded by so few for so long. The more traditional Richardson and Smollett were more frequently imitated. What gives the period its limited interest is that some of its many 'poor novelists' were 'persons of strong views and strong feelings [who] tried out such special varieties of fiction as the novel of sensibility, the tale of terror, and the revolutionary or discussion novel, and so bequeathed a lesson or a warning for those who were to come even a long time later' (5: 12).

Baker clearly believes that had the later eighteenth-century novelists had the sense to follow Fielding, better novels would have been written. Instead, under the joint influence of the needs of the circulating libraries and the demands of middle-class readers and critics for heavy didacticism, the period was flooded with novels that ranged from mediocre to poor. He sees no need to address the worst, the bestsellers and Harlequin Romances of the day. Instead, he turns to minor novelists and minor forms of the novel. He begins with two 'middling talents,' Sarah Fielding and Charlotte Lennox, tracing their 'fitful reactions ... to literary fashions and climatic changes' in the novel (37). He had already discussed Fielding in volume 4, in one of his chapters on her brother, expressing his view that she was more an essayist in the Addisonian mode than a novelist; *David Simple* is clumsy in dialogue, awkward in plot, and generally chaotic in structure (4: 119). He now looks at her other novels, finding her mixture of her brother and her friend Richardson unable to produce great fiction. His favourite of her novels is *The Countess of Dellwyn*, a somewhat unusual choice, but not surprising from Baker when he declares it her closest approximation to her brother's kind of novel. He finds Lennox old-fashioned and overly dependent on the French, especially Prévost and Marivaux. Her most successful novels are *Harriot Stuart* (1750) and *The Female Quixote*. The former is over-blown sentimental fiction in the manner of *Cleveland* (1731); the latter is better, 'pleasantry done to death, though partly redeemed by the character of Arabella, whose imperiousness some-how becomes her' (5: 41). Baker also endorses the common view that the novel is weakened by Johnsonian sententiousness.

Discussion of Fielding and Lennox is followed by analysis of a number of male and anonymous novelists; some are familiar, others had rarely if ever appeared in a standard history before Baker. His account includes Paltock, Cleland (both *Fanny Hill* and *Memoirs of a Coxcomb*), Shebbeare, Sir John Hill, Johnstone, William Combe, and Coventry, as well as several novels by unidentified authors. This chapter on the minor novelists is fol-lowed by one on the 'Oriental Story from *Rasselas* to *Vathek*.' Baker con-siders it a minor, artificial genre, at its best in exotic if inaccurate description and as satire of contemporary Britain. It 'was bound to be transient and to leave no indelible mark upon the history of fiction' (56). Baker traces the vogue for the Oriental from its French origins through the periodical essay, noting both its didactic and satiric tendencies, to the following British examples: *Rasselas*; Ellis Cornelia Knight's sequel, *Dinarbas* (1792) ('the style is a close imitation of Johnson's; not unsuccess-ful, except that his strength and fearlessness are lacking, and the apho-risms are mere platitudes' [5: 64]); Hawkesworth's *Amoran and Hamet*; Sheridan's *Nourjahad* (the latter two are both seen as rationalistic apo-logues, anticipating Radcliffe's technique of explaining away the appar-ently supernatural; he considers Sheridan's tales full of 'brilliant scenes' [5: 66]); *The Citizen of the World*; Reeve's short *The History of Charoba* (1785) ('admirable' in both 'form and diction' [5: 71], and important as the inspi-ration for Landor's *Gebir*); Bage's *The Fair Syrian* (1787); and the 'most imaginative' of them all, *Vathek*.

The chapter on the Oriental tale is followed by one curiously titled 'The Afterglow of the Augustans.' Baker tries here to collect those authors who resisted 'the progress and triumph of sentimentalism' (5: 77), by which he means the sentimentalism of the generation after Richardson, one without his moral solidity. Not surprisingly, no wom-en are found among the naysayers. The group is limited to Gold-smith (whose *The Vicar of Wakefield* is described as 'the best-read book from that day to now, all the world over, of the books of the Fielding epoch'), Graves, Charles Jenner, Herbert Lawrence, George Brewer (Jenner, Lawrence, and Brewer are very minor figures for Baker), and Cumberland. The legacy of Fielding in the eighteenth century is a great disappointment to Baker.

Baker then turns to the legacy of Richardson in a chapter entitled 'The Novel of Sentiment.' His narrative tells of realism 'giving way to melodramatic romance' (5: 91). The implied judgment is clear. He begins with more minor figures: William Guthrie, Susannah and Margaret Minifie, Susannah's daughter Elizabeth, Maria Susanna Cooper, Mrs Woodfin, Thomas Hull, and Hugh Kelly. None of these writers produced important novels; each is presented as a close imitator of Richardson. For Richardson, sensibility was not an end in itself; after Sterne, novelists increasingly provided it for its own sake, sometimes in earnest, sometimes with Sterne's disregard for morality. Sterne's followers include Thomas Bridges, 'Peter Pennyless,' Lawrence, Isaac Brandon, Jane Timbury, 'Courtney Melmoth' (Samuel Jackson Pratt), Elizabeth Bonhote, William Combe, George Keate, James Thistlethwaite, Joseph Cradock, and John Williams. Pratt and Bonhote seem to Baker the best of this mediocre lot. A twelve-page account of Mackenzie is followed by a brief account of his successors, including Mary Robinson. The chapter ends with five pages on Henry Brooke.

Baker continues with a chapter entitled 'The Novel of Sensibility,' which he distinguishes from 'The Novel of Sentiment' largely as a French import, though one based on the French response to English sentiment. A full account (twenty pages) of the French novel from the heroic romance to the 'reign of sensibility, the absolutism of feeling and instinct,' is provided. When he arrives at the English responses, Baker finds *Sidney Bidulph* 'the most distinguished novel' (5: 141) in the French-influenced line from Richardson. It is 'the extreme example in English of pathos for the sake of pathos, of a banquet of woe deliberately provided for the epicure of sensibility' (5: 142). Despite its excess, a three-page account identifies sufficient good qualities to warrant the attention. In the same mould, though inferior in both conception and construction, is the work of Frances Brooke.

Baker's conclusion is that the novel-writing world, especially the world of the circulating libraries, was caught up in imitating the French, particularly the French of Prévost and Riccoboni. He asserts, without apparent evidence, that the majority of novels in the libraries were written by women. When he returns to individual novelists, he briefly cites John Heriot and William Renwick before turning to Elizabeth Griffith, 'whose novels, not undeservedly, had a vogue far superior to these occasional writers' (5: 149). He endorses Reeve's view that Griffith was a solid second-rate novelist. She is followed by 'two perfervid exponents of the sentimental theme,' Mary Robinson and Helen Maria Williams. Williams is the better of the two, able to present plot and character effectively, and sincere in her overblown use of sentiment. A single sentence on Wollstonecraft's *Mary* (1788) notes that she 'paid a heavy tribute to sensibility when she stressed the value of passion in her novel of purpose' (5: 151). The chapter concludes with mention of three more minor writers, Lady Hawke, George Monck Berkeley, and Sir Samuel Egerton Brydges, and an appreciative glance at Beckford's parodies of sensibility, *Modern Novel Writing* and *Azemia*.

Baker can now turn his attention to a writer more to his taste, the only one to be given a chapter of her own in this volume:

> Fanny Burney provides an interlude of natural comedy in the long monotone of solemn and pretentious sentimentalism. She was not entirely immune from the chief foible of her time. But she was aware of that foible, she laughed at its aberrations in others, and she usually succeeded in checking it in herself ... In comparison with her fellow-novelists she was an anti-sentimentalist. If she is compared with such men and women of her own world as Walpole, Mrs. Delany, or Mrs. Montagu, the attitude in this respect is much the same in her novels and their letters. All were still under the sway of the didactic spirit, prone to moralize, apt to drop into a sentimental mood. Sane as they were, it did not take much to melt them. (5: 154)

I quote this passage at length because it reveals so much about early twentieth-century attitudes to the eighteenth-century novel. Baker is not uncommon in rejecting the sentimental, especially on aesthetic grounds. He is unusually open in his declaration of his personal preferences, but his are also very much the preferences of the time – just as Burney captures the preference of her time. Burney is preferred because she is able to distance herself from the excesses of her numerous contemporaries. She becomes the model against which they are measured, and helps to explain why they were so often rejected by Baker and his contemporaries.

Even Burney is not, for Baker, in the first group of novelists. She was 'a rather prim young woman, admirably brought up, not too intelligent and not too intellectual at all' (a note seconds Annie Raine Ellis's view that Burney was 'backward though not a dunce' [Ellis was the Victorian editor of Burney's early diaries]). Burney's contribution stems from her gift of being able to provide 'a direct transcript of life,' that is, her observations were transferred to her novels with minimal 'simplifying, ordering, or interpreting.' Unlike Fielding or later great novelists, Burney seems free of conscious artistry. 'At her best, she seems to reproduce what she sees' (5: 156). Hers, in other words, is an inadvertent, superficial realism.

Baker clearly enjoys *Evelina*, especially for its comedy. Burney's mixture of satire and sentiment places her with the best of her contemporaries. *Cecilia* is 'more ambitious' and 'more elaborate' (5: 164). Though a 'clever melodrama,' it is 'mechanical, not motived': 'Fanny Burney does not understand the fundamentals of character; her concern is with the differences and oddities of human nature, not with that which is universal. Hence, apart from a few scenes of concentrated comedy, her novels are inferior to the diaries in the very characteristics which are her strength' (5: 165). Baker retains many of the responses of his Victorian predecessors while adding to them the requirements of a modernist critic. The result is particularly hard on most eighteenth-century women novelists. When even the best cannot pass the complex tests applied to them, the remainder are almost certainly doomed to banishment. Baker provides comprehensive support for his contemporaries, most of whom did not share his need to read the novels they rejected.

Baker joins his predecessors in seeing Burney's career as going downhill after *Cecilia*. He prefers *Evelina* of all her novels as her only genuine success at creating the illusion 'of having transferred reality, unimproved and untampered with, to the printed page.' By the time of *Camilla*, she 'labours the insignificant and relates at great length and in conscientious detail what merits no attention, until the reader is bored to death.' To make matters still worse, 'she writes with a forced vivacity vacant of charm, and at times with a formality and Johnsonian pedantry that benumb' (5: 171). *The Wanderer* opens more promisingly, but soon degenerates. So much for the greatest novelist of her generation. Burney's influence upon Smith as well as on two competent, minor novelists, Agnes Maria Bennett and Eliza Blower, is noted. She also influenced Austen, and thus can claim to stand 'somewhere between the broad realism of Fielding and the finer portraiture of her successor, and between his rich comedy and her demure irony' (5: 173).

From Burney, Baker proceeds to 'The Gothic Novel.' Baker's take on the Gothic differs from that of most of his predecessors: he sees it as 'the popular variant of the fiction of sensibility' (5: 175), and traces it to French rather than English sources. Given his clearly stated assessment of the novel of sensibility, his evaluation of the Gothic is immediately predictable. Prévost is the key to origins of the Gothic, Baculard d'Arnaud the other important player. The French influences arrived at a time when native interests also revealed 'a growing interest in the past … the rage for the mediæval, the awakening of the historical spirit.'

When coupled with the simultaneous increase in taste for 'abnormal forms of sensibility' such as 'the literature of death and the sepulchre' (5: 176) as well as superstition and the supernatural, the result was the Gothic. The rise of the Gothic is, for Baker, tied to the rise of the historical novel; Leland's *Longsword* is seen as inspired by Prévost's *Cleveland*. *The Castle of Otranto* is likewise viewed in this context, a minor curiosity of little importance until 'Clara Reeve undertook to show how it ought to have been written' (5: 179).

*The Old English Baron* offers a far more appropriate model for understanding the Gothic. Reeve's attempt to unite romance and common sense forces her to limit her use of Gothic 'awe and dread' to what can sustain rational explanation. She 'aims at correctness; but the correctness is unhistorical, and the characters and manners are those of her own time. It is a modern sentimental story in a sham-antique frame' (5: 179–80). Baker considers the Lees more important to the development of the ·Gothic genre, though 'their craftsmanship was halting, and their imagination limited' (5: 181). *The Recess* is another imitation of *Cleveland* (a point acknowledged by Harriet Lee). He devotes three pages to *Canterbury Tales*, with special attention given to 'Kruitzner' and 'The Landlady's Tale.' The importance of the Lees to Scott and Byron is, of course, stressed. Brief mention is made of Anne Fuller and the burlesques of the Gothic by James White. This is followed by a six-page discussion of Smith's novels, with special attention devoted to her part in the Gothic movement as a fringe player who shared an interest in mystery and terror and as an accomplished painter of sentimental landscapes. His overall summary of Smith as a novelist places her firmly among the second-rate: 'Mrs. Smith recounts facts without realism; this was all she was competent to do. She could not draw a striking character; but she had a sound knowledge of human nature in general, and her creations act upon reasonable and well-defined motives. Her criticism of the state of society is also effective' (5: 191).

From Smith, Baker moves to 'the best phase of the genre,' the high point before its degeneration into the excesses of Lewis and Maturin. This high point is of course Radcliffe, whose name is 'almost a synonym for Gothic romance' (5: 192). Twelve pages describe the work of this most ordinary-seeming of women. He assumes that she had a standard education and little experience of the world, and considers the novel of sensibility the most formative influence on her development as a writer, with Prévost and Rousseau the most important writers. To them he adds the painters of the sublime, Poussin, Claude, Salvator Rosa, and Guido

Reni, all known favourites of Radcliffe. Smith is also credited as an important influence. He joins the chorus of those who think her work would have been better if she had not always explained away the apparently supernatural. Radcliffe uses terror as just another emotion in the repertory of sensibility, no different in kind from pathos. He sees her greatest artistic triumph as the ability to create 'atmosphere': 'Landscapes, seascapes, picturesque ruins, skies and storms evoke it, and make the right psychical accompaniment to the emotional drama. It was not something absolutely new in fiction, but no one had used atmosphere before as a principal element, and no one had used it so consciously' (5: 203). Her stories themselves offer nothing new; they are all 'sentimental dramas.' Radcliffe remained to the end 'a firm believer in the sentimentalist doctrine that virtue never goes without its reward' (5: 204). Baker's reduction of the Gothic to a sub-genre of the sentimental limits its potential to produce a work he can recognize as first rate.

Baker concludes this chapter with a discussion of the Gothic after Radcliffe, beginning with her narrowest imitators, Sir Egerton Brydges and Regina Maria Roche. More important is Lewis, who took the Gothic in another direction, away from beauty, towards horror. Brockden Brown is given full coverage, followed by a writer greatly influenced by him, Mary Shelley. Aside from *Frankenstein*, he finds her novels dull. Maturin and the parodists, Edgeworth (in *Angelina*), Mary Charlton, Benjamin Thompson, Sarah Green, and Barrett, are the final authors considered in the chapter.

The volume ends with 'The Novel of Doctrine,' a predictable, inevitable development of the novel in the hands of reformers and revolutionaries. These novelists took the domestic novel, even the romantic and sentimental novel, and used it for their own polemical purposes. Not surprisingly, a considerable number were women:

Women are sure to concentrate upon domestic fiction, and to seize the opportunities this offers for edification. The sex is more sentimental, more moralistic, more censorious, than men. Hence the insistence on fine sentiments, elegant taste, delicacy, high principle, the sense of duty, the dependence of happiness upon character and conduct. Here are the germs of the problem novel; they could be discerned in several of Charlotte Smith's stories, and even in the high-pitched novels of sensibility. They can be seen, too, in the emergence of a definite subject, idea, point of view, especially in novels by women, women having a graver sense of the issues involved, feeling their responsibility as authors more acutely, disliking the comic attitude of a Fielding, which they think flippant, though at bottom it may be more serious than their own earnest but less catholic vision. (5: 229)

No passage in Baker more fully captures his reservations about women novelists – or the sources of those reservations. Once again, they stem from a model of what the novel should be based on Fielding. Novelists who turned away from the master – and most women novelists did – can never attain the pantheon of the greatest novelists.

That said, Baker nonetheless finds that the leaders among novelists of doctrine are men, Bage, Holcroft, and Godwin. Five pages on Moore are followed by five on Bage, two on Holcroft, and six on Godwin. He then turns to Inchbald, finding *A Simple Story* a mix of sensibility (especially in the first half), and doctrine (especially in the second half). *Nature and Art* is more purely a novel of doctrine. Baker's two pages on Inchbald are followed by a single paragraph on Opie and Wollstonecraft (and Thomas Day). Baker finds *Mary* 'a moving story,' but one limited by too much 'analysis of sensibility' (5: 252). Opie is described as a writer who shares with Wollstonecraft and Day strong views about education, views at odds with those of Wollstonecraft. Mary Hays's *Emma Courtney* (1796) also fits the template of doctrine; in this case, the target is middle-class morality and the repression of women. Hypocrisy is the problem, but Baker is hardly more sympathetic than Hays's first readers: she was 'unwise to select a case of morbid hysteria as her illustration' (5: 253). The chapter and volume end with a page on Elizabeth Hamilton's satire on the novels of doctrine in general, and on Hays in particular, in *Memoirs of Modern Philosophers* (1800).

Baker covers the well-trod field of the late eighteenth-century novel in this volume, providing still more thorough coverage than his predecessors. He includes a full range of women novelists and considers one of them, Burney, the best novelist of her age. Yet it is hard to come away from this volume with a sense of encountering a sympathetic reading. His accounts are balanced; Baker always points to strengths as well as weaknesses. But he does not like the kinds of novels that dominated the period. He is hostile to sentiment and sensibility, and he remains opposed to heavy-handed didacticism or polemics in the novel. A bias for realism informs his tastes and judgments, just as a bias for the standards of modernist formalism inflects his sense of realism. To that mix must be added a gendering of novelists, that is, an assumption that women, whether by nature or nurture, produce certain kinds of fiction and not others. When combined, these biases produce a critic with a clearly limited capacity for appreciating late eighteenth-century women novelists. They also produce a history, however inclusive, that values most those works that best accord with his critical principles.

This is not to suggest that Baker is a critic ill-equipped to appreciate any woman novelist. Volume 6 is devoted to 'Edgeworth, Austen, Scott.' Edgeworth and Austen, for Baker, provide welcome transitions to the nineteenth-century novel. 'Without any shock of surprise or startling change of scenery, we gradually find that the past has been left behind and we are entering upon the present.' Manners no longer 'seem strange or antiquated; still less is there in the bearing and workmanship of the novelist that requires the reader to make allowances' (6: 11). And since Baker believes that English society improved over the course of the history of the novel, he finds the realistic novel a key indicator of that improvement as well as a form on its own trajectory of progress. Fielding remains the touchstone for determining excellence, and his range, largely a function of his gender, gives him an advantage over even these two women. Scott could match him in range, but Scott's romanticism biases his view of his society. (Baker here enunciates the common twentieth-century objection to Scott.)

The volume devotes two, three, and four chapters respectively to its title novelists, with a final chapter on other Scottish novelists of the age. Edgeworth follows the novelists of doctrine in her inclusion of social philosophy in her novels; but she is free from their polemics. She was not a profound or original thinker, instead getting her ideas from her father and his friends. Utilitarianism provided her with some access to the developing modern notions of the individual, notions necessary for the leap forward in the novel of the nineteenth century. Baker repeats the familiar tale of her father's influence (more benign for Baker than for most), especially on the didactic nature of her writing. *Castle Rackrent* is an exception, a holiday from educational theory. 'She was the first writer to render the racial peculiarities of the Irish with the charm of perfect comprehension' (6: 18). *Castle Rackrent* is also 'probably the first novel to give the history of a family through several generations.' Using the simple Thady as the source of the narrative is another noteworthy innovation (6: 32). But unlike Fielding or Austen, Edgeworth is 'not one of our great comic novelists': 'life to her was a practical affair, and therefore moral above everything' (6: 33).

The second chapter on Edgeworth discusses the rest of her novels. Baker's favourites are *The Absentee* and *Ormond* (1817). He appreciates her attacks on sentimentalism and much of her social satire as well as her portrayals of Irish life. The ongoing problem remains her didacticism. The chapter ends with two of her like-minded contemporaries, More, whose didacticism is still more damaging to her fiction, and Brunton, whose novels 'are far too melodramatic to carry conviction, and hence inferior as didactic stories to either Maria Edgeworth's or Hannah More's' (6: 53–4). The following chapters turn to Austen and Scott, 'beyond challenge the greatest novelists between Fielding and Dickens' (6: 122). It is worth noting that Baker's discussion of Austen places her firmly in the context of her predecessors, particularly the women novelists he has chronicled up to this point.

The other Scottish novelists include Ferrier, Galt, and Hogg. Baker sees Ferrier as a talented amateur with a gift for character and manner but little else:

> Miss Ferrier's style was notably spirited, pungent, and graceful. But she lacked Jane Austen's irony, and also the reticence which was one of the subtlest gifts of the English novelist. It is an old mistake to compare the two. Her sparkling and more or less satirical cartooning of the superficies of character, the fops and prattlers, fools and eccentrics, is much more like Fanny Burney's; and she has the same proneness to repeat a situation, to show her oddities performing their tricks over again. The earnestness of her moralizing, also, a habit that grew upon her, is nearer to Dr. Johnson's 'character-monger' than to Miss Edgeworth's regular didacticism. (6: 229)

So ends the relevant section of what remains the fullest account of the English novel to date. Embedded in it are most of the objections, implicit as well as explicit, to women novelists before Austen. Despite his extensive coverage of these women novelists, Baker provides little support for their claims to more serious attention.

### J.B. Priestley (1894–1984)

At the opposite extreme to Baker's comprehensive survey is J.B. Priestley's brief primer, *The English Novel* (1927). Priestley's very popular book traces the novel chronologically, but from 'the point of view of an ordinary intelligent reader of our own time.' His principle of selection, accordingly, is a novelist's 'value to us, here and now' (6). He allows two pages for prose fiction before the eighteenth century, mentioning Malory, Lyly, Sidney, Lodge, Nashe, the imitators of French romance, Behn, and Bunyan. He credits Behn (in *Oroonoko* and *The Fair Jilt*) with 'making some approach to reality' (8); Defoe is the first to achieve 'the complete illusion of reality' (11). Swift and Addison are important, but they failed to produce novels proper. It was Richardson who added realistic character to Defoe's realistic stories and details to achieve a novel as Priestley understands it.

Priestley's treatment of Richardson is representative of the dominant response of his time. He is 'a little fat bookseller' (16) whose strength was in producing 'a slow-motion picture of human life on its purely sentimental side.' His readers were largely women and the new middle class; he 'spent far more of his time among women than among men' (17), and was able to give his women readers exactly what they wanted. 'There is, indeed, something curiously feminine about him. Sir Charles Grandison is a sanctimonious spinster's idea of a fine gentleman.' Though Richardson was able to capture enormous numbers of readers in his lifetime, he was unable to hold them: 'no novelist who has been given so much praise is now so seldom read.' The main cause is 'the quality of his mind.' It is 'not that of a great novelist' (18). The first great novelist was Fielding; Priestley urges his readers to return to *Joseph Andrews* and *Tom Jones*.

In Priestley's account Smollett is a talented novelist, but not a novelist of genius. Sterne has genius (Priestley is also taken with the perfection of his art); Mackenzie is the best of the failures who tried to imitate him. Johnson's *Rasselas* is an important book, but too weighed down with morality. *The Vicar of Wakefield* makes far better reading. The late-century revival of romantic fiction begins with Walpole, and its best exponents before Scott were Radcliffe, Lewis, and Maturin. Priestley considers their tales of terror equivalent to the detective novels of his own time. The best (*The Mysteries of Udolpho* ranks highest) 'are not entirely without literary power, but, nevertheless, what was chiefly demanded of them was ingenuity and not imagination' (36–7). The devices that worked well on their early readers have become so familiar that they can no longer thrill twentieth-century readers. Priestley dismisses Godwin and his followers in a single paragraph for combining 'a passion for the most barren and abstract social theorizing' with 'the absurdities of ultra-romantic story-telling.' The result is a 'holiday' from common sense that refuses 'to look steadily at reality' (37). Mary and Percy Shelley are Priestley's examples of Godwin's followers. Scott and Austen, near total opposites, are both counted among the great novelists. Austen is credited with being the first 'to exploit characteristically feminine sides of life and points of view' (46–7), though Burney is mentioned in passing as her single important predecessor.

Priestley's canon is very small, and his responses to the writers he discusses offer few new insights. What distinguishes his work from earlier surveys of the novel is a focus, shared by Baker, on realism and formal artistry as the keys to greatness in fiction. He downgrades the novel of sentiment, the political novel, and the Gothic novel, the principle forms of the novel before Austen taken up by women. To be fair, Priestley does not advance the cause of very many early male writers of fiction to fill the void; he is quite content with a highly selective and restrictive set of criteria that admits only a few to greatness. For the purposes of this study, it is important to note that his values and approach remove many of the most important eighteenth-century novelists from consideration – and as always, significant numbers of the neglected novelists are women.

### Walter Allen (1911–1995)

In between Baker's comprehensive history and the very compact history of Priestley lies Walter Allen's *The English Novel: A Short Critical History* (1949). Written from the perspective of 'someone who follows the craft of fiction himself' (9), Allen's is another history aimed at the general reader, though it was also read widely by students. He begins by announcing that Dickens is the greatest English novelist and proceeds to argue that literary historians who attempt to establish a long genealogy for the novel are under the misguided impression that it is synonymous with fiction. The novel is a new form for Allen, one which appears in the late seventeenth century with Bunyan and is developed soon after by Defoe and Richardson. He does not offer a precise definition, but says enough to reveal his basic sense of what a novelist does: 'He is making an imitation, an imitation of the life of man on earth. He is making, it might be said, a working model of life as he sees and feels it, his conclusions about it being expressed in the characters he invents, the situations in which he places them, and in the very words he chooses for those purposes' (12). Allen is a believer in formal unity, and he has a clear notion of the realism he considers central to the novel.

Allen's opening chapter, 'The Beginnings,' discusses why the best early fiction cannot be described as novels. His list of 'the best' includes Chaucer, Henryson, Malory, Lyly, Sidney, Greene, Lodge, Dekker, Deloney, Nashe, the French heroic romances and their (unnamed) English imitators, and Head. Bunyan was the first to capture the real in fiction, a major breakthrough for the novel. The best of the professional fiction writers of his time (all of whom are his inferiors) was Behn. *Oroonoko* is, predictably, the work he discusses, and Allen finds in it several innovations, most importantly the 'attempt to engraft verisimilitude onto a conventional story of romance' (32). It was an attempt of historical importance for the young novel, and one that impressed its readers with its novelty. But as novelists and their readers became more sophisticated in their understanding of fictional reality and how to represent it, Behn's achievement lost its appeal. Readers also became more sophisticated about history, and Behn's fictional account of Surinam was increasingly found unsatisfactory. Allen links the growing sense of history, just emerging in seventeenth-century England, to the development of the novel.

Allen includes Congreve among the early developers of novelistic realism, but the next central figure after Bunyan is Defoe. New in his discussion of Defoe is Allen's emphasis on the importance of *A Journal of the Plague Year* and *Moll Flanders* as well as *Robinson Crusoe*. He repeats the familiar line that 'the first great flowering' (40) of the English novel began with *Pamela* and ended with *Humphry Clinker*. Richardson and Fielding are the best novelists of their time; Allen sees them as opposites, but recognizes their different kinds of greatness. His long discussion of *Clarissa* is an important attempt to re-establish its eminence among English novels. Allen considers *Pamela* a worthy first attempt at what *Clarissa* later achieved, but finds *Grandison* much less successful, a novel 'too much of its time' (48). Richardson's 'analysis of emotion and motive, introspection in the widest sense, and ultimately the belief in the value of emotion and of feeling for their own sakes' (49) had an enormous influence on novelists for at least the next hundred years. Still more influential was Fielding, who established 'the main tradition of the English novel' (50), for Allen a tradition founded in social criticism, morality, satire, and irony.

Smollett and Sterne round out Allen's presentation of the early masters. Allen argues that the twenty years following these four masters were 'a relatively barren period' (76) for the novel. There was no shortage of new novels; the novel-reading public increased regularly, but they were not very demanding in what they chose to read. The best new novels came not from professional novelists, since they were content meeting demand, but from amateurs or writers who were not primarily novelists, such as Goldsmith, Johnstone, and Graves. Henry Brooke and Mackenzie follow, but each is limited as a novelist by the pernicious influence of sensibility. *The Fool of Quality* is a 'remarkable book,' but 'it is one of the worst novels ever written' (81). While *The Man of Feeling* offers an interesting response to Rousseau, that does not make it a good novel.

Allen looks to *Rasselas* and *Vathek* for his examples of the Oriental tale; the latter is pronounced a 'masterpiece' (86). He then moves to the Gothic, beginning with Walpole. Reeve, he argues, tried to make Walpole's form more probable. The result was that 'she did little more than tell a sentimental story in a sham-mediaeval setting, with the supernatural reduced to a few hollow groans. The flowering of the Gothic novel was still to come.' But before moving to Radcliffe, Allen turns to Burney, a writer whose 'historical importance is undeniable, though her actual achievement has been over-valued.' Burney's claim to fame comes from combining the traditions of Richardson and Fielding. From Richardson she derives the theme of the development of the mind and emotions of a young woman. 'But the exploration of emotion and moral impulse' is not her strength. Allen compares Burney unfavourably to Inchbald, finding the first 'adequate expression of the attitude towards men of a strong-willed, imperious, beautiful young woman' in *A Simple Story*. 'Beside Mrs Inchbald's Miss Milner, Fanny Burney's Evelina is a priggish mouse.' Burney's real strength is in social comedy. 'Her work represents the feminization of Fielding's art' (89). The result is necessarily a reduction to the frame of reference of a young woman of the middle class: 'To read Miss Burney is rather like having a mouse's view of the world of cats: the cats are very terrifying, but the mouse's sense of the ridiculous could not be keener. As an almost necessary corollary, the cats are only convincing as characters when they are ridiculous: Lord Orville, the hero of *Evelina*, a young girl's dream of a nobleman based on Richardson's Grandison, could scarcely be more wooden' (90). Allen credits Burney with introducing class conflict into the English novel, but considers her range so narrow that when she tried to extend it, she was doomed to fail. He mentions none of her other novels.

Allen considers Burney overrated; Smith, by contrast, he declares underrated. Smith, for Allen, means *The Old Manor House*, a novel he admires greatly for several reasons. It is a well-made novel with its parts successfully 'fused into an organic whole.' Smith has incorporated new end-of-century tastes; she is 'probably the first novelist to use descriptions of natural scenery as a matter of course,' and she integrates them fully into the structure of her novel. She has a modern sense of history. The Gothic elements are subordinated to the story, and she brings to her story, 'without in the least distorting her fiction to propaganda ends … a body of ideas which gives the novel a real strength' (91–2). Radcliffe is important as a major innovator. Not only did she write the first successful thriller, but, far more significantly, she was the first to add to the novel a close and poetic relationship between character and environment. In her novels, 'the ambience in which the characters move is as important as the characters themselves.' Each is 'impregnated' with the other; the result is a 'symbolic' relationship central to the structure and power of the novel (93). In Allen's view Radcliffe is the first to succeed at this romantic use of landscape and scenery, as well as the first to manage to manipulate suspense so effectively. Her influence on Lewis and Maturin was 'enormous' (94), as was her influence on Poe and countless others.

Allen ends his account of the eighteenth-century novel with the political or 'doctrinaire' novel, a form that contributed to the fine novels of the 1790s. The master of the form is Godwin, because he exceeded its inherent limitations by writing 'from profounder impulses than the purely political' (97). Bage is the representative novelist of doctrine. No others are mentioned. Allen begins his next chapter, on the early nineteenth century, with Edgeworth, 'nearly a great novelist,' and one of greater historical importance than Austen. Radcliffe had brought landscape for its own sake to the novel; Edgeworth 'gave fiction a local habitation and a name' (98). In doing so, she incorporated her characters into the local landscape and thereby created the regional novel. Edgeworth's strengths include rounded characters of the highest order, though her heroes are rarely successful. *Castle Rackrent* and *The Absentee* are her best works; *Belinda* exemplifies her major weakness as a writer, her didacticism. Long accounts of Austen and Scott are followed by shorter, but still generous, accounts of Ferrier, Galt, and Hogg. Ferrier's is 'an admirable talent that scarcely took itself seriously enough.' The lively, interesting characters and fine sense of social satire are too much compromised by the conventional and the 'pedagogically moral' (120).

Allen's canon is quite catholic, but far more limited than most of his predecessors who wrote comprehensive histories of the English novel. He focuses on the greats, and rarely moves below the second rank. Originality remains a signal virtue, and his judgments are consistently informed by a sense of artistry that comes from modernist aesthetics and formalist structure. He is opposed generally both to sensibility and didacticism in the novel, and his canon is especially thin in novelists well disposed to either.

## Critical Studies of the Novel

### Norman Collins (1907–1982)

The period also includes a number of influential studies of the English novel that are more concerned with exploring key texts than with providing thorough history. Although they are usually organized chronologically, their object is generally to present the best for the benefit of twentieth-century readers, including students. Norman Collins's *The Facts of Fiction* (1932) provides a useful, influential example. His goal is to capture the best novelists 'in something like their essential originality' (10). He begins with Richardson, after explaining why all of Richardson's predecessors were not novelists. Malory, Nashe, Dekker, Deloney, Behn, Bunyan, Swift, and Defoe are rejected by name; Defoe's claim receives the fullest explanation for rejection.

Richardson is both 'the father of fiction' and 'the father of psychological fiction' (19), though Collins believes that he intended to be neither. Rather, Richardson's goal was to be a moral writer. His real gift was as a writer who intuited the interests of his largely female readership, particularly in sex. 'Women always adore stories about womanly women and male men; the luscious landscape of love where every prospect pleases and only man is vile satisfies feminine curiosity and vanity simultaneously.' His weakness was his need to moralize, to explain away the psychological truths he represented so well. Richardson, for Collins, is 'essentially a feminine author.' He was 'the first important woman novelist in the language. His thoughts all moved in skirts. His novels are the apotheosis of vapours and virtue. He wrote as women write; only a little better' (17). It is difficult to find a more thoroughly misogynistic passage in a study of the English novel by an influential critic. It is also difficult to find a passage that better illustrates my contention that the fates of many eighteenth-century women novelists were linked to the fate of Richardson. Given his view of Richardson, it would be shocking if Collins had much time for early women novelists.

Collins's view of Fielding is anything but predictable from his response to Richardson. He has serious reservations about Fielding's morals, and still more serious reservations about his sense of humour. He even rejects Fielding's claim to be a realist; for Collins, Fielding was 'a hopeless romantic' (45). Collins does recognize Fielding's importance, and he has some grudging respect for him as an artist and moralist, especially in *Joseph Andrews*. But his hesitation, a hesitation that extends well beyond

Fielding to most of his contemporaries and immediate successors, is captured well by the following summary: 'Anyone who cannot enjoy Fielding will probably have a thin enough time in the rest of English fiction. Just as anyone who persists in calling *Tom Jones* the greatest novel in the language must have had a thin enough time already' (55).

Collins's next two chapters are on Smollett and Sterne. Smollett is described as a crude writer, focused on low, often cruel humour; Sterne, though clearly an artist of quality himself, is accountable for being 'the founder of sentimental fiction' (77). That inferior form is exemplified by Mackenzie, who adds Richardson's morality to Sterne's narrative technique. The result is 'unreadable' (81). The following chapter is on 'The Major Minor Novelists,' Johnson, Walpole, and Goldsmith, none really a novelist (hence minor), but each 'men of genius' (hence major) (82). The chapter ends with 'The Arrival of Female Genius' in the person of Burney, 'the first recorded specimen of a now familiar English bird often shot on these shores, the woman novelist, who could write a really admirable novel, yet remain a foolish young thing all her life' (98). He genuinely admires *Evelina* if not its author; it is the only one of Burney's novels he mentions.

Sandwiched between chapters on Austen and Scott is the final chapter relevant to this study, 'The Reign of Terror and the Noble Savage.' Walpole is credited with fathering both Gothic fiction and Gothic romance, producing a period of extravagant fiction Collins has little respect for. The first to follow Walpole was Reeve, 'who wrote her first novel at the mature and unlikely age of fifty-one.' (It is interesting that Richardson's similarly late start is not 'unlikely.') Reeve's 'unexcitable middle-age' seems to have been the cause of her attempt to explain away the supernatural in *The Old English Baron* (117). Radcliffe was much better suited for the task and was able to create 'a world not unlike that of a sick child's nightmare' (118). For Collins the 'Romantic Revival or Renaissance of Wonder was the child of Protestant reason' (119). English readers enjoyed the lure of the alien, Catholic settings exploited so effectively by Radcliffe and her followers, Maturin and Lewis. Parodies by Austen, Edgeworth, and Barrett bear tribute to the holding power of the mystery and terror conveyed in the Gothic.

The other branch of new fiction at the end of the century comes from the impact of Rousseau and the idea of the noble savage. Pedagogical fiction was Rousseau's vehicle for reaching a wide audience, and his English imitators followed suit. Collins sees Day's *Sandford and Merton* as 'a handbook of gentle Bolshevism' (127). *Caleb Williams*, similarly, is a 'Tolstoyan tract' (128), and Holcroft's novels 'the didactic stories of the nursery' (131). No other novelists of the period are mentioned. Collins's canon is quite limited, and inflected by his general dislike of all eighteenth-century fiction. To that must be added a more intense dislike for most fiction by women. His sympathetic readers were unlikely to come away with a desire to explore novels he leaves unmentioned.

### F.R. Leavis (1895–1978)

'The great English novelists are Jane Austen, George Eliot, Henry James, and Joseph Conrad' (9). The famous opening line of F.R. Leavis's *The Great Tradition* (1948) takes Collins's approach to its logical conclusion. The operative word in Leavis's title is 'great,' and greatness is awarded with the utmost caution. The great novelists 'are significant in terms of that human awareness they promote; awareness of the possibilities of life' (10). His discussion of Austen clarifies somewhat the criteria he advances here: 'She is intelligent and serious enough to be able to impersonalize her moral tensions as she strives, in her art, to become more fully conscious of them, and to learn what, in the interests of life, she ought to do with them. Without her intense moral preoccupation she wouldn't have been a great novelist' (16). Add to this a preoccupation with form, with striving for a 'formal perfection' that for Leavis 'can be appreciated only in terms of the moral preoccupations that characterize the novelist's peculiar interest in life' (17), and the argument for Austen as the first modern English novelist, the first great novelist, and the creator of the great tradition falls into place. Leavis's tradition is reserved exclusively for the greats.

The implication for novelists before Austen is clear. Leavis, nonetheless, spells it out in a few pages largely on Fielding and Richardson. He acknowledges that novelists can have historical importance without lasting value: 'Fielding deserves the place of importance given him in the literary histories, but he hasn't the kind of classical distinction we are also invited to credit him with. He is important not because he leads to Mr J.B. Priestley but because he leads to Jane Austen, to appreciate whose distinction is to feel that life isn't long enough to permit of one's giving much time to Fielding or any to Mr Priestley' (11).

The English novel in some sense begins with Fielding; the great tradition does not. Leavis shares Collins's low opinion of Fielding, and, like Collins, prefers Richardson. He is drawn to Richardson's superior skill in the 'analysis of emotional and moral states' and recognizes *Clarissa* as 'a really impressive work' (13). But it is too limited and too long to remain in the canon of great novels even though Richardson, too, was an important influence on Austen. Leavis credits Burney with providing the link between Richardson and Austen 'by transposing him into educated life' (13). The line that runs from Richardson through Burney to Austen is important for the English novel, but once it reaches Austen and the breakthrough to greatness, Richardson and Burney – and the many (unnamed by Leavis) other novelists Austen read and absorbed – become little more than specimens for literary historians.

Leavis's canon is one of the most exclusive in English criticism. All eighteenth-century novelists are excluded. To his credit, he seems free of gender bias: half his greats are women. But his interest in reading and recommending women novelists before Austen is virtually nil. Since it is hard to overestimate the influence of his judgments on several generations of students and readers, it is essential to include Leavis's particular kind of hostile approach in any account of the neglect of women novelists before Austen throughout most of the twentieth century.

## Arnold Kettle (1916–1986)

A third example of an approach in this tradition is found in Arnold Kettle's two-volume *An Introduction to the English Novel* (1951). Kettle provides a historical survey, though not a history. He has no interest in being inclusive, though what he includes is not based entirely on quality. He follows Collins and Leavis in his commitment to the principle that 'the ultimate concern of the study of literature is evaluation' (1: 12). Kettle also shares Leavis's concern with morality and life. He sees two traditions in English fiction, one the moral fable developing from medieval allegory, the other a less directed interest in life developing from the picaresque in writers who have accepted middle-class values in place of the earlier values of the aristocracy. In both cases, the novelists share a 'search for an adequate philosophy of life' (1: 24), whether consciously or not.

What distinguishes Kettle from the others is his attempt to historicize his evaluations. It is not accidental, he argues, that the novel appears in the eighteenth century, with all due respect to the contributions made by ancient, medieval, and heroic romances, and by such writers as Rabelais, Lyly, Sidney, Greene, Ford, Cervantes, Congreve, Behn, and Bunyan. For Kettle, the novel is 'a realistic prose fiction,' where realistic means 'relevant to real life' (1: 26). Non-realistic fiction is romance. Relevance is the key for Kettle: *Gulliver's Travels* is realistic; *The Mysteries of Udolpho* is not. And realism is clearly an honorific. The novel is the realistic response to earlier romances (hence Cervantes and Bunyan are the closest to novelists in the above list of precursors). The novel arose when it did to meet the demands of a new reading public, especially women. And the novel 'grew with the middle class, a new art-form based not on aristocratic patronage but on commercial publishing, an art-form written by and for the now powerful commercial bourgeoisie' (1: 28). Kettle then offers an extensive analysis of the relation between romance and the novel to the class interests each supported. His study is thus a curious mixture of evaluative criticism and a kind of soft Marxist historicism.

When he turns to the novel proper, Kettle deliberately limits his study to a few of its most important examples. The great novelists of the period, Defoe, Richardson, Fielding, and Sterne, tried to unite the traditions of moral allegory and the picaresque. He begins with the moral fable, looking at *The Pilgrim's Progress* and *Jonathan Wild*, as models. The form doesn't die in response to the true novel; writers like Day, Inchbald, Godwin, Edgeworth, and More continue to produce moral fables even beyond the end of the century. Defoe exemplifies the picaresque tradition in the eighteenth century. With Richardson, Kettle finds the novel with relevance that he so values. Richardson is guilty of indulging in some of the practices of the romance writer, 'the titillation of emotion for its own sake and the explicit recommendation of a bogus philosophy of life' (1: 65). But he was also the first to achieve genuine tragedy in fiction when 'he stumbled on one of the real, contemporary dilemmas of his own time,' particularly 'the inability of class society' to meet the demands of women for emancipation. In so doing, he 'achieved an art which has relevance' to our time (1: 66).

When Kettle turns to Fielding and Sterne, he turns from tragic to comic, but, unlike Leavis, he is able to recognize impressive achievement in this form too. (He dismisses Leavis's remarks on Fielding as 'patronising strictures' [1: 67].) While he finds shortcomings in both Fielding and Sterne, each passes his test for great fiction. From Sterne, he moves directly to Austen. No other early novelist is mentioned. Like Leavis, Kettle does not make judgments based on gender bias. Half the nineteenth-century novelists in his study are women. But he too demonstrates the lack of interest in women novelists before Austen found in Collins and Leavis. Their approach to the novel through the greats was shared by many other critics and absorbed by many of their students. It contributed significantly to the neglect of the eighteenth-century novel in general, and of the women novelists in particular that was so acute at the end of the period covered by this study.

## Studies of Women Novelists

### Joyce M. Horner (1903–1980)

I have chosen three representative studies of women novelists from this period, two of limited interest, the third of far greater importance. The first is Joyce M. Horner's *The English Women Novelists and their Connection with the Feminist Movement (1688–1797)* (1929–30). Horner's study was published in two parts, and it continues to read like two separate studies. The first is a historical study of the growth of the woman novelist; the second, also a historical study, focuses on distinctly female qualities in the novels by women. Horner's method consists of tracing the growth of the psychological novel and the evolution of the heroine in English fiction.

Horner begins with 'The Fair Triumvirate of Wit': Behn, Manley, and Haywood. Behn is the first woman novelist, as well as the first professional woman writer. *Oroonoko* is the only one of Behn's works that Horner admires; she is especially taken with it for its anticipation of Rousseau and for its critique of English policy in the West Indies. She finds Behn less hampered by her sex than other women of her time and for some time after, but also argues that Behn wrote 'like a man' (3). She is troubled by the lack of morality in Behn's work, but defends it as reflecting the values of its time. Manley is considered an inferior writer, and her chosen forms, the scandal chronicle and fictionalized autobiography, are of historical importance only. Haywood wrote whatever was popular with book buyers, and while Horner admires her ability to please her public, she does not see her as a particularly gifted writer. Overall, Horner admires the courage, energy and versatility of the three pioneers, if not their work itself.

The next chapter in this study is on the emergence of the 'lady' novelist. Horner notes the increasingly respectable work by increasingly respectable writers in the period between Addison and Richardson. Her examples are Rowe, Aubin, and Barker, and to Barker she awards the title of 'the first "lady" novelist. She was not great enough to establish the respectability of the novel; but she was, nevertheless, a novelist and respectable' (24). The arrival of Richardson had an enormous impact on women novelists. With *Pamela*, he established the virtue rewarded plot, as well as the 'need for greater realism' and the value in fiction of 'the everyday things of life' (32). The first two writers to profit from his success were Sarah Fielding and Charlotte Lennox.

The period of the bluestockings is important for the recognition of at least some women for their intellectual and artistic abilities. Horner finds the inclusion of women in Johnson's circle a significant sign of this change and surveys the bluestockings themselves (though they are not novelists) for the same reason. She then turns to Burney, whose *Evelina* is 'the first book with which the woman novelist came into her own' (61). Fielding and Lennox had made progress, as had Sheridan and Brooke, but Horner seconds Brimley Johnson's view that the key to Burney's claim is that she wrote the best book. She also benefited from writing after the great male novelists were dead, at a time when there was little competition among active novelists. Horner shares the standard view that the subsequent trajectory of Burney's career as a novelist is downhill; *Cecilia* is still worth reading, but the final two novels are best forgotten.

Horner's final group explored ways to make a living as novelists. Inchbald and Smith wrote in many forms, the novel being only a partial source of income for them. Radcliffe could have made a living as a novelist had she set herself up as a professional writer. Horner admires her novels for their 'natural scenery' (72) and considers Radcliffe an 'early master of the ghost story' (69). Given her enormous success, she must also be recognized as 'a formative influence in the history of the novel' (76). Horner takes notice of women writing political novels, particularly Wollstonecraft and Smith, before ending with a brief mention of some novelists who are now 'only names' (77): Brooke, Sheridan, Mrs Kier, Griffith, and the Minifies.

With the arrival of Jane Austen, Horner can point to 'the woman novelist who showed the heights which were capable of being reached by her sex, and for whom the earlier writers were unconsciously preparing the way' (78). Horner's is another Whig history, justified ultimately by the achievements of those who surpassed the subjects of her study. The second part makes the same argument by tracing the development of the themes that are central to the great novels by women from Austen on.

## Muriel Masefield (fl. 1927–1953)

Muriel Masefield's *Women Novelists from Fanny Burney to George Eliot* (1934) shares much in common with Horner's discussion of the novel. Her focus is on the novel of 'life and manners' (7) in the hundred years following the publication of *Evelina*. The novel, for Masefield, begins with Richardson, as does the 'feminine type of novel.' The four great male novelists established the original forms of the genre and, following Macaulay, Masefield credits Burney with bravely entering a hitherto largely all-male world. 'In doing this Fanny Burney brought about a literary revolution: the novel was freed from the reproach of coarseness ... and the natural story of life and manners came into its kingdom' (23). *Cecilia* 'is not as good as *Evelina*, although it contains the strongest dramatic scene she ever wrote – that of the evening at Vauxhall' (29). It has a clever plot, but less sprightly dialogue, and it is too long to maintain the reader's interest. With *Camilla*, the 'deterioration is obvious' (30), though Masefield defends its representation of 'the rich panorama of society' (31) and its acute capturing of the social values of the day. She offers no similar defence for *The Wanderer*. Burney's strength came from the youthful quality of her writing. As she lost it her novels became increasing worse, and Burney compounded the problem by imitating Johnsonian prose, a disaster for the kind of novels she wrote. But Burney excelled at creating characters who represent particular places in the class and social structure of her time, and she played a crucial role in preparing the way for the much greater Austen.

Masefield details her reasons for her high opinion of Austen before moving to shorter chapters on Edgeworth and Ferrier, as novelists who represented Irish and Scottish life respectively. Edgeworth's importance is for her Irishness. *Castle Rackrent* represents her greatest success in capturing Irish characters; *The Absentee* exhibits her most successful plot. The rest of her novels offer interesting views of Irish life, but are all too long. Edgeworth's strengths were drawn from her 'knowledge of the world (and particularly of Ireland)' and from her 'trenchant characterization and humour' (81). Ferrier, her Scottish counterpart, has analogous strengths: 'the glory of Susan Ferrier's books is the character-drawing, in which lively satire is just sufficiently mitigated by touches of tenderness' (83).

Burney, Austen, Edgeworth, and Ferrier are the only novelists Masefield addresses in this study. Her view of the woman's novel, or at least one subgenre of it, recognizes nothing of value before Burney. This remained the dominant view throughout most of the twentieth century.

### B.G. MacCarthy (1904–1993)

By far the most comprehensive and important study of women novelists in this period – and in my study – is B.G. MacCarthy's two-volume

*The Female Pen: Women Writers and Novelists 1621–1818* (1944–7 reprinted in one volume 1994). MacCarthy wrote in response to Virginia Woolf's *A Room of One's Own*, to answer the questions Woolf raised about the causes that impeded the development of women writers in England. She sees the origin of the novel in ancient texts such as *Daphnis and Chloe*, texts based in 'actuality,' not 'fancy.' With Marie de France and Margaret of Navarre, women become writers of fiction 'because they had for subject-matter themes and events most familiar, if not in their own lives, then certainly in the lives of those about them' (2). For MacCarthy, realism is essential to the novel and the natural mode for women. When fiction turned to the pastoral under the influence of Sidney, Lady Mary Wroth followed his lead, with unfortunate results, including a long delay in the development of the novel as well as in the development of other good women writers. MacCarthy links the two inseparably.

MacCarthy then establishes a second major contention in response to critics who for centuries maintained that women's limited experience provided insurmountable obstacles to their becoming great writers (an argument that should by now be familiar): 'We know that the material on which creative imagination may work can be found in daily life no matter how limited in extent. Experience need not be wide for human or literary fulfilment, but it must be deep, and, for literary purposes, it must be artistically realized, and it must be expressed ... Creative imagination transforms experience into a work of art, but it can only give artistic form when it is familiar with such forms ... It requires training and familiarity' (3). The major obstacle for women writers was their lack of education. MacCarthy cites Fielding's description of the qualities required of a great writer: '*Genius, Learning, Conversation*, and "*a good heart*"' (4). The first and last are natural endowments, but the middle two come from education.

MacCarthy continues the general outline of her study with a quick tour of the line of women writers in England, from the pastoral through the drama, Restoration fiction and poetry, and finally the eighteenth-century novel proper. She ends with Austen who, in her opinion, symbolizes the arrival of the mature woman novelist in England. The obstacles for women include external obstacles, particularly male opposition based largely on 'a double fear: fear that women's new occupation might change their attitude towards domestic and social duties, and fear that women's achievements might eclipse those of men' (8). She acknowledges a third fear, too, a fear of the moral corruption that often comes with writing. This corruption, exemplified in Behn, Manley, and the 'Restoration school of female desperadoes' (22), is especially abhorrent in women, and MacCarthy to some extent shares the concern. But MacCarthy's reservations are not sufficient to cause her to overlook their superiority as writers to their near contemporary, Katherine Philips, who earned a high reputation by avoiding fiction in favour of artificial, *précieuse* poetry. Philips's mediocrity went unnoticed by many during her lifetime because she was so adept at choosing forms acceptable to her audience. MacCarthy can credit her only with being 'the first sentimental writer in the English language' (18).

For MacCarthy, the coming of age of women writers coincides with the coming of age of the English novel. Women became full and equal partners in the novel as its various subgenres emerged. Her study thus traces the parallel developments of women novelists and the genre in which they flourished.

MacCarthy begins her detailed account with 'The Pastoral Romance,' a chapter dedicated to Lady Mary Wroth and Anne Weamys. As the first woman to write prose fiction, Lady Mary is the more important of the two. Her *Urania* is largely a Sidneian romance, but in the process of writing her pastoral she included a number of short, digressive 'realistic little stories' (49) in the manner of the French *novelle*, thereby introducing an important innovation in the direction of the novel. The seventeenth century also saw the rise of biographies written by women, a development MacCarthy maintains also contributed to the novel, since biography required a realistic presentation of an artful narrative of a human life. Her chapter on biography examines the work of Anne Clifford, Countess of Montgomery and Pembroke; Margaret Cavendish, Duchess of Newcastle; Lucy Hutchinson; and Anne, Lady Fanshawe.

The following chapter is devoted to Newcastle as a writer of fiction. MacCarthy praises her for contributing a number of 'embryonic ideas' to the novel as well as for turning her back on the 'decadent' heroic romances so much favoured by contemporary women of her class (121). This is followed by a chapter surveying the range of popular forms during the Restoration, beginning with the heroic romance, a form MacCarthy dislikes for its resistance to realistic story-telling as well as for its class biases. She finds the Restoration stage dominated by the same romance spirit in its serious plays, though the comedies provide an indication of the possibility of preferable alternatives. Prose alternatives were also available in the *novelle* and *novella*, along with the picaresque tale and the new fiction of Lafayette. She assumes that the Restoration was a time when no woman not desperate for money would write, and that any woman driven to writing would likely be drawn to stage comedy or short fiction both by inclination and by the marketplace.

This discussion is by way of introducing 'the first and the greatest of the literary swashbucklers,' Aphra Behn. Behn wrote for bread. Her 'success depended on writing as the men wrote, and the men wrote to please the lewd and cynical tastes of the rich and leisured. The influential public wanted in plays or in stories a representation of life as they knew it, and life as they knew it stank to heaven.' Behn, like other women writers for money, understood the job description: 'If one chooses to be a miner one expects to be blackened from head to foot in the course of one's work' (130). MacCarthy finds Behn (overly) influenced by the heroic romance, an influence she regrets but excuses as unavoidable, given the central place of the romance in the culture of the age. But she also sees some important innovations in Behn's work, particularly in anticipating the techniques of Defoe that made fictional events and characters seem real. She provides detailed accounts of all of Behn's fiction (her assumption throughout the study is that full accounts, including plot summaries, are necessary because so few people have actually read the fiction she is discussing) before turning to her great novel, *Oroonoko*, 'which carried her far beyond all the novelists of the age' (151). It shares with her other fiction a mix of romance, realism, and claims for authenticity, but transcends them 'because the gap between her experience and her idealism, realized suddenly with deadly clarity, wrings from her something nobler than she guessed' (162).

After a discussion of realistic satire by women and mention of the realism of Defoe and Swift, MacCarthy turns to the followers of Behn. Manley and Haywood have their brief moment before 'the ethical focus returns to fiction.' She contrasts 'their artificial and poisonous concoctions' (194) with the realism of *Moll Flanders* and *Roxana*. They remain, however, the bridge between Behn and the more wholesome world of Barker, Davys, Aubin, and Rowe: 'Before we can arrive at this God-fearing and piously sentimental ground we must pass through noxious swamps. Here be crocodiles, here be stenches! Let us clench our teeth, hold our noses and advance' (195). She begins with *The New Atalantis*, a shameless scandal chronicle without redeeming value. It remains unread, MacCarthy notes, by all but historians of the novel. Not only is it highly suspect on moral grounds, but it is also devoid of artistic merit: 'Had this work been distinguished by intelligent construction, a graceful style, or by wit, however mordant, these qualities would suffice to triumph in a great measure over the ephemeral nature of the subject. But actually *The New Atalantis* is devoid of such characteristics. The construction is execrable. It consists of endless conversations between vague individuals, or rather monologues so long and so involved that we forget the speaker and are surprised when a question or a reply reminds us of their existence. There is either no effort or no ability to achieve verisimilitude' (198).

MacCarthy has read Manley's works with care, but she is far too committed to the realistic novel, and to the more general aesthetic principles of her time, to tolerate Manley's near total disregard of them. Add to that her moral distaste, and it is not surprising that she can find little good to say about Manley's work. MacCarthy nevertheless devotes seventeen pages to her, and acknowledges the occasional effectiveness of her sharp wit. But even Manley's 'triumphs of vindictiveness' are rare. 'Obscenity and slanderous *tours de force*' are her norm' (202). Her short novellas occasionally contain realistic elements, but they are insufficient to salvage the whole. MacCarthy ends with *Rivella* (1714), a work she finds pathetic in its accurate representation of the author's life.

Haywood inevitably follows Manley, and is given similar and near equal billing with sixteen pages. Her prolific fiction writing is divided into three types: 'the sentimentalized *novella*,' 'the key-novel,' and 'the novel of domestic sentiment and of manners' (212). MacCarthy explains in some detail why neither of the first two subgenres is worthy of great attention. In the novella, her 'melodramatic fustian bears a superficial resemblance to Aphra Behn's worst novels, but without Aphra Behn's power and without her flashes of realism. Of Mrs Haywood's key-novels one can only say that they are as scurrilous and as prurient as those of Mrs Manley, with similar flashes of mordant pithiness' (215–16). Having sinned against the changing tastes of the middle of the eighteenth century, Haywood was able eventually to adapt. 'It is to this opportunism that her only notable achievements are due' (219); late in life she produced work more in line with the new morality, and still later with the novel as developed by Richardson, Fielding, and Smollett. *Betsy Thoughtless* is too full of excess incident and mannerism to qualify as well made, even by eighteenth-century standards, but it is Haywood's best novel, with traces of realism and credible characterization. It perhaps influenced Burney, but any comparison with *Evelina* is entirely to Haywood's disadvantage.

MacCarthy finishes her chapter on the generations immediately after Behn with discussions of minor writers. Arabella Plantin wrote outmoded and highly artificial romances. *Love Led Astray* (1727), for example, is 'an absurd travesty of the pastoral tradition' (227). Elizabeth Rowe's religious tracts in the guise of novella or pastoral romance are full of 'unctuous moralizing' that pleased her readers and was encouraged by the likes of Watts, Pope, Prior, and Johnson: 'These excellent men were willing to accord to piety an admiration which expressed itself in literary criticism. Pious mediocrity did not set their teeth on edge, and was indeed regarded as peculiarly womanly. When Hannah More became the apotheosis of the Rowe tradition, she found her pedestal awaiting her' (229). Jane Barker also wrote heavily didactic novels, hardly better than Rowe's. Mary Davys is in the same mould. MacCarthy much prefers Penelope Aubin to either. Despite 'her obvious didacticism,' Aubin was able to blend realism with romance; she was an early contributor to the development of the Oriental tale; she made good use of the theme of 'the virtuous maiden pursued by the charming rake'; and 'she was one of the very few women who essayed the picaresque' (231). Elizabeth Boyd's claim to attention is also for the picaresque, but the most important writer of picaresque fiction at this time was Sarah Fielding, who managed to blend it with Richardsonian sensibility. *David Simple* is too heterogeneous a mixture of essays, sermonizing, satire, and story to be a novel. Its characterization is weak, especially the 'cardboard' title character, an uninteresting 'bloodless, moralizing sentimentalist' (233). The internal conflict between 'external events' and 'character analyses' leads to the book's failure. But Fielding is praised for 'her inward approach to character,' an approach that anticipated the direction of the modern novel (237). MacCarthy summarizes her view of the women novelists immediately after Behn as 'for the most part, merely hacks' who achieved 'nothing much' in their 'mediocre' work (238). Their importance is largely historical, 'but they prepared the way for the greatness to come' (239).

The final chapter in volume 1 focuses on a particular stream in which the preparatory work of early women novelists was especially important: the epistolary novel. This chapter shows that Richardson's form for *Pamela* was anything but new when he arrived at it. MacCarthy traces the emergence of fictional letters in the late seventeenth century, and the many contributors to the subgenre before Richardson, paying special attention to the influence Newcastle, Behn, and Rowe must have had on him. She notes the strengths and weaknesses of the form, and its special suitability to Richardson's sensibility. She also identifies the feminine nature of his art by the following analogy: 'As women ordinarily turned to letter-writing to give vent to their love of intimate outpourings and familiar gossip, and for the expression of views so often denied them in daily intercourse, so Richardson, that retiring and sedentary man, that unobtrusive egoist, had been a voluminous correspondent all his life long.' Her description of his mind only reinforces the connection: 'His mind was a hot-house within which a strange luxuriance of emotions fed on a sickly-sweet corruption, and grew out of all proportion in the vitiated air. It was an essential of his being, and consequently it was the habit of a lifetime, to observe minutely, to dissect every mood, impulse, reaction, and motive, to magnify the emotions, and to luxuriate in sensibility' (242). Richardson's habits of mind, of course, had enormous influence on later women novelists. MacCarthy's point in this chapter is to revisit the claims for his inventing the epistolary novel by demonstrating 'that women writers of fiction played their part in preparing the raw materials' (262).

MacCarthy organizes her second volume by dividing the novel into five subgenres. She begins with the Oriental novel, and traces its development over the century from its Continental sources through the periodical essays and Johnson to its greatest triumph, *Vathek*. She then discusses the women who wrote Oriental fiction. Aubin, Laetitia Pilkington, and Reeve are given brief mention; Haywood receives fuller treatment for *The Adventures of Eovaai* (1736), only to be dismissed for producing just another scandal chronicle, 'this time in a turban' (273). The best contributions by women were of the moral kind, and the best by far among this group was Sheridan's *Nourjahad*. 'This charming story is excellently constructed, and the magical effects are most ingeniously and convincingly suggested and reasonably explained. The moralizing is not in the least overdone' (276). Greatly inferior is Knight's *Dinarbas*, a 'moralizing' continuation of Johnson's 'philosophic novel.' Knight adds no novelistic interest to Johnson's tale while failing to continue the philosophic argument that gave the original its importance. MacCarthy ends her account with a characteristic, short-tempered dismissal: 'Indeed it seems that she wrote a moralistic tale because philosophy was beyond her scope' (279). The chapter concludes with a brief discussion of Edgeworth's *Murad the Unlucky* (1804), a story of 'sheer edification' without 'the more imaginative touches of *Nourjahad*,' but nonetheless 'well told' (279).

'The Novel of Sentiment and of Sensibility' merits a much longer chapter. MacCarthy begins by revealing a number of her attitudes and assumptions about the second half of the eighteenth century. Social class relations determine a great deal of activity in this society, and she clearly finds the rigid hierarchy and resulting behaviour repulsive. She has nothing but contempt for heightened sensibility which ignores real social problems while wallowing in sentiment. The growth of the middle class and its increasing prosperity created an enormous appetite for fiction, and most of the novelists were content to provide 'pabulum' to meet demand. Yet at mid-century there was 'a spontaneous flowering in fiction' thanks to the work of the 'Great Four,' Richardson, Fielding, Sterne, and Smollett, the 'men of genius' who raised the novel to new heights and established it as a 'branch of literary art' (284).

Though Fielding was the greatest novelist of the century, and Sterne, Smollett, and Goldsmith were all great artists, it was Richardson who made the greatest initial impact on his readers, 'not because they realized his greatness as an artist, but because he had so much in common with their outlook and again because, in a general sense, he was more easily imitable' (285). His readership was steeped in the romance tradition and three-quarters of it MacCarthy asserts, were women. Sensibility was the watchword for many novel readers. It differed from sentiment 'mainly in degree,' and was characterized by 'excessive vulnerability to feeling,' arising from 'an idealization of spiritual delicacy.' MacCarthy clearly considers it a doctrine without merit supporting the worst hypocrisies of its society: 'It eventually perished of its own falsity' (286). A full catalogue of the qualities and values associated with sensibility reveals just how fully MacCarthy is predisposed against it.

This was also the time of a great influx of women novel writers. Given that 'the cult of sentiment and sensibility was so effeminate and the trend of moral earnestness so decorous' (289), it was completely predictable that women novelists would be drawn to the subgenre. It was both the most natural and the most respectable kind of novel for women to write. It was also the novel of choice for the circulating libraries: there was a 'ready market for rubbish' much to the benefit of even the most 'untalented woman writer' (290). The novels by most women novelists of the period are of great historical interest, particularly for providing a key to the basic, common principles that defined the way most middle-class women led their lives, but few have much artistic merit. MacCarthy is consistently clear about the views that inform her discussions of individual writers. In this case, her readers are well-prepared for the harsh criticism that even the most interesting of these writers will receive.

She begins with a writer who preceded the influx of the largest numbers of women novelists, Charlotte Lennox. MacCarthy devotes eleven pages to Lennox's novels. Her favourites are *The Female Quixote* and *Henrietta* (1758). The former is a thoroughly enjoyable send-up of the heroic romance, a bit repetitious and a bit sententious, but successful despite these shortcomings. Lennox is not, however, contrary to the view of some critics, comparable to Cervantes: 'One was a genius. The other was a clever wit. One, intending to write a satire, achieved an immortal work of art: the other, intending to write a burlesque – wrote a burlesque' (301). *Henrietta* is an 'interesting novel,' in fact, one of the best from the 1750s. It is filled with 'much energy, vividness, and acute observation.' The influence of Richardson is apparent, but it does not extend to his Christian charity. Instead, there is 'an attitude of acid criticism, chiefly exerted on the *nouveaux riches* and on the nobility who are shown as haughty and heartless, willing to lower their pride only for money' (304). Finally, MacCarthy finds *Henrietta* humourless, superficial, and crude. It is worth emphasizing that this is the criticism she offers of a novel she likes, and one that appeared before the unfortunate dominance of sensibility.

The account of Lennox is followed by five pages on Susannah and Margaret Minifie. Their early novels are 'poor in construction and unduly sentimental' (305), but they improve with time. Susannah's *The Memoirs of Mary* (1793), written under her married name, Gunning, is, for MacCarthy, 'one of the best of the lesser novels of the period' (308). Not least of Gunning's achievements is writing 'the least sentimental work of this group of women novelists' (309). Elizabeth Bonhote, Maria Susanna Cooper, and Mrs Woodfin all provide examples of more sentimental novelists who focus on issues of domestic morality. They provide a brief introduction to the best of the novelists of sensibility, Frances Sheridan. Five pages are devoted to *Sidney Bidulph*, a novel written under the direct aid and encouragement of Richardson. MacCarthy agrees with the traditional view that the novel is too long and too full of suffering, but she notes the link between sensibility and 'endurance.' She also praises Sheridan for presenting 'the feminine point of view' (312) on issues hitherto not represented in fiction and, more generally, for presenting a woman's mind. '*Sydney Bidulph*,' she concludes, 'is an original, vivid, and charming book. It is, above all human,' successful in making its characters 'live before our eyes' (315).

MacCarthy's final group of novelists of sensibility, Frances Brooke, Elizabeth Griffith, Helen Maria Williams, and Mary Robinson, are similarly drawn to excessive misfortune, though none have the power and originality of Sheridan. Brooke consistently suffers from the influence of overly idealized sensibility, even in her elaborate descriptions of nature, which too often resemble pastoral. Though Griffith's *The Delicate Distress*

(1769) consists of 'graceful letters' (318) and a more controlled representation of sensibility, her plot and characters fall short of credible, as does
her valuing of gentleness as the supreme female virtue. *The History of
Lady Barton* (1771) 'is a very poor novel indeed' (320), mechanical, badly
constructed, entirely wanting in characterization, sententious, and melodramatic. And Griffith is rarely able to see beyond the male point of
view about women. She is a model for all that MacCarthy dislikes about
the novels of sensibility. Williams too is found wanting. Her commit-
ments to the principles of the French Revolution did not make her a
good novelist; Williams's novels are excessively emotional, and they are
almost entirely lacking in any connection to reality. Robinson is similarly
removed from reality and unable to create a credible character. 'But however smothered by high-falutin' nonsense, there is sincere feeling for
scenery, and it is evident also that Mary Robinson had taken the Gothic
hint from Mrs Radcliffe.' Robinson's novels are 'a curious mixture of
vulgarity, ignorance, and poetic feeling' (327). The chapter concludes by
summarizing the importance of these novelists of sensibility, despite
their many faults, in establishing a female point of view in the novel, in
other words, of women writing as women.

MacCarthy's thirty-six-page chapter 'The Domestic Novel' is devoted
entirely to Burney. Its length probably provides the clearest indication of
MacCarthy's valuing of Burney: the chapter is full of heavily qualified
praise mixed with censure. An unfavourable comparison is made to the
Brontës, who 'were born with powers which "little Burney" never
possessed, and which she would have feared even to imagine' (336).
MacCarthy thinks that *Evelina* was initially overvalued by her friends
and family because they had so severely undervalued its author prior to
its appearance. She is startled by Burney's lack of interest in reading,
given that she had access to a fine library, and rejects the notion that
Burney pretended to ignorance, offering instead the view that 'Fanny's
affectation really lay in pretending to hide under an appearance of womanly ignorance, knowledge which she certainly did not possess' (338).
Burney's diaries are the principle source for her view, and MacCarthy
attributes Burney's gift as a novelist to her family situation: 'Since Fanny
Burney had the mind of a newspaper reporter with a keen sense of the
ridiculous, it was fortunate for her that she lived in such a maelstrom of
events, albeit merely social events. The Burney ménage was the perfect
environment for such talents, because a ceaseless tide of life flowed
swiftly in at the front door through the drawing room and music room,
and so out again. Not such a tide as moving seems asleep, but the most

charming, shallow, babbling, frothy stream in the world' (339). MacCarthy sees Burney as a passive receptacle, taking in the surface events around her without inquiring into the motives or feelings that informed them. She was incapable of creating three-dimensional characters because her perceptions remained on the surface.

MacCarthy argues that in following Richardson's lead Burney found the right form for her talents in the epistolary novel. Aside from Mr Villars, the characters produce letters that understandably caught the interest of Burney's reading public. It had been some time since the four great novelists had captured the attention of that public; Burney was the best novelist to appear since the death of Smollett, and she brought genuine innovation to the novel. She was the first to create real women characters, 'the first to create a convincing heroine,' and the first 'to show us real life through a woman's eyes' (347). Not for Burney was the traditional male view of women found even in the novels by women that preceded her.

Burney is also important for her influence on Austen, though Austen is, of course, the far superior writer. Her heroines, unlike Burney's, refuse to acquiesce in the male values that controlled so much of women's lives, a strong plus for MacCarthy. *Evelina* is Burney's best novel because it is her shortest and because 'its subject-matter was least likely to expose her superficiality' (351). Her characters, even in *Evelina*, remain caricatures, and her lack of judgment too often leads to vulgarity: 'This lack of good taste is the plague spot in Fanny Burney, and to it we may trace all the worst faults in her writings. It shows itself always in a want of restraint, in the deplorable way in which she always tended to exaggerate, whether it was a character, an emotion, or a style' (354). That lack of restraint is most revealing, MacCarthy finds, when Burney attempts to represent depth of feeling. Even characters who had seemed convincing are suddenly reduced to 'cardboard' (356). Lack of restraint in style manifests itself as 'pretentious pedantry' and 'euphuistic pomposity' (357).

All of these shortcomings can be identified in *Evelina*, and when MacCarthy turns to Burney's other novels she finds Burney's excesses magnified beyond her point of tolerance. The decision to switch from an epistolary format to a narrative in Johnsonian English is further evidence of Burney's lack of judgment. *Cecilia* is distinctly inferior to *Evelina*, and it is only 'with reluctance' that MacCarthy speaks of *Camilla* and *The Wanderer* at all (362). They make no contribution to the development of the novel, and reveal the decline of a novelist who had produced one great, if superficial, novel. MacCarthy's explanation is that after her years at court Burney was so consumed by 'extreme refinement and decorum' that she was reduced to only the 'veriest trifles for her subject' (363). Her late novels are interesting only as an example of a once fine artist losing her powers.

From the domestic MacCarthy moves to 'The Gothic Novel.' She echoes the opinion that the Gothic revival was a late product of the cult of sensibility as well as part of the Romantic revival. She traces the development of the various components of the Gothic revival, in architecture and poetry, and early attempts at the historical novel and the novel of terror (both physical and supernatural) before turning to Walpole. *The Castle of Otranto* is of historical importance, but a failure both as Gothic and historical novel: MacCarthy is unable to take it at all seriously. She agrees with Reeve's criticism of Walpole, and is disappointed that Reeve could not transfer her theoretical approach to the Gothic novel to her practice. *The Old English Baron* (like Reeve's subsequent novels) is clear, commonsensical, and moral to a fault. 'Clara Reeve writing a Gothic novel calls up a picture of a maiden lady in elastic-sided boots, endeavouring to control a mustang' (380).

Reeve's greatest importance for MacCarthy lies in her influence on Harriet Lee; Lee was influenced by Reeve's *The Exiles* (1788) in writing her 'Kruitzner.' MacCarthy considers the Lee sisters 'women who really caught the Gothic spirit' and 'aided its development in fiction' (381). She devotes nine and a half pages to them, compared to the three and a half allotted to Reeve. She acknowledges the probable influence of *The Recess* on Scott, but does not think the better of it for that: 'Genius can find an inspiration in the most unexpected and even worthless material. That *The Recess* is worthless there is little doubt' (381). Its use of history is laughable; its emphasis on tears at best unfortunate, and MacCarthy clearly takes offence at what she finds a grotesquely inaccurate representation of Ireland. She greatly prefers the *Canterbury Tales* to *The Recess*, largely for Harriet's Gothic contributions. *Kruitzner* is the best of her works, and it is significant for its title character, for in Kruizner, Lee presented 'not merely Gothic mysteries, but the mysteries of a soul' (390).

MacCarthy's discussion of the Lees is followed by eight pages on Charlotte Smith. Smith's particular importance is in her gift in presenting landscape as part of her fiction; in this she anticipated and influenced Radcliffe. Smith's work blends sensibility and doctrinal didacticism with a growing use of the Gothic. When her didacticism dominates, as in

*Desmond*, MacCarthy finds Smith least interesting and effective. In her best work, *The Old Manor House*, the elements are blended evenly and to good purpose and Smith succeeds in realizing character for the first time. MacCarthy's summary of Smith is interesting in its emphasis on the importance of the Gothic elements in her work, not a frequent refrain in most of the earlier criticism: 'In her effort to unite the Gothic, domestic, and *tendenz* genres she attempted the impossible, yet, as a reflection of the chief trends in the second half of the eighteenth century, her novels repay careful examination. Their chief value lies in their Gothic aspect. That Charlotte Smith and Mrs Radcliffe had the same conception of Gothicism is quite clear, and Mrs Smith's best claim to remembrance rests in the fact that she provided Mrs Radcliffe with some of the raw materials of the Gothic craft (398).

Fifteen pages on Radcliffe immediately follow. Radcliffe's importance stems from her ability to consolidate its various elements into 'the most characteristic type of English Gothic fiction' (398). After two artistic failures she succeeded in uniting beauty and terror in the novel, realizing the sublime effects anticipated in the work of Smith. This is the gift of a poet, and MacCarthy feels that Radcliffe should have been one. But her verse is 'worthless,' so she was diverted into producing the kinds of prose poems that highlight her work. 'She is the supreme example of genuine literary power misdirected for want of education' (403). Radcliffe was incapable of realizing character, pretentious, and either naïve or vulgar. She lacked the ability to be a great novelist, and the discipline and training to be the great poet MacCarthy thinks she could have been. And she was too successful to learn from her critics, most of whom were entirely too encouraging. MacCarthy admits that she does not care for the Gothic novel in any form; this antipathy makes her disappointment in its being the form in which Radcliffe wasted her genius the more acute. She is most positive about *The Mysteries of Udolpho* and *The Italian*; the latter is Radcliffe's best novel, despite its mindless hostility to Roman Catholicism. 'With all her faults (and they are great),' MacCarthy concludes, 'Mrs Radcliffe deserves to be remembered amongst these who have permanently influenced English literature' (415). She is thinking especially of subsequent generations, for she considers *Frankenstein* the only novel of value to appear from her immediate followers.

From the Gothic MacCarthy moves to 'The Didactic Novel,' which she also calls the *tendenz* novel. She distinguishes it from the novel of sensibility by virtue of its genuine concern for social issues, as opposed to the mere wallowing in emotion for its own sake that she associates with sensibility. The idealism of the *tendenz* novelists arose in response to a number of wholly admirable concerns, and MacCarthy seems far more in sympathy with the politics of the didactic novel than virtually all of her predecessors. Her modernist aesthetic, however, does not sit well with those that put propaganda ahead of art. Bage and Holcroft offer models of the problems inherent in the didactic novel. There is enough of the Gothic in *Caleb Williams*, however, to make it 'in a sense a masterpiece' despite its 'sociological purpose' (421).

Women, too, were drawn to the didactic novel, with its educational objectives. But they had a harder time being taken seriously when they entered the world of radical politics than their male counterparts. Smith met with great resistance to *Desmond*, and others had still more hostile or dismissive receptions. With Wollstonecraft (six pages), the political agenda takes on issues that are clearly feminist. Yet, while an interesting philosopher and social thinker, she had no skills as a novelist. All of her fiction is poorly conceived as fiction, and equally poorly executed.

Mary Hays (two pages) follows in Wollstonecraft's wake, but lacks her 'greatness of mind' (429). MacCarthy focuses on Hays's 'morbid psychology' and on her failure to do much with the novelistic potential of her favourite theme, the ruined woman. She then turns to Elizabeth Hamilton (nearly three pages), a writer whose novels oppose the radical politics of Hays and Godwin. Hamilton's *Memoirs of Modern Philosophers* is a curious mixture of ridicule and didacticism; her gift was for the former and she was far less successful at presenting opposing arguments in a more serious form. Not only do these two approaches conflict in a single text, but when Hamilton departs from burlesque she is a dull story teller, and her 'direct moralizing has really no place in a work of fiction' (434).

Another contrast to Hays is found in Elizabeth Inchbald, the one woman in 'Godwin's group of philosophic enthusiasts' capable of being 'doctrinal without abating her femininity' (434). Seven and a half pages demonstrate why MacCarthy feels that Inchbald's novels deserve a better reputation than they have had. She admires Inchbald's gift for social satire, her ability to tell a story, her characterization, and her control over her didactic intentions. Four pages on Amelia Opie follow. Opie, who wrote her novels after the excesses of the French Revolution were well known, tries to negotiate a path between her 'revulsion' at those excesses and her ongoing moral and social concerns, concerns that evolved from an early affinity with the radicals to a commitment to Quakerism. Her novels teach with 'generosity and charm. She had a pleasant, simple narrative style, and was particularly praised in her own day for her pathos, but she had not a sure touch, and, by comparison with Maria Edgeworth, she appears mediocre' (442). MacCarthy finds *Adeline Mowbray* an effective, sympathetic treatment of the life of Wollstonecraft; it is also Opie's best novel. Unfortunately, she was unable to maintain work of this level. Her late novel, *Temper* (1812), 'is really a wretched novel' (445).

MacCarthy's single paragraph on Hannah More mixes hostility with dismissal. 'Since it cannot be said that she contributed anything to the art of fiction, and since her stories are nearer to direct pedagogy than to literature, it would serve no useful purpose to consider them in any detail' (445). But she cannot refrain from expressing her indignation at *Cœlebs*: 'We are asked to contemplate this characterless prig, this sententious vacuum, while he scours England for one who might be worthy to marry him. To endure his interviews with hopeful parents and marriageable daughters, one must laugh.' She finds More's still more overtly didactic tales her best fiction, but doubts that they succeeded in keeping readers from experiencing novels 'intended for their betters' (446).

From More MacCarthy moves to Edgeworth, 'the greatest of the didactic moralists' (446). Eleven pages are devoted to an account of her use of fiction to further the educational theories she shared with her father (whose contributions to her work get a mixed review). Like More, Edgeworth wrote moral tales in support of the social order. But what is intolerable in More is transformed by Edgeworth's 'gift' into fiction genuinely praiseworthy: 'We read her shallow stories and swallow her specific for happiness as a hypochondriac might swallow quack medicine – not because we believe, but because it seems so easy and infallible' and 'because they are presented with charm and wit' (449). Edgeworth shares with Austen an instinct for commonsense, 'but Jane's commonsense and her instinct for the ludicrous could never have allowed her to reduce the whole of life to a tract. Jane's commonsense was the reasoning of a satiric genius; Maria's was the blind earnestness of a second-rate mind' (450).

Edgeworth is acknowledged as the first regional novelist. *Castle Rackrent* is her best novel; the other Irish novels increasingly deal with the social and political conditions of Ireland, conditions Edgeworth approaches as a well-intentioned outsider without the stomach or interest to take them on directly or in adequate depth. Ultimately, MacCarthy considers Edgeworth a writer often overrated: 'The claim of didactic preeminence is in itself sufficient to range a novelist on a lower artistic level. The question of her Irish sketches remains. Her interest in local colour was secondary to her didactic purpose except in one single work – *Castle Rackrent*, on which must be based her surest claim as a novelist. Her greatest achievement lies in the fact that, although she had no clearly conceived intention and imagined no corresponding artistic form, her novels did suggest the idea of regionalism to later writers' (457).

This chapter ends with four pages on the Scottish Edgeworth, Susan Ferrier. MacCarthy finds Ferrier less didactic and more realistic, less sympathetic and more satiric. Ferrier shares Burney's instinct for caricature and Edgeworth's weakness in plot construction. But where Edgeworth is frequently diverted by her didacticism, Ferrier's diversion stems from her 'intense pleasure in vivisecting her eccentrics' (458). Ferrier is important for the development of Scottish literature, and she is an impressive satirist, albeit without the skill or subtlety of Austen.

MacCarthy concludes her study with a chapter on the first genuinely great woman novelist, Austen. She makes clear that she considers Austen the finest artist among the women novelists, just as she considers Emily Brontë the greatest genius. That perspective informs her judgments of their predecessors, but she concedes their importance in having fought for and succeeded in establishing the rights and abilities for women to write novels, and to write them on their own terms. MacCarthy's aesthetic is not friendly to the work of the early women novelists, but her study remains one of the most important works predating the renewed interest in these novelists in the past thirty or so years (as recognized by Janet Todd's reprinting *The Female Pen* with an introduction praising MacCarthy for her pioneering study). The fact that even MacCarthy, one of the best read and most sympathetic critics of the twentieth century, could not recommend much of the fiction by women before Austen speaks volumes about the critical resistance to their work throughout the century.

## Specialized, Academic Studies

### J.M.S. Tompkins (1897–1986)

The general increase in scholarly publication during the middle of the twentieth century included a significant number of specialized, often academic, studies of topics relevant to early women novelists. The most important of these was probably J.M.S. Tompkins's *The Popular Novel in England, 1770–1800* (1932). Tompkins discusses large numbers of women novelists in her study, including a significant number of largely forgotten writers. She justifies her subject, 'tenth-rate fiction,' in terms of three key questions: 'What sort of novels were read between 1770 and 1800? What interests, tastes and principles do they reflect? What types do they exhibit?' (v). She notes without objection the standard judgment that there are no great novelists between Smollett and Austen, but recognizes that many novels were consumed with great pleasure by an eager readership in the final three decades of the eighteenth century. The sources of that pleasure provide her with an interesting subject to explore.

Tompkins does not attempt to recover neglected greatness, and she has no declared interest in revising the canon of the novel. But her efforts invariably cause her readers to revisit their previous assumptions, and it is arguable that she intended to generate renewed respect for a small number of the writers she surveys. She is a demanding critic, one who does not offer praise easily. No novelist of the period she studies was able to maintain the quality that the four great mid-century novelists had established. Moreover, 'the good work that was published bore no proportion to the bad, and the bad was very bad indeed and infected the reputation of the good' (3). The novels that earn her approbation have passed a test that should impress her readers.

Tompkins begins with a discussion of the literary marketplace for novels, one that provided the working environment for the better novelists of the period. They had to compete in that marketplace, and they had to try to distance themselves from the ordinary purveyors of pulp for the booksellers. An account of how late-century novelists developed what they learned from their predecessors follows. Richardson's imitators wrote epistolary novels of virtue under attack, full of pathos; none are worth revisiting. Graves, Jenner, and Cumberland provide far better fare among the followers of Fielding. Smollett has no genuine followers; picaresque novels continue, but none of genuine worth. Sterne's followers are legion, but only Mackenzie transcends the tired imitation that is the norm. Older forms, too, continue, particularly romances, and critics continue to protest their gross violations of probability. 'The reasonable plots of Mrs. Brooke and Miss Burney, though the future lay with them, are insignificant in number beside the unreasonable ones' (60).

Having provided the context for the novel in 1770, Tompkins moves on to the new developments that characterize the most interesting work of her period. A chapter on didacticism and sensibility argues that conduct was 'the prevailing intellectual interest of the age' (70), and that it holds a prominent place in the novels of that age. She lists a number of the favourite topics that recur in the novels; they are usually domestic, and they often focus on the appropriate conduct of women. She discusses the cult of sensibility, again with special emphasis on the centrality of women and female feeling. She also notes the virtual absence of the comic novel.

Tompkins then turns to the 'female novelists,' in a chapter that provides an unusually comprehensive survey. She begins with a discussion of the conditions that led to increased participation by women in the literary marketplace and the conventions for female authorship that followed. Women wrote for three reasons, two of them expected and acceptable: to teach and to support themselves and their families. The third group, those who wrote for pleasure, took the greatest risks and achieved the best results. That group includes Radcliffe, Reeve, Griffith, and Burney, those few women who were considered beyond the narrowly defined and well-contained class of women writers. But even they failed to write in a realistic mode, instead sharing with inferior women writers the roles of 'moralists, satirists and dreamers. In their hands the novel was not so much a reflection of life as a counterpoise to it, within the covers of which they looked for compensation, for ideal pleasures and ideal revenge' (129). Tompkins's low opinion of the quality of much of the fiction she discusses results in part from the privileging of realism so common in the criticism of the early twentieth century.

Tompkins is still more forthright about the impact of the 'moral code of the woman's novel' (140). She finds the eighteenth-century idea of prudence, 'self-government in the interests of the community' (141), the centrepiece of that moral code. Since it informs the treatment of women in virtually all the novels of the period, it must be understood by subsequent critics. Tompkins clearly considers the code both a severe limitation on the novelists and a disincentive for readers.

Few positive evaluative comments emerge in the first half of her study, but when she reaches her chapter 'New Life in the Novel,' and charts the appearance of new voices amidst the increased novelistic activity of the 1780s, Tompkins refers to Bage, Sophia Lee, Smith, Radcliffe, and Moore as 'filling the old forms with new interest and striking out new forms of their own,' drawing 'the novel nearer to life' while probing hitherto unexplored 'realms of imagination' (174). They offered the earliest evidence that declarations of the death of the novel were premature; instead, she finds the precursors of the greater Victorian novelists preparing the way for triumphs to come. The novel, in short, is becoming more realistic, more democratic, and more open to risk-taking. For Tompkins, there could be no better indication of the progress that she finds in the development of the novel.

Tompkins welcomes the increasingly individualized characters, regional and exotic settings, and serious intellectual content of the novels of the 1780s and 1790s. Her first extended discussion of an individual novelist is of Bage, and she makes it clear that she considers him better than the vast majority of his contemporaries. Her following chapter, on the revival of romance and the early historical novel, focuses on Reeve, Walpole, and Lee, again largely for reasons of quality. The Gothic romance is then given its own chapter. Tompkins distinguishes between the native version, exemplified by Radcliffe, and the German-inspired version exemplified by Lewis. Radcliffe is the greatest of the Gothic novelists; her novels surpass the genre they so successfully established: 'Ann Radcliffe, mighty enchantress of Udolpho, Shakespeare of Romance-writers and first poetess of romantic fiction, has during the last ten years resumed her proper place in the eye of criticism, and her very real though limited talent is no longer obscured by critical amusement, or by the excess of its own charms. The importance of her novels as a contribution to fiction has never been doubted, but recent studies, cutting through their redundancies to the vigorous imagination that inspired them, have put the reader in a position to understand, even if he does not wish to echo, the exuberant praises shed on her by her contemporaries' (248). Tompkins goes on to praise Radcliffe's novels for their 'picturesque beauty' intensified by 'fear and awe,' their boldness and assurance of touch at a time when such qualities were rare in the novel, their unabashed romanticism, and their 'conscientious' craft (248–9). No other novelist receives such high praise or extensive coverage. Radcliffe is, for Tompkins, simply the greatest novelist of her age.

Tompkins then turns her attention to the philosophic novel of the 1790s. With the exception of *Caleb Williams*, the novels in this group offer little that is new to the form. That the novel became, at least for a brief period, a forum for propaganda and occasionally philosophic debate increased its stature, but did little to improve its quality. The novel acquired a new relevance in the general debates that captured so much of the intellectual energy of the times, but Holcroft, Wollstonecraft, Hays, Inchbald, and their many followers and opponents made no lasting contributions to the novel as a literary form.

The final chapter brings together and develops Tompkins's thoughts on the theory and technique of novel writing in the late eighteenth century. She is heartened by the return of formal considerations by century's end, encouraged by the attention to plot required by the Gothic novel. She notes a renewed attention to character, aided by dramatists like Inchbald who had turned their hand to fiction. She recounts the increased profile of physical description epitomized by Radcliffe. Finally, she returns to the slow progress of realism in this period, a progress unaided by the desire for heightened poetical effects in the novel.

Though the 'popular' novel of the period is the subject of Tompkins's study, it is difficult to determine what she has excluded. She mentions many long-forgotten texts and authors, but her focus remains on the figures who recur in the criticism discussed above. While it is not her stated intention to address issues related to the canon she is an evaluative critic, and her taste is very much in line with that of other critics of her time. *The Popular Novel in England* thus does not encourage a rethinking of the canon. Returning to forgotten writers has no impact on what is to be read in the twentieth century; Tompkins has no quarrel with the canon she received, and no desire to promote change.

## Q.D. Leavis (1906–1981)

Tompkins's study of the late eighteenth-century popular novel appeared the same year as Q.D. Leavis's *Fiction and the Reading Public*, and Leavis provides an explanation for Tompkins's apparent inability to differentiate popular from canonical fiction. Twentieth-century readers, Leavis argues, no longer have access to or contact with the best literature. An inferior, alternative literature emerged as good writers produced increasingly inaccessible work for readers increasingly unwilling to grapple with challenging literature. She sees the eighteenth century as the great age of novels written for a single, unified audience. Bunyan and Defoe wrote for a Puritan, middle- and working-class readership; Behn wrote for an educated, court-based readership. With the *Spectator* came a unified readership, one Haywood and Barker, and then Richardson and Fielding, succeeded in reaching in their novels. With the arrival of the circulating libraries that audience began to divide, and by the twentieth century the divide was absolute. Leavis mentions few novels; she is not providing a history of the novel. But her list of important novelists before Austen includes nearly equal numbers of men and women.

## James R. Foster (b. 1890)

The proliferation of scholarship in the twentieth century witnessed many specialized studies of aspects of the early novel, often doctoral dissertations published with little or no revision. A good example is Godfrey Frank Singer's (b. 1905) University of Pennsylvania thesis, published as *The Epistolary Novel: Its Origin, Development, Decline, and Residuary Influence*. Singer has chapters on the epistolary novel before Richardson, on Richardson, and on the epistolary novel to 1800. His is a thorough survey, with a focus on changes to the subgenre as it develops; he has little interest in evaluation. I have passed over studies of this kind in the interest of space, with one exception: James R. Foster's *History of the Pre-Romantic Novel in England* (1949). Foster's survey attempts to include 'any novel possessing literary value' from a group he considers victims of critics who approached them from the perspective of realistic novels and found them wanting. He argues that these novels are important for the influence they had on later, better ones and is unwilling to condemn their lofty goals: 'They preached the religion of the tender heart, stirred the emotions and the imaginations, and planted in many a breast the desire for higher ideals, tolerance, and benevolence' (vii).

Foster traces the novel of sensibility, his central focus, to the medieval romance. He sees *La princesse de Clèves* as inaugurating the modern novel of sensibility (or sentimental novel – the terms are roughly equivalent for him), 'first of all a story of love, and second a story of trials and tribulations' (16). French models remain central in Foster's study, and he includes discussions of many English translations of influential French writers. He considers Marivaux and Prévost of great importance to the English sentimental novel, listing Sarah Fielding, Lennox, Collyer, Frances Brooke, the Lees, and Burney as followers of Marivaux, and Sarah Fielding, Frances Sheridan, Reeve, the Lees, Bage, and Radcliffe among the smaller group to be influenced by Prévost. The French model was anglicized by Behn, but her appreciation of sentimental values was soon found wanting, and her lack of delicacy cost her many a later reader. Manley was similarly lacking in modesty and delicacy. Much more in the sentimental mode was Penelope Aubin; Foster accordingly describes her novels in greater detail. Haywood, too, merits significant coverage for much of her later work.

Foster's fourth chapter turns to the English novelists themselves. He begins with Sarah Fielding, a writer he admires for her learning and graciousness, despite her 'chief weakness' of 'letting her passion for moralizing and essay writing get out of hand' (74). He considers *David Simple* her best novel, a successful combination of the novels of her brother and Richardson. The others, by contrast, are 'mere potboilers' (75). He next turns to Lennox, whom he places in the school of Marivaux and Richardson. While he does not consider her of the first rank, Foster does think she was a novelist of 'better than average ability' (83). *The Female Quixote* is clearly her finest effort. He then turns to Mary Collyer, because of her originality in writing the first deist novel and, more generally, in introducing a sentimental novel in which ideas drive the narrative. The chapter ends with sections on Shebbeare,

Amory, and Dodd, providing some gender balance among a group of novelists that does not break down on clear gender lines.

Foster follows his chapter on the early sentimentalists with one on novelists he considers much greater: Richardson, Goldsmith, Fielding (mainly *Amelia*), Smollett (late), and Sterne. He then returns to the minor novelists, beginning with Frances Sheridan. For Foster, '*Sidney Bidulph* is one of the best English sentimental novels.' He admires the style, and the 'insight into the feminine heart' (142). It was more popular with readers than critics, but while he recognizes its imperfections, particularly the improbability of the plot, Foster, unlike most, is untroubled by Sheridan's desire to represent the suffering of the virtuous. Frances Brooke is his next example, and he finds in her work a successful blend of French and English sensibility, of Rousseau and Richardson. *Emily Montague* (1769) is his favourite Brooke novel, in part for its descriptions of the Canadian landscape. In the same school of novelists but inferior in quality are the Minifie sisters. Griffith is classed with them too, but judged nearly as good as Brooke. Hugh Kelly and Anne Amelia Masterman also get brief mention in this group.

Other authors singled out from this period as worthy, second-rate figures are Arthur Young, Edward Bancroft, Henry Brooke, Mackenzie, Samuel Jackson Pratt (Courtney Melmoth), Treyssac de Vergy, William Combe, Cumberland, and Charles Jenner. For Foster, sentimentalism is not limited to women novelists. It is also interesting to note how many of the figures he treats in depth have been ignored in most of the more general histories of the novel.

The final two decades of the eighteenth century round out Foster's tale as the pre-Romantic is realized in the Romantic. He sees the 1780s and 1790s as decades of increasing interests in earlier history as well as in the recent events in France. These stimulants produced the Gothic novel, a novel Foster defines through the lens of later Romanticism:

> Although undoubtedly influenced by the growing thirst for historical knowledge, the Gothic romance does not represent a serious attempt to reproduce in fiction an exact picture of the minds and manners of men and women who lived in past ages. There is usually some kind of historical background but usually not much genuine history. What novel readers wanted more than anything else was romantic love, thrilling adventure, dramatic action, and something to invite their imaginations to go vagabonding away from the here and now. The Gothic romance, especially as written by eighteenth-century ladies, is a sentimental novel in which the characters are tricked out in costumes belonging to some past epoch but

rarely concealing the fact that the minds and manners of the wearers really belonged to the century of enlightenment. (186)

Foster's fresh view from the perspective of romantic fiction shows its limitations in this passage, in his imposition of a model that the Gothic cannot realize. The best that the pre-Romantic can do is, necessarily, prepare the way for the Romantic.

When he turns to novels to demonstrate his view of the Gothic Foster begins with Leland's *Longsword*, the novel he considers 'the first English historical romance' (187). Other early influences come from the novels of Baculard d'Arnaud, Sir Herbert Croft, Ann Burke, and Elizabeth Bromley. *The Castle of Otranto*, not itself a pre-Romantic novel for Foster, was more important for the development of the Gothic as first realized by Reeve in *The Old English Baron*. Foster credits Reeve's mixture of Gothic trappings, rational world-view, and strong moral sensibility with providing the ground rules for the flood of Gothic novels to follow. He finds her interesting, but no great novelist. He is more impressed by the Lees, particularly Sophia Lee's *The Recess*, 'the most important novel blending historical characters with fictitious incidents between *Longsword* (1762) and *Waverley* (1814)' (209). He considers Harriet Lee's *The Errors of Innocence* (1786) her best novel, and he endorses the widely held view that 'Kruitzner; the German's Tale' is her best story and best work overall. The Lees, in Foster's view, seem to have best realized in English the tradition of Prévost's *Cleveland*, and *The Recess* in particular inspired subsequent novelists.

Its influence can be seen in *The Old English Baron*, and both influenced the novels of Anne Fuller, a writer he finds important largely for her influence in turn on the Porters. Anna Maria Mackenzie is the most important of the remaining host of novelists inspired by *The Recess*.

In his discussion of Burney's novels Foster emphasizes the sentimental side, looking to Richardson, Riccoboni, Frances Brooke, *Betsy Thoughtless*, Marivaux, and Prévost for conscious models Burney had read and assimilated. He sees Elizabeth Blower trying to duplicate Burney's special blend of wit, social satire, and sentiment, but without anything like equal success.

Foster's next chapter is on the 'doctrinaire novel,' a form he considers a development of the sentimental novel, and one differing more in degree than kind (225). He begins with Bage, whose novels he places in the line of Collyer, Shebbeare, Amory, Bancroft, and Henry Brooke. Next comes Smith, who, for Foster, is very similar to Bage in her political and social views. She differs in lacking his 'wit and humor,' producing novels about 'romantic loves and female distresses' in the tradition of Sheridan, the

Lees, Mackenzie, Prévost, and Rousseau (240). Her contribution to this tradition is the addition of abundant description of sublime and picturesque landscapes. Foster considers Smith's influence on Radcliffe significant, while acknowledging that she later borrowed in turn from the master of the Gothic. He also considers her superior to Radcliffe at poetic description of landscape. His full discussion of her work focuses on the early novels (as innovative), *Desmond* (for its contribution to the fiction of the French Revolution), and *The Old Manor House*, her best novel. He concludes that Smith was 'industrious, ingenious, and talented, but not a genius' (250).

The other writers Foster considers from the group that includes Smith and Radcliffe are Eliza Parsons, Helen Maria Williams, and Mary Robinson. They derive from similar moulds but are clearly inferior to Smith or Radcliffe as novelists. He then turns to the Godwin circle, starting with Inchbald, a novelist he considers good, but limited. He shares the common view that the less didactic *A Simple Story* is better than *Nature and Art*. He finds Wollstonecraft's novels interesting for their desires and for their influence, first and foremost on Mary Hays, who developed more fully many of the ideas in Wollstonecraft's short, unfinished fiction. But though he finds these novels interesting, Foster remains less than enthusiastic about this subgenre.

Foster's final chapter is on Radcliffe and her followers. He sees them emerging from the line of Richardson, Prévost, D'Arnaud, Mackenzie, Reeve, the Lees, and Smith. Radcliffe culminates a particularly imaginative tradition of sentimental novelists: 'She was the inventor of melodrama in Technicolor, the great impresario of beauty, wonder, and terror' (262). He recognizes the power of Radcliffe's work, particularly *The Romance of the Forest*, *The Mysteries of Udolpho*, and *The Italian*; he also recognizes that her version of the Gothic went out of fashion with the introduction of more supernatural events and greater horror in Lewis's *The Monk*. Elizabeth Helme, Regina Maria Roche, and George Walker are followers of Radcliffe worthy of notice. Foster ends with Godwin's debunking of the cult of feeling in *Fleetwood* (1805), noting that such attacks were rare; instead, the man of feeling was transformed into the romantic hero. In his discussion of Radcliffe, Foster cites Trollope's contempt for readers who could prefer Gothic romance to realism. Foster himself provides a discerning reading of the novels informed by sensibility, though he is unable to detach himself from the approach of Trollope and his many twentieth-century followers in privileging realism as the key to great novels. But in the process of surveying the other tradition in the eighteenth century, he manages to construct a canon of women novelists of unusual depth and thoughtfulness for the middle of the twentieth century.

# Conclusion

I conclude my study with the 1956 and 1957 appearance of two highly formative studies of the eighteenth-century novel for my generation: Alan Dugald McKillop's (1892–1974) *The Early Masters of English Fiction* and Ian Watt's (1917–99) *The Rise of the Novel*. Both books incorporate the dominant views of mid-century; in the process each also inadvertently contributed to a later, more thorough, re-evaluation of the early novel in general, and, more particularly, of the importance of early women novelists. McKillop's is the more traditional study, and it proved far less influential. More than Watt, he attempts to promote the 'early masters'; that is, he writes from a position that assumes the need to establish the importance of '*les cinq grands*' (vii), and, by extension, of the novel before Austen. Eighteenth-century studies are still on the defensive for McKillop.

McKillop is also a more traditional scholar than Watt, more interested in description and explication than evaluation. His title and choice of authors is, of course, evaluative, but McKillop's evaluations have taken place before he begins to write about his 'masters': they are assumed, not argued. His choices are also as predictable as possible. They accept the judgments of his predecessors while incorporating standards of judgment developed early in the twentieth century. Like Leavis, he is for a small canon of greats only. His 'greats' are the novelists whose originality contributed to the development of the novel. For example, McKillop points to Defoe's 'conception of character as brought out by immediate practical problems, his sense of social and economic reality, his selective and vivid presentation of detail significant for action, his application of a bourgeois success philosophy in a dangerous hinterland beyond the limits of respectability' (28). McKillop has chosen a number of aspects of Defoe's art that conform to modernist standards of the novel. While *Robinson*

*Crusoe* had been central to the history of the novel since Reeve and Dunlop, Defoe's other novels had rarely figured at all. McKillop discusses all of them, and for him, as for E.M. Forster, it is *Moll Flanders*, not *Crusoe*, that best represents Defoe as a novelist. McKillop was not the first critic to take Defoe's other novels seriously, but his advocacy of *Moll Flanders* and *Roxana*, despite subject matter that had rendered them untouchable for generations, made it that much easier for subsequent critics to reconsider other long-untouchable work such as the novels of the triumvirate.

When McKillop turns to Richardson, he turns to the central focus of his own scholarly career. He was the pre-eminent Richardson scholar of the first half of the twentieth century, a pioneer in the recovery project that ultimately restored Richardson to his earlier stature in the history of the novel. McKillop emphasizes his importance for the development of the realistic, psychological novel: 'He remains the novelist of introversion and introspection, of scrutinized motives and attitudes, of the interplay of impulse and interest with code and convention that constantly ripples the surface of society and sometimes subjects the individual to an ordeal of crucial importance' (97). He considers his own generation the first since the early nineteenth century to appreciate Richardson's achievement and contribution to the novel, and he notes Austen's respect for Richardson, pointing to him as a major influence. In the process, he neglects the many other novelists who bridged the time between them. For McKillop there are no women among the 'early masters,' although he is certainly aware of the existence of early women novelists: Aubin, Collier, Cooper, Sarah Fielding, Griffith, and Haywood are mentioned in passing. But I would argue that his reassessment of Defoe and Richardson contributed to a critical climate that soon allowed for a reassessment of their female contemporaries, the multitude of women novelists excluded from his own study.

What is true for McKillop is more dramatically true for Watt. *The Rise of the Novel* has remained in print for nearly fifty years and has probably had more readers than any other study of the eighteenth-century novel. Watt limits his study to the earliest three of McKillop's masters, and his interest in them is generated by his desire to develop a more sophisticated theory of realism than what he found in earlier critics, and to demonstrate that it was realism as he understands it – a 'narrative technique' that he calls 'formal realism' – that provided 'the lowest common denominator of the novel genre as a whole' (34). The development of that technique was crucial for the rise of the novel as we know it. Defoe, Richardson, and Fielding are the major players in that development. Watt shares McKillop's conviction that *Moll Flanders* is Defoe's most representative work, the work that best repays critical attention, while his account of 'formal realism' reads Richardson as at least Fielding's equal. (Fielding critics have objected to Watt's treatment of their favourite ever since.)

It is only in his brief final chapter (he calls it a 'Note') that Watt considers the aftermath of the founding of the novel through the discovery of formal realism. He begins with the commonplace view that the novel went into decline in the second half of the eighteenth century: only Smollett, Sterne, and Burney 'rose above the level of mediocrity and worse' (290) that characterizes novels of the period, and Watt considers all three inferior to the earliest masters. He argues that neither Richardson nor Fielding fully resolved the narrative challenges of formal realism. Sterne's importance comes from his attempt to work through those challenges, although his solutions were not entirely successful; Smollett is less interesting because he was not engaged in this central issue for eighteenth-century fiction.

In Austen Watt finds the 'desired resolution, that is, the successful union of the best of what Richardson and Fielding brought to the novel. Burney's earlier attempts provided an important model for Austen, hence her claim to a place of honour in Watt's history of the novel. It is in the context of his discussion of Burney and Austen that Watt observes that 'the majority of eighteenth-century novels were actually written by women, but this had long remained a purely quantitative assertion of dominance' (298), the throw-away line – based on no acknowledged quantitative data – that so incensed Dale Spender. In its context, one that suggests that Burney, Austen, and Eliot are central figures in the history of the novel, it is clear that Watt's motive is not to conspire against women writers. Like McKillop, he is aware of many earlier women novelists; he mentions Behn, Collier, Sarah Fielding, Griffith, Haywood, Manley, More, and Reeve. But he does not consider them important players in the history of the novel. Watt's contempt for the 'various fugitive literary tendencies such as sentimentalism or Gothic terror' (290) provides a rationale for his lack of interest in most later eighteenth-century women novelists, and the male novelists who worked in these forms fare no better.

Watt summarizes the modernist biases that dominated so much of novel criticism in the first half of the last century. For him, the novel is tied to 'formal realism,' a realism that began in the eighteenth century and developed continuously over the next two hundred years. The great novels are the products of this tradition, and they are few. Watt shares the progressive theory of the history of the novel that had remained virtually unchallenged since Dunlop's time and, like most progressive critics, he is not very interested in exploring the neglected byways of the early novel. His road is straighter and more narrow.

McKillop and Watt represent the nadir of the critical fortunes of women novelists before Austen. Neither critic had any interest in renewing attention to early women novelists. Their highly influential studies, however, paved the way for the feminist revival of the next generation by restoring Richardson to his central position in the history of the novel and by attending to Defoe's novels other than *Crusoe*, particularly *Moll Flanders*. With Defoe's novels of the female under- world made respectable, it became easier to make the case for recon- sidering Behn, Manley, and Haywood. And with the renewal of Richardson's reputation, his full line of the novel, including Watt's 'fugitives,' became more inviting to scholars and critics of the early novel. Current histories of the novel bear little resemblance to those that dominated my undergraduate education. Nowhere is this more dramatically evident than in the treatment of women novelists before Jane Austen.

# Appendix: Novels Cited

Amory, Thomas. *The Life and Opinions of John Buncle, Esq.; Containing Various Observations and Reflections, Made in Several Parts of the World*. London, 1755–66.

[Anon.] *A Narrative of the Life and Astonishing Adventures of John Daniel, A Smith at Royston in Hertfortshire*. London, 1751.

[Anon.] *The Travels and Adventures of William Bingfield, Esq*. London, 1753.

[Anon.] *Arabian Nights' Entertainments. Consisting of One Thousand and One Stories told by the Sultaness of the Indies*. Trans. 'E.W.' London, 1706.

Aubin, Penelope. *The Noble Slaves: or, The Lives and Adventures of Two Lords and Two Ladies, who were Shipwreck'd*. London, 1722.

Austen, Jane. *Emma*. London, 1816.

– *Mansfield Park*. London, 1814.

– *Northanger Abbey*. London, 1818.

– *Persuasion*. London, 1818.

– *Pride and Prejudice*. London, 1813.

– *Sense and Sensibility: A Novel*. London, 1811.

Bage, Robert. *The Fair Syrian, A Novel*. London, 1787.

– *Hermsprong: or Man as He Is Not*. London, 1796.

Barrett, Eaton Stannard. *The Heroine, Or Adventures of a Fair Romance Reader*. London, 1813.

Beckford, William. *An Arabian Tale, from an Unpublished Manuscript*. London, 1786.

– *Azemia: A Descriptive and Sentimental Novel*. London, 1797.

– *Modern Novel Writing, or The Elegant Enthusiast; and Interesting Emotions of Arabella Bloomville. A Rhapsodical Romance*. London, 1796.

– *Vathek*. London, 1787.

Behn, Aphra. *The Adventure of the Black Lady* in *All the Histories and Novels Written by the Late Ingenious Mrs. Behn*. London, 1698.

– *Agnes de Castro, or, The Force of Generous Love* in *Three Histories by … Mrs. A. Behn*. London, 1688.

– *The Fair Jilt, or, Tarquin and Miranda* in *Three Histories*. London, 1688.
– *The History of the Nun: or, The Fair Vow-Breaker*. London, 1689.
– *Love-Letters Between a Nobleman and his Sister*. London, 1684.
– *The Lucky Mistake*. London, 1689.
– *Memoirs of the Court of the King of Bantam* in *Histories and Novels*. London, 1698.
– *Oroonoko, or, The Royal Slave* in *Three Histories*. London, 1688.
Bennett, Anna Maria (Agnes Maria). *Anna; or, Memoirs of a Welch Heiress, Interspersed with Anecdotes of a Nabob*. London, 1785.
Berington, Simon. *The Memoirs of Signor Gaudentio di Lucca: Taken from his Confession and Examination before the Fathers of the Inquisition at Bologna in Italy*. London, 1737.
Bernardin de Saint-Pierre, Jacques-Henri. *The Indian Cottage*. 1790. London, 1791.
– *Paul and Virginie*. 1787. London, 1788.
Brontë, Charlotte. *Jane Eyre*. London, 1847.
– *Shirley: A Tale*. London, 1849.
Brooke, Frances. *The Excursion*. London, 1777.
– *The History of Emily Montague*. London, 1769.
– *The History of Lady Julia Mandeville*. London, 1763.
Brooke, Henry. *The Fool of Quality; or, The History of Henry Earl of Moreland*. London, 1766–70.
Brown, Charles Brockden. *Edgar Huntly; or, Memoirs of a Sleep-Walker*. Philadelphia, 1799.
– *Wieland; or, The Transformation*. New York, 1798.
Brunton, Mary. *Discipline*. Edinburgh, 1814.
– *Self-Control: A Novel*. Edinburgh, 1811.
Bunyan, John. *The Life and Death of Mr. Badman*. London, 1680.
– *The Pilgrim's Progress*. London, 1678–84.
Burney, Frances. *Camilla: or, A Picture of Youth*. London, 1796.
– *Cecilia, or Memoirs of an Heiress*. London, 1782.
– *Evelina, or, A Young Lady's Entrance into the World*. London, 1778.
– *The Wanderer; or Female Difficulties*. London, 1814.
Cervantes, Miguel de. *Exemplary Novels*. London, 1720–22.
– *The History and Adventures of the Renowned Don Quixote*. 1605–15. Trans. Tobias Smollett. London, 1755.
– *The History of the Renowned Don Quixote de la Mancha*. Trans. John Ozell. London, 1700.
– *Instructive and Entertaining Novels: Designed to Promote Virtue, Good Sense, and Universal Benevolence*. Trans. James Mabbe. London, 1742.

– *The Life and Exploits of the Ingenious Gentleman Don Quixote de la Mancha.* Trans. Charles Jarvis. London, 1742.

Cleland, John. *Memoirs of a Coxcomb.* London, 1751.

– *Memoirs of a Woman of Pleasure.* London, 1748–49.

Congreve, William. *Incognita: or, Love and Duty Reconcil'd.* London, 1692.

Coventry, Francis. *The History of Pompey the Little, or, The Life and Adventures of a Lap-Dog.* London, 1751.

Darwin, Erasmus. *The Loves of the Plants.* London, 1789.

Day, Thomas. *The History of Sandford and Merton, A Work Intended for the Use of Children.* London, 1783–89.

Defoe, Daniel. *The Fortunate Mistress or a History...of the Lady Roxana.* London, 1724.

– *The Fortunes and Misfortunes of the Famous Moll Flanders, &c.* London, 1722.

– *A Journal of the Plague Year.* London, 1722.

– *The Life, Adventures and Pyracies of the Famous Captain Singleton.* London, 1720.

– *The Life and Strange Surprizing Adventures of Robinson Crusoe.* London, 1719.

Edgeworth, Maria. *Belinda.* London, 1801.

– *Castle Rackrent, An Hibernian Tale.* London, 1800.

– *Harrington, A Tale; and Ormond, A Tale.* London, 1817.

– *The Modern Griselda: A Tale.* London, 1805.

– *Moral Tales for Young People.* London, 1801.

– *Murad the Unlucky* in *Popular Tales.* London, 1804.

– *Tales of Fashionable Life.* London, 1812.

Eliot, George. *The Mill on the Floss.* London, 1860.

Ferrier, Susan. *The Inheritance.* Edinburgh, 1824.

– *Marriage, A Novel.* Edinburgh, 1818.

Fielding, Henry. *Amelia.* London, 1751.

– *An Apology for the Life of Mrs Shamela Andrews.* London, 1741.

– *The History of the Adventures of Joseph Andrews, and his Friend Mr. Abraham Adams. Written in Imitation of the Manner of Cervantes, Author of Don Quixote.* London, 1742.

– *The History of Tom Jones, A Foundling.* London, 1749.

– *The Life and Death of Jonathan Wild the Great.* London, 1743.

Fielding, Sarah. *The Adventures of David Simple.* London, 1744–53.

– *The History of the Countess of Dellwyn.* London, 1759.

– *The History of Ophelia.* London, 1760.

– *The Lives of Cleopatra and Octavia.* London, 1757.

Fielding, Sarah, and Jane Collier. *The Cry; A New Dramatic Fable.* London, 1754.

Gaskell, Elizabeth. *Mary Barton, A Tale of Manchester Life.* London, 1848.

Gibbes, Phebe. *Hartly House, Calcutta.* London, 1789.

Godwin, William. *Fleetwood, or, The New Man of Feeling*. London, 1805.
– *St. Leon: A Tale of the Sixteenth Century*. London, 1799.
– *Things as they Are; or, The Adventures of Caleb Williams*. London, 1794.
Goldsmith, Oliver. *The Citizen of the World; Or Letters from a Chinese Philosopher, Residing in London, To his Friends in the East*. London, 1762.
– *The Vicar of Wakefield: A Tale. Supposed to be Written by Himself*. London, 1766.
Grafigny, Mme de. *Letters Written by a Peruvian Princess*. Anon. trans. London, 1748.
Graves, Richard. *Columella; or, The Distressed Achoret*. London, 1779.
– *The Spiritual Quixote: or, The Summer's Ramble of Mr Geoffrey Wildgoose. A Comic Romance*. London, 1773.
Green, Sarah. *Romance Readers and Romance Writers*. London, 1810.
Griffith, Elizabeth. *The Delicate Distress: A Novel* in *Two Novels: In Letters*. London, 1769.
– *The History of Lady Barton, A Novel*. London, 1771.
Hamilton, Elizabeth. *The Cottagers of Glenburnie; A Tale for the Farmer's Ingle-Nook*. London, 1808.
– *Memoirs of Modern Philosophers*. London, 1800.
Hawkesworth, John. *Almoran and Hamet: An Oriental Tale*. London, 1761.
Hays, Mary. *Memoirs of Emma Courtney*. London, 1796.
Haywood, Eliza. *The Adventures of Eovaai*. London, 1736.
– *The Fruitless Enquiry; Being a Collection of Several Entertaining Histories*. London, 1727.
– *The History of Jemmy and Jenny Jessamy*. London, 1753.
– *The History of Miss Betsy Thoughtless*. London, 1751.
– *Idalia: or the Unfortunate Mistress*. London, 1723.
– *The Invisible Spy; By Exploralibus*. London, 1755.
– *Memoirs of a Certain Island Adjacent to Utopia*. London, 1725.
Head, Richard and Francis Kirkman. *The English Rogue Described, in the Life of Meriton Latroon*. London, 1665–71.
Inchbald, Elizabeth. *Nature and Art*. London, 1796.
– *A Simple Story*. London, 1791.
Jacson, Frances. *Rhoda. A Novel*. London, 1816.
– *Things by their Right Names; A Novel*. London, 1812.
Johnson, Samuel. *The Prince of Abyssinia. A Tale*. London, 1759.
Johnstone, Charles. *Chrysal; or, The Adventures of a Guinea*. London, 1760.
Knight, Ellis Cornelia. *Dinarbas; A Tale: Being a Continuation of Rasselas, Prince of Abyssinia*. London, 1792.
Lafayette, Marie-Madeleine. *La princesse de Clèves*. Trans. 'A Person of Quality.' 1678. London, 1679.

– *Zayde. A Spanish History, being a Pleasant and Witty Novel.* 1669–71. Trans. 'P. Porter, Esq.' London, 1678.

Langhorne, John. *Solyman and Almena.* London, 1762.

Lee, Harriet. *The Errors of Innocence.* London, 1786.

Lee, Sophia. *The Recess; or, A Tale of Other Times.* London, 1783–5.

Lee, Harriet and Sophia Lee. *Canterbury Tales for the Year 1797.* London, 1797–99.

Leland, Thomas. *Longsword, Earl of Salisbury. An Historical Romance.* London, 1762.

Lennox, Charlotte. *The Female Quixote; or, The Adventures of Arabella.* London, 1752.

– *Henrietta.* London, 1758.

– *The Life of Harriot Stuart. Written by Herself.* London, 1750.

Lesage, Alain-René. *The Adventures of Gil Blas.* 1715–35. Trans. Tobias Smollett. London, 1749.

– *The History and Adventures of Gil Blas de Santillane.* London, 1716.

Lewis, Matthew Gregory. *The Bravo of Venice.* London, 1805.

– *The Monk: A Romance.* London, 1796.

Lyly, John. *Euphues: The Anatomy of Wit.* London, 1578.

Mackenzie, Henry. *Julia de Roubigné, A Tale. In a Series of Letters.* London, 1777.

– *The Man of Feeling.* London, 1771.

Manley, Delarivier. *The Adventures of Rivella.* London, 1714.

– *The Power of Love: In Seven Novels.* London, 1720.

– *The Secret History of Queen Zarah, and the Zarazians.* London, 1705.

– *Secret Memoirs and Manners of Several Persons of Quality, of both Sexes. From the New Atalantis, an Island in the Mediteranean.* London, 1709.

Marmontel, Jean-François. *Moral Tales.* London, 1763–5.

Maturin, Charles Robert. *Fatal Revenge; or the Family of Montorio.* London, 1807.

– *Melmoth The Wanderer: A Tale.* Edinburgh, 1820.

– *The Wild Irish Boy.* London, 1808.

Melville, Herman. *Moby-Dick, or, The Whale.* London, 1851.

Minifie Gunning, Susanna. *The Memoirs of Mary, A Novel.* London, 1793.

Moore, John. *Zeluco. Various View of Human Nature, Taken from Life and Manners, Foreign and Domestic.* London, 1789.

More, Hannah. *Cœlebs in Search of a Wife. Comprehending Observations on Domestic Habits and Manners, Religion and Morals.* London, 1808.

Morgan, Lady (Sydney Owenson). *Florence Macarthy: An Irish Tale.* London, 1818.

– *The O'Briens and the O'Flahertys; A National Tale.* London, 1827.

– *O'Donnel. A National Tale.* London, 1814.

– *The Wild Irish Girl; A National Tale*. London, 1806.

Neville, Henry. *The Isle of Pines, or, A Late Discovery of a Fourth Island near Terra Australis*. London, 1668.

Opie, Amelia. *Adeline Mowbray, or The Mother and Daughter: A Tale*. London, 1805.

– *The Father and Daughter, A Tale: In Prose*. London, 1801.

– *Temper, or Domestic Scenes: A Tale*. London, 1812.

– *A Wife's Duty: A Tale*. London, 1828.

Orrery, Roger Boyle, earl of. *Parthenissa*. London, 1651–69.

Paltock, Robert. *The Life and Adventures of Peter Wilkins, A Cornish Man*. London, 1750.

Parsons, Eliza. *The Castle of Wolfenbach*. London, 1793.

Plantin, Arabella. *Love Led Astray, or the Mutual Constancy*. London, 1727.

Polidori, John. *The Vampyre: A Tale*. London, 1819.

Porter, Anna Maria. *Artless Tales*. London, 1793–95.

– *Don Sebastian, or the House of Braganza: An Historical Romance*. London, 1809.

– *The Hungarian Brothers*. London, 1807.

– *The Knight of St.John: A Romance*. London, 1817.

– *The Recluse of Norway*. London, 1814.

– *Walsh Colville: or a Young Man's First Entrance into Life*. London, 1797.

Porter, Jane. *The Pastor's Fireside*. London, 1815.

– *The Scottish Chiefs. A Romance*. London, 1810.

– *Thaddeus of Warsaw*. London, 1803.

Prévost, Abbé Antoine-François. *The Life and Entertaining Adventures of Mr Cleveland, Natural Son of Oliver Cromwell, Written by Himself*. 1731–9. London, 1734–5.

Radcliffe, Ann. *The Castles of Athlin and Dunbayne: A Highland Story*. London, 1789.

– *The Italian, or, The Confessional of the Black Penitents. A Romance*. London, 1797.

– *The Mysteries of Udolpho, A Romance*. London, 1794.

– *The Romance of the Forest*. London, 1791.

– *The Sicilian Romance*. London, 1790.

Radcliffe, Mary-Anne. *Manfroné; or, The One-Handed Monk: A Romance*. London, 1809.

Reeve, Clara. *The Champion of Virtue. A Gothic Story*. Colchester, 1777. Reissued as *The Old English Baron: A Gothic Story*. London, 1778.

– *The Exiles: or Memoirs of the Count de Cronstadt*. London, 1788.

– *Memoirs of Sir Roger de Clarendon, The Natural Son of Edward Prince of Wales*. London, 1793.

Richardson, Samuel. *Clarissa: or, The History of a Young Lady.* London, 1747–8.

– *The History of Sir Charles Grandison. In a Series of Letters.* London, 1753–4.

– *Pamela; or, Virtue Rewarded. In a Series of Familiar Letters from a Beautiful Young Damsel, to her Parents.* London, 1740.

Roche, Regina Maria. *The Children of the Abbey, A Tale.* London, 1796.

Scott, Walter. *Ivanhoe: A Romance.* Edinburgh, 1820.

– *Old Mortality.* Edinburgh, 1817.

– *Quentin Durward.* Edinburgh, 1823.

– *Waverley; or, 'Tis Sixty Years Since.* Edinburgh, 1814.

Scudéry, Madeleine de. *Artamenes, or, The Grand Cyrus.* Trans. 'F.G. Gent.' 1649–53. London, 1653.

Shelley, Mary. *Frankenstein; or, The Modern Prometheus.* London, 1818.

Shelley, Percy Bysshe. *St. Irvyne or the Rosicrucian: A Romance.* London, 1811.

– *Zastrozzi: A Romance.* London, 1810.

Sheridan, Frances. *The History of Nourjahad.* London, 1767.

– *Memoirs of Miss Sidney Bidulph, Extracted from her own Journal.* London, 1761.

Sidney, Philip. *The Countesse of Pembroke's Arcadia.* London, 1590.

Smith, Charlotte. *Desmond. A Novel.* London, 1792.

– *Emmeline, The Orphan of the Castle.* London, 1788.

– *Ethelinde, or The Recluse of the Lake.* London, 1789.

– *The Old Manor House. A Novel.* London, 1793.

Smollett, Tobias. *The Adventures of Peregrine Pickle. In Which are Included, Memoirs of a Lady of Quality.* London, 1751.

– *The Adventures of Roderick Random.* London, 1748.

– *The Expedition of Humphry Clinker.* London, 1771.

– *The Life and Adventures of Sir Launcelot Greaves.* London, 1762.

Staël, Germaine de. *Corinne.* London, 1807.

Sterne, Laurence. *The Life and Opinions of Tristram Shandy, Gentleman.* York and London, 1759–67.

– *A Sentimental Journey Through France and Italy.* London, 1768.

Stowe, Harriet Beecher. *Uncle Tom's Cabin; or, Life Among the Lowly.* Boston, 1852.

Strutt, Joseph and Walter Scott. *Queenhoo-Hall, A Romance.* Edinburgh, 1808.

Swift, Jonathan. *Travels into Several Remote Nations of the World ... By Lemuel Gulliver.* London, 1726.

Thackeray, William Makepeace. *The History of Henry Esmond.* London, 1852.

– *Vanity Fair: A Novel Without a Hero.* London, 1848.

Walpole, Horace. *The Castle of Otranto, A Story.* London, 1764.

West, Jane. *The Advantages of Education, or, The History of Maria Williams, A Tale for Misses and their Mammas*. London, 1793.

Wollstonecraft, Mary. *Mary: A Fiction*. London, 1788.

Wroth, Mary. *The Countesse of Montgomerie's Urania*. London, 1621.

# Notes

## Introduction

1  There has been considerable research on the early novel in the fifty years since Watt made his claim. The number of women novelists writing in the eighteenth century cannot be determined with precision, but a very good attempt is found in Raven, 'Introduction' (summarized well in table 4) and Raven, 'Historical Introduction' (summarized well in figure 6).

## 1: The Eighteenth Century

1  Early examples of attempts to separate the novels of Richardson and Fielding from their connections with earlier traditions of prose fiction can be seen in Richardson's prefatory material and defences of *Pamela*, in Fielding's preface to *Joseph Andrews*, and in the anonymously published *An Essay on the New Species of Writing Founded by Mr. Fielding*. Critics continue to argue that the 'novel' began in 1740. Sheldon Sacks provides a good example of that argument two hundred years later. Arguments for the newness of the species and for its distinctness from its fictional predecessors also have a long tradition, documented in this study. Recent feminist criticism is especially relevant. See, for example, Ballaster, *Seductive Forms*, Doody, *True Story of the Novel*, and Spencer, *Rise of the Woman Novelist*.

2  Coventry is the probable author of *An Essay on the New Species of Writing Founded by Mr. Fielding*, in which he attributes the source of this diseased form of literature to the French models embraced all too eagerly by English authors and readers a century earlier (xiv).

3  The narrative of the English novel as the product of rival traditions begun respectively by Richardson and Fielding dates from Fielding's attacks on

Richardson in *Shamela* and *Joseph Andrews* and has continued to dominate
accounts of the novels ever since (many of which are traced below). Blanchard
offers a classic, if less than balanced, example of a study built around the
Fielding versus Richardson dialectic. For more balanced, more recent discussions, see Kreissman, *Pamela-Shamela*, and Park, 'Fielding and Richardson.'

4  Christopher D. Johnson, Fielding's most recent editor, still buys into this
history. His discussion of Fielding's sources, and his placement of the *Lives*
(following Ann Marilyn Parrish) in the *Mirrour for Magistrates* tradition
continues to ignore both influence by and continuity with earlier eighteenth-century prose fiction.

5  See, for example, Forster (both 'Introductions'), Bartolomeo, *New Species of
Criticism*, Donoghue, *Fame Machine*, Mayo, *The English Novel*, Roper,
*Reviewing*, and Tompkins, *The Popular Novel in England*.

6  Seward's outrage is captured by the following examples: 'There is but one
way of accounting for a decision so senseless. The *English Baron*, charming
as it is, can stand on no line of equality with *Grandison*, and the yet greater
*Clarissa*; ... and the heart of Clara Reeves, less candid and sincere than her
imagination is happy, with the co-operation of that eternal misleader self-
conceit, suggested this too common practice of disingenuous spirits, to
attempt the degradation of a superior writer, by extolling a work of his,
which they know they can *themselves* excel, *above* those *higher* efforts of his
genius, which they feel unattainable ... No person endowed with any
refinement of perception, any accuracy of judgement, can think *Pamela*
superior to *Grandison*, and *Clarissa*' ('Letter,' 16).

7  My thanks to Thomas Bonnell for sharing his knowledge of eighteenth-
century publishers and their various series.

8  Mayo, Roper, and Tompkins (see note 5 above) all make persuasive cases in
defence of the reviewers.

## 2: 1800–1840

1  Barbauld's interest in the novel can be traced back at least as far as her
youthful 'On Romances, an Imitation' [of Samuel Johnson], in Aikin,
*Miscellaneous Pieces*.

2  The British Novelists consists of the following novels: Richardson,
*Clarissa, Sir Charles Grandison*; Defoe, *Robinson Crusoe*; Fielding, *Joseph
Andrews, Tom Jones*; Reeve, *The Old English Baron*; Walpole, *The Castle of
Otranto*; Coventry, *Pompey the Little*; Goldsmith, *The Vicar of Wakefield*;
Lennox, *The Female Quixote*; Johnson, *Rasselas*; Hawkesworth, *Almoran and
Hamet*; Brooke, *Lady Julia Mandeville*; Inchbald, *Nature and Art, A Simple*

*Story*; Mackenzie, *The Man of Feeling, Julia de Roubigné*; Smollett, *Humphry Clinker*; Graves, *The Spiritual Quixote*; Moore, *Zeluco*; Smith, *The Old Manor House*; Burney, *Evelina, Cecilia*; Radcliffe, *The Romance of the Forest, The Mysteries of Udolpho*; Bage, *Hermsprong*; Edgeworth, *Belinda, The Modern Griselda*.

3  This concern is related causally to another of Barbauld's concerns, that the novel be mistaken for real life. See Kraft, 'Anna Barbauld's Edition of the British Novelists.'

4  Scott, *Biographical Memoirs*, 3:181. The fourteen novelists in the original series are: Richardson, Fielding, Smollett, Cumberland, Goldsmith, Johnson, Sterne, Walpole, Reeve, Radcliffe, Lesage, Johnstone, Bage, and Mackenzie.

5  Robertson, in *Legitimate Histories*, notes that 'Scott's reputation for generosity has undermined his claims to be taken seriously as a literary critic' (57).

6  For a detailed, if extremely partisan account, see Blanchard, *Fielding the Novelist*.

7  In his discussion of Scott in *The Spirit of the Age* Hazlitt makes light of the fact that all of Scott's readers are not admirers with the following anecdote: 'For we met with a young lady who kept a circulating library and a milliner's shop, in a watering-place in the country, who, when we inquired for the Scotch Novels, spoke indifferently about them, said they were "so dry she could hardly get through them," and recommended us to read Agnes. We never thought of it before; but we would venture to lay a wager that there are many other young ladies in the same situation, and who think "Old Mortality" "dry"' (11:59).

8  Wellek emphasizes Jeffrey's 'literary nationalism with its stress on the glories and independence of the English' even though he finds it incongruous when mixed with Jeffrey's 'Scottish nationalism' (*History of Modern Criticism*, 2:119–20).

9  The authors are: D'Arblay, Barbauld, Bennet, Charlton, Curties, Edgeworth, Fontaine, Genlis, Godwin, Gunning, Hamilton, Helme, Holcroft, Hunter, Inchbald, Lathorn, Lathy, Le Brun, Le Noir, Lee, Mavor, Meeke, Moore, More, Opie, Parsons, Pilkington, Plumbtree, Porter, Pratt, Radcliffe, Reeve, Robinson, Roche, Siddons, Smith, Staël, Surr, Walker, West, Williams, and Young [*sic* throughout].

10  For an account of the influence of the Evangelicals, see Jones, *Ideas and Innovations*.

11  Kelly, 'Unbecoming a Heroine,' 220–41. Kelly reads *The Heroine* purely for its ideology; he ignores its more literary concerns and is indifferent to its playfulness.

## 3: 1840–1880

1 For discussions of Taine's theory of literature see Wellek, *History of Modern Criticism*, and VanderWolk, 'Hippolyte Taine.'

2 For an account of *Oroonoko* as abolitionist tract, see Spencer, *Aphra Behn's Afterlife*, chap. 6.

3 For the classic example, see Knights, 'Restoration Comedy.'

4 G.B. Smith's essay on Fielding provides a good example of the neglect of women novelists to become more common after 1880 (see chapters 4 and 5).

# Bibliography

Aikin, J. and A.L. *Miscellaneous Pieces, in Prose*. London: J. Johnson, 1773.

Alison, Archibald. 'The Historical Romance.' *Blackwood's* 58 (1845): 341–56. Reprinted in Eigner and Worth, 58–83.

Allen, Walter. *The English Novel: A Short Critical History.* 1954. Reprint, Harmondsworth: Penguin, 1958.

Altick, Robert. *The English Common Reader: The Social History of the Mass Reading Public, 1800–1900*. 2nd ed. Columbus: Ohio State University Press, 1988.

Alves, Robert. *Sketches of a History of Literature*. 1794. Reprinted with an introduction by Patrick O'Flaherty. Gainesville, FL: Scholars' Facsimiles and Reprints, 1967.

Angus, Joseph. *The Handbook of English Literature*. London: Religious Tract Society, [1865].

Armstrong, Nancy. *Desire and Domestic Fiction: A Political History of the Novel*. Oxford: Oxford University Press, 1987.

Arnold, Thomas. *A Manual of English Literature: Historical and Critical*. Boston: Ginn, 1887.

Ashton, Rosemary. *The German Idea: Four English Writers and the Reception of German Thought, 1800–1860*. Cambridge: Cambridge University Press, 1980.

Backsheider, Paula R., ed. *Revising Women: Eighteenth-Century 'Women's Fiction' and Social Engagement*. Baltimore: Johns Hopkins University Press, 2000.

Backsheider, Paula R., and Catherine Ingrassia, eds. *A Companion to the Eighteenth-Century Novel and Culture*. Oxford: Blackwell, 2005.

Baker, Ernest A. *A Guide to the Best Fiction in English*. 1903. Reprint, New York: Macmillan, 1913.

– *The History of the English Novel*. 10 vols. London: Witherby, 1924–39.

– *History of Fiction: A Guide to the Best Historical Romances, Sagas, Novels, and Tales*. 2 vols. London: George Routledge, 1907.

Ballaster, Ros. *Seductive Forms: Women's Amatory Fiction from 1684 to 1740*. Oxford: Clarendon Press, 1992.

Barbauld, Anna Laetitia, ed. *The British Novelists*. 50 vols. London: Rivington, 1810.

– 'Life of Richardson.' In *The Correspondence of Samuel Richardson*, edited by Anna Laetitia Barbauld. Vol. 1. London: Richard Philips, 1804.

Barber, Giles. 'Galignani and the Publication of English Books in France from 1800 to 1852.' In *Studies in the Booktrade of the European Enlightenment*, 353–72. London: Pindar, 1994.

Barrett, Eaton Stannard. *The Heroine*. 1813. Introduction by Walter Raleigh. London: Henry Frowde, 1909.

– *The Heroine*. 1813. Edited by Michael Sadleir. London: Elkin Mathews and Marrot, 1927.

Bartolomeo, Joseph F. *A New Species of Criticism: Eighteenth-Century Discourse on the Novel*. Newark: University of Delaware Press, 1994.

– '"Tenth Rate Fiction," First-Rate Criticism: The Legacy of J.M.S. Tompkins.' *Eighteenth-Century Novel* 2 (2002): 179–92.

Baugh, Albert C., ed. *A Literary History of England*. New York: Appleton-Century-Crofts, 1948.

Beattie, James. 'On Fable and Romance.' In *Dissertations Moral and Critical*, 503–74. London: W. Strahan and T. Cadell, 1783.

Beckford, William. *Modern Novel Writing (1796) and Azemia (1797)*. Reprinted with an introduction by Herman Mittle Levy, Jr. Gainesville, FL: Scholars' Facsimiles and Reprints, 1970.

Beers, Henry. *An Outline Sketch of English Literature*. New York: Chautaugua, 1886.

Bell, A.F. *Leaders of English Literature*. London: G. Bell, 1915.

Bernbaum, Ernest. *The Mary Carleton Narratives, 1663–1673: A Missing Chapter in the History of the English Novel*. Cambridge, MA: Harvard University Press, 1914.

Bisset, Robert. *Modern Literature: A Novel*. 3 vols. London: Longman and Rees, 1804.

Black, Frank Gees. *The Epistolary Novel in the Late Eighteenth Century: A Descriptive and Bibliographical Study*. Eugene: University of Oregon Press, 1940.

Blair, Hugh. *Lectures on Rhetoric and Belles Lettres*. 1783. 2nd ed. 3 vols. London: W. Strahan and T. Cadell, 1785.

Blakey, Dorothy. *The Minerva Press, 1790–1820*. London: Bibliographical Society, 1939 (for 1935).

Blanchard, Frederic T. *Fielding the Novelist: A Study in Historical Criticism*. New Haven, CT: Yale University Press, 1926.

Blewett, David, ed. 'Reconsidering the Rise of the Novel.' *Eighteenth-Century Fiction* 12.2–3 (2000), 141–499.

Block, Andrew. *The English Novel, 1740–1850: A Catalogue Including Prose Romances, Short Stories, and Translations of Foreign Fiction*. London: Dawsons of Pall Mall, 1961.

Bowen, Elizabeth. *English Novelists: Britain in Pictures*. 1942. Reprint, London: Collins, 1947.

Brett, R.L. 'George Henry Lewes: Dramatist, Novelist and Critic.' *Essays and Studies*, n.s. 11 (1958): 101–20.

Brontë, Charlotte. *The Letters of Charlotte Brontë: With a Selection of Letters by Family and Friends*, edited by Margaret Smith. 3 vols. Oxford: Clarendon Press, 1995–2004.

Brooke, Stopford. *English Literature*. Literature Primers. 3rd ed. Toronto: James Campbell, 1877.

Brown, Homer Obed. *Institutions of the English Novel from Defoe to Scott*. Philadelphia: University of Pennsylvania Press, 1997.

Buchan, Susan. *Lady Louisa Stuart: Her Memoirs and Portraits*. London: Hodder and Stoughton, 1932.

Buckland, Anna. *The Story of English Literature*. London: Cassell, 1890.

Burney, Frances. *Evelina*. 1778. Edited by Edward A. Bloom. London: Oxford University Press, 1968.

Burton, Richard. *Masters of the English Novel: A Study of Principles and Personalities*. 1909. Reprint, New York: Henry Holt, 1932.

Cecil, David. *Early Victorian Novelists: Essays in Revaluation*. London: Constable, 1934.

– 'Fanny Burney's Novels.' In *Essays on the Eighteenth Century: Presented to David Nichol Smith in Honour of His Seventieth Birthday*, 212–24. Oxford: Clarendon Press, 1945.

Chambers, Robert, ed. *Cyclopædia of English Literature: A Series of Specimens of British Writers in Prose and Verse. Connected by a Historical and Critical Narrative*. 2 vols. Edinburgh: William and Robert Chambers, 1843.

*Chambers's Cyclopædia of English Literature: A History Critical and Biographical of Authors in the English Tongue from the Earliest Times Till the Present Day with Specimens of their Writings*. 3rd ed., edited by Robert Carruthers. 2 vols. London: W. and R. Chambers, 1876.

*Chambers's Cyclopædia of English Literature: A History Critical and Biographical of Authors in the English Tongue from the Earliest Times till the Present Day with Specimens of their Writings*. Edited by David Patrick, revised by J. Liddell Geddie. 3 vols. London: W. and R. Chambers, 1925–7.

Chandler, Frank Wadleigh. *The Literature of Roguery*. 2 vols. Boston: Houghton Mifflin, 1907.

Chew, Samuel C. 'The Nineteenth Century and After (1789–1939).' In *A Literary History of England*, edited by Albert C. Baugh, 1109–1605. New York: Appleton-Century-Crofts, 1948.

Clery, E.J. *Women's Gothic from Clara Reeve to Mary Shelley.* Horndon, Tavistock, Devon: Northcote House in Association with the British Council, 2000.

Cleveland, Charles D. *English Letters of the Nineteenth Century on the Plan of the Author's 'Compendium of English Literature,' and Supplementary to It. Designed for Colleges and Advanced Classes in Schools as well as for Private Reading.* Philadelphia: E.C. and J. Biddle, 1857.

Colby, Robert A. *Fiction with a Purpose: Major and Minor Nineteenth-Century Novels.* Bloomington: Indiana University Press, 1967.

– '"Rational Amusement": Fiction vs. Useful Knowledge.' In *Victorian Literature and Society: Essays Presented to Richard D. Altick,* edited by James Kincaid and Albert J. Kuhn, 46–73. Columbus: Ohio State University Press, 1984.

Collier, William Francis. *A History of English Literature in a Series of Biographical Sketches.* 1861. Reprint, Toronto: James Campbell, 1871.

Collins, Norman. *The Facts of Fiction.* London: Victor Gollancz, 1932.

Compton-Rickett, Arthur. *A History of English Literature.* London: T.C. and E.C. Jack, 1918.

Conant, Martha Pike. *The Oriental Tale in England in the Eighteenth Century.* 1908. Reprint, New York: Octagon, 1966.

Coppée, Henry. *English Literature Considered as an Interpreter of English History: Designed as a Manual of Instruction.* 1872. 3rd ed. Philadelphia: Claxton, Remsen, and Haffelfinger, 1874.

Cordasco, Francesco. *The Bohn Libraries: A History and a Checklist.* New York: Burt Franklin, 1951.

Corman, Brian. 'Early Women Novelists, the Canon, and the History of the British Novel.' In *Eighteenth-Century Contexts: Historical Inquiries in Honor of Phillip Harth,* edited by Howard D. Weinbrot, Peter J. Schakel, and Stephen E. Karian, 232–46. Madison: University of Wisconsin Press, 2001.

Courtney, William Prideaux. *The Secrets of Our National Literature: Chapters in the History of the Anonymous and Pseudonymous Writings of Our Countrymen.* London: Archibald Constable, 1908.

Coventry, Francis. *An Essay on the New Species of Writing Founded by Mr. Fielding.* 1751. Reprint edited by Alan D. McKillop. Los Angeles: William Andrews Clark Memorial Library, 1962.

– *The History of Pompey the Little.* 1751. Edited by Robert Adams Day. London: Oxford University Press 1974.

Craik, George L. *A Compendious History of English Literature and of the English Language From the Norman Conquest.* 2 vols. London: Charles Griffin, 1878.

– *Sketches of the History of Literature and Learning in England: With Specimens of the Principal Writers.* 4 vols. London: Charles Knight, 1844–5.

Crane, R.S. Review of *A History of English Literature*, by Émile Legouis and Louis Cazamian. *Philological Quarterly* 7 (1928): 161.

Croker, John Wilson. Review of *Melmoth the Wanderer*, by Charles Robert Maturin. *Quarterly Review* 24 (1821): 303–11.

– Review of *The Wanderer*, by Frances Burney. *Quarterly Review* 11 (1814): 123–30.

– Review of *Waverley*, by Sir Walter Scott. *Quarterly Review* 11 (1814): 354–77.

Cross, Wilbur L. *The Development of the English Novel*. 1899. Reprint, New York: Macmillan, 1919.

Cruse, Amy. *English Literature through the Ages: Beowulf to Stevenson*. London: George G. Harrap, 1919.

Cunningham, Allan. 'British Novels and Romances. From "Biographical and Critical History of the Literature of the Last Fifty Years."' *The Athenaeum* (November 16 and 30, 1833). Reprinted in Olmstead 1:145–61.

Daiches, David. *The Novel and the Modern World*. 1939. Reprint, Chicago: University of Chicago Press, 1948.

Dalgleish, M. Scott. *The Great Authors of English Literature: Their Lives and Selections from their Writings*. London: Thos. Nelson, 1891.

Davis, Lennard J. *Factual Fictions: The Origins of the English Novel*. New York: Columbia University Press, 1983.

Dawson, W.J. *The Makers of English Fiction*. New York: Fleming H. Revell, 1905.

Day, Geoffrey. *From Fiction to the Novel*. London: Routledge and Kegan Paul, 1987.

De Bellis, Jack. 'Sidney Lanier.' *Dictionary of Literary Biography* 64 (1988): 136–47.

De Quincey, Thomas. 'Goldsmith.' In *Collected Writings*, edited by David Masson, 4:288–320. London: A. and C. Black, 1897.

Dobson, Austin. *Eighteenth-Century Vignettes*. 1st series. 1892. Reprint, London: Chatto and Windus, 1897.

– *Eighteenth-Century Vignettes*. 2nd series. London: Chatto and Windus, 1894.

Dodd, Philip. 'Edmund Gosse.' *Dictionary of Literary Biography* 57 (1987): 108–18.

Donoghue, Frank. *The Fame Machine: Book Reviewing and Eighteenth-Century Literary Careers*. Stanford, CA: Stanford University Press, 1996.

Donovan, Josephine. *Women and the Rise of the Novel, 1405–1726*. New York: St Martin's, 1999.

Doody, Margaret Anne. *The True Story of the Novel*. New Brunswick, NJ: Rutgers University Press, 1996.

Dryden, John. 'An Essay of Dramatic Poesie.' In *The Works of John Dryden*, vol. 17: *Prose 1668–1691*, edited by Samuel Holt Monk, 1–81. Berkeley: University of California Press, 1971.

Dunlop, John Colin. *The History of Fiction*. 1814. 3rd ed. 2 vols. London: Longman, 1845.

Dykes, Eva Beatrice. *The Negro in English Romantic Thought: A Study of Sympathy for the Oppressed*. Washington, DC: Associated Publishers, 1942.

Eagles, John. 'A Few Words about Novels: A Dialogue in a Letter to Eusebius.' *Blackwood's Edinburgh Magazine* 64 (October 1848): 459–74. Reprinted in Olmsted 1:579–96.

Edgar, Pelham. *The Art of the Novel*. New York: Macmillan, 1934.

Edgeworth, Maria. *Practical Education*. London: J. Johnson, 1798.

Eigner, Edwin M., and George J. Worth, eds. *Victorian Criticism of the Novel*. Cambridge: Cambridge University Press, 1985.

Eliot, George. 'The Progress of Fiction as an Art.' *Westminster Review* (October 1853): 342–74. Reprinted in Olmsted, 2:71–105.

– 'Silly Novels by Lady Novelists.' *Westminster Review* 66 (1856): 442–61. Reprinted in Olmsted, 2:277–98.

Elton, Oliver. *A Survey of English Literature, 1730–1780*. 2 vols. London: Edward Arnold, 1928.

– *A Survey of English Literature, 1780–1830*. 2 vols. London: Edward Arnold, 1912.

Elwood, Anne K. *Memoirs of the Literary Ladies of England from the Commencement of The Last Century*. 2 vols. 1843. Reprint, New York: AMS, 1973.

*Encyclopædia Britannica*. 11th ed. Cambridge: Cambridge University Press, 1911.

Entwistle, William J., and Eric Gillett. *The Literature of England, A.D. 500–1942: A Survey of British Literature from the Beginnings to the Present*. London: Longmans, Green, 1943.

Ernle, Right Hon. Lord. *The Light Reading of Our Ancestors*. New York: Brentano's, 1927.

Ezell, Margaret J.M. *Writing Women's Literary History*. Baltimore: Johns Hopkins University Press, 1992.

Fairchild, Hoxie Neale. *The Noble Savage: A Study in Romantic Naturalism*. New York: Columbia University Press, 1928.

Fenwick, Gillian. *Women and the Dictionary of National Biography: A Bibliography of DNB Volumes, 1885–1985, and Missing Persons*. Aldershot, UK: Scolar Press, 1994.

Ferris, Ina. *The Achievement of Literary Authority: Gender, History, and the Waverley Novels*. Ithaca, NY: Cornell University Press, 1991.

Fielding, Henry. 'Preface.' In *Joseph Andrews*, edited by Martin C. Battestin, 3–11. Oxford: Clarendon Press, 1967.

Fielding, Sarah. *The Lives of Cleopatra and Octavia*. 1757. Reprint edited by Christopher D. Johnson. Lewisburg, PA: Bucknell University Press, 1994.

Fisher, Mary. *Twenty-Five Letters to English Authors*. 1895. Reprint, Chicago: Scott, Foresman, 1900.

Ford, Ford Madox. *The English Novel: From the Earliest Days to the Death of Joseph Conrad*. Philadelphia: J.B. Lippencott, 1929.

Forster, Antonia. 'Introduction.' In *Index to Book Reviews in England, 1749–1774*, 3–18. Carbondale: Southern Illinois University Press, 1990.

– 'Introduction.' In *Index to Book Reviews in England, 1775–1800*, xiii–xliii. London: British Library, 1997.

Forster, E.M. *Aspects of the Novel*. New York: Harcourt, Brace, 1927.

Forsyth, William. *The Novels and Novelists of the Eighteenth Century in Illustration of the Manners of the Age*. London: John Murray, 1871.

Foster, James R. *History of the Pre-Romantic Novel in England*. New York: MLA, 1949.

Fox, Ralph. *The Novel and the People*. London: Lawrence and Wishart, 1937.

Garside, Peter, James Raven, and Rainer Schöwerling, eds. *The English Novel 1770–1829: A Bibliographical Survey of Prose Fiction Published in the British Isles*. 2 vols. Oxford: Clarendon Press, 2000.

George, W.L. *A Novelist on Novels*. London: Collins, 1918.

Gerould, Gordon Hall. *The Patterns of English and American Fiction: A History*. Boston: Little, Brown, 1942.

Gallagher, Catherine. *Nobody's Story: The Vanishing Acts of Women in the Marketplace, 1670–1820*. Oxford: Clarendon Press, 1994.

Gosse, Edmund. *A History of Eighteenth-Century Literature (1660–1780)*. London: Macmillan, 1889.

– *A Short History of Modern English Literature*. London: William Heinemann, 1897.

Grabo, Carl H. *The Technique of the Novel*. 1924. Reprint, New York: Gordian, 1964.

Graham, Kenneth. *English Criticism of the Novel, 1865–1900*. Oxford: Clarendon Press, 1965.

Greenhunt, Norris. 'George Henry Lewes as a Critic of the Novel.' *Studies in Philology* 45 (1948): 491–511.

Gregory, Allene. *The French Revolution and the English Novel*. 1914. Reprint, New York: Haskell House, 1966.

Griffith, Elizabeth, ed. *A Collection of Novels, Selected and Revised*. 3 vols. London: G. Kearsley, 1777.

Gross, John. *The Rise and Fall of the Man of Letters: Aspects of English Literary Life since 1800*. London: Weidenfeld and Nicolson, 1969.

Guillory, John. *Cultural Capital: The Problem of Literary Canon Formation*. Chicago: University of Chicago Press, 1993.

Gwynn, Stephen. *The Masters of English Literature*. New York: Macmillan, 1904.

Hale, Sarah Josepha. *Woman's Record; or Sketches of all Distinguished Women, from 'The Beginning' Till A.D. 1850. Arranged in Four Eras with Selections from Female Writers of Every Age*. New York: Harper, 1853.

Halleck, Reuben Post. *History of English Literature*. New York: American Book Co., 1900.

Hamilton, Catherine J. *Women Writers: Their Works and their Ways*. 2 vols. London: Ward, Lock, Bowden, 1892–3.

Hammond, Brean, and Shaun Regan. *Making the Novel: Fiction and Society in Britain, 1660–1789*. Basingstoke, UK: Palgrave, 2006.

Hannay, James. *A Course of English Literature*. London: Tinsley, 1866.

Hays, Mary. *Female Biography; or, Memoirs of Illustrious and Celebrated Women, Of All Ages and Countries*. 6 vols. London: Richard Phillips, 1803.

Hazlitt, William. *Lectures on the English Comic Writers*. In *The Complete Works of William Hazlitt*, edited by P.P. Howe, 6:1–168. London: Dent, 1931.

– Review of *The Wanderer*, by Frances Burney. *Edinburgh Review* 24 (1815): 320–38.

– *The Spirit of the Age*. In *Complete Works*, 11:5–184.

Heidler, Joseph Bunn. *The History from 1700–1800, of English Criticism of Prose Fiction*. Urbana: University of Illinois Press, 1928.

Herford, C.H. *The Age of Wordsworth*. 1889. 12th ed. London: Bell, 1919.

Hinchman, Walter S. *A History of English Literature*. New York: Century, 1918.

Hinchman, Walter S., and Frances B. Gummere. *Lives of Great English Writers: From Chaucer to Browning*. Boston: Houghton Mifflin, 1908.

Hirshberg, Edgar W. *George Henry Lewes*. New York: Twayne, 1970.

Horne, Charles Francis. *The Technique of the Novel: Elements of their Art, their Education and Present Use*. New York: Harper, 1908.

Horner, Joyce M. *The English Women Novelists and their Connection with the Feminist Movement (1688–1797)*. 1929–30. Reprint, Folcroft, PA: Folcroft Library Editions, 1973.

Howells, William Dean. *Heroines of Fiction*. 2 vols. New York: Harper, 1901.

Hudson, William Henry. *An Outline History of English Literature*. London: Bell, 1913.

Hughes, Helen Sard. 'English Epistolary Fiction Before *Pamela*.' In *The Manly Anniversary Studies in Language and Literature*, 156–69. Chicago: University of Chicago Press, 1923.

Hunter, J. Paul. *Before Novels: The Cultural Contexts of Eighteenth-Century English Fiction*. New York: Norton, 1990.

– 'Canon of Generations, Generation of Canons.' *Modern Language Studies* 18 (Winter 1988): 38–57.

Inchbald, Elizabeth. 'To the Artist.' *Artist* 14 (June 1807). Reprinted in William McKee, *Elizabeth Inchbald Novelist*. Washington, DC: Catholic University of America, 1935.

Ingrassia, Catherine. *Authorship, Commerce, and Gender in Early Eighteenth-Century England: A Culture of Paper Credit*. Cambridge: Cambridge University Press, 1998.

Jeaffreson, J. Cordy. *Novels and Novelists, from Elizabeth to Victoria*. 2 vols. London: Hurst and Blackett, 1858.

Jeffrey, Francis. *Contributions to the Edinburgh Review*. Boston: Phillips, Sampson, 1856.

Johnson, Charles F. *Outline History of English and American Literature*. New York: American Book Co., 1900.

Johnson, R. Brimley. *The Women Novelists*. London: Collins, 1918.

Jones, Ann H. *Ideas and Innovations: Best Sellers of Jane Austen's Age*. New York: AMS, 1986.

Jones, Dorothy Richardson. *'King of Critics': George Saintsbury, 1845–1933, Critic, Journalist, Professor*. Ann Arbor: University of Michigan Press, 1992.

Jusserand, J.J. *The English Novel in the Time of Shakespeare*. Translated by Elizabeth Lee. 1890. Reprint, London: Ernest Benn, 1966.

Justice, George. *The Manufacturers of Literature: Writing and the Literary Marketplace in Eighteenth-Century England*. Newark: University of Delaware Press, 2002.

Kaminsky, Alice R. *George Henry Lewes as Literary Critic*. Syracuse, NY: Syracuse University Press, 1968.

Kavanagh, Julia. *English Women of Letters: Biographical Sketches*. Leipzig: Tauchnitz, 1862.

Kelly, Gary, ed. *Sarah Scott and Clara Reeve*. Vol. 6 of *Bluestocking Feminism: Writings of the Bluestocking Circle, 1738–1785*. London: Pickering and Chatto, 1999.

– 'Unbecoming a Heroine: Novel Reading, Romanticism, and Barrett's *The Heroine*.' *Nineteenth-Century Literature* 45 (1990): 220–41.

Kettle, Arnold. *An Introduction to the English Novel*. 2 vols. London: Hutchinson University Library, 1951–3.

Kinnaird, John. *William Hazlitt: Critic of Power*. New York: Columbia University Press, 1978.

Kirkland, E.S. *A Short History of English Literature for Young People*. Chicago: A.C. McLurg, 1892.

Klancher, Jon P. *The Making of the English Reading Audiences, 1790–1832*. Madison: University of Wisconsin Press, 1987.

Knights, L.C. 'Restoration Comedy: The Reality and the Myth.' In *Explorations: Essays In Criticism, Mainly on the Literature of the Seventeenth Century*, 131–49. London: Chatto and Windus, 1946.

Knox, Vicesimus. *Essays Moral and Literary.* 1778. 13th ed. 3 vols. London: Charles Dilly, 1793.

Kraft, Elizabeth. 'Anna Barbauld's Edition of the British Novelists and the Making of a Canon.' Ninth International Congress on the Enlightenment. University of Münster, 25 July 1995.

Krapp, George Philip. *The Rise of English Literary Prose.* New York: Oxford University Press, 1915.

Kreissman, Bernard. *Pamela-Shamela: A Study of the Criticisms, Burlesques, Parodies, and Adaptations of Richardson's 'Pamela.'* Lincoln: University of Nebraska Press, 1960.

Krutch, Joseph Wood. *Five Masters: A Study in the Mutations of the Novel.* New York: Jonathan Cape and Harrison Smith, 1930.

Lang, Andrew. *History of English Literature from 'Beowulf' to Swinburne.* 1912. 2nd ed. London: Longmans, Green, 1914.

Lanier, Sidney. *The English Novel and the Principle of Its Development.* 1883. Revised as *The English Novel: A Study in the Development of Personality,* New York: Scribner's, 1897.

Lanser, Susan Sniader. *Fictions of Authority: Women Writers and Narrative Voice.* Ithaca, NY: Cornell University Press, 1992.

Lathrop, Henry Burrows. *The Art of the Novelist.* 1919. Revised edition, New York: Dodd, Mead, 1927.

Leavis, F.R. *The Great Tradition: George Eliot, Henry James, Joseph Conrad.* London: Chatto and Windus, 1948.

Leavis, Q.D. *Fiction and the Reading Public.* London: Chatto and Windus, 1932.

Legouis, Émile, and Louis Cazamian. *A History of English Literature.* 2 vols. London: J.M. Dent, 1926–7.

Lerenbaum, Miriam. '"Mistresses of Orthodoxy": Education in the Lives and Writings of Late Eighteenth-Century English Women Writers.' *Proceedings of the American Philosophical Society* 121 (1977): 281–301.

Lewes, George Henry. 'The Lady Novelists.' *Westminster Review* 58 (July 1852): 129–41. Reprinted in Olmsted 2:37–51.

– 'The Novels of Jane Austen.' *Blackwood's Edinburgh Magazine* 86 (July 1859): 99–113. Reprinted in Olmsted 2:441–57.

– 'A Word about *Tom Jones.*' *Blackwood's Edinburgh Magazine* 87 (March 1860): 331–41. Reprinted in Olmsted, 2:653–65.

Lister, T.H. *Review of Women as They Are; or, the Manners of the Day,* by Catherine Gore. *Edinburgh Review* 51 (July 1830): 444–62. Reprinted in Olmsted, 1: 51–61.

'Literary Spy.' *Ladies Monthly Museum* 4 (1808): 19–22, 121–3, 196–9, 306–7; 5 (1808): 29–33.

Litz, A. Walton, Louis Menand, and Lawrence Rainey, eds. *The Cambridge History of Literary Criticism.* Vol. 7. *Modernism and the New Criticism.* Cambridge: Cambridge University Press, 2000.

Long, William J. *English Literature: Its History and its Significance for the Life of the English Speaking World: A Text-Book for Students.* Boston: Ginn, 1909.

Lovell, Terry. *Consuming Fiction.* London: Verso, 1987.

Lovett, Robert Morss, and Helen Sard Hughes. *The History of the Novel in England.* Boston: Houghton Mifflin, 1932.

Lubbock, Percy. *The Craft of Fiction.* 1921. Reprint, London: Jonathan Cape, 1963.

Lynch, Deidre Shauna. *The Economy of Character: Novels, Market Culture, and the Business of Inner Meaning.* Chicago: University of Chicago Press, 1998.

Lytton, Edward Bulwer. 'On the Art of Fiction.' *Monthly Chronicle* (March–April 1838). Reprinted in *Pamphlets and Sketches*, 318–52. London: Routledge, 1875.

– 'Lady Blessington's Novels.' *Edinburgh Review* 67 (1838): 349–57. Reprinted in Olmsted, 1:255–65.

Macaulay, Thomas Babington. *Critical, Historical, and Miscellaneous Essays.* 6 vols. New York: Sheldon, 1860.

MacCarthy, B.G. *The Female Pen: Women Writers and Novelists, 1621–1818.* 2 vols. 1944–7. Reprinted in one vol. with preface by Janet Todd. New York: New York University Press, 1994.

Mackintosh, Robert James, ed. *Memoirs of the Life of the Right Honourable Sir James Mackintosh.* 2nd ed. 2 vols. London: Edward Moxon, 1836.

Maginn, William. Review of *The Dominie's Legacy,* by Andrew Picken. *Fraser's Magazine* I (1830): 318–35. Reprinted in Olmsted, 1:19–28.

Magnus, Laurie. *English Literature in Its Foreign Relations, 1300–1800.* London: Kegan Paul Trubner, 1927.

Masefield, Muriel. *Women Novelists from Fanny Burney to George Eliot.* 1934. Reprint, Freeport, NY: Books for Libraries Press, 1967.

Masson, David. *British Novelists and their Styles: Being a Critical Sketch of the History of Prose Fiction.* Cambridge: Macmillan, 1859.

Matthew, E.J. *A History of English Literature.* London: Macmillan, 1901.

Mayo, Robert D. *The English Novel in the Magazines: 1740–1815.* Evanston, IL: Northwestern University Press, 1962.

McCullough, Bruce. *Representative English Novelists: Defoe to Conrad.* New York: Harper, 1946.

McGhee, Richard D. 'Francis, Lord Jeffrey.' *Dictionary of Literary Biography* 107 (1991): 114–24.

McKeon, Michael. *The Origins of the English Novel 1600–1740.* Baltimore: Johns Hopkins University Press, 1987.

McKillop, Alan Dugald. *The Early Masters of English Fiction*. Lawrence: University of Kansas Press, 1956.

– *Samuel Richardson: Printer and Novelist*. Chapel Hill: University of North Carolina Press, 1936.

McKnight, Natalie J. 'George Henry Lewes.' *Dictionary of Literary Biography* 144 (1994): 166–78.

Mellor, Anne K. 'A Criticism of Their Own: Romantic Women Literary Critics.' In *Questioning Romanticism*, edited by John Beer, 29–48. Baltimore: Johns Hopkins University Press, 1995.

– *Mothers of the Nation: Women's Political Writing in England, 1780–1830*. Bloomington: Indiana University Press, 2000.

Michie, Allen. *Richardson and Fielding: The Dynamics of a Critical Rivalry*. Lewisburg, PA: Bucknell University Press, 1999.

Minto, William. *The Literature of the Georgian Era*. New York: Harper, 1895.

Moir, George. 'Modern Romance and the Novel.' In *Treatises on Poetry, Modern Romance, And Rhetoric; being the Articles Under Those Heads Contributed to the Encyclopædia Britannica, Seventh Edition*, 159–271. Edinburgh: Adam and Charles Black, 1839.

Moody, William Vaughn, and Robert Morss Lovett. *A History of English Literature*. 1902. Reprint, New York: Scribner's, 1905.

Moore, Catherine E. '"Ladies … Taking the Pen in Hand": Mrs. Barbauld's Criticism of Eighteenth-Century Women Novelists.' In *Fetter'd or Free? British Women Novelists, 1670–1815*, edited by Mary Ann Schofield and Cecilia Macheski, 383–97. Athens: Ohio University Press, 1986.

Moore, John. 'A View of the Commencement and Progress of Romance.' In *The Works of Tobias Smollett*, 8 vols., 1:v–xcv. London: B. Law, 1797.

More, Hannah. *Hints towards Forming the Character of a Young Princess*. 1805. Reprinted in *Works*, vol. 4. London: Bohn, 1853.

Morell, John Daniel. *A Biographical History of English Literature, Being an Elementary Introduction to the Greater Writers. With Four Hundred Exercises*. London: W. and R. Chambers, n.d. [18 –].

Morgan, Charlotte E. *The Novel of Manners: A Study of Prose Fiction between 1600 and 1740*. New York: Columbia University Press, 1911.

Morgan, Peter F. 'Scott as Critic.' *Studies in Scottish Literature* 7 (1969): 90–101.

Morley, Henry. *A First Sketch of English Literature*. 1873. Reprint, London: Cassell, 1890.

Muir, Edwin. *The Structure of the Novel*. 1928. Reprint, London: Hogarth, 1928.

Murch, Jerom. *Mrs Barbauld and Her Contemporaries; Sketches of Some Eminent and Scientific Englishwomen*. London: Longmans, Green, 1877.

Murray, H. *Morality of Fiction; or, An Inquiry into the Tendency of Fictitious Narratives*. Edinburgh: Mundell, 1805.

Napier, Elizabeth. 'Clara Reeve.' *Dictionary of Literacy Biography* 39 (1985): 372–7.

Neill, S. Diana. *A Short History of the English Novel*. London: Jarrolds, 1951.

Nesbit, H.B., and Claude Rawson, eds. *The Cambridge History of Literary Criticism*. Vol. 4. *The Eighteenth Century*. Cambridge: Cambridge University Press, 1997.

Newcomer, Alphonso Gerald. *English Literature*. Chicago: Scott, Foresman, 1907.

Nicoll, Henry J. *Landmarks of English Literature*. New York: D. Appleton, 1886.

*The Novelist's Magazine*. 23 vols. London: Harrison, 1780–8.

O'Connor, Frank. *The Mirror in the Roadway: A Study of the Modern Novel*. New York: Knopf, 1956.

Oliphant, Margaret. *The Literary History of England in the End of the Eighteenth Century and Beginning of the Nineteenth Century*. 3 vols. London: Macmillan, 1882.

Olmsted, John Charles, ed. *A Victorian Art of Fiction: Essays on the Novel in British Periodicals*. 3 vols. New York: Garland, 1979.

'On British Novels and Romances, Introductory to a Series of Criticisms on the Living Novelists.' *New Monthly Magazine* 13 (1820): 205–9.

'On the Female Literature of the Present Age.' *New Monthly Magazine* 13 (1820): 271–5, 633–8.

Oram, Richard W. 'George Saintsbury.' *Dictionary of Literary Biography* 57 (1987): 240–8.

Orel, Harold. *Victorian Literary Critics: George Henry Lewes, Walter Bagehot, Richard Holt Hutton, Leslie Stephen, Andrew Lang, George Saintsbury, and Edmund Gosse*. London: Macmillan, 1984.

Pancoast, Henry J. *An Introduction to English Literature*. 1894. Reprint, New York: Henry Holt, 1902.

Park, William. 'Fielding and Richardson.' *PMLA* 81 (1966): 381–8.

Pennell, Elizabeth Robins. *Mary Wollstonecraft Godwin*. London: W.H. Allen, 1885.

Perry, Bliss. *A Study of Prose Fiction*. Boston: Houghton Mifflin, 1902.

Perry, Ruth. *Novel Relations: The Transformation of Kinship in English Literature and Culture, 1748–1818*. Cambridge: Cambridge University Press, 2004.

– *Women, Letters, and the Novel*. New York: AMS, 1980.

Perry, Thomas Sargeant. *English Literature in the Eighteenth Century*. New York: Harper, 1883.

Phelps, William Lyon. *The Advance of the English Novel*. New York: Dodd, Mead, 1916.

Poovey, Mary. *The Proper Lady and the Woman Writer*. Chicago: University of Chicago Press, 1984.

Prescott, Sarah. *Women, Authorship and Literary Culture, 1690–1740*. Basingstoke, UK: Palgrave Macmillan, 2003.

Price, Leah. *The Anthology and the Rise of the Novel*. Cambridge: Cambridge University Press, 2000.

Priestley, J.B. *The English Novel*. 1927. Reprint, London: Thomas Nelson, 1938.

Probyn, Clive T. *English Fiction of the Eighteenth Century*. London: Longman, 1987.

Rabb, Melinda Alliker, ed. 'Making and Rethinking the Canon: The Eighteenth Century.' *Modern Language Studies* 18 (Winter, 1988): 3–16.

Railo, Eino. *The Haunted Castle: A Study of the Elements of English Romanticism*. New York: George Routledge, 1927.

Raleigh, Walter. *The English Novel: Being a Short Sketch of Its History from the Earliest Times to the Appearance of Waverley*. London: John Murray, 1903.

– *On Writing and Writers*, edited by George Gordon. London: Edward Arnold, 1926.

Ransome, Arthur. *A History of Story-Telling: Studies in the Development of Narrative*. London: T.D. and E.C. Jack, 1909.

Raven, James. 'Historical Introduction: The Novel Comes of Age.' In *The English Novel, 1770–1829: A Bibliographic Survey of Prose Fiction Published in the British Isles*, edited by Peter Garside, James Raven, and Rainer Schöwerling, 2 vols, 1:15–121. Oxford: Oxford University Press, 2000.

– 'Introduction.' In *British Fiction, 1750–70: A Chronological Check-List of Prose Fiction Printed in Britain and Ireland*, 1–42. Newark: University of Delaware Press, 1987.

– *Judging New Wealth: Popular Publishing and Responses to Commerce in England, 1750–1800*. Oxford: Clarendon Press, 1992.

Raven, James, Helen Small, and Naomi Tadmor, eds. *The Practice of Representation of Reading in England*. Cambridge: Cambridge University Press, 1996.

Reeve, Clara. *The Progress of Romance*. 2 vols. Colchester: W. Keymer, 1785.

Richardson, Samuel. 'Preface by the Editor' and Letters to the Editor. In *Pamela; or Virtue Rewarded*, edited by Thomas Keymer and Alice Wakely, 3–10. Oxford: Oxford University Press, 2001.

Richetti, John, ed. *The Cambridge Companion to the Eighteenth-Century English Novel*. Cambridge: Cambridge University Press, 1996.

– *The English Novel in History, 1700–1780*. London: Routledge, 1999.

– *Popular Fiction before Richardson: Narrative Patterns, 1700–1739*. Oxford: Clarendon Press, 1969.

Richter, David H., ed. *Ideology and Form in Eighteenth-Century Literature*. Lubbock: Texas Tech University Press, 1999.

Robert, Marthe. *Origins of the Novel*. Translated by Sacha Rabinovitch. Bloomington: Indiana University Press, 1980.

Robertson, Fiona. *Legitimate Histories: Scott, Gothic, and the Authorities of Fiction*. Oxford: Clarendon Press, 1994.

Rogers, Katharine M. 'Anna L. Barbauld's Criticism of Fiction: Johnsonian Mode, Female Vision.' *Studies in Eighteenth-Century Culture* 21 (1991): 27–41.

Roper, Derek. *Reviewing before the 'Edinburgh': 1788–1802*. London: Methuen, 1978.

Ross, Trevor. *The Making of the English Literary Canon: From the Middle Ages to the Late Eighteenth Century*. Montreal: McGill-Queen's University Press, 1998.

Rossetti, Lucy Madox. *Mrs Shelley*. London: W.H. Allen, 1890.

Runge, Laura L. *Gender and Language in British Literary Criticism, 1660–1790*. Cambridge: Cambridge University Press, 1997.

Rutherford, Mildred Lewis. *English Authors; A Hand-Book of English Literature from Chaucer to Living Writers*. Atlanta: Constitution, 1890.

Sacks, Sheldon. *Fiction and the Shape of Belief: A Study of Henry Fielding with Glances at Swift, Johnson, and Richardson*. Berkeley: University of California Press, 1964.

Sackville-West, V. *Aphra Behn: The Incomparable Astrea*. London: Gerald Howe, 1927.

Sadleir, Michael. 'Introduction.' *The Heroine*, by Eaton Stannard Barrett, 7–15. London: Elkin Mathews and Marrot, 1927.

– *XIX Century Fiction: A Bibliographical Record Based on His Own Collection*. 2 vols. London: Constable, 1951.

Saintsbury, George. *The English Novel*. London: Dent, 1913.

– *A First Book of English Literature*. 1914. Reprint, London: Macmillan, 1919.

– *A History of Criticism and Literary Taste in Europe from the Earliest Texts to the Present Day*. 3 vols. Edinburgh: William Blackwood, 1904.

– *The Peace of the Augustans: A Survey of Eighteenth-Century Literature as a Place of Rest and Refreshment*. London: Bell, 1916.

– *A Short History of English Literature*. 1898. Reprint, London: Macmillan, 1900.

Salzman, Paul. *English Prose Fiction 1558–1700: A Critical History*. Oxford: Clarendon Press, 1985.

Schellenberg, Betty A. *The Professionalization of Women Writers in Eighteenth-Century Britain*. Cambridge: Cambridge University Press, 2005.

Scott, Walter. *Biographical Memoirs of Eminent Novelists and Other Distinguished Persons. Miscellaneous Prose Works*, vols 3–4. Edinburgh: Robert Cadell, 1834.

– 'To Lady Louisa Stuart.' In *The Letters of Sir Walter Scott*, edited by H.J.C. Grierson, Vol. 10: *1826–1828*, 95–7. London: Constable, 1936.

Seccombe, Thomas. *The Age of Johnson (1748–1798)*. London: Bell, 1900.

Senior, Nassau W. *Essays on Fiction*. London: Longman, Green, 1864.

Seward, Anna. Letter. *Gentleman's Magazine* Jan. 1786, 15–17.

Shattock, Joanne. *Politics and Reviewers: The 'Edinburgh' and the 'Quarterly' in the Early Victorian Age.* London: Leicester University Press, 1989.

Shaw, Thomas B. *A History of English Literature*, edited by Sir William Smith. 1867. Reprint, London: John Murray, 1892.

– *Outlines of English Literature.* 1846. New American edition with *A Sketch of American Literature* by Henry T. Tuckerman, Philadelphia: Blanchard and Lea, 1852.

Shepperson, Archibald Bolling. *The Novel in Motley: A History of the Burlesque Novel in English.* Cambridge: Harvard University Press, 1936.

Sherburn, George. 'The Restoration and Eighteenth Century (1660–1789).' In *A Literary History of England*, edited by Albert C. Baugh, 697–1108. New York: Appleton-Century-Crofts, 1948.

Sholto-Douglas, Nora I. *Synopses of English Fiction.* London: George C. Harrap, 1926.

Singer, Godfrey Frank. *The Epistolary Novel: Its Origin, Development, Decline, and Residuary Influence.* Philadelphia: University of Pennsylvania Press, 1933.

Siskin, Clifford. *The Work of Writing: Literature and Social Change in Britain, 1700–1830.* Baltimore: Johns Hopkins University Press, 1998.

Skinner, John. *An Introduction to Eighteenth-Century Fiction: Raising the Novel.* Basingstoke, UK: Palgrave, 2001.

Smith, G.B. 'Henry Fielding.' *Macmillan's Magazine* 30 (May 1874): 1–18. Reprinted in Olmsted, 3:81–100.

Spalding, William. *The History of English Literature; with an Outline of the Origin and Growth of the English Language.* 1853. Reprint, New York: D. Appleton, 1862.

Spencer, Jane. *Aphra Behn's Afterlife.* Oxford: Oxford University Press, 2000.

– *The Rise of the Woman Novelist: From Aphra Behn to Jane Austen.* Oxford: Basil Blackwell, 1986.

Spender, Dale. *Mothers of the Novel: 100 Good Women Writers before Jane Austen.* London: Pandora, 1986.

Staël, Germaine de. 'Essay on Fictions.' In *Major Writings of Germaine de Staël*, edited and translated by Vivian Folkenflik, 60–78. New York: Columbia University Press, 1987.

Stang, Richard. *The Theory of the Novel in England, 1850–1870.* New York: Columbia University Press, 1959.

Stanton, Judith Phillips. 'Statistical Profile of Women Writing in England from 1660 to 1800.' In *Eighteenth-Century Women and the Arts*, edited by Frederick M. Keener and Susan E. Lorsch, 247–54. New York: Greenwood, 1998.

Steeves, Harrison R. *Before Jane Austen: The Shaping of the English Novel in the Eighteenth Century.* New York: Holt, Rinehart and Winston, 1965.

Stephen, [James] Fitzjames. 'The Relation of Novels to Life.' In *Cambridge Essays Contributed by Members of the University,* 148–92. London: Parker, 1855.

Stephen, Leslie. *English Literature and Society in the Eighteenth Century.* London: Duckworth, 1904.

– 'Richardson's Novels.' *Cornhill Magazine* 17 (January 1868): 48–69. Reprinted in Olmstead, 2:597–620.

– 'Some Words about Sir Walter Scott.' In *Hours in a Library,* 3 vols., 1:218–55. London: Smith, Elder, 1874.

Stuart, Lady Louisa. *Selections from Her Manuscripts,* edited by James Home, 232–6. New York: Harper, 1899.

Summers, Montague, ed. *The Works of Aphra Behn.* 6 vols. London: William Heinemann, 1915.

Sutherland, J.A. *Victorian Novelists and Publishers.* Chicago: University of Chicago Press, 1976.

Taine, H.A. *History of English Literature.* Translation of *Histoire de la Littérature Anglaise* (1864) by Henri Van Laun. 1872. 3 vols. Reprint, London: Chatto and Windus, 1890.

Taylor, John Tinnon. *Early Opposition to the Novel, 1760–1830.* New York: King's Crown, 1943.

Thackeray, William Makepeace. *Critical Papers in Literature.* London: Macmillan, 1904.

– *The English Humourists of the Eighteenth Century.* 1853. Reprinted in *Miscellanies,* 8:133–362. London: Smith Elder, 1877.

Thomson, Alexander. *Essay on Novels: A Poetical Epistle.* Edinburgh: P. Hill and J. Watson, 1793.

Thomson, Clara Linklater. *Samuel Richardson: A Biographical and Critical Study.* 1900. Reprint, Folcroft, PA: Folcroft Press, 1969.

Thorndike, Ashley H. *Literature in a Changing Age.* 1920. Reprint, New York: Macmillan, 1925.

'Thoughts on Novel Writing.' *Blackwood's Magazine* 4 (1819): 394–6.

Tieje, Arthur Jerrold. *The Theory of Characterization in Prose Fiction Prior to 1740.* Minneapolis: Bulletin of the University of Minnesota, 1916.

Todd, Janet. *The Sign of Angellica: Women, Writing, and Fiction, 1660–1800.* London: Virago, 1989.

Todd, William B., and Ann Bowden. *Tauchnitz International Editions in English, 1841–1955: A Bibliographical History.* New York: Bibliographical Society of America, 1988.

Tompkins, J.M.S. *The Polite Marriage.* Cambridge: Cambridge University Press, 1938.

– *The Popular Novel in England, 1770–1800*. 1932. Reprint, Lincoln: University of Nebraska Press, 1961.

Trollope, Anthony. *An Autobiography*. 1833. Reprinted with an introduction by Michael Sadleir. London: Oxford University Press, 1953.

– 'On English Prose Fiction as a Rational Amusement.' In *Four Lectures*, edited by Morris L. Parrish, 94–124. London: Constable, 1938.

Tuchman, Gaye, with Nina E. Fortin. *Edging Women Out: Victorian Novelists, Publishers, and Social Change*. New Haven, CT: Yale University Press, 1989.

Tuckerman, Bayard. *A History of English Prose Fiction from Sir Thomas Malory to George Eliot*. New York: Putnam's, 1882.

Turner, Cheryl. *Living by the Pen: Women Writers of the Eighteenth Century*. London: Routledge, 1992.

Ty, Eleanor. *Unsex'd Revolutionaries: Five Women Novelists of the 1790s*. Toronto: University of Toronto Press, 1993.

VanderWolk, William. 'Hippolyte Taine.' In *The Johns Hopkins Guide to Literary Theory And Criticism*, edited by Michael Groden, Martin Kreisworth, and Imre Szeman, 900–1. Baltimore: Johns Hopkins University Press, 2005.

Van Ghent, Dorothy. *The English Novel: Form and Function*. New York: Holt, Rinehart and Winston, 1953.

Verschoyle, Derek, ed. *The English Novelists: A Survey of the Novel by Twenty Contemporary Novelists*. New York: Harcourt, Brace, 1936.

Wagenknecht, Edward. *Cavalcade of the English Novel*. New York: Holt, Rinehart and Winston, 1943.

Walford, Lucy B. *Twelve English Authoresses*. 1893. Reprint, Freeport, NY: Books for Libraries Press, 1972.

Walpole, Hugh. *The English Novel: Some Notes on its Evolution: The Rede Lecture 1925*. London: Cambridge University Press, 1970.

Ward, A.W. and A.R. Waller, eds. *The Cambridge History of English Literature*. 15 vols. Cambridge: Cambridge University Press, 1907–16.

Ward, Robert Plumer. *De Vere; or, the Man of Independence*. 1827. Reprint, Stuttgart: Belser, 1989.

Warner, William B. *Licensing Entertainment: The Elevation of Novel Reading in Britain, 1684–1750*. Berkeley: University of California Press, 1998.

– 'Licensing Pleasure: Literary History and the Novel in Early Modern Britain.' In *The Columbia History of the British Novel*, edited by John Richetti, 1–22. New York: Columbia University Press, 1994.

Watt, Ian P. *The Rise of the Novel: Studies in Defoe, Richardson, and Fielding*. London: Chatto and Windus, 1957.

Watt, William W. *Shilling Shockers of the Gothic School: A Study of Chapbook Gothic Romances*. 1932. Reprint, New York: Russell and Russell, 1967.

Wellek, René. *A History of Modern Criticism*. 8 vols. New Haven, CT: Yale University Press, 1955–92.

Welsh, Alfred H. *Development of English Literature and Language*. 1882. 2 vols. Reprint, Chicago: S.C. Griggs, 1890.

Weygandt, Cornelius. *A Century of the English Novel: Being a Consideration of the Place in English Literature of the Long Story; together with an Estimate of its Writers from the Heyday of Scott to the Death of Conrad*. New York: Century, 1925.

Wharton, Edith. *The Writing of Fiction*. New York: Scribner's, 1925.

[Whately, Richard.] Review of *Northanger Abbey* and *Persuasion*, by Jane Austen. *Quarterly Review* 14 (1821): 352–76. Reprinted in Walter Scott, *Miscellaneous Prose Works*, 18:209–49. Edinburgh: Robert Cadell, 1835.

Whiteford, Robert Naylor. *Motives in English Fiction*. New York: Putnam's, 1918.

Williams, A.M. *Our Early Female Novelists and Other Essays*. 1904. Reprint, New York: Haskell House, 1971.

Williams, Ioan, ed. *Novel and Romance, 1700–1800: A Documentary Record*. London: Routledge and Kegan Paul, 1970.

Williams, Jane. *The Literary Women of England. Including a Biographical Epitome of All The Most Eminent to the Year 1700; and Sketches of the Poetesses to the Year 1850; With Extracts from their Works, and Critical Remarks*. London: Saunders, Otley, 1861.

Wilson, Mona. *These Were Muses*. London: Sidgewick and Jackson, 1924.

Winchester, C.T. *An Old Castle and Other Essays*. New York: Macmillan, 1922.

Woolf, Virginia. *The Common Reader*. New York: Harcourt, Brace, 1925.

– *The Common Reader: Second Series*. London: Hogarth Press, 1932.

– Review of *The Women Novelists*, by R. Brimley Johnson. *TLS*, 17 October 1918. Reprinted in *Women and Writing*, edited by Michèle Barrett, 69–72. 1979; Toronto: Quadrant, 1984.

– *A Room of One's Own*. London: Hogarth Press, 1929.

Wright, J.C. *Outline of English Literature*. London: John Heywood, 1889.

Yonge, Charles Duke. *Three Centuries of English Literature*. London: Longmans, Green, 1872.

Yonge, Charlotte M. *Hannah More*. London: W.H. Allen, 1888.

Zimmern, Helen. *Maria Edgeworth*. London: W.H. Allen, 1883.

# Index of Authors/Critics and Their Works

Numbers in **bold face** indicate pages devoted specifically to the author or critic in question.

182; Lovett, 112, 195; Moody, 112;
Thomson, 172
Gregory, Allene, **172–3**; *The French
Revolution and the English Novel*,
172–3
Griffith, Elizabeth
– critics on: Alves, 25; Baker, 207;
Barbauld, 33; *Critical Review*, 22;
Foster, 248; Hale, 107; Horner, 226;
Hughes, 197; Lovett, 197; MacCar-
thy, 235–6; McKillop, 252; *Monthly
Review*, 22; Reeve, 18, 19; Sherburn,
191; Tompkins, 244; Watt, 253
– works of:
*A Collection of Novels*, 21
*Count de Belflor and Leonora de Ces-
pedes* (translation of), 21
*The Delicate Distress*, MacCarthy
on, 235
*Fruitless Enquiry* (abridged and
expurgated by Griffith), 21
*Lady Barton*, MacCarthy on, 236
*The School for Rakes*, source text of,
21
*Zayde* (translation), 21
Griffith, Richard: Cross on, 154
Gross, John: on Saintsbury, 141–2
[Guilleragues, Gabriel Joseph de la
Vergne, vicomte de], *The Portu-
guese Letters*, Staël on, 23
Gunning, Elizabeth. *See* Plunkett,
Elizabeth (née Gunning)
Gunning, Susannah Minifie
– critics on: Baker, 207; Barbauld, 33;
Beckford, 26; Foster, 248; Horner,
226; 'The Literary Spy,' 51, 265n9;
MacCarthy, 235
– *Memoirs of Mary*, MacCarthy on,
235
Guthrie, William: Baker on, 207

Hale, Sarah Josepha: on Haywood,
93; treatment of women novelists,
107
– works of: biography of Behn, 92;
*Woman's Record*, 106–7
Hall, Joseph: Lovett and Hughes on,
195
Hamilton, Catherine J., **171**; *Women
Writers: Their Works and Their
Ways*, 171
Hamilton, Elizabeth
– critics on: Baker, 212; *Cambridge
History*, 126; Chambers/Carruth-
ers, 67, 72, 73; revised *Chambers*,
188; Elton, 180; Elwood, 107; Gosse,
132; Hale, 107; Herford, 118; 'The
Literary Spy,' 51, 265n9; MacCarthy,
240; Masson, 62, 64; Murch, 107;
'On the Female Literature of the
Present Age,' 52; Scott, 40; Shaw,
108; Lady Louisa Stuart, 40
– works of: *The Cottagers of Glen-
burnie*, Baker on, 162; Chambers
on, 72; *Memoirs of Modern Philoso-
phers*, Baker on, 212; MacCarthy
on, 240
Hanaway, Mary J.: Gregory on, 173
Hannay, James, *A Course of English
Literature*, on Burney, 95; on Scott,
98
Har(r)ington, James: Baker on, 160
Harrison, James (publisher), *The
Novelist's Magazine*, 21
Hawke, Lady (Cassandra Hawke):
Baker on, 208
Hawkesworth, John: Beattie on, 14;
Sherburn on, 191 .
– *Almoran and Hamet*, critics on:
Baker, 206; Barbauld, 264n2;
Hughes, 197; Lovett, 197; More, 24